THE
MIND

'2012

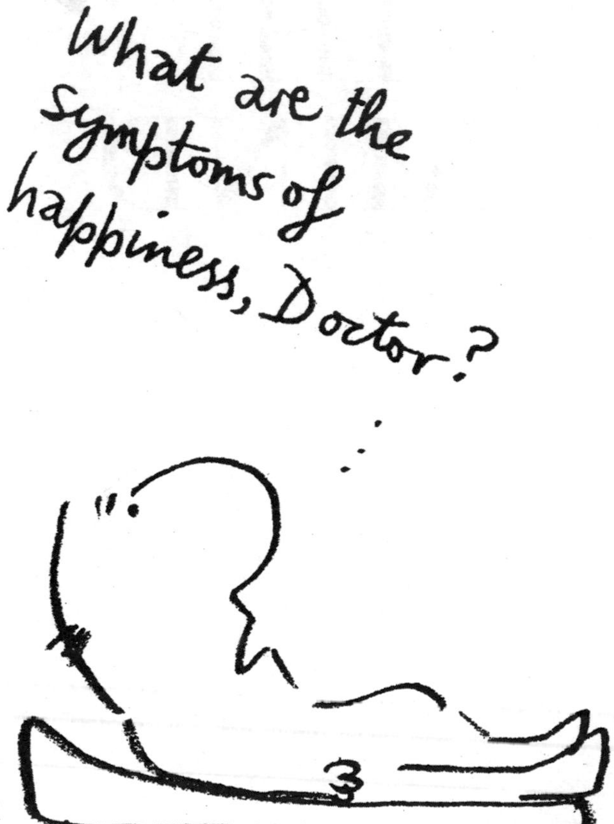
What are the symptoms of happiness, Doctor?

THE MIND
A USER'S GUIDE

Consultant Editor
Dr Raj Persaud

BANTAM PRESS

LONDON · TORONTO · SYDNEY · AUCKLAND · JOHANNESBURG

TRANSWORLD PUBLISHERS
61–63 Uxbridge Road, London W5 5SA
a division of The Random House Group Ltd
www.booksattransworld.co.uk

First published in Great Britain
in 2007 by Bantam Press
a division of Transworld Publishers

A CIP catalogue record for this book
is available from the British Library.

ISBN 9780593056356

Addresses for Random House Group Ltd companies outside the UK
can be found at: www.randomhouse.co.uk

The Random House Group Ltd Reg. No. 954009

The Random House Group Ltd makes every effort to ensure that the papers
used in its books are made from trees that have been legally sourced from
well-managed and credibly certified forests. Our paper procurement policy
can be found at: www.randomhouse.co.uk/paper.htm

Set in 10.5/14.5pt Nofret Light by
Falcon Oast Graphic Art Ltd.

Printed and bound in Great Britain by
William Clowes Ltd, Beccles, Suffolk

2 4 6 8 10 9 7 5 3

We dedicate this book to the '1 in 4' of us who will, some time in their life, experience mental health problems and those who care for them. We hope that this book will be a useful guide to those who are seeking help and that it will show that not only are mental health problems common, but that the majority are treatable and should not attract discrimination.

Acknowledgements

The Royal College of Psychiatrists would like to acknowledge the contributions from psychiatrists, all other mental health professionals, patients, carers and College staff who took part in the production of this book. We would also like to thank the team at Transworld for their support and particularly their belief that a book should be published addressing the complex and misunderstood world of mental health.

Contents

Part Two: Managing the Mind

Part One

Disorders of the Mind

Preface

I don't want to worry you about the state of your mind, but here are some sobering statistics:

❖ At any one moment in the UK, roughly 10 per cent of the population report feeling seriously down or depressed, and 15.5 per cent report loss of interest or pleasure in activities formerly considered enjoyable.

❖ Of those who are diagnosed as severely depressed, only 12.5 per cent report that they have received treatment for their depressive disorder.

This somewhat worrying state of affairs doesn't just apply to depression; most mental health problems in the community are seriously *underdetected*. Indeed, some research conducted by Professor Robin Priest and colleagues from St Mary's Hospital Medical School shows that health professionals are often very reluctant to refer patients to the appropriate specialists, such as psychiatrists. This disturbing finding may also explain the startling statistic that over 90 per cent of psychotropic medicines – designed to help people with psychological problems such as depression or psychosis – are prescribed by general medical practitioners in the UK. In other words, the vast majority of those people diagnosed as mentally ill are never seen by a psychiatrist, psychologist or any other kind of mental health specialist.

This relates to what academics refer to as the 'clinical iceberg'. This term is used to highlight the fact that psychiatrists treat only a tiny percentage of people with mental health problems and there is a great mass of people lurking below the surface in society who are never seen by mental health professionals.

Professor Priest's study was even gloomier about the possibility of improving this worrying situation and reminds us that general practitioners often do not get enough psychiatric training. Research has shown that even with proper training in the diagnosis of mental illness, in many cases the majority of GPs still failed to diagnose depressive illness.

Professor Paul Bebbington, a research psychiatrist then at the Institute of Psychiatry in London (now at University College London), recently led a study that found that about 1 in 3 women and 1 in 5 men will suffer from depression at some time in their lives. This study was based on an inner-city part of London and may therefore not be representative of the rest of the country. Nevertheless, these findings are really quite startling, particularly for women.

Psychiatric disorders are not only very common, but they tend to bring other problems with them; they don't seem to exist in isolation. For example, in one twelve-month period, two thirds of people with a mood disorder such as depression will also experience anxiety, or an alcohol or drug problem, while 1 in 2 people with depression will also suffer problems like agoraphobia and post-traumatic stress disorder. Equally worrying is the fact that 1 in 3 of those with depression will relapse in the first year, and in the long term 70–80 per cent will experience at least one further episode.

When the amount of disability caused by psychiatric illness is measured using instruments such as Disability Adjusted Life Years, which encompass both mortality and disability, depression ranks fourth across the world as a leading cause of disability, third in Europe and first in the Americas. And in studies of those at work in offices in the UK, psychiatric disorder, largely neurosis, is found to be the second most common cause of very long work absences.

Given how common and disabling psychiatric illnesses are, it's perplexing that they remain so neglected by health services worldwide, not just in the UK.

One problem is that, while it might be evident to everyone around you that you have indeed broken your leg – they can see you hobbling about, the plaster cast on your leg and the crutches you have to use – by their very nature, mental health problems such as depression often remain hidden and undetected. Neither the sufferers nor those closest to them necessarily have any obvious signs to help them identify the problem. Another reason why we fail to recognize psychological problems may relate to the fact that many people find these difficulties simply too mysterious and incomprehensible to deal with, so they are ignored or swept under the carpet until the person desperately needs help.

There is also a profound stigma still associated with psychiatric illness. This stigma may have its roots in a previous age when the greatest fear of developing a psychological problem was that the 'men in white coats' would be called to 'take you away' and you would never be seen again – living out the rest of your life locked away in the back ward of some institution.

The taboo surrounding psychological problems isn't just about incurability – it is also about the fear that suffering from such difficulties might make you dangerous, unpredictable or unpleasant to be with.

The reality is that all these various stigmas are misplaced and problems of the brain and mind are eminently treatable today, thanks to huge advances in the field of scientific research. The more we know about these problems, the more likely we are to prevent them from occurring.

It is important to recognize, however, that psychiatric illness, if not properly diagnosed and treated, can lead sooner or later to tragic results. The suicide rate for those suffering from depression is thirty times higher than that of the general population.

But it's not just suicide that we have to worry about in terms of mortality. Research shows that depression raises your chances of an accidental death by about 50 per cent, and almost doubles the death rate from other medical causes. So, depression and other mental illnesses can dramatically alter your physical health as well.

Yet psychological and psychiatric research has led to many notable advances in our understanding and recently there have been many break-throughs in treatment. Today, the prognosis for much mental illness is probably better than it is for comparable serious medical disorders.

Knowledge in this area is gathering at an ever-increasing rate – and it is constantly illuminating and deepening our understanding. However, it is important to realize that there is still much that remains a mystery – particularly in relation to serious psychological problems such as schizophrenia.

For example, the proportion of people with schizophrenia born during the winter months is about 5–15 per cent higher than at other times of the year. We don't know whether this is caused by the mother being infected with a virus at a crucial moment in foetal brain development, by an alteration in maternal diet, or by other factors affecting foetal development. But what we do know is that neuroscience and psychological study is helping us better to understand the brain and the mind – and that treatment is crucial.

So the widespread belief that psychological problems are not open to being treated effectively, that there is no expertise in the field beyond sheer 'common sense', or that stepping forward and seeking help will merely alarm and alienate your neighbours, colleagues, family and friends, can now be definitely shown to be nothing more than ignorant prejudice.

In order to confront these issues for the first time comprehensively, the Royal College of Psychiatrists in the UK has entered into a unique collaboration with Transworld Publishers, and the product is the book you now hold in your hands. This volume is intended to assist anyone who has an interest in maintaining their mental health, and therefore educating themselves in a variety of ways. It is also a guide that will help you to decide on what to do next if you recognize symptoms described here. It will help to clarify, and in some cases dispel, the myths relating to mental health issues and is designed to empower people who may already have encountered problems and who have some experience of mental health services or self-help materials.

The College has recruited distinguished experts and has challenged them to write in a jargon-free, concise and accessible manner practically everything you need to know about the latest thinking in brain and mind sciences in order to safeguard your mental health. So, where a medical encyclopedia has pictures showing you what lumps or bumps to look out for, this handbook has distinctive descriptions of behaviour, feelings and thoughts which will similarly assist. As Consultant Editor, I have written the conclusions to all the chapters (except for Chapter 11 on Gender Disorders and Chapter 43 on Stigma and Discrimination Against People with Mental Illness) which I hope summarize some of the most challenging and current thinking around mental health.

Although you may not recognize any symptoms described here in relation to yourself, it is important to realize just how common these kinds of problems are throughout our lifespan. This guide may well prove invaluable to you or to a relative at some time in the future – a handy 'encyclopedia' that will help you to clarify or better understand worrying symptoms of the mind. These symptoms remain not just some of the most widespread medical problems, but also appear in many instances to be increasing in incidence, for what remain largely mysterious reasons.

Our bodies are undoubtedly wondrous biological machines, the complexity of which is unmatched in nature. Yet another scale of intricacy altogether is that relating to the brain and mind, which remain the most complicated mechanisms in the known universe. This is why, although we are all born with brains and minds that are amazing, those who research and treat the symptoms of psychological and psychiatric disorder, including the authors of this book, firmly believe we would all find our lives enhanced by a user's guide to the mind.

Dr Raj Persaud

References

Jan Scott and Barbara Dickey, 'Global Burden of Depression: The Intersection of Culture and Medicine', *British Journal of Psychiatry*, August 2003, 183: 92–94.

Eugene S. Paykel, Traolach Brugha, Tom Fryers, 'Size and Burden of Depressive Disorders in Europe', *European Neuropsychopharmacology*, August 2005, 15: 4, 411–23.

Evelyn J. Bromet and Shmuel Fennig, 'Epidemiology and Natural History of Schizophrenia', *Biological Psychiatry*, 1 October 1993, 46: 7, 871–81.

Maurice M. Ohayon, Robin G. Priest, Christian Guilleminault, Malijaï Caulet, 'The Prevalence of Depressive Disorders in the United Kingdom', *Biological Psychiatry*, 1 February 1999, 45: 3, 300–307.

P. E. Bebbington, R. Kats, P. McGuffin, C. Tennant, J. Hurry, 'The Risk of Minor Depression Before Age 65: Results from a Community Survey', *Psychol. Med.*, 1989, 19: 393–400.

R. D. Goodwin, C. Faravelli, S. Rosi, F. Cosci, E. Truglia, R. de Graaf, H. U. Wittchen, 'The Epidemiology of Panic Disorder and Agoraphobia in Europe', *European Neuropsychopharmacology*, August 2005, 15: 4, 435–43.

Introduction:
Your Brain and
How It Works

The big picture

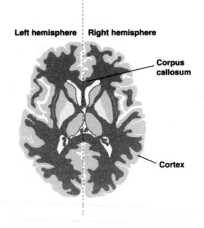

Left hemisphere | Right hemisphere

Corpus
callosum

Cortex

Bearing more than a passing resemblance to a slice through a cauliflower, this is a diagram of a horizontal section of the human brain.

You'll see that it is separated into two halves: the left and right *cerebral hemispheres*. They are joined in the middle by the *corpus callosum*. You'll see that the surface is very folded; we've evolved this way to increase the surface area of the outer layer of brain, known as the *cortex*.

An easy way of understanding the different bits of the brain is to think of it in layers, like an onion. The inner part of the brain, the *central core*, looks after basic functions such as breathing, sleeping, eating and drinking, temperature control and sex.

In the middle layer is the *limbic system*. It controls our emotions.

The outer layer is the *cortex*. This controls everything else, including movement, sensation, speech, vision, hearing and even our personality.

Under the microscope

The brain contains about 100 billion nerve cells, or *neurones*, mostly located within a few millimetres of the surface of the cortex. The neurones are surrounded by several times as many supporting, or glial, cells which protect the neurones from damage. Some of our nerve cells are very long, starting in the brain and running all the way down our spine.

The nerve cells use electrical pulses to transmit nerve impulses or messages very quickly along their length. Messages can also jump from one nerve cell to another by releasing tiny amounts of a chemical, or *neurotransmitter*, which jump across a tiny gap between the cells and trigger the next nerve cell. These gaps between cells are called *synapses*.

There are many different neurotransmitters. They each have a specific 'shape', which can be 'recognized' by a specific receptor in the synapse, rather like a key fitting a lock.

Neurones can talk to several other neurones simultaneously, including those in different areas of the brain. This means very complex messages can be put together.

For example, when you pick up a very hot dish, your brain will be informed that something hot, painful and potentially damaging is touching a hand. The brain would send a message to the hand to drop the plate. However, that message could also be influenced by a message from another part of the brain – let's say the sound of your partner's voice saying, 'My mother gave us that: if you drop it she'll kill you!', and at the same time a message from your memory reminds you of your mother-in-law when she's angry. Then you might override the basic response to drop the dish and 'think twice'.

What does the brain actually do?

The cortex
If you stripped off your ear and skull and looked at your brain from the side,

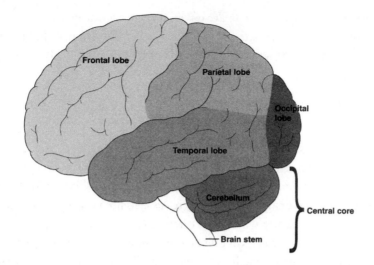

you'd notice that each hemisphere is divided into four lobes, as in the picture above.

The left hemisphere in most people is said to be *dominant* over the right (the dominant hemisphere processes language and mathematical or logical problems, whereas the non-dominant one concentrates on things like music, vision and our ability to see things relative to each other).

The occipital lobe

This lobe, at the back of the brain, is primarily involved with processing information from our eyes and generating everything that we see.

The temporal lobe

This processes what we hear through our ears. It links with the occipital lobe to help us recognize *what* we see. It is also involved with memory – usually visual memory on the right and verbal memory on the left. Lastly, the left temporal lobe is where spoken sound is decoded into language so that we can understand what is being said.

The parietal lobe

This area has two main functions. It is where all messages from all our touch and pain nerve cells are processed. It also links into our visual processing, helping us to understand what we see.

In this lobe, the brain also holds a map of the body surface so that each touch input goes to its own designated area for processing. The most sensitive parts of our bodies, such as our fingers, our mouth or our genital areas, are given the most space in the parietal lobe as they have to process the most information.

The frontal lobe

This lobe controls many of the extra things that we do that make us human. These are often called *executive functions* and include tasks such as concentration, planning, reasoning and judgement – abilities which help us make complex decisions and solve problems.

A large area of the frontal lobe is reserved for sending outputs to the muscles in the body, telling them to move when we want them to. The left frontal lobe also helps us speak and links up with the area in the left temporal which helps us understand language.

The frontal lobe links with the limbic system (see below) and controls how we behave in different situations.

The limbic system

This area, in the middle layer of the brain, has a big role to play in regulating our emotions. It also helps us to store memories. It exerts control over the primitive central core, making us, hopefully, more adaptable and less like slaves to hunger or sexual urges.

The *hippocampus* is the bit of the limbic system needed to store new memories. While memories do not live in the hippocampus, information has to pass through it to be remembered. People who damage this bit of the brain cannot make any new memories, although they can remember most facts they learned before the damage happened.

Another part of the limbic system, the *amygdala*, is critical in experiencing certain feelings, such as fear. It is also important in making emotional memories, both positive and negative, through its close links with the hippocampus.

There is a theory that people with post-traumatic stress disorder may have a problem with the hippocampus and the amygdala. This may explain the vivid flashbacks and anxiety that people experience with this condition.

Inputs

The brain constantly receives inputs from the body in order to keep us updated on how we are and what's happening around us. Some of these inputs are noticeable to us, like those from our five senses, but we aren't generally aware of others, such as messages which control how quickly we breathe or when to blink our eyes.

To illustrate this, have a look at the picture below. This is you, reading this book. Your hand is touching the pages. This sends a message up your arm in a nerve to the spinal cord, up the spinal cord, through a hole at the base of your skull and into the brain, ultimately arriving in the parietal cortex.

On their way into the cortex to be processed, inputs pass through an area in the central core called the *thalamus*. It acts a bit like a gatekeeper, sorting out which inputs go where. It can also increase or decrease the 'volume' of the input from different senses, if the cortex tells it that the input is more or less important.

Consider the picture again. You prob-ably weren't aware that your hand was touching the page until we drew your attention to it – or, more accu-rately, until your cortex told your thalamus to increase the volume on the touch sensation.

Outputs

Everything that the brain tells the body to do is, at a basic level, a message to a muscle telling it to contract or relax. This may be something we've actively thought about doing, a *voluntary output*, like holding on to that hot dish on page 7.

We are unaware of other outputs, the *involuntary* ones, such as those telling our breathing muscles to move, or telling our heart to beat faster. There wouldn't be room for much else if we had to think and remember to breathe all the time, so this division of outputs into voluntary and involuntary is useful.

Voluntary movements are controlled by an area in the frontal lobe. Involuntary movements, like breathing, are controlled by the central core. The bit of the central core called the *cerebellum* has a particular role in main-taining posture, balance and controlling movement.

The emotional brain

An emotion has many parts. There are physical sensations – like your heart pounding in a threatening situation; an awareness of an emotion – when you actually *feel* frightened; and thoughts and memories from the cortex stemming from similar experiences in the past that influence how you feel, and what you do as a result.

A physical sensation in itself does not tell you how you are *feeling*. Your body can't differentiate frightened or excited – for example, in both feelings the heart beats faster and the pupils dilate. It is the amygdala in the limbic system that decides whether you will feel fear or excitement. People with damage to this bit of the brain are incapable of feeling scared, and might be the sort to take very big risks.

The frontal lobe is also involved in emotions, telling us how to respond appropriately in social settings. It helps us to read emotional cues, reminds us of the past consequences of our actions, and helps us to judge what is socially and morally acceptable. This is perhaps the most complex bit of our emotional response.

Brain chemicals and emotion

As we have mentioned, the brain communicates using a combination of electrical and chemical activity. We've already met neurotransmitters, the chemicals involved with passing on messages at synapses. In this section, we'll go through them in a bit more detail, as they are pretty crucial.

We know of at least seventy different brain chemicals or neurotransmitters so far. They are not equally distributed in the brain, but vary depending on brain function at particular locations.

Serotonin is a neurotransmitter involved in mood regulation (feeling happy, sad or depressed). It is found in the limbic system. Antidepressant drugs seem to work on this chemical.

Dopamine acts in the neuronal pathways associated with rewards and motivation. Roughly speaking, the more dopamine, the more we perceive that we want something. This is true of 'natural' rewards, like food, or artificial rewards, like cocaine. It is thought that too much dopamine activity in some areas of the limbic system causes schizophrenia, whereas too little in other brain areas causes Parkinson's disease.

Endorphins are naturally occurring neurotransmitters that cause pain relief and increase pleasure. Opiate drugs, like heroin and morphine, mimic endorphins, thus causing the same effect. Safe ways in which we can increase our ability to get a 'natural high' include taking exercise and eating chocolate or spicy food. In addition, some complementary therapies, like acupuncture, work by increasing the brain's endorphin levels.

Dr Mona Freeman
and Dr Hind Khalifeh

Dr Persaud's conclusion

Medicine's understanding of how the brain works still lags to some extent far behind our knowledge of the rest of our body. This is without doubt linked to the greater complexity of the brain compared to our other body organs. The brain is the most complex object in the known universe.

Are we going to blame our brains for our behaviour – argue that it was a trigger-happy amygdala that made us feel so threatened by someone that we hit them? Brain-scanning results are being used in courts of law in the USA to assist defendants. We now know that the brain scans of those convicted of so called 'motiveless' homicides are different from those of other perpetrators.

Mental health may involve learning how to be in charge of our emotions, and therefore our brains, rather than being a victim of them. We also have recently found that the brain changes produced in treating depression with antidepressants are remarkably similar to those that psychotherapy achieves, so learning to change our brains may involve more than one mechanism.

Alzheimer's and Other Dementias

A man who forgot he had retired

GERALD HAS NEVER considered there to be a problem. Cynthia, Gerald's wife, on the other hand, has been worried for over three years, since just after Gerald retired from his job in a factory.

The first thing Cynthia noticed was that Gerald began to make mistakes when the couple were playing cards (a pastime they both loved). Then one day Gerald got lost while driving to his daughter's home – a route with which he was very familiar.

As time progressed, Cynthia noticed more problems: Gerald had always paid the bills, but now was not doing this, and was hiding the reminders; he forgot their anniversary (for the first time in forty-two years) and began to forget appointments. He also lost interest in his hobbies – gardening and horse-racing.

At first Cynthia thought these difficulties were because

he had retired, but about two years ago she was worried enough to take Gerald to the family doctor. The doctor listened patiently to Cynthia, but then reassured the couple that this was nothing more than 'just getting on a bit' – some loss of memory was to be expected as Gerald got older.

Cynthia was reassured, but as time progressed things got worse. Gerald began to forget conversations and started repeating the same things again and again. On a few occasions, quite uncharacteristically, he flew into a rage when his wife reminded him that they had already spoken about something.

One night, at about 3.00am, he got up and dressed, telling his wife it was morning and he had to go to work, despite having been retired for over eighteen months; he would not accept that it was the middle of the night. On another occasion, while the couple were out shopping, Gerald met an old friend in the street but didn't recognize him.

The last straw came when he not only forgot his grandson's birthday, but could not recall his name. As Gerald had always doted on the boy, now aged eight, Cynthia was very worried and took him back to the doctor.

This time the doctor referred Gerald to the local old–age psychiatry services. They visited Gerald and Cynthia at home and listened to the account of Gerald's difficulties. They arranged for him to have some investigations, including in–depth memory tests by a psychologist and a brain scan. An occupational therapist also visited the couple to assess whether Gerald needed any help in completing everyday tasks. She looked at safety in the home and recommended various changes, including placing a large clock on Gerald's bedside table so he could see the time if he woke at night.

After a few weeks, the consultant spoke with Gerald and Cynthia and gave them the results of all these investigations: Gerald had Alzheimer's disease.

Gerald was started on a dementia treatment known as

donepezil, a medicine designed to slow down the memory loss in dementia. In the weeks after the diagnosis, a nurse visited regularly to provide counselling and support for Gerald and to monitor the effects of the medication. An occupational therapist visited to provide support and advice to Cynthia. Meanwhile, the consultant advised Gerald to stop driving. Gerald began to attend the day clinic at the local hospital, which ran a self–help group for people with dementia, to help them come to terms with the diagnosis and to understand the disease. Cynthia was put in touch with the local Alzheimer's Society group and began to attend their weekly evening meetings.

One year on, Gerald has got a little worse – he is more forgetful, sometimes puts his shirt on inside–out when getting dressed, and has wet himself a few times. With help from the GP, who put the couple in contact with the local incontinence service, his occasional accidents do not cause any major problems.

However, he rarely goes out on his own now, because he got lost on a couple of occasions while going to the shops. He still repeats conversations, but although Cynthia finds this frustrating, she has now learned to take it in her stride.

There are a lot of things Gerald can still do – he enjoys playing cards and watching the horse–racing; he and Cynthia still do the gardening together; and he loves visiting his daughter and grandson.

What is dementia?

Dementia is a term used to describe loss of brain function, which is usually progressive. Over 100 different causes of the condition have been recognized (see overleaf).

Dementia usually starts in a very mild way. In the early stages, people may have particular problems with learning new things, or forget what they have just said or done, even though they can often recall clearly events that happened many years ago. Their sense of time and place may be lost. People with dementia may develop problems with finding words, and it becomes increasingly difficult for them to learn new information and to do new things.

As time goes on, they need help to perform even the most basic tasks of everyday living, including washing, dressing and eating. Eventually, people with dementia may become uncommunicative and incontinent. Sometimes there are severe behavioural problems. Most people with dementia will eventually require 24-hour care.

There are over 100 different types of dementia. The most common are Alzheimer's disease, vascular dementia and Lewy body dementia, which together account for approximately 95 per cent of cases. Dementia currently affects approximately 750,000 people in the UK.

What causes dementia?

Causes of dementia include:
* Alzheimer's disease, which accounts for about 60 per cent of all cases. People with this type have memory loss and loss of other brain functions, which progresses slowly over the years.
* Vascular dementia, which usually results from brain damage due to tiny strokes, and can follow a more erratic course than Alzheimer's disease.
* Lewy body dementia, a disorder which often causes visual hallucinations (seeing things) and symptoms similar to those of Parkinson's disease (shaking and stiffness).
* Fronto-temporal dementia, in which there are often striking changes in behaviour before the memory problems appear.
* Huntington's disease, also sometimes called Huntington's chorea, which is characterized by jerky movements in addition to dementia.
* AIDS-related dementia.
* Creutzfeld Jakob disease, or CJD, a very rare form of dementia which usually progresses very rapidly.
* Dementia due to an excessive intake of alcohol over an extended period of time.

❖ Dementias due to various treatable causes, including vitamin deficiency, hormone deficiency and syphilis.

A lot of people are aware of dementia now – just a generation ago there was little understanding among the public, and some doctors, of dementia and its consequences. As a result, there is now intense public debate about some issues, and several controversies have emerged. Some of the more complicated of these are:

❖ Paying for personal (non-nursing) care at home or in residential homes. In Scotland, all care for people with dementia is provided by the state. In England, individuals with dementia have to pay for the care if they can afford it.

❖ Prescribing dementia drugs. There is some controversy in England and Wales as to which treatments should be used for people with moderate dementia.

❖ To tell or not. Researchers have found that most people want to be told the diagnosis if *they* have dementia, but many are reluctant for their relative with dementia to be told.

❖ Treating psychological behavioural symptoms. About 50 per cent of people with dementia will experience hallucinations or behavioural symptoms (such as aggression). Whether these symptoms should be treated with drugs (usually used to treat schizophrenia; see p. 196) is controversial.

What does it feel like?

Dementia affects people in different ways. Some people inhabit a bewildering and frightening place, while others seem totally unconcerned that their faculties are failing. Although dementia progresses gradually over time, it is sometimes helpful to consider the common symptoms at three phases: early, middle and late.

Early symptoms

The early stage of Alzheimer's disease is often overlooked, being incorrectly labelled by professionals, relatives and friends as 'old age', or as a normal part of the process of ageing. Because the onset of the disease is gradual, it is difficult to identify exactly when it begins.

The person may:

❖ show difficulties with language – for example, not remembering the right word for something
❖ experience memory loss – having particular problems with learning new facts and remembering recent events and conversations, or forthcoming appointments
❖ be disorientated in time – losing track of time or thinking night is day
❖ become lost in familiar places
❖ display difficulty in making decisions
❖ lack initiative and motivation
❖ show signs of depression and aggression
❖ show a loss of interest in hobbies and activities

Middle symptoms

As the disease progresses, problems become more evident and restricting, to the extent that people can no longer manage to live alone without difficulties. At this stage the person may:

❖ become very forgetful – forgetting names of family members and important anniversaries, or leaving cooking on the stove; bills will go unpaid; they may even forget to eat
❖ be unable to cook, clean or shop
❖ need assistance with personal hygiene, including visiting the toilet, bathing and washing; they may become extremely dependent
❖ need help with dressing
❖ have increased difficulty with speech
❖ wander and sometimes get lost
❖ show various behavioural abnormalities, such as aggression or constantly following a carer round the house
❖ experience hallucinations or depression

Late symptoms

This stage is generally one of significant dependence and loss of activity. Memory problems are very serious, and the physical side of the disease becomes more obvious. The person may:

❖ have difficulty eating
❖ not recognize relatives, friends and familiar objects
❖ have difficulty understanding and interpreting events

❖ be unable to find his or her way around in the home
❖ have difficulty walking
❖ suffer bladder and bowel incontinence
❖ display inappropriate behaviour in public
❖ be confined to a wheelchair or bed

It is important to remember that, as we get older, our memory does get worse – this is normal. For example, we have more difficulty remembering people's names, or things we are going to buy in the shop. We may also forget appointments. Someone with ordinary forgetfulness, however, can still remember the details associated with the thing they have forgotten. For example, you may briefly forget your friend's name, but you still know that the person you are talking to is your friend and you remember other things about them.

People with dementia not only forget the details, but the entire context. They usually also have other problems, such as changes in behaviour or personality, and they may lose the ability to perform everyday tasks, or have problems with their speech.

What can be done to help?

If anyone develops symptoms suggestive of dementia that don't appear to be getting any better, it is important to get a proper medical diagnosis. There are some conditions that can mimic dementia, such as depression (see p. 76), underactive thyroid gland or Parkinson's disease. Infections or constipation can also cause temporary confusion, as can some medicines, such as strong painkillers or tranquillizers.

If the diagnosis is dementia, then getting this diagnosis confirmed is important, because it allows the individual (and their family) to make plans for the future, and to get the right support and treatment. Many GPs will refer someone they suspect of having dementia to a specialist – usually a psychiatrist or neurologist, who can help make the diagnosis and plan treatment and care.

Investigations

A diagnosis of dementia is usually made on the basis of a patient's symptoms and mental abilities – there are no specific tests for any of the common causes of dementia. To obtain as much information as possible, the doctor will talk to the patient, and probably to someone else who knows the patient well, such as a family member or friend. They will probably do a physical examination and ask for some blood tests to rule out the rare, treatable causes of dementia. A psychologist may be asked to do extensive tests of memory and brain function.

It is often difficult to make a conclusive diagnosis of Alzheimer's disease, vascular dementia or Lewy body dementia in the early stages. Sometimes a brain scan or in-depth memory tests can help, but often the diagnosis is made only after observing how a patient's condition develops over a period of several months.

Treatment

Treatment is centred around maximizing existing abilities and preventing decline. Some general tips include:

❖ stop smoking and don't drink too much (keep well within the recommended weekly maximum of 14 units for women and 21 units for men)

❖ get gentle, regular exercise and eat a balanced diet

❖ keep the brain active – try to maintain interests in hobbies, do 'brain exercises', such as reading or crosswords

❖ have regular physical check-ups and ensure that general health, such as blood pressure, is monitored

In addition, there are four main treatment approaches:

Maximize ability. Health professionals, such as psychologists or occupational therapists, can provide advice to help compensate for loss of memory. For example, using techniques to maximize memory, including keeping a diary and scribble pad, or placing reminder cards by the front door ('remember your keys').

An occupational therapist may be able to provide advice on various aids and adaptations to help, such as clothing that can be done up easily or devices to warn if the bath is overfilling.

Individualized patient care. Consequences of dementia can include depression, hallucinations (seeing things that are not there), delusions (false beliefs, such as believing someone has stolen a handbag) and behaviour that causes problems for carers, such as wandering, agitation, aggression and sleeplessness.

The first approach here should be to obtain as much information as possible about the individual, their background and the circumstances of the problem, in order to see the difficulties in the context of the person. Sometimes, observing symptoms over a period of time can give clues to what is causing them. For example, a person may be distressed on and off. Careful observation may show this occurs at mealtimes – a clue to the fact the agitation is caused by a missing filling resulting in toothache.

Medication. Behavioural approaches are always preferable to drugs. In general, it is best to try to avoid tranquillizers or drugs that cause sedation. However, sometimes small doses of such drugs, prescribed with care and reviewed regularly, are necessary to relieve distress in patients and their carers. Antidepressants can often brighten mood in someone who is depressed.

Drugs to improve memory. Over the last ten years several drugs have become available: donepezil (Aricept), galantamine (Reminyl) and rivastigmine (Exelon) all belong to the same class of drugs (cholinesterase inhibitors). These have been shown in clinical trials to provide a small improvement in memory function to some people – about 1 in 5 people will see a noticeable improvement.

The drugs do have side-effects, such as headaches, feeling sick and tummy pain, but most people find little problem taking them.

Tips for families and friends

❖ Don't be put off if a doctor does not agree that there is a problem – if you are worried, seek a second opinion. Getting a diagnosis early is helpful.
❖ Keep a list (or diary) of problems you notice before you see the doctor or specialist.
❖ Once a diagnosis has been made, contact organizations that provide support and help.
❖ Good communication with the GP and other health professionals can make a big difference. It's best to have the name of a professional you can contact.
❖ Plan for the future, including making arrangements – such as taking a

longed-for holiday, writing a will and sorting out an enduring power of attorney.

❖ Don't keep it secret from friends and family. Being aware of the diagnosis will help them come to terms with changes in function, personality and behaviour.

❖ Make contact with social services – they may be able to help with day care, home care, etc.

❖ Look after your own health. Caring for someone with dementia can be time-consuming and demoralizing. Make sure you get the benefits due to you and organize respite care.

Dr Nori Graham
and Dr James Warner

Dr Persaud's conclusion

There is some recent evidence that even in later life taking up leisure activities such as reading, board games, playing musical instruments, dancing, exercise and walking are linked with a reduced risk of developing dementia.

General good mental and physical health care may be something one should take more seriously and be more vigorous about as one gets older, rather than being resigned to viewing ageing as a process of inevitable decline.

Regular blood-pressure checks and care of the cardiovascular system, like monitoring cholesterol levels, are important because we know that looking after your heart is similar to caring for your brain; dementia often results from the 'mini-strokes' that characterize a circulatory system which is also prone to heart disease.

We also know that depression in your younger years might foretell a future depression, so good care of one's emotional health continues to be important as the years go by. So, as we get older, retire and experience the loss of roles we are used to, finding new or more enduring reasons to embrace life and look after ourselves is essential.

SUPPORT ORGANIZATIONS

Age Concern England: Astral House, 1268 London Road, London SW16 4ER; helpline: 0800 009 966; *www.ace.org.uk*

Alzheimer's Disease International: information about dementia associations worldwide. 64 Great Suffolk Street, London SE1 0BL; tel: 020 7981 0880; *www.alz.co.uk*

Alzheimer Scotland – Action on Dementia: 22 Drumsheugh Gardens, Edinburgh EH3 7RN; helpline: 0808 808 3000; *www.alzscot.org.uk*

Alzheimer Society of Ireland: 43 Northumberland Avenue, Dun Laoghaire, Co. Dublin, Ireland; helpline: 1800 341 341; *www.alzheimer.ie*

Alzheimer's Society: 10 Greencoat Place, London SW1P 1PH; helpline: 0845 300 0336; *www.alzheimers.org.uk*

Benefits Enquiry Line (BEL): benefits information for people with disabilities or for their carers. Freephone for England, Scotland and Wales: 0800 882 200; Freephone for Northern Ireland: 0800 220 674; *www.dwp.gov.uk*

WEBSITES OUTSIDE THE UK

Australia:
www.alzheimers.org.au

New Zealand:
www.alzheimers.org.nz

Canada:
www.alzheimer.ca

South Africa:
www.alzheimers.org.za

India:
www.alzheimerindia.in

FURTHER READING

Dementia at Your Fingertips (second edition), Harry Cayton, Nori Graham and James Warner, Class Publishing, 2001

Dancing with Dementia: My Story of Loving Positively with Dementia, Christine Bryden, Jessica Kingsley Publishers, 2005

Dementia Reconsidered, Tom Kitwood, Open University Press, 1997

Anxiety and Panic

2

A man who couldn't be reassured

ROBBIE WAS THIRTY-FOUR and waiting at a bus stop to go to work. He was running a little late, having had an argument with his wife over his daughter's attitude to school. He was feeling stressed and tense. He became aware of a tightness in his chest and thought he felt a tingling in the fingers of his left hand. He had read that a chest pain going into the left hand is a sign of a heart attack. He began to worry about it and what would happen to his family if he couldn't work any more and, worse, if he suddenly dropped dead.

Robbie started to breathe heavily and felt dizzy; he thought he was going to faint. His pulse was racing and his chest pain got worse. He had to sit down.

Someone at the bus stop called an ambulance and he was taken to hospital. He had an ECG and was examined by a junior doctor who said he 'thought the heart was normal' and that he had probably had a panic attack. He referred him to the cardiology clinic – a decision which only confirmed Robbie's fears that there might be something seriously wrong with him.

He was slightly reassured by the normal results of the angiogram, but continued to worry about his heart. When his second panic attack happened 'out of the blue' a few weeks later, he became very concerned about his health and got a second opinion.

Robbie's story is that of a man who misread his own feelings of stress and developed negative thinking patterns. This led to repeated panic attacks, with fears and preoccupations about his health. Had he been aware that this was a normal physical response to feeling mildly stressed because he was late for work, because of domestic stress and too much coffee for breakfast, things would not have got out of hand. He is now on the verge of a serious anxiety disorder, which could be treated successfully if recognized early.

What is anxiety disorder?

Anxiety is a normal human feeling linked to the sensation of fear when faced with threatening and difficult situations. It can be a positive experience. It can improve our performance and increase our awareness, as part of the 'fight or flight response'. However, when the feelings become very severe, either in strength or time, it becomes an anxiety disorder. This can result in losing our enjoyment of life and our performance is affected.

Anxiety is a feeling that we have and stress (see p. 241) is something that happens to make us feel anxious. Nevertheless, stress and anxiety are often considered to be the same thing and this can result in confusion.

There are several types of anxiety disorder:

Generalized anxiety disorder

Generalized anxiety disorder is a condition where people feel very anxious and worried for no obvious reason. You may have physical (headaches, chest pains) or emotional (tiredness, tension) symptoms. The anxiety can be caused by environmental stress or can result from internal factors. The condition can last for a long time, although it can vary in strength.

Panic

This is the sudden unexpected surge of anxiety which is often accompanied by physical sensations such as chest pain, dizziness or breathing difficulties. It usually leads to a person having to get quickly out of whatever situation they happen to be in. Someone who has panic attacks may worry excessively about the significance of their symptoms. They may avoid situations they believe will result in further panic attacks. In a severe case, a person will not leave the security of their home and will develop agoraphobia (see below).

Phobias

A phobia is a strong fear of a specific object or situation – for example a fear of spiders, snakes or furry things – which is not dangerous and which most people do not find troublesome. As many as half the population have some particular phobia. (See also Chapter 18, p. 166.)

Agoraphobia is a fear of leaving the security of the home. In the most severe cases, people become 'housebound housewives' – they can go out only in the company of someone else, for security. Claustrophobia (the fear of confined spaces) is commonly associated with it.

Social phobia is an extreme version of shyness where people are frightened of, for example, speaking in public or other situations where they may be the subject of scrutiny by others. This can be quite debilitating for someone who functions normally in every other aspect of their life.

Anxiety can be found in association with many other conditions, especially depression, post-traumatic stress disorder and obsessive compulsive disorder (see pp. 76, 187 and 149).

What causes anxiety?

There are two elements in anxiety:

❖ **Our constitution**, or our genetic vulnerability to anxiety – some people are born worriers, while others are calm and easy-going.

❖ **Our environmental situation** at the time, which may lead to a person becoming anxious at times of particular stress.

It is the mixture of these two factors, the underlying vulnerability and the external stressor, which results in the development of symptoms.

What does it feel like?

The feeling is essentially one of fear and worry about what might happen in the future. Anxiety produces both psychological (mind) and physical (body) symptoms.

Mind
❖ worrying all the time
❖ trouble concentrating
❖ feeling irritable and tired
❖ poor sleep

Body
❖ irregular heartbeat, 'palpitations'
❖ sweating
❖ tension and pains in the muscles
❖ heavy breathing
❖ dizziness and faintness
❖ indigestion and diarrhoea, or a desire to pass water

Many patients consult their GP because of the bodily symptoms of anxiety, which they do not immediately recognize as being caused by psychological factors. Anxious patients frequently go to their doctor over minor physical complaints for which there is no obvious physical cause.

What can be done to help?

The majority of people with anxiety do not consult their doctor about their symptoms. They know what is causing them, and in most cases the symptoms disappear when the problematic situation is resolved. However, a lack of understanding of what is happening, and of how the body responds to stress, can be as much of a problem as the underlying problem itself. Therefore, it is important to recognize the condition for what it is – a self-limiting, normal physical and mental response to outside stresses. It is also important for people to understand that they *can* have control over their situation.

If symptoms are more severe, professional help may be necessary. Simple counselling is generally available through your GP. If this is not enough, medication or more structured therapy with a specialist may be indicated (see below). If there is no obvious cause for the condition, it is worth excluding some physical illness which can mimic anxiety, most notably an overactive thyroid.

Self-help

If the anxiety is relatively mild, gaining an understanding of the condition and learning simple relaxation techniques may be all that is needed. Avoiding excessive alcohol and stimulant drugs, such as caffeine, and doing more exercise can also do much to help.

There are many self-help groups, books and cassettes available from bookshops, health food shops, GPs' surgeries, public libraries and through mental health organizations. They explain the condition and offer simple self-help and/or relaxation techniques. These self-help tools should be the first port of call and often are all that is needed to resolve the problem.

Talking treatments

This is generally the treatment of choice for anxiety disorders. Counselling helps clarify the underlying causes of the anxiety (if there are causes, such as environmental stress or lifestyle issues). Talking through the problem with a counsellor may help you understand the issues and find simple solutions.

If the problem is more deep-rooted, cognitive behavioural therapy (CBT; see p. 427) may be recommended. CBT can help you to change how you think ('cognitive') and what you do ('behaviour'). These changes can help you understand and manage your thoughts and behaviour, and so feel better. Unlike some of the other talking treatments,

No – I'm fine ...
Just to say I'm at the airport...
I'm fine. Are you? Sure?
I know I just left but –
well ...I could cancel my trip
if you like ...I didn't want
to go ...but you said I should.
Anyway ...so long as you're
O.K. ...I'll be back
tomorrow... or maybe
before then ...
Look – why don't you
come with me?

CBT focuses on the 'here and now' problems and difficulties. CBT is done with a therapist, either individually or with a group of people. If individual, a course is usually from 5–20 weekly or fortnightly sessions, which usually last between 30–60 minutes.

You may be asked to monitor your symptoms to note how these vary in severity, depending on the situation. You can be taught to relax when you feel tense, and how to have some control over your symptoms. For instance, you learn that a racing heart is not a sign of a heart attack, but the normal physical response of a healthy heart to something stressful. As avoidance is unhelpful, you can learn, through gradual exposure, how to build up tolerance for the situation or object, thereby lessening the anxiety it causes.

Changing unhelpful thinking patterns is important. For example, you may think that others see you as a failure and that you will not be successful at the task you have to perform. However, if you think it through, you realize that you have done it well in the past and that you can do it as well, or better, than other people. Even if it's not perfect, doing it reasonably well may be good enough.

Psychoanalysis (see p. 440) deals with underlying emotional conflicts. It can help clarify why a person is vulnerable to anxiety in certain situations, and what it is about situations that remind them of anxieties in the past. For example, someone may be anxious and fearful in relationships and this could be traced back to their relationship problems with their parents, and possible child abuse. Dealing with problems in a psychoanalytical way is a complex, lengthy process, which may not cure the symptoms at first, but leads to an understanding of how the problems have developed. Cognitive analytic therapy (see p. 441) combines psychoanalytical and CBT techniques.

Therapy is an active process and the person must be willing to work on their problems themselves. Not everyone will be able to do this.

Medication

Medication can be prescribed by your GP and is helpful in controlling symptoms, but not necessarily in resolving problems. As skilled 'talking' therapists are in short supply, drugs can help to control the more severe symptoms to give therapy the time to work. For the more severe symptoms, there are many medicines available.

Benzodiazepines, such as diazepam (Valium) and lorazepam, as well as sleeping tablets such as temazepam and zopiclone, are highly effective treatments to relieve the symptoms, and they work within a matter of minutes – they will quickly cut short a panic attack. The drawback is that they only work properly for a matter of days or weeks. There is also a risk of dependency – the person cannot stop taking the medication, even when they are better. Therefore, these controversial drugs should only be used in the short term or from time to time.

Beta–blockers, such as propranolol, are drugs that control the heart rate and the physical symptoms of anxiety. They are particularly good for performance anxiety, such as in driving tests and for exam nerves, because they do not have any strong mental effects. They are relatively safe, mild treatments and are used by heart patients for long–term treatment of raised blood pressure.

Antidepressants are widely used to control the symptoms of general anxiety. They are effective for social phobias, and reduce the frequency and severity of panic attacks. Rather than a cure, they control the symptoms to a manageable degree, whilst the condition either resolves itself or other treatments and therapies are used to deal with the underlying issues. Other drugs for anxiety include buspirone and pregabalin.

Doctors tend to prescribe tranquillizers in low doses because of the fear of dependency. Tranquillizers can relieve some of the symptoms of anxiety.

Complementary therapies

These are physical and non–drug ways of dealing with symptoms and problems. However, the effectiveness of many treatments is unproven. They can include acupuncture, massage, herbal remedies and dietary supplements. Many simple, over–the–counter remedies are helpful in encouraging sleep and as mild sedatives. Fish oils and folic acid are also popular. Exercise and a healthy lifestyle are important complements to any more formal treatment.

Tips for families and friends

Families can provide support and advice on limiting alcohol and other self–destructive behaviours. They can encourage the person to see a counsellor. They should not collude with the person and their anxiety because this can encourage avoidance, which may progress to agoraphobia. Individuals need to be encouraged to confront their fears in a structured manner, rather than simply avoid them.

Dr Cosmo Hallstrom

Dr Persaud's conclusion

Severe anxiety is one of the most aversive experiences in the pantheon of psychological distress, so it is understandable that most of us will move heaven and earth to avoid it, and indeed will seek to leave an anxiety-provoking situation immediately.

When it comes to treatment, there is bad news and good news. First the bad news – the most effective treatments inevitably involve us confronting our fears and staying in situations we would rather avoid, rather than fleeing them.

Now the good news – all anxiety is completely treatable using these graded exposure methods. The key is to find a graded approach which works for you. This may require a therapist with the motivational skills to help us do something we would really rather not. However, the startling thing about graded exposure is that it can be done successfully without a therapist at all.

i

SUPPORT

SUPPORT ORGANIZATIONS

Mind, 15–19 Broadway, London E15 4BQ; tel: 020 8519 2122; fax: 020 8522 1725; email: contact@mind.org.uk; information helpline: Mind*info*Line: 0845 766 0163; *www.mind.org.uk*

National Phobic Society, Zion CRC, 339 Stretford Road, Hulme, Manchester M15 4ZY; tel: 0870 122 2325; fax: 0161 226 7727; email: info@phobics-society.org.uk; *www.phobics-society.org.uk*

WEBSITES OUTSIDE THE UK

Australia:
www.anxietyaustralia.com.au

New Zealand:
www.phobic.org.nz

Canada:
www.anxietycanada.ca

South Africa:
www.anxiety.org.za

India:
www.indianpsychiatry.com

FURTHER READING

Living With Fear, Isaac Marks, McGraw Hill Education, 2005

Anxiety: Your Questions Answered, Trevor Turner, Churchill Livingstone, 2003

Autism and Asperger's Syndrome

A boy who didn't want to be cuddled

WHEN JAMES WAS a baby, his parents took pride in every new development, such as smiling and recognizing them. He was like any other child. However, when he was about eighteen months old, things began to change. He stopped babbling and responding to his parents' cuddles. His mum says, 'He didn't seem to know us, and wasn't interested in us the way he had been.'

He began to stare at lights and at the corner of the ceiling. Their doctor explained that many children go through phases like this, and that he still seemed healthy and well. The parents were reassured – after all, James had been developing normally. Over the next two to three months, however, he did not make any sounds. He became withdrawn and was upset by loud noises, but he still ate well and put on weight.

By his second birthday, it was clear that he was not

developing as well as some of the other children they knew. Their doctor arranged for them to see a paediatrician, who watched James to see how he played and asked his parents if any members of the family had similar problems. James's father mentioned that one of James's cousins had special needs at school and had been slow to start talking. The paediatrician commented that James was not interested in play in the usual way and did not explore the room as most children would. He noted that, left to himself, James was content to fiddle with pieces of cloth or scrunch up pieces of paper. Also, he did not seem to seek his parents' interest in what he was doing; this was something that had always upset them a lot.

The paediatrician explained that James was not developing in the way most children do, and that he would need to have some tests. His parents asked if he might be deaf, or was having funny turns. The paediatrician said that his hearing would be tested, and that he would have a brain scan and a test for epilepsy. He would also be having blood tests.

The results were all normal, but James was still not talking and was still distant. His parents began to wonder if autism was the problem. The paediatrician agreed that this was the next thing to test for at the Child and Family Mental Health Service, where there were developmental psychiatrists, psychologists and speech and language therapists. The assessments were done over two visits by members of the team.

Afterwards, the psychiatrist explained that James did have autism, but that, with the right support, he and his parents could be helped a lot. He encouraged them to visit the National Autistic Society website, where they would find the stories of many families who had been through the same thing.

When it was time for James to go to school, his parents found a local school with a learning-support unit. The school team explained James's problems to the other pupils, in a way they could understand, and the children became quite caring and protective of James. James, in turn, did well. He began to talk, although mostly in single words concerning things he wanted, or repeating the words other people said to him.

The psychiatric team kept in contact over the years. James remained a solitary boy, but not unhappy. With attention to his need for routine, and remembering his dislike of loud noises, his parents were able to avoid his getting upset. Life with James was demanding, but fulfilling.

What are autism and Asperger's syndrome?

Autism and Asperger's syndrome are caused by abnormalities in the way the brain works. Autism usually shows itself in the first three years of life. Asperger's syndrome is less severe and may not be recognized until later.

The book *The Curious Incident of the Dog in the Night-time* is a useful insight into the mind of a young person with Asperger's syndrome, while one of the best-known portrayals of autism is Dustin Hoffman's Raymond Babbitt in the film *Rain Man*. In fact, it is rare for people to be as mathematically gifted as Hoffman's character, but autistic people are often knowledgeable about numbers and shapes. Rain Man is affected by autism to the extent that he has to live in an institution, but most people with autism socialize better than this. Raymond is a caricature rather than an accurate portrayal of autism.

What are the signs?

People with autism or Asperger's syndrome have difficulties with:
❖ socializing
❖ communication
❖ behaviour

These problems may be noticed soon after birth, but more often they become apparent after a year or two of normal development.

Socializing

Children. Children with autism tend to ignore other people, or appear insensitive to others' needs, thoughts or feelings. They do not make the usual eye contact, or use facial expressions in social situations. They are less likely to use gestures, such as pointing, to communicate.

They tend to find it difficult to co-operate, share or take turns with others. They prefer to play alone and show no interest in imaginative play. They get on best with adults. Socializing and forming friendships is hard for them. Children with Asperger's syndrome have milder problems.

Adults. Adults affected by autism and Asperger's syndrome also have problems socializing. They do not form relationships easily and tend to live alone. Some live with their parents and relatives; others find it preferable to live in a group home with staff who understand the condition. Such residential facilities are for people who are more severely affected and are mostly run by charities, such as the National Autistic Society.

The choices of occupation and leisure made by people with autism or Asperger's syndrome will typically reflect their preference for a solitary lifestyle.

Communication

Not being able to communicate properly is a particularly handicapping aspect of autism.

Children. Problems with communicating are often the thing that first causes concern to parents and others. Nearly all affected children will have problems understanding and speaking; more severely affected children may never learn to speak. If they do begin to talk, they may simply echo what they have just heard, or speak in an odd way.

Children with Asperger's syndrome are not slow to learn to speak, but their language may sound formal or mechanical.

Adults. Most learn to talk, or to communicate in some way, but some, especially those with severe autism, never learn to speak. Sometimes their speech will be unique to them, as if they have a language of their own. The subject matter is often dominated by their particular interest, which may be spoken about in a way that others find offputting or even wearing.

The adult with Asperger's syndrome will often talk in a mechanical way, lacking expression and rhythm.

Unusual behaviour

Children. Children with autism will prefer familiar routines, and tend to resist change. They may have unusual interests, such as the outline of maps, or electronic gadgets. They may be very sensitive to tastes, smells and sounds – some find loud noises very upsetting.

More severely affected children may have odd body movements, such as hand-flapping or finger-twiddling. Attempts to stop these activities can result in furious protests and distress. When upset, they may have tantrums, be hyperactive or injure themselves. Some children have special talents or gifts for drawing, music or calculation.

Adults. They have similar problems to children, and in many cases their habits can be very ingrained. Attempts to change routine should be made very carefully.

One of the features of autism and Asperger's syndrome is an inability to see things from other people's points of view, or to appreciate how other people might think about something. For example, if a family member is upset or sad about something, the person with Asperger's syndrome is genuinely unable to see why. It is important that families appreciate this, and do not regard it as a callous lack of concern – it's just the way the person thinks.

What causes autism and Asperger's syndrome?

There is a lot we don't know, but both conditions appear to be partly genetic.

Most medical experts believe that there is no evidence that autism is caused by vaccine damage. This has been studied very carefully in large groups of children. However, many families remain convinced that their child has been damaged by a vaccine.

Some causes of learning disability (see p. 130), including a condition called Fragile X syndrome, also cause autism. People with this kind of autism have special problems and need a lot of support.

There is no evidence that autism and Asperger's syndrome are becoming more common. But over the last twenty years we have become much more aware of the conditions, and this has resulted in more people being diagnosed.

What can be done to help?

Diagnosis and assessment

Parents, teachers and doctors need to recognize that a child is not developing normally and to arrange for an assessment. This is usually carried out by a specialist service, where medical, psychological and language aspects can be assessed, and other conditions can be identified. It may involve blood tests and other special investigations, as well as psychological testing.

Obtaining a correct diagnosis is an important first step. It helps us to understand the child's behaviour and work out what help they will need.

Education and language

Education, with speech and language therapy, is the best way to make sure that the child reaches his or her full potential. The type of education needed should be decided after a detailed assessment. Depending on what resources are required, a child may do best in a mainstream school that provides support for children with communication difficulties, or in a special school for children with autism.

Planning home life: specialist advice

Parents have a very important part to play in providing the love, understanding and consistency that their child needs. Many find that life at home goes more smoothly if they use similar strategies to those employed by teachers or other professionals. However, a child's behaviour can vary enormously in different environments. Advice from a clinical psychologist or child psychiatrist may be needed.

Social Services

Social Services may have a role to play in providing practical support and help for the child and family. They can provide help in the home, respite care, and advice on attendance and disability allowances. Many families also value support from their local Mencap or autism society.

Complementary therapies

Families will readily invest in 'cures', such as swimming with dolphins or other unusual, if enticing, possibilities. There is little evidence that many of these treatments work.

However, some approaches, such as diets high in fish oils, may be useful. The best advice is to question any claim of a 'miracle cure'. Support groups will often include families who have tried different treatments and will be able to share their experiences.

Medication

There is no drug cure for autism, but medication can help. It is important to treat associated conditions such as epilepsy. Depression and severe anxiety are common among people with autism and Asperger's syndrome (see pp. 76 and 24).

Many young adults with Asperger's syndrome get very depressed and anxious about their problems. Drug treatment with a selective serotonin re-uptake inhibitor (SSRI) can be very helpful. Some people can have very severe obsessions, which may be coupled with anxiety about socializing. Again, medication can be helpful.

The most important things are for others to understand and respect the person's need for routine and order, to treat other health problems, to get help with language and education, and to ensure that all people who regularly come into contact with the person understand them and – as far as possible – make allowances for their unusual nature.

Tips for families and friends

❖ Don't believe anyone claiming a 'miracle cure' for autism.
❖ Join a support group.
❖ Ask lots of questions of your doctors and educators.
❖ Respect the person's need for order and routine.

But

❖ Routines and obsessions can be changed, gradually and gently.
❖ Be aware that if one routine or obsession is removed, it will probably be replaced by another.

❖ Some routines and obsessions can become assets for the person. Look for ways of exploring this, whether through drawing, music or an interest in numbers.

Professor Greg O'Brien

Dr Persaud's conclusion

There has been much more media interest in autism recently for many reasons, including controversy over whether a widely used vaccine might be an unsuspected cause.

Rates of autism appear, according to some, to be rising. The debate continues as to whether this might merely reflect increased education and recognition of the disorder rather than some new burgeoning environmental cause.

Careful assessment by a specialist is vital before diagnoses are made and this needs to be emphasized more now than ever. Because of the media interest, modern parents are likely to worry more about autism than their own parents did. A core problem around the disorder is having to interact not just with a healthcare system, but an educational one as well. So the stress around autism can be enormous.

New psychotherapeutic approaches are being pioneered to assist with the treatment of autism, which need more funding as the whole family is likely to be affected in ways more profound than with most other childhood problems.

SUPPORT ORGANIZATIONS

The National Autistic Society: information and advice for parents and families. 393 City Road, London EC1V 1NG; helpline: 0845 070 4004; email: *autismhelpline@nas.org.uk; www.nas.org.uk*

MENCAP National Centre, 123 Golden Lane, London EC1Y 0RT; tel: England: 020 7454 0454; Northern Ireland: 02890 691351; Wales: 02920 747588; helpline: 0808 808 1111; email: *information@mencap.org.uk; www.mencap.org.uk*

WEBSITES OUTSIDE THE UK

Australia:
www.autismaus.com.au

New Zealand:
www.autismnz.org.nz

Canada:
www.autismcanada.org

South Africa:
www.autismsouthafrica.org

India:
www.indiapsychiatry.com

FURTHER READING

The Curious Incident of the Dog in the Night-time, Mark Haddon, Vintage, 2004

Bipolar
Disorder

A woman who would fight with anyone

SUSAN WAS TWENTY–EIGHT when she first became depressed. Her doctor treated it with antidepressants. However, after a few months, she found that she was becoming very restless and had difficulty sleeping and times when she felt over–excited. Her mind became 'full of ideas' about how to improve her job, yet she couldn't focus on work. After two years of repeated depression, antidepressants and spells of restlessness, she decided to leave her job, as she thought she could improve her situation.

She started a new job in a bank, but the cycle began again and after six months she left and returned home. She was referred to a psychiatrist.

At her first visit to the psychiatrist, she described being in the restless phase. She was extremely irritable and said, 'At the moment I fight with everyone and anyone.' She had gained a lot of weight due to her increase in appetite over a two-week period. She felt out of control, extremely excited and couldn't sleep.

Susan had had a happy and stable childhood; her parents were still alive and had always been very loving. She had a cousin whom she knew suffered from manic depression (or bipolar disorder), and her mother had been depressed several years earlier, but was now well.

After a few visits, the psychiatrist was able to see the changes in Susan's mood and agreed that she was showing signs of bipolar disorder, with both episodes of depression and periods of being high. She was started on a drug called sodium valproate which helped stabilize her mood. She returned to work in the bank, and is now in the process of buying a house.

What is bipolar disorder?

Bipolar disorder used to be called manic depression. It is an illness where people experience both depression (see p. 76) and episodes of being high or elated. These mood swings are greater and much more severe than the usual mood changes that most of us experience. The episodes are often unpleasant and, even when feeling elated, the person feels out of control and irritable. Occasionally the person may feel very happy in a high, but those around them will see it as excessive.

The mood swings are often independent of anything that is happening in the person's life. They are often caused by the problems of day-to-day living. For example, getting up for work may be impossible during the depressed phase. During a period of elation, people may behave in a way that is out of character for them. They may, for instance, spend money excessively or make reckless and unwise decisions on the spur of the moment.

How common is it?
Between one and four people in every 100 are affected by bipolar disorder.

Can anyone get it?

Bipolar disorder is slightly more common in women than men, and typically begins in the mid-twenties. It is rare for bipolar disorder to begin in the over-sixties. It often runs in families, and occurs in all races and cultures.

What does it feel like?

In the depressed phase, you will feel very low in mood and have difficulty getting any pleasure from life, even from things that would normally be a source of happiness. Sometimes you will feel like crying, although when deeply depressed it is hard to cry. You may find yourself wishing you were dead or may even start thinking about suicide.

You may lose your appetite, have difficulty sleeping and experience aches and pains. Feelings of tension and restlessness may make you agitated. Your concentration and energy will be reduced and you may lose all your self-confidence.

In the high phase, your mood may be elated or you may feel irritable and angry, particularly with people around you. Your thoughts are likely to race as you have lots of great ideas, perhaps about making loads of money or setting up a new business. It is likely that you would have bags of energy and confidence and won't seem to need any sleep.

In a severe or manic state, you may be convinced that you have special powers or that you have a special relationship with film stars or royalty. Your judgement is likely to be impaired, so you may behave very unwisely on a financial or sexual front. This can leave you facing major problems when you recover.

Sometimes people have a mixture of depression and elation at the same time; we call this a mixed state.

There is usually a gap between episodes when the person is completely well – this may vary from months to years.

What causes bipolar disorder?

Genes play a part, so there is a 5 to 10 per cent chance that the child of someone with bipolar disorder may have the condition.

We don't really know what causes the mood swings, but we think it has something to do with the way certain chemicals work in the brain. Stress and life events, such as bereavement or financial problems, may trigger the illness, although relapses often occur for no obvious reason.

What can be done to help?

Medicines can play an important role in treating the episodes and in preventing the person becoming unwell again (relapse). Psychotherapy – talking treatments – also has a role to play in helping people manage their illness.

Preventing relapse

Lithium is the main drug prescribed. It is taken as a long-term treatment even when the person is completely well and reduces the risk of relapse. This drug has been used since the late 1940s.

Before starting lithium, various physical checks are carried out to make sure your heart, kidneys and thyroid gland are working normally. When you are taking the drug, blood tests are carried out about every three months to make sure the level in the body is right. Side-effects include weight gain, thirst and interference with the thyroid gland, but the blood tests keep a check on this.

Other drugs can also be used to prevent relapse, including carbamazepine, sodium valproate and lamotrigine.

Depressed phase

The depressed phase is sometimes treated with antidepressants, but there is a risk that they can make some people high.

High phase

This can be treated with a mood stabilizer, such as lithium or sodium valproate. Sometimes antipsychotics are used, especially if someone is very over-excited and restless. Sleeping tablets or mild tranquillizers, such as diazepam or lorazepam, are also used to help calm people.

Psychotherapy

Cognitive behavioural therapy (CBT; see p. 427) can help prevent relapse, especially into depression. CBT can help you to change how you think ('cognitive') and what you do ('behaviour'). These changes can help you understand and manage your thoughts and behaviour, and so feel better. Unlike some of the other talking treatments, CBT focuses on the 'here and now' problems and difficulties.

Helping a person to understand their illness, and helping them to recognize the early signs of relapse so that they can take steps to prevent it, is important and effective. If the illness has caused strain in the family, then couple, family or interpersonal therapy may help (see pp. 444 and 442).

If this is your MANIC phase — I dread your depressed one ...

Complementary therapies

Some people think that omega-3 fish oils may be useful when used in combination with a mood stabilizer. It is best to avoid using St John's Wort as this can cause people to 'switch' into a high. It can also reduce the effectiveness of other medications.

Stopping treatment

There is often a temptation to reduce or stop treatment when feeling well, especially if there have been no symptoms for a few years. However, bipolar disorder is a long-term illness for which there is no cure, though it can be effectively controlled with maintenance medication. Stopping treatment may well lead to relapse. If you are determined to come off treatment, then it must be done slowly, otherwise there is a very high chance that you will become unwell again.

Special considerations

❖ Pregnancy is the most important. Most mood stabilizers can damage the unborn baby, so it is very important that appropriate contraceptive precautions are taken. If a couple wish to conceive, they should seek specialist advice.

❖ Both valproate and carbamazepine are thought to be safe to take when breastfeeding, but lithium should be used only with extreme caution and the safety of lamotrigine is uncertain. Breastfeeding may be associated with sleep deprivation in the mother, so this must be carefully considered, as it may induce relapse.

❖ When stopping lithium, it must be reduced over at least two weeks, as 'rebound mania' can occur if the drug is stopped suddenly.

❖ If more than one mood stabilizer is used, the dosage must be carefully monitored, as the drugs may interact with each other.

❖ Always inform your doctor if you are on any other medication, since a variety of commonly used drugs can alter the effectiveness of mood stabilizers.

Tips for patients

❖ Sticking to your treatment is essential if you are to stay well.

❖ Learn to listen to your body and your mind – in this way you will be able to identify subtle changes in your behaviour, your sleep pattern or your mood before these become noticeable to others. This will allow you time to seek treatment early and hopefully prevent relapse. For example, one person always changed into brighter clothes when she was relapsing, whilst another began to send text messages more frequently. Sometimes this self-knowledge does not come immediately, and may only develop after a few relapses.

❖ In the early stages of recovery it is helpful to keep a mood diary, as this will allow you to track your recovery and will assist in deciding the extent to which your treatment is controlling your mood swings.

❖ If substances such as cannabis are used, you may find that it upsets your mood; this should be avoided.

❖ Be cautious in your use of alcohol, especially in the early period of treatment.

❖ Take care to avoid jet lag. Sleep deprivation from other causes, such as partying, can also make the illness more unstable and may provoke relapses.

❖ Consider meeting others with bipolar disorder. This may happen informally in the outpatient clinic. A number of organizations exist that provide more formal support and information to those with bipolar disorder and to their relatives.

❖ Try to understand your illness by reading about it, or joining one of the support organizations that can update you on the latest scientific advances.

Tips for families and friends

❖ Do not try to protect the person from stresses. It is up to each person to identify their own vulnerabilities, as these are different for everybody. Overprotection will add to the stigma and the annoyance (even anger) that some feel at having a psychiatric illness.

❖ With the permission of your family member, it might be helpful to their psychiatrist if you keep an independent diary of the mood changes *you notice* in them. This should be based on your own observations rather than on what the person tells you. Your diary may help in deciding whether the illness is being brought under control.

❖ Encourage them to stick with the treatment and to keep in touch with the doctor or other members of the mental health team.

Professor Patricia Casey

Dr Persaud's conclusion

Bipolar disorder is probably as serious a problem as schizophrenia, and yet it receives much less publicity in the media for reasons that remain mysterious, given that it is probably just as common, if not more so.

One consequence of its relative neglect is that even doctors don't receive as much training in its diagnosis and treatment as they do with schizophrenia. This could mean that bipolar disorder is one of the most missed psychiatric diagnoses and could even be one of the most misdiagnosed. This is a great pity, as again the prognosis is excellent with the right treatment.

A recent development is the idea that prescribing antidepressants might be unhelpful and could even be dangerous for sufferers, and so the management of the illness requires specialist input and constant review.

People with bipolar disorder frequently appear very sensitive to relatively minor life upsets, and therefore benefit from the newly developed psychological approaches designed to improve coping skills and enhance early self-recognition of relapse.

SUPPORT ORGANIZATIONS

Manic Depression Fellowship, Castleworks, 21 St George's Road, London SE1 6ES; helpline: 08456 340 540; fax: 020 7793 2693; www.mdf.org.uk

www.lucidinterval.org This site is written by a person with bipolar disorder and provides very useful hints for identifying relapses in their early stage.

Bipolar Aware: www.bipolaraware.co.uk

Aware, 72 Lower Leeson Street, Dublin 2, Ireland; helpline: +353 190303 302; www.aware.co.ie

WEBSITES OUTSIDE THE UK

Australia:
www.blackdoginstitute.org.au

New Zealand:
www.balance.org.nz

Canada:
www.mooddisorderscanada.ca

South Africa:
www.lifeline.org.za

India:
www.namiindia.com

FURTHER READING

An Unquiet Mind, Kay Redfield Jamison, Picador, 1997

*i*SUPPORT

Body Image Disorders

A man who camouflaged himself

BRETT IS A TWENTY–FIVE–YEAR–OLD man who has just been diagnosed with body dysmorphic disorder (BDD). He is a graphic designer who lives alone and is not currently in a relationship. Brett, a shy boy, was teased by his classmates when he was younger; this continued into adolescence and now adulthood. The teasing took the form of remarks about his mild acne and lack of popularity.

The problem began when Brett was fifteen and a comment was made during a school dance about his nose being crooked. When he arrived home that night, he went straight to the mirror and began to study his nose in depth. He indeed found a slight bump. His mirror–checking gradually worsened as he got older. He now checks his appearance in mirrors and other reflective surfaces between fifteen and twenty times a day.

Brett always looks towards the ground when he walks

along, as he thinks that people are less likely to see his nose. He avoids eye contact when talking to people and frequently pretends to scratch his face so that he has an excuse to have his hand over his nose. He feels very uncomfortable when people are able to see his profile. He will always choose a seat that he believes will not allow people to see his face from angles that accentuate his nose. He avoids having his picture taken. In the train, he changes seats often because he feels that people sitting next to him are criticizing his nose. Brett always compares his nose to other people's, and avoids social gatherings and being out in public whenever he can.

He assumes other people's lives must be much better than his, based solely on the shape of their noses. He is constantly planning cosmetic surgery in his mind, but he doesn't have the money to do it. The thought of no longer camouflaging himself, or not looking in the mirror, makes him panic. His heart rate increases and he starts sweating, especially in the palms of his hands. Brett eventually decides he needs help.

Body dysmorphic disorder is usually overcome using cognitive behavioural therapy (CBT), although sometimes it may also require the person to take antidepressants called SSRIs (selective serotonin re-uptake inhibitors). The CBT will help his behaviour, such as the continual mirror-checking and looking towards the ground. The therapist will refocus Brett on what he enjoys in life so that, despite feeling anxious, he can do things he has been avoiding for quite some time. He will also be asked to attend group therapy with other people who have BDD.

After Brett has finished his CBT, he still notices himself comparing his features to those of others. However, he now understands that just because their noses appear to him to be more attractive, it does not mean they have a better life than he does. Although comparing his features with others' has not stopped completely, he has learned not to give in to his previous behaviour, but to observe it and let it pass.

Brett still attends his group therapy once every two weeks and is reminded of the positive changes in his life. He can walk down the street without holding his hand to his nose, and he attends social events. He now speaks to others who have been diagnosed with BDD and helps them to change their lives as he has done.

What is body dysmorphic disorder?

Body dysmorphic disorder is the name given to a condition in which a person spends a lot of time concerned about their appearance. They may compare their looks with other people's, worry that they are physically imperfect, and spend a long time in front of a mirror trying to hide what they believe is a defect.

In diagnosing BDD, healthcare professionals will look for signs of real distress, an inability to socialize and to work, or other behaviours that stop people leading their lives as they should. The healthcare professionals will also make sure that this preoccupation about a certain aspect of the body is not caused by another mental health problem, such as anorexia nervosa (see p. 93).

The most common preoccupations found in patients with BDD are with the nose, skin, hair, eyes, eyelids, mouth, lips, jaw and chin. However, any part of the body may be involved, and the preoccupation is frequently focused on several body parts.

Complaints often involve perceived or slight flaws on the face, the size of body features (too small or too big), hair thinning, acne, wrinkles, scars, visible blood vessels, paleness or redness of the complexion, asymmetry or lack of proportion. Sometimes the complaint is extremely vague; it may amount to no more than the patient feeling generally ugly.

Some patients with BDD spend hours in front of a mirror, whilst others keep away from them (sometimes by covering them or removing them) to avoid the distress of seeing their own image. BDD is a hidden disorder and many patients do not seek help from mental health professionals. When people with BDD do seek help, they may also have symptoms of depression or social phobia (see pp. 76 and 166) and will not reveal the main problem unless they are specifically questioned.

Individuals with BDD are often very secretive about their problems because they think they will be seen by others as vain and self-absorbed. It is important that friends and family of people with BDD are sensitive to their feelings and understand that their 'defects' are in fact real in their eyes, and also extremely disabling.

BDD patients generally have a poor quality of life. They are often unemployed or disadvantaged at work, can be socially isolated or housebound, and are at high risk of committing suicide.

Many patients with BDD seek help from cosmetic surgeons or experts in skin problems (dermatologists). Approximately 5–10 per cent of patients seeking a cosmetic procedure will have BDD. These patients are often dissatisfied with their surgery and their symptoms of BDD are the same, or worse, after it. In general, it is not recommended that individuals with BDD have a cosmetic procedure, as research has found that it does not help or make their life any easier.

When does a concern with one's appearance become body dysmorphic disorder?

A person with BDD usually avoids a wide range of social and public situations to prevent themselves feeling uncomfortable and worrying that people are rating them negatively. Sometimes they will socialize, but feel very self-conscious.

They may camouflage themselves excessively to hide their perceived defect by using heavy make-up, brushing their hair in a particular way, changing their posture, or wearing heavy clothes.

They may spend several hours a day thinking about their perceived defect and asking themselves questions that cannot be answered (for example, 'Why was I born this way?' 'If only my nose was straighter and smaller'). They may feel forced to repeat frequently certain time-consuming behaviours such as:

❖ checking their appearance in a mirror or reflective surface
❖ seeking reassurance about their appearance
❖ checking by feeling their skin with their fingers
❖ cutting or combing their hair to make it 'just so'
❖ picking their skin to make it smooth
❖ comparing themselves with models in magazines or people in the street

Why does body dysmorphic disorder develop?

There has been very little research into the development of BDD. In general terms, there are two different levels of explanation – one biological and the other psychological.

The biological explanation would be that a person has a genetic predisposition to a mental disorder, which may make it more likely for them to develop BDD. Another risk factor for developing BDD can be that the person is more aesthetically sensitive, e.g. being well educated, or working in art or design.

Certain stresses or life events, especially during adolescence, such as teasing or abuse, may bring on the disorder. Once it has taken hold, the person may also develop an imbalance of chemicals in the brain.

The psychological explanation would be that a person's low self-esteem, and the way they judge themselves almost exclusively by their appearance, can cause BDD to develop. They may worry about being alone and isolated.

Once the disorder has developed, the excessive self-focused attention and ruminating about having a defect or being ugly keeps it going. This leads the person to thinking about how they are going to fix the defect and ways they can avoid situations, or to activities such as excessive checking in mirrors. They may also constantly compare themselves with others, and seek reassurance about their features from other people.

What does it feel like?

Many BDD sufferers are preoccupied with minor or imaginary flaws, usually on some part of their face, but they may also focus on several other aspects of their body. Typical flaws include:

❖ perceived acne, scars, hair thinning, wrinkles and veins
❖ lack of symmetry of the body
❖ body parts are seen as too big or too small
❖ some aspects of the body are out of proportion with others

This may lead to:
❖ troubling thoughts and images about the defect

❖ mirror-checking or mirror-avoidance

❖ either vague feelings of ugliness, or specific complaints about the imagined 'defect'

❖ seeking reassurance about their feature(s)

❖ seeking referrals to dermatologists or plastic surgeons

What can be done to help?

There are two recommended treatments for individuals with BDD:

Cognitive behavioural therapy (CBT) is a psychological therapy that can help you to change how you think ('cognitive') and what you do ('behaviour'). These changes can help you to feel better. Unlike some of the other talking treatments, CBT focuses on the 'here and now' problems and difficulties. Instead of concentrating on the causes of your distress or symptoms in the past, it looks for ways to improve your state of mind now. (See also p. 427.)

CBT helps someone with BDD approach situations or activities that are associated with their anxieties to test out whether they have a *problem* with their appearance, or whether the problem is *worrying* about their appearance.

With the support of the therapist, the patient is 'exposed' to whatever makes them frightened or anxious (for example, allowing someone to see their nose from the side), so they can learn to deal with the anxiety until it gradually goes away. CBT may also help someone stop getting into the constant comparative thought pattern and the rumination that goes with it.

CBT often requires a person to work on an aspect of their treatment between sessions by keeping a diary, or listing things that lead them to be distressed.

Antidepressants. As an adult with BDD, you may be given an anti-depressant called fluoxetine. Research has shown that for people with BDD fluoxetine works better than other SSRIs. You will need to take the tablets for at least three months to find out whether they help. If you do not respond to fluoxetine, another SSRI or clomipramine may be tried.

The main problem with the SSRIs is that there may be a high rate of relapse when the drug is stopped; so if it does work, the medication may need to be taken for a few years. Side-effects of SSRIs most commonly include nausea, gastrointestinal disturbance, abdominal pain, agitation and anxiety, sedation, sleep disruption and headache.

There is no evidence that BDD benefits from drugs used for psychotic disorders, even delusional types of BDD (delusions are also a symptom of psychosis).

Which treatment is right for me?

❖ If someone has BDD and their symptoms are mild, they should be offered brief (time-limited) CBT to address their symptoms.
❖ If a person has BDD and the symptoms are more severe, they should be given a choice of an SSRI or CBT to address their symptoms. These treatments are often offered in combination.

Tips for families and friends

✔ Do

❖ give practical and emotional support
❖ learn how BDD develops and about the treatments that help
❖ ask the professionals any questions you may have to gain a better understanding
❖ help the professionals during their assessments, if asked
❖ avoid talking about appearances altogether

✘ Don't

❖ tell the person with BDD they are vain or narcissistic
❖ compare the person with BDD to another person or celebrity
❖ talk about your own (or other people's) appearance with the person with BDD
❖ respond to reassurance-seeking, or discussions about whether a feature is camouflaged or can be seen; focus more on why the person is

seeking reassurance, and whether it helps them to function better in the long term

Whenever possible, it can be helpful for everyone if healthcare professionals work not only with the person with BDD, but also with their family and carers.

Jessica Colon
and Dr David Veale

Dr Persaud's conclusion

One dilemma at the heart of BDD is that the cosmetic surgeon is often hovering in the background, yet many people cannot see what actual physical difference surgery has made to a person who is so obsessed with a tiny difference in their face or body.

However, it's also the case that sometimes surgery does appear massively to alleviate the suffering of someone who is so preoccupied with their appearance. The problem is that no one can reliably tell who is going to be helped by surgery and who isn't.

There are many tragic stories of sufferers seeking excessive surgery and becoming ever more distressed by the outcome. This is one of the most difficult problems to resolve, because at its centre is a conflict between patient and clinician – the patient thinks they have a physical problem, while the clinician believes it's a psychological one. The two sides need to develop a working relationship, perhaps based on a more sensible approach, realizing when something is working and when it isn't, and who is going to shoulder the responsibility for the result of an important and irreversible process such as surgery.

i
SUPPORT

SUPPORT ORGANIZATIONS

OCD Action: a charity focused on obsessive compulsive and related disorders, including BDD. 22–4 Highbury Grove, Suite 107, London N5 2EA; helpline: 0845 390 OCDA (6232); email: info@ocdaction.org.uk; *www.ocdaction.org.uk*

OCD Foundation: an international not-for-profit organization composed of people with OCD and related disorders. 676 State Street, New Haven, CT 06511, USA; tel: +1 203 401 2070; *www.ocfoundation.org*

BDD Central: a comprehensive website for sufferers of BDD. *www.bddcentral.com*

WEBSITES OUTSIDE THE UK

Australia:
www.disability.vic.gov.au

India:
www.namiindia.com

Canada:
www.cwhn.ca

New Zealand:
www.tki.org.nz

FURTHER READING

The Broken Mirror: Understanding and Treating Body Dysmorphic Disorder, Katharine Phillips, Oxford University Press, New York, USA, 2005

Feeling Good About the Way You Look: A Program for Overcoming Body Image Problems, Sabine Wilhelm, Guilford Publications, New York, USA, 2006

The BDD Workbook: Overcome Body Dysmorphic Disorder and End Body Image Obsessions, James Claiborn and Cherry Pedrick, New Harbinger Publications, Oakland, California, USA, 2002

6
Cravings

A woman who avoids walking behind smokers

DEVINA HAD BEEN smoking for more than thirty years. She had been taught to smoke by her best friend Micha, on the no. 31 bus on the way to and from school, and especially how to inhale properly. She had her first menthol cigarette when she was twelve.

Devina's father had died of lung cancer at the age of fifty-six and she had watched him suffer over the last few years of his life. He'd started smoking as a very young child when still living in Jamaica. Somehow, Devina never believed that this would happen to her.

However, as the years wore on, and more and more of her friends stopped smoking, she started to feel like a pariah and realized that she was truly addicted. She gave up for a year, but started again when she put on weight. Finally, after years of struggling to stop, going cold turkey, nicotine patches and gum, she finally gave up by using a self–help book.

It's been six months now, but she still craves a cigarette. She knows that this feeling will never go away, but it lessens every day. It's the little things in life which trigger her cravings: walking behind someone in the street who is smoking, having an argument with her partner, a bad day at work, a glass of wine in the evening, the long boring wait in an airport, the interval at a concert and, worst moment of all, her first cup of coffee in the morning.

She still avoids parties or events in pubs where she knows there will be a lot of smokers. Her fridge is full of fruit for those moments when she has a desperate craving for a cigarette. She has started running in her local park twice a week with another ex–smoker. She feels much happier and no longer wakes up every morning with that hungover feeling – but she knows that she has to take every day as it comes.

What is craving?

Craving can be hard to understand if you have not experienced it. It can vary from a mild sensation to something very unpleasant and it often occurs in people who are dependent on drugs that affect the mind. These addictive drugs can be illegal (such as heroin, cocaine and cannabis), legal (such as alcohol or nicotine) or prescribed (such as diazepam or temazepam). See also Chapter 34, p. 329.

Some drugs are more addictive than others. A high proportion of people using cocaine or nicotine become addicted, whereas a smaller proportion of people drinking alcohol or using cannabis become addicted (less than 10 per cent). When someone becomes addicted, one of the common features is that it is difficult to stop taking the drug and then stay off it. When an addicted person stops taking the drug, they can crave for it, and this often leads to their going back on the drug.

Of smokers trying to give it up, about 15 per cent remain abstinent after fifty-two weeks. This indicates that, once addicted, even motivated smokers find it difficult to remain abstinent. Over 90 per cent of teenagers who smoke three to four cigarettes a day will be trapped into a career of regular smoking which lasts typically for some thirty to forty years. About 18 per cent of people who try cocaine become dependent. Nicotine is probably even more addictive than cocaine and both are more addictive than other substances commonly misused.

What does it feel like?

Craving is usually an unpleasant experience, with feelings of tension, anxiety, restlessness, irritability, feeling on a 'short fuse', or intense hunger. There are often physical symptoms of muscle tension, sweating, heart racing, light-headedness or headache. Feeling anxious or stressed because of problems in your life can make the craving worse.

Craving is usually more intense when someone does not have access to the drug. However, some people also experience craving as pleasant, almost like the effects of the drug itself, even though they have not consumed it for some time. This seems to be more common with stimulant drugs like cocaine and amphetamine.

When does craving happen?

Craving occurs when withdrawing from an addictive drug. With some drugs, it can start a few hours after the last dose, but it can sometimes take up to several days. Once withdrawal has begun, craving generally reaches a peak after a few days and then gradually declines. Some people experience craving many weeks or months after the withdrawal has ended.

Craving can be started by external reminders (cues), such as seeing someone smoking a cigarette, an advertisement for alcohol, or walking past a pub. Cues can also be internal, such as feeling stressed or depressed.

What can be done to help?

Craving is relieved by further use of the drug. However, this effect is only temporary. Further episodes of craving may be experienced once the effects of the drug have worn off. So in the short term taking the drug helps, but many people find it problematic in the long term. As tolerance develops, more and more of the drug is needed to relieve the craving.

Treatments for craving can target both the addiction and the craving itself.

Addiction and dependence can be treated with medication, but talking therapies – such as counselling and psychotherapy – are also important. People with addictions often need to make changes in their lifestyle – such as how they spend their leisure time, how they work and how they manage their personal lives.

Treatment is aimed at changing both people's behaviour and their relationship with their drug, so that they use it in a less damaging way or stop using it altogether.

Craving improves over time once the drug has been stopped and the withdrawal process is over. While craving can be intense in the first few days or weeks after stopping a drug, this usually improves if the person manages to stay drug free. So the good news is that time is a great healer.

Self-help

The simplest approach to reducing craving is to avoid situations in which you are likely to come into contact with reminders of the drug – including the drug itself, situations, places and people. Sometimes this is easier said than done, but with careful planning it is usually possible to minimize the level of temptation. For example, if you are trying to stop drinking and have been invited to a social event where you know there will be a lot of drinking and pressure on you to drink, you need to ask yourself if it is a good idea to go at all.

If it is not possible to avoid the situation, what could you do to stay safe and avoid temptation? Some people find it helpful to write down on a card all the reasons why they decided to stop taking the drug and all the problems it has caused them. They can carry this with them and, when the craving occurs, use it to remind themselves that there are good reasons not to use the drug. This is sometimes called 'urge surfing'.

Another effective way is to distract yourself by turning your mind to something more pleasant, or engaging in an unrelated activity, such as exercise or watching a film. Sometimes, calling a non-drug-using friend or family member and talking it through or, even better, talking about something completely different, can help.

Self-help groups, such as Alcoholics Anonymous or Narcotics Anonymous, can provide support. It is often helpful to talk to someone who has been through the same things that you are experiencing, and so can provide advice and support.

Other techniques, including relaxation, deep breathing, massage, hypnotherapy, acupuncture, exercise and eating sugar, have all been tried and are sometimes helpful.

It is worth finding out what's available locally. If these treatments are not beneficial, it doesn't mean that you can't be helped. You may just need to try something else.

Some people suffer so much that they do better in a drug-free residential setting for the first few weeks or months after stopping a drug.

Complementary therapies

Few complementary therapies for craving have been tested by research. So they may be costly and without benefit. We just don't know.

Medication

A number of medications can be used to help addicts overcome their cravings. See also p. 448.

Nicotine

Tobacco products all contain the drug nicotine. Nicotine replacement therapy (NRT) helps to reduce craving. NRT products can be bought over the counter in chemists or obtained on prescription. They work by releasing nicotine into the body so that nicotine craving is tackled without needing to smoke: 'substitution therapy'. NRT is available as a patch that is placed on the skin, as a chewing gum that is chewed and kept in the mouth, and as a nasal spray that is inhaled. Over time, the NRT is gradually reduced and stopped, so that the nicotine craving is minimized.

Bupropion, although not a form of NRT, also reduces the need for people to smoke.

Alcohol

Acamprosate reduces the risk of relapse for some people. We don't know how it works, but it reduces the strength and frequency of craving rather than removing it altogether.

Naltrexone is thought to work by reducing the pleasurable effects of alcohol. It is not commonly used and then only by an addiction specialist.

Disulfiram (Antabuse) is also used to treat alcohol dependence, but is not thought to work by reducing craving.

Heroin

Craving can be treated by replacing heroin with a drug that has similar effects (substitution therapy). Methadone is the drug that is often used. Buprenorphine is another option. Both reduce craving for opiates, but because these drugs are like heroin, at some point in the future when the person plans to stop taking them they will still experience withdrawal and craving. This is minimized by gradual withdrawal of the drugs.

Cocaine

Unfortunately, no drug has been found to be effective in treating cocaine craving, but the search continues.

Benzodiazepines (e.g. diazepam, temazepam)

There is no effective treatment to combat craving for benzodiazepines. However, it is usually helpful to substitute a long-acting drug such as diazepam for a shorter-acting one such as temazepam or lorazepam. It seems to be easier to withdraw gradually from the longer-acting drugs.

Talking treatments

Most services treating people with addiction have access to counselling services. At a basic level, this aims to provide information and support to help the individual cope better with their addiction.

Cognitive behavioural therapy (CBT; see p. 427) helps you modify thoughts, feelings and behaviours. CBT can help you to change how you think ('cognitive') and what you do ('behaviour'). These changes can help you understand and manage your thoughts and behaviour, and so feel better. Unlike some of the other talking treatments, CBT focuses on the 'here and now' problems and difficulties. Motivational enhancement therapy empowers people to make positive changes; and relapse prevention helps people to identify and manage triggers for relapse, and encourage effective ways of coping.

One promising approach is cue-exposure treatment. This involves exposing the abstinent drug or alcohol user to cues associated with former use (such as the sight and smell of a favourite drink, or pictures of drugs and injecting equipment) in a safe, supportive environment, such as a hospital. There is some evidence that repeated exposure over several days can reduce craving, and the risk of relapse, in alcohol dependence. However, this approach is still experimental and is not yet widely available.

Where are these treatments available?

Local provision will vary, depending on where you live. Checking on the internet, a local phone directory, or using the resources at the end of this chapter may help.

The first point of contact for many people is their GP, who should know what is available in the area. They may be able to offer treatment themselves, or put you in touch with local services. The National Health Service (NHS), as well as private and charitable bodies, may all offer treatment for these issues. Most people would be able to find some useful help from these agencies.

If you want to stop smoking, either a GP or a pharmacist will be able to help. Nicotine Replacement Therapy is widely available, either over the counter or on prescription. The NHS also provides smoking clinics for people who need additional support.

Drug and alcohol dependence can be treated by your GP, but there is also a wide range of voluntary, NHS and private treatment agencies that can provide more specialized help. Substitution treatment, such as methadone, is widely available in the UK; and talking therapies are becoming more commonplace. People who need in-patient treatment, or residential rehabilitation, should be able to access this through their local addiction-treatment agency, and local authority care managers for addiction.

Alcoholics Anonymous and Narcotics Anonymous have groups and meetings throughout the UK, and can easily be found in the phone book or on the internet.

Tips for families and friends

Craving can be intense, so you may notice changes in the way that somebody behaves. They may become more irritable, bad-tempered, distracted, stressed or lower in mood than usual. However, support from a friend or loved one can go a long way.

Craving can come in short bursts, and even pass without the need to turn to the drug. So simply talking about the experience, or even trying to take their mind off it, may help. Try listening to what they have to say or asking them what they would prefer, if you feel comfortable with this.

You could suggest that they try some of the strategies described above. When things are more settled, you may want to talk about the possibilities of addiction, and whether they should try to seek treatment. It may help them to take the first useful steps towards getting specialist help.

Dr Billy Boland
and Professor Colin Drummond

Dr Persaud's conclusion

Coping with craving is a particularly tough part of the thorny area of psychological dysfunction, but it is important to bear in mind that this is part of the more general problem of how to cope with distress. Many patients have difficulty with the concept that suffering is not something that just happens to you, but is coloured by your attitude and the way you cope.

Patients often turn to doctors to relieve their distress and become upset if modern medicine appears unable to help them.

'Toughing it out' is obviously all too easy for people to suggest if they have never experienced terrible craving themselves. The reality is, however, that some distress in life you have to learn to tolerate. The methods suggested above, including distraction, can help. We shouldn't expect our distress to be 'medicined' away.

It is particularly interesting that it is largely the non-medicine approaches, such as those used by movements like Alcoholics Anonymous and Narcotics Anonymous, that appear to be adopted most around the world by successful recoverers.

SUPPORT ORGANIZATIONS:

Action on Smoking and Health: www.ash.org.uk

Alcohol Concern: tel: 020 7928 7377; www.alcoholconcern.org.uk

Alcoholics Anonymous: helpline: 0845 769 7555;
www.alcoholics-anonymous.org.uk

Al Anon (help for families): tel: 020 7403 0888; www.al-anonuk.org.uk

Benzodiazepine.org: www.benzodiazepine.org

Drugscope: tel: 020 7928 1211; www.drugscope.org.uk

Frank phoneline: National drugs helpline: tel: 0800 77 66 00;
www.talktofrank.com

WEBSITES OUTSIDE THE UK

Australia:
www.ranzcp.org

New Zealand:
www.nzna.org

Canada:
www.drugaddictiontreatment.ca

FURTHER READING

The Craving Brain: A Bold New Approach to Breaking Free from Drug Addiction, Overeating, Alcoholism, Gambling, Ronald A. Ruden and Marcia Byalick, Harper Paperbacks, 2003

Overcoming Problem Drinking, Marcantonio Spada, Constable and Robinson, 2006

i SUPPORT

Dangerousness and Mental Disorder

Two people – how dangerous are they?

A man with a knife and nowhere to go

KEVIN IS NINETEEN, just out of prison, and very angry. He is the fifth of eight children, most with different fathers, and can't remember his own. He was always teased at school and was hardly there in the last three or four years. He can barely read. He spent most of his time with a group of boys who drank and did drugs together, and went stealing, shoplifting or mugging. Kevin has had convictions for theft, drug possession, reckless driving and violence.

When he was twelve he attacked a school inspector, who spent several weeks in hospital with head and rib injuries. Kevin saw a child psychiatrist and was to see a psychologist and a social worker, but neither he nor his family kept any appointments. He recently knifed one of his 'friends' while they were both high on drugs. He left prison yesterday, and went straight to his mother's – but she has a new man who threatened him. So he has nowhere to live, no money, no job and nothing to do.

A librarian who keeps his wife hostage

Ernest was the city's chief librarian. He was fifty-nine and had been married to Mary for thirty-five years. His son David noticed a difference in him after getting back from a year away travelling. He asked Susie, his sister, what she thought. She hadn't seen Ernest for weeks because she'd been busy with her new baby, but felt it was strange that her mother had not visited recently.

That night, David noticed that his father had drunk nearly a whole bottle of whisky. Ernest said that Mary had been 'spending all our money, so I have to stay at home to keep an eye on things.' David's mother would 'clam up' with Ernest in the room, so Susie found an excuse to talk to her alone.

'At first Mum wouldn't say much, but I found out that six months ago there had been the threat of job losses at the library where Dad works. He had been concerned for his staff, but then started to worry about his own job. That's when he started drinking, and waking up in the middle of the night.

'After a month or two of this, he got the idea that Mum was taking money from their bank accounts so that she could leave him. He got angry and insisted that she shouldn't go out any more. She says it's easier not to argue, and that's why she hasn't been round.'

What is the risk of dangerousness in mental illness?

It is commonly believed that violence is an integral part of mental disorder. A survey of TV dramas found that nearly three-quarters of characters with a mental illness were also portrayed as violent. Although the media hugely exaggerate the amount of violence due to mental illness, there is some connection.

For example, people with schizophrenia are about four times more likely to be violent – even so, only 3 per cent of the violence in society is caused by people with schizophrenia. The truth is, people with such serious mental disorders are more likely to become victims of crime.

Shouldn't risky people just be locked up?

As so little of the violence in society is due even to severe mental illness, locking up everyone with schizophrenia would do very little towards creating a safer society.

Can't we tell who is going to be dangerous?

Not very well. People are complicated, and there are too many unpredictable factors involved.

Predicting risk is in itself risky because the consequences can be so serious. If we get it wrong by overestimating risk, a person can be wrongfully accused or labelled as being dangerous, or even locked up. If we are wide of the mark by underestimating risk, harm may come to someone else.

So, how can we assess dangerousness? We start by looking at a number of different factors in a person's life.

'**Static' factors** are the things that won't change – they include gender (men are more likely to be violent than women), a violent or abusive upbringing, and a past history of violent acts to people or animals. We can't do anything about these, but they give us an idea about someone's 'baseline' risk of being violent.

'Dynamic' factors are the things that might change for better or worse. They include the use of drugs or alcohol, whether someone has accepted psychological help, or whether they continue to see mental health professionals and take their medication.

Patterns of behaviour are important – is the violent behaviour becoming more or less frequent, or more or less serious? These are important factors because we can often do something about them. They can be used in two ways:

❖ 'Actuarial' assessments are like the risk tables used by insurance companies. They predict the likelihood that an event will occur in a group of people, based on their (mainly 'static') risk factors. They cannot predict whether an individual will offend or not.

❖ Clinical assessments are done with the individual. They tend to take into account rather more of the 'dynamic' factors mentioned above. They also involve an interview and some attempt to develop a psychological understanding.

The actuarial assessment may miss important changes that have happened in someone's life. The clinical assessment may neglect important background factors. So both are usually used.

In practice, psychiatrists want not just to assess risk, but actually to help their patients. Even if you have an idea of risks for an individual, it doesn't take away the need to establish a rapport with them, to listen to what they are saying and to understand what they are meaning.

Risk assessment in real life

In our first case study, Kevin had a long list of 'static' factors predicting violence:

❖ a long history of violence

❖ violence started when he was young

- ❖ employment problems
- ❖ conduct disorder
- ❖ he had not co-operated with efforts to help him

Most assessment systems would predict that he would return to violence. However, Kevin's probation officer managed to find him a place with a special project for the homeless. He was able to get to know a worker there and join a work scheme. He met Judy, a young woman with whom he was able to go to adult literacy classes.

Two years later, Kevin seemed to be coping well with good social support, and was planning to live with Judy. He had not used drugs or alcohol at all in that period, was working on a building site and training in carpentry. He had not been violent.

Those things that could be changed had been changed – his negative attitudes had shifted, he was able to use help, he was beginning to plan appropriately and, for the first time in his life, he had a close personal relationship. This meant that he no longer felt he had to fit in with his old group of 'friends' and their drink and drugs.

However, after two years Kevin was still only twenty-one and did not yet have strong inner resources. Judy had started to talk about wanting a baby, and this brought up a new set of questions. Would a baby divert too much of Judy's attention from this needy man? Could he cope with the stress of having to rely on himself, as well as having to look after a vulnerable partner and her baby? Would he return to his old habits of drugs, alcohol and violence? Changes of this sort mean that services have constantly to re-evaluate risk in the light of new situations.

In our other case, Ernest had none of the 'static' risk factors. Most assessment would have predicted a very low risk of violence. His doctor had known him, for many years, as a sensible, reasonable and kindly person.

Although at first Ernest had refused to visit his family doctor, and even to speak to him when he called at the house, he finally did so and the doctor was reassured. He correctly diagnosed a serious depression (see p. 76) with some psychotic features. He suggested to Ernest that it would be wise to have some treatment, and perhaps to start that treatment in hospital.

Ernest became very angry, saying that the problems were all his wife's doing. He accused the doctor of being the man his wife was interested in, and threatened him. Mary asked the doctor to leave, assuring him that she could cope. The doctor did so, deciding to return the next day. However, that night Ernest attacked his wife and tried to kill himself.

There was very little in his past to suggest that this might happen. Whatever a formal risk assessment predicted, earlier recognition and treatment of Ernest's illness would almost certainly have prevented this incident.

What can be done – risk management

Assessing risk is just a means to an end – knowing what to do to reduce the risk of dangerous behaviour and how and when to do it: a risk management plan. This plan is more likely to be accurate if the psychiatrist has a good relationship with the person and any carers, but this may not always be possible when someone is very ill.

In Kevin's case, his risk factors were recognized and dealt with so that he was able to change his behaviour. In Ernest's case the picture was rather less obvious, because of the lack of background (or 'static') risk factors. In his case, the 'dynamic' factors were of paramount importance – his symptoms had become worse, he had developed delusional ideas, and he perhaps became suddenly more paranoid and fearful following the doctor's visit. The risk involved in situations – and its assessment – can change quickly.

This does not mean that any person who poses any risk needs to be admitted to hospital. The general rule is that the minimum level of security that is compatible with safety should be used. In most cases this means constructing, and carrying out, a plan to manage the separate risk factors involved – outside hospital.

People are often aware that there is a problem and they can be helped without going into hospital. However, occasionally it will be necessary to keep someone in hospital against their will. So if someone's mental illness means that they pose a risk to themselves or others, they can be detained under mental health legislation – even if no harmful act has yet taken place. (See Appendix One, p. 463.)

But hospital admission is nearly always a fairly brief episode in the context of someone's whole life. Outside hospital, risk factors must still be managed – for example, if someone is threatening members of his or her family, they may have to live away from them until the threat has resolved.

The best security for a person with mental disorder – and for the people around them – is effective help and treatment. This will often include medication, but almost always other treatments as well, usually psychotherapy or cognitive behavioural therapy (see pp. 440 and 427). Nearly always, such people will return to ordinary life outside hospital or prison. Good risk management ensures that each person recovers as much freedom as possible, as early as possible and as safely as possible.

In Ernest's case, it is likely that if he had been admitted to hospital immediately, his illness would have responded to treatment. As he felt better and regained insight, the risk would have reduced, and he would have been able to return home to receive longer-term help as an outpatient.

Professor John Gunn and Professor Pamela Taylor

Dr Persaud's conclusion

Part of the work of mental health professionals is to identify people at risk of harming themselves or others. Risk assessment enables us to prevent harm and to plan the right treatment and help. Assessing risk linked to psychological dysfunction is uniquely part of the specialist training of psychiatrists. Policymakers, users of mental health services and carers should make better use of psychiatric expertise by asking more about risk. There should be greater awareness of risk as an issue in mental health services.

It is important to remember that people with mental disorder contribute little to society's violence. Contrary to reports in the media, there is no evidence that community care has led to any increase in violence by the mentally ill in the UK. We can never predict and prevent all violence caused by mental disorder – but the evidence in fact suggests that we are getting better at it.

Governments and newspaper headline writers often become particularly concerned with mental healthcare policy when a tragedy occurs and someone dies or is seriously injured as a result of another's severe mental illness.

By the time anyone develops a dangerous psychiatric disorder, managing the situation has already become complex and difficult for all concerned. Far better in terms of prevention of these tragedies would be the provision of high-quality accessible services, so that at the very earliest stage psychological problems could be addressed vigorously, so preventing them from later developing into something dangerous.

SUPPORT ORGANIZATIONS

There are no non-statutory organizations that we know of which provide specific support for people with mental disorder, or for their relatives and friends, in the event of concern about 'dangerousness'. The following, however, may be helpful:

Samaritans: 24-hour confidential emotional support for people who are experiencing distress or despair, including feelings that may lead to suicide. Tel: 08457 909090 (Ireland: 1850 609090); text: 07725 909090 (Ireland: 0872 609090); email jo@samaritans.org; *www.samaritans.org*

SANELINE: national confidential out-of-hours telephone helpline offering practical information, crisis care and emotional support to anybody affected by mental health problems; the service is open every day and receives calls from patients, family members, carers and health professionals. Tel: 0845 767 8000; *www.sane.org.uk*

If people have been detained in a secure institution because of actual or predicted dangerous behaviour, then it may also be important for them, and for their families, to be able to access support in relation to getting the fact or the conditions of the detention.
The Mental Health Act Commission may be able to help or advise. Tel: 0115 943 7100; *www.mhac.org.uk*

The Mental Welfare Commission for Scotland: advice line: 0800 389 6809; *www.mwcscot.org.uk*

WEBSITES OUTSIDE THE UK

Australia:
www.ranzcp.org

New Zealand:
www.ranzcp.org

Canada:
www.schizophrenia.com

FURTHER READING

Evil: Inside Human Violence and Cruelty, Aaron T. Beck (Foreword), Roy F. Baumeister, Aaron Beck, Owl Books, 1999

75

Depression

A man who thought he would be better off dead

HARRY IS MARRIED with three children. He has worked for many years on the oil rigs in the North Sea. For the past few years he has been team leader, working two weeks on and two weeks off. He usually enjoys life. He is fit and healthy, and rarely sees doctors.

For the past month, however, Harry has been feeling fed up and tired all the time. He is snappy with his family and workmates. He sometimes thinks he would be better off dead, but decided that would make life too difficult for his wife and family. He says, 'I just feel like crying for no reason.' He is tired and edgy, restless at night and has lost his appetite. He finds it difficult to concentrate. He can't see much point in anything, and he's worried that he is letting his family down. He is anxious about returning to work. He does not get on with the other team leader who does the shifts when he is not there.

His wife is supportive but he is worried about letting her get too close to him. He doesn't think it's right to burden her with how he is feeling.

Harry and the doctor agree that he needs some time off work and he is given a sick note for two weeks. The doctor suggests that he is depressed and might benefit from drug treatment. He says he is prepared to 'give anything a go if it helps', so the doctor prescribes him an antidepressant and arranges to see him again in a fortnight.

After two weeks he tells the GP he is a bit better. He says he has more good days than bad ones, though he finds he gets intense feelings of irritation at times, especially in shops. He is keeping himself busy, mainly doing weight training in the local gym and working in his garden. The doctor provides him with another fortnight's sick note.

The next time the GP sees him he is feeling worse, which he puts down to a conversation with his manager about the problems that are building up in work while he is off. He says he is very tense and finds he worries about 'lots of small silly things'. The doctor tells him that he has very high expectations of himself and strongly encourages him to talk to his wife about what has been happening to him recently. The doctor signs him off work for another four weeks, and repeats his antidepressant prescription.

After another two weeks he tells the GP that he is now feeling fine. He has been able to talk things through with his wife and is much happier as a result. He has just come back from a few days' holiday with his family, the first time they have been away together for several years. He's been told that the other team leader in his work is leaving, which is good news. He now intends to return to work in two weeks' time, when his current sick note runs out.

What is depression?

Depression is a common condition, and fortunately there are a number of effective treatments. It is an illness that people are often embarrassed to talk about, as they see it as a sign of weakness. It often overlaps with anxiety (see p. 24), and it is sometimes hard to distinguish depression from common physical illnesses, particularly those that cause pain and fatigue. Depression is often made worse by problems in life, and it can be difficult to decide if someone is depressed or just understandably unhappy.

Why do people become depressed?

There will sometimes be an obvious reason, such as a disappointment, frustration, or losing something or someone important. Sometimes, though, it isn't clear why we feel depressed: we're just 'down' and we don't know why.

❖ It is normal to feel depressed after a bereavement (see p. 279), a divorce or losing a job. After a while we usually come to terms with what's happened, but some of us get stuck in a depressed mood that doesn't lift.

❖ If we are alone, have no friends around, are stressed (see p. 241), have other worries or are physically run down, we are more likely to become depressed.

❖ Depression often strikes when we are physically ill. People may also become depressed after viral infections, like flu or glandular fever.

❖ Anyone can become depressed, but some of us are more likely to suffer than others. This may be because of the make-up of our body, or because of experiences in our life.

❖ Many people who drink too much alcohol (see p. 269) become depressed. It often isn't clear which came first – the drinking or the depression.

❖ Women seem to get depressed more than men. Perhaps men are less likely to admit their feelings, more likely to bottle them up, or to express them through aggression or through drinking heavily.

❖ Depression can run in families.

What about manic depression?

About 1 in 10 people who suffer from serious depression will also have periods when they are high and overactive. This is called manic depression or bipolar disorder (see p. 42).

Isn't depression just a form of weakness?

Depression can happen to the most determined of people. It is not a sign of weakness – even powerful personalities can experience depression. Winston Churchill called it his 'black dog'.

What does it feel like?

If you are depressed you may feel low in mood, have reduced energy and lose your enjoyment of life. You may find it difficult to concentrate on ordinary things and find yourself worrying about things that would not usually bother you. You may feel useless.

You may have disturbed sleep, often waking early in the morning and not being able to doze off again. Your appetite can be affected, causing you to eat either more or less than usual, which leads to changes in weight. You are likely to lose interest in sex. You may have thoughts of ending your life, and perhaps make plans to act on these thoughts (see p. 250).

What can be done to help?

Self–help

❖ Don't keep it to yourself – if you've had bad news, try to tell someone how you feel. It often helps to talk over a painful experience.

❖ Do something – try to take exercise. This will help you keep fit and you may sleep better.

❖ Eat well – try to eat a good, balanced diet, even though you may not feel like eating.

❖ Beware of alcohol – it makes depression worse.

❖ Sleep – try not to worry about finding it difficult to sleep. It may help to get up and listen to the radio, or watch TV while you're lying down, even if you can't sleep.

❖ Tackle the cause – if you know what is behind your depression, it can help to write down the problem and then think of ways to tackle it.

❖ Keep hopeful – remind yourself that many other people have gone through depression. You will come out of it.

Talking treatments

Talking things through with a trained counsellor or therapist can help you get things off your chest and see things more clearly. There are many different sorts of psychotherapy available, though in some countries they are in short supply, so you may find yourself waiting for several months.

Cognitive Behavioural Therapy (CBT) helps overcome the negative thoughts that happen in depression. CBT can help you to change how you think ('cognitive') and what you do ('behaviour'). These changes can help you understand and manage your thoughts and behaviour, and so feel better. Unlike some of the other talking treatments, CBT focuses on the 'here and now' problems and difficulties. (See also p. 427.)

Interpersonal or psychodynamic therapies can be helpful if you find it difficult to get on with other people. Talking treatments take time to work, so you might need anywhere from five to thirty sessions. (See also pp. 442 and 440.)

Complementary therapy

St John's Wort is a herbal remedy available from chemists and is effective in mild to moderate depression. It seems to work in the same way as some antidepressants, but some people find that it has fewer side-effects. If you are thinking of taking St John's Wort, you should consult your doctor as it can produce manic episodes in some vulnerable people, including those with bipolar disorder. If you are taking other medication, you should consult your family doctor, as it can reduce their effectiveness.

This isn't a depression - it's a pit...

Antidepressants

If your depression is severe or goes on for a long time, your doctor may suggest a course of antidepressants. They can help you to feel and cope better, so that you can start to enjoy life and deal with your problems effectively again. You may need to take them for 2–3 weeks before you notice an improvement.

For more information on antidepressants, see Chapter 44, p. 427.

How do antidepressants work?

To be honest, we don't know, but most experts think that they boost the action of two compounds in the brain – serotonin and noradrenaline. These compounds help to transmit messages from one brain cell to another, and we think they play a part in depression.

Problems with antidepressants

Like all medicines, antidepressants have side-effects. The newer antidepressants – selective serotonin re-uptake inhibitors (SSRIs) – may make you feel a bit sick or a little more anxious for a short while. The older antidepressants (called tricyclics) can cause a dry mouth and constipation. Unless the side-effects are very bad, your doctor is likely to advise you to carry on with the tablets.

Make sure your pharmacist gives you an information leaflet with the medication. Many people wonder if these tablets will make them drowsy. Generally, medicines which make you sleepy are taken at night, so any drowsiness can then help you to sleep. However, if you feel sleepy during the day, you should not drive or work with machinery until the effect wears off.

It's best to stay on antidepressants for at least 4 months after you feel better, but your doctor may advise longer. You may get withdrawal symptoms if you stop taking an antidepressant suddenly – these can include anxiety, diarrhoea, vivid dreams or even nightmares. This can usually be avoided by slowly reducing the dose before stopping.

Which treatment is right for me?

In mild depression, talking treatment is usually best. In moderate depression, talking treatments or antidepressants can be equally effective, or you can have both together. If your depression is severe, you are more likely to need antidepressants.

Some people just don't like the idea of medication and some don't like the idea of psychotherapy, so there is a degree of choice.

When you are low, it can be difficult to work out what you should do. Talk it over with your family or people you trust. They may be able to help you decide.

What will happen if I don't get any treatment?

The good news is that 4 out of 5 people with depression will get better without any help. This will probably take 4–6 months (or sometimes more). However, depression is very unpleasant and may affect your ability to work. It may affect your relationships, and your family will be worried about you. Your confidence and enjoyment of life will be affected, and a small number of people with depression will commit suicide.

Taking up some of the suggestions in this chapter may shorten the depression. If you can overcome it by yourself, then that will give you a feeling of achievement. However, if the depression is severe, or if it goes on for a long time, then a course of treatment will help bring it to an end.

Tips for families and friends

❖ Be a good listener. It's best not to offer advice unless it's asked for.

❖ If the depression has an obvious cause, you may be able to help the person find a solution.

❖ It's helpful just to spend time with someone who is depressed. You can encourage them, help them to talk and help them to keep going.

❖ You can reassure them that they will get better, but you may have to repeat this over and over again.

❖ Make sure that they are eating enough.

❖ Help them to avoid alcohol.

❖ If they are getting worse, and start hinting at harming themselves, take them seriously. Make sure that they tell their doctor.

❖ Try to get them to accept help. Don't discourage them from taking medication or from seeing a therapist.

Professor Chris Dowrick

Dr Persaud's conclusion

There is some controversy as to whether the incidence of depression is increasing in modern times, leading to the suggestion that there are some widespread structural problems in our society which account for this. The reality is, whatever the final truth about rising rates, it is only ever a minority of the population who are suffering from depression at any one time – sizeable though that minority might be.

It is also the case that no single life event, no matter how awful, reliably causes someone to become depressed. There is an enormous variability in susceptibility to depression across the population. It now appears that it's not the bad thing that happens to you that explains why you might get depressed; instead, low mood arises out of how you actually cope with things and with the awful environmental change that is upsetting you.

The good news is that learning to transform our coping responses helps enormously with depression and that, with proper treatment and support from friends and relatives, this psychological problem has in fact a good prognosis. The problem with depression is that it makes you pessimistic about life generally, and therefore people don't always seek help. It's vital that those with depression are encouraged to continue with their treatment, as the condition is also associated with one of the worst outcomes of all in psychiatry – suicide.

i SUPPORT

SUPPORT ORGANIZATIONS

Depression Alliance, 212 Spitfire Studios, 63–71 Collier Street, London N1 9BE; tel: 0845 123 23 20; email: information@depressionalliance.org; *www.depressionalliance.org*

Manic Depression Fellowship, Castle Works, 21 St George's Road, London SE1 6ES; tel: 08456 340 540; fax: 020 7793 2693; *www.mdf.org.uk*

Samaritans: tel: 08457 909090 (Ireland: 1850 609090); text: 07725 909090 (Ireland: 0872 609090); email: jo@samaritans.org; *www.samaritans.org*

WEBSITES OUTSIDE THE UK

Australia:
www.ranzcp.org

New Zealand:
www.balance.org.nz

Canada:
www.mooddisorderscanada.ca

South Africa:
www.anxiety.org.za

India:
www.indianpsychiatry.com

FURTHER READING

Beyond Depression: A New Approach to Understanding and Management, Christopher Dowrick, Oxford University Press, Oxford, 2004

Speaking of Sadness: Depression, Disconnection and the Meaning of Illness, David A. Karp, Oxford University Press, New York, USA, 1996

Mood Gym: Delivering Cognitive Behavioural Therapy for the Prevention of Depression, *www.moodgym.anu.edu.au*

Diagnosis: What Have I Got?

A man who was told to jump to his death

JOHN HAD BEEN hearing voices. There were several of them, and they had been talking with each other about what he was doing – an obscene running commentary he found very difficult to deal with. The voices also told him to do things like jump off a multi–storey car park. A doctor told him he had schizophrenia and put him on antipsychotic medication.

On leaving hospital, John stopped taking the medication because he thought it was making him lethargic and he had started to put on a lot of weight. He hated the diagnosis and stated that the doctor was wrong – God was sending the voices to him. He was hospitalized under a section of the Mental Health Act several more times, once dramatically from his house with some of his neighbours watching.

Finally he was put on a medication which, for him, had very few side–effects, and he also learned coping skills that allowed him to live with the voices. However, he found that because of his psychiatric diagnosis some people treated him differently from other people – especially one of the neighbours, who ran indoors whenever John was around.

John actually continued to be the same gentle person he had always been, but a lot of his friends stopped seeing him because they had recently read about someone with schizophrenia who had killed a man when he was ill.

In the end, John lost confidence. He hated anyone calling him a 'schizophrenic', so he cut himself off and, apart from going to the day centre once a week, led an increasingly lonely life.

A woman who was told to jump in the river

JULIE HAD BEEN hearing voices. There were several of them, and they had been talking with each other about what she was doing, an obscene running commentary she found very difficult to deal with. The voices also told her to do things, and she was hospitalized for trying to jump in the river because she had become worn down by their constant telling her to do so. She was diagnosed as having schizophrenia and put onto antipsychotic medication.

When she got home she used the word 'psychosis' to do some research on the internet. She wanted to see if there were other medications, because the one she was on was making her lethargic and she was putting on weight. She also wanted to find out about her diagnosis, and perhaps meet others who had it, to find out how to live with the problem. She gave the information she found to her friends so that they could understand her better.

Although Julie was 'upbeat' about her diagnosis, remained healthy and had very good references, when she tried to change occupations she found that no one asked her for an interview. She found this very frustrating, but in the end decided to work freelance, helping to train mental health professionals. Although this was not the job she really wanted, it was the only area where she was not stigmatized by her illness.

A woman who liked a good time

JOSIE LIKED MEETING new friends in the pub every night and having a good time. In the course of the evening, she would drink several glasses of wine, but was always able to get up and go to work the next day.

After several years, Josie found herself needing to drink more to enjoy herself. She found it harder to get up in the morning and occasionally took the day off because she felt so unwell. She felt tired, was not working well and even stopped enjoying her evenings quite as much. She often had a drink in the morning to try to 'pick herself up'.

Eventually Josie plucked up the courage to go to an Alcoholics Anonymous meeting with a friend. She heard people saying, 'Hello, my name is Tom/Dick/Harry and I'm an alcoholic', and then going on to talk about their drinking problems. The first time Josie said, 'Hello, my name is Josie, and I'm an alcoholic', she felt liberated, as if by labelling herself in this way she could now begin to try to sort herself out. After a hard struggle, she gave up drinking.

For years after, she continued to think of herself as an 'alcoholic', as it helped to remind her that drinking controlled her. Josie didn't like other people calling her an alcoholic, but she did want her real friends to use the word, as this helped her to stay sober.

Labelling by doctors

When you become ill, you experience changes in the way you feel, think and move compared to when you are well. These are called symptoms. If you don't understand your symptoms, you will probably go to see your doctor, who will talk to you, examine you and perhaps do some tests. Often they can then give you a diagnosis, which means giving the condition a name or a label. This diagnosis helps you to understand what might happen without treatment, and what needs to be done to get better. It also helps friends and family to know what is wrong. In the case of physical illness – for example, a broken leg or bronchitis – we usually accept the doctor's diagnosis and wear the plaster cast or take the antibiotics in order to get better.

Mental health problems are sometimes more complicated. If someone is thinking strangely, it can be due to an obvious physical cause – for example, being drunk or having had a stroke. These problems can be diagnosed using examination, questioning and tests in the normal way.

However, strange thoughts and behaviours can also occur when someone is physically healthy, and they may be given a label of mental illness – for example, schizophrenia or bipolar disorder (see pp. 196 and 42).

There are no blood tests that can be done to make sure doctors have given someone the right psychiatric label. Various manuals have been written that help the doctor to choose the correct label.

Correct diagnosis also depends on the doctor and the patient understanding each other's cultural and religious background – for example, the belief that God is talking to you will be interpreted differently, depending on your background and your doctor's awareness of that. To establish what 'abnormal' thoughts are, there has to be an agreement within a cultural group about how the mind works normally. Not everyone in that community will necessarily agree about this, and there are no definite boundaries when moving from 'normal' thoughts to 'eccentric (but acceptable)' thoughts to 'abnormal' thoughts.

In England in the late nineteenth century, women who had children outside marriage were often regarded as being 'morally insane' and placed in psychiatric asylums. This would not happen now. In Russia during the communist era, some people who questioned the political regime were told they had dysfunctional thinking, and were locked in a psychiatric hospital. And thirty years ago in the United States of America, homosexuality was listed as a psychiatric problem in the diagnostic manual.

Another difficulty with psychiatric diagnosis is that, in many countries, it can allow doctors to take away someone's liberty (to 'lock them up') and forcibly medicate them, if they are considered dangerous to themselves or others. This does not happen in the case of severe and infectious physical illnesses – even very serious ones such as HIV or tuberculosis.

Some people with a psychiatric diagnosis might agree, when they are well again, that being detained in hospital was the right thing to have happened. But there are others who will resent the interference in their life, disagree with the diagnosis and state that there was nothing wrong with them.

Finally, all labels carry lots of baggage, both good and bad. 'Christmas' does not just mean a Christian celebration on 25 December, but also specific food and music, visiting people you like and hate, eating too much, church, the office party, bad (or good) television programmes, and a wealth of other things.

In the same way, 'psychotic' can mean symptoms of schizophrenia (hallucinations and delusions), the film *Psycho*, people who smoke too much cannabis, a famous footballer, the person acting strangely on the bus, a murderer you read about in the paper, etc., etc. In studies of people's attitudes to someone with mental health problems, a psychiatric label *always* makes attitudes worse towards that person.

Labelling by others

Unfortunately, some mental illness diagnoses carry especially negative and stereotypical images. Until the twentieth century there was no reliable cure for many mental health problems, and people who were severely affected by them were locked up in an asylum, often for life.

It was common for families to be very ashamed that a family member was 'mad', and they would often be 'hidden' and not mentioned outside the family. This trend was made worse by Victorian novelists, in whose stories madness sometimes played a central part of the plot, usually designed to scare the reader. Many people who read Robert Louis Stevenson's *Dr Jekyll and Mr Hyde* think it's about someone with schizophrenia. It isn't. In Charlotte Bronte's *Jane Eyre* there is a character who is 'mad', who is hidden and guarded, but still escapes to stab someone and set furniture alight. It also became fashionable at that time for well-to-do people to tour the big asylums (for a fee) to see very distressed patients living in basic conditions.

Today there are effective treatments for mental illnesses. Occasionally, someone with a psychiatric diagnosis does kill or hurt someone badly, but many more people are killed or hurt by people who are not mentally ill. In fact, in 2004–2005, nearly as many people in Britain were killed by a speeding police car than by someone with mental illness.

The majority of people with a psychiatric diagnosis are just ordinary people. The stigma of these illnesses means they will find it difficult to get a job. They may also be stopped from doing things other people can do, such as jury service, or joining a uniformed service. And they may be shunned by neighbours, who think they are dangerous. (See also Chapter 43, p. 417.)

Labelling by self

For most of us, a diagnostic label of either a physical or a mental disorder can change our lives. If you have developed diabetes, you have to rethink your diet and the way you live. A mental health diagnosis can change the way other people react, with the outside world taking a positive or negative attitude, as illustrated by the three case studies.

However, as we saw in the study of Josie, who drank too much, labelling helped her to accept and overcome her problem. Julie also found the diagnosis assisted her and her friends to understand the problem, and helped her to stay well. Unfortunately, she still found that the illness label didn't help when it came to finding a new job.

Knowing about labelling and stereotypes is an important first step towards reducing prejudice.

Janey Antoniou and Dr Peter Byrne

Dr Persaud's conclusion

A diagnosis can be helpful if it leads to a management plan that helps the person sporting the label. If no treatment or action that can help is immediately suggested, and if the label has negative connotations, then it's reasonable to wonder what the point of the diagnosis is.

Many psychiatrists and psychologists find themselves in the slightly odd situation of trying not to label patients – who seem, in contrast, rather keen on having a diagnosis. A label can be reassuring, suggesting that someone somewhere knows what is going on, when of course a word or term may carry no such guarantee.

Labels may help people avoid taking responsibility for their actions, while on the other hand they can galvanize services into deploying resources.

Whatever your view on labels, they are powerful things which need to be used carefully and wisely.

DID YOU KNOW . . .

Did you know that whilst hearing voices can occur in psychiatric illnesses (schizophrenia, depression and bipolar disorder), it can also occur in Parkinson's disease, Alzheimer's disease, high fever, when using street drugs, in infections, epilepsy, lead poisoning, sleep deprivation, post-traumatic stress disorder, withdrawing from alcohol and while taking some prescription medications?

i SUPPORT

USEFUL WEBSITES

www.stigmaresearch.org   www.nami.org

www.rethink.org

WEBSITES OUTSIDE THE UK

www.who.int/en

FURTHER READING

Don't Call Me Nuts: Coping with the Stigma of Mental Illness, Patrick Corrigan and Robert Lundin, Recovery Press, Chicago, USA, 2001

Changing Minds: Our Lives and Mental Illness, Rosalind Ramsay (ed.), Gaskell Publications, Royal College of Psychiatrists, London, 2002

Eating Disorders

10

A girl who gained control by losing weight

DEBBIE WAS THE youngest child of two teachers. Her elder brother had always been rebellious; he would stay out late and didn't care much about his college work. Debbie, on the other hand, had always been labelled the 'clever one' and the 'good one'. She was keen to please her parents by doing well at school, by keeping her room in order and by looking after her mother when she had her 'low days'.

Debbie's parents didn't get on well, and she had always felt distanced from her dad, particularly in her teens – a time when she began to feel more self-conscious and shy.

When Debbie started at sixth-form college, her sense of security was disrupted. She struggled to adapt to the more relaxed environment. In her new peer group, appearance, fashion and boys seemed to rank higher than academic achievement, and she no longer felt as 'safe' and 'special' as she had at school. She described feeling 'alone', 'afraid' and uncertain about the future. She believed it was impossible to discuss these feelings with others because she felt it was unacceptable for her to have needs, or to ask for help.

Debbie began to cycle the 8 miles to and from college. The teachers commented that she had lost weight, and she started to feel a bit 'special' and 'in charge' of her destiny again. In her usual 'all–or–nothing' way, she made the best use of these new feelings by reducing the amount and types of food she ate.

Before too long, she was cycling 16 miles a day and eating just four crackers with jam for lunch, with a small bowl of soup for her evening meal. Her mother became worried about the rapidity of her daughter's weight loss, but there was no way Debbie would break her ever–tightening rules around food and exercise. Controlling her weight gave her freedom from emotional pain, and a sense of achievement and control in what seemed to her a chaotic and frightening world. Her periods stopped, which she took as a marker of her 'success' and willpower.

Debbie's college work suffered and there were conflicts in her family around mealtimes. Then her course tutor raised concerns about her weight loss. She was suspended from college and her GP referred her to the local eating disorders service.

A girl who binged

GEMMA WAS THE middle child of busy business people. Although the children were fed and clothed, and went to good schools, there wasn't much time for close communication, fun or play. While the parents worked, a succession of nannies cared for Gemma and her two brothers. A nanny she felt close to left when Gemma was twelve and this loss hit her like a bolt.

Gemma's parents assumed she would step in and help look after her two brothers, but she felt lonely and ill-equipped to deal with them, and started to eat for comfort. At first this made the loneliness and emptiness a little more tolerable, but then she began to feel 'fat', 'unlovable' and 'out of control'.

After her family commented that she was getting podgy, Gemma tried to regain some sense of control by dieting, but the hunger pangs made the urges to binge stronger. She had a friend at school who made herself sick if she felt 'too full'. Gemma thought this might be the solution for her.

Before long she was bingeing on large quantities of food and then making herself sick up to four times a day. Before the binge she felt a slight sense of excitement; during the binge she felt nothing at all; and after making herself sick she had to weather painful feelings of self-disgust, emptiness, loneliness and shame.

The urges to binge grew, and by the time she was twenty-five, Gemma would binge and then vomit whenever she felt alone, anxious, rejected or even when she felt too many positive emotions all in one go. She was scared of her emotions, believing they were too much for other people to handle, and kept them bottled up.

Gemma also started spending lots of money on clothes, which gave her a similar buzz, followed by low, empty feelings some time later.

In the context of a new relationship, she decided to try to get herself out of this rut. She went with a friend to see her GP. She was open and honest, though at first she felt worried about telling the doctor of her problems; she thought she was the only person in the world to spend so much of her time bingeing and vomiting. She felt reassured when she discovered that other people had dealt with similar issues. The GP arranged a referral to the local eating disorders service.

What are anorexia and bulimia?

Anorexia nervosa (AN) and bulimia nervosa (BN) are the two main eating disorders. People with anorexia lose large amounts of weight by rigidly limiting the food they eat. They may also further control their weight by exercising excessively, making themselves sick or taking laxatives. People with AN are terrified of gaining weight, but often do not see themselves as severely underweight.

People with bulimia nervosa tend to binge-eat – that is, they eat large quantities of food in a short space of time, then afterwards make themselves sick or abuse laxatives to try to compensate for the food they have eaten. People with bulimia are usually within the normal weight range.

Eating disorder symptoms can range from mild (such as infrequent episodes of bingeing and vomiting) through to life-threatening (such as the emaciated state of people with severe AN). Approximately 90 per cent of people with eating disorders are female. AN often starts in the mid-teenage years and BN somewhat later, but people of all ages can develop eating disorders.

AN and BN are often thought of as two separate diseases, but in reality many people with these disorders do not fit neatly into one category. They may have symptoms from both categories, or just a few symptoms from one category. Binge-eating disorder is an example of this. In this condition people have episodes of binge-eating, but do not try to compensate for it.

People with eating disorders often find their problem difficult to talk about because they feel ashamed, and may hide some symptoms – e.g. bingeing and vomiting. They may not be interested in seeking help if a 'scared' part of them is clinging to the illness.

Carers often report feeling powerless, and at a loss over how to help the person with AN or BN. In AN especially, carers are vital in helping the person recover.

The following summary describes the key features and treatment approaches for AN and BN separately, but often people with these disorders have a mixture of the two.

Anorexia nervosa

What to look out for

With AN, you restrict your food intake so that you reach an unhealthy low weight.

❖ You feel driven to control and limit your eating so that you lose an unhealthy amount of weight. The thought of gaining weight is terrifying. You often refuse to admit you are underweight.

❖ At the start of the illness, you may feel cheerful and full of energy, in spite of eating little.

❖ You may become secretive, trying to ward off the attention of others. For example, you may pile your plate high with salad, so it appears you are having a normal portion, or you may secretly throw food away, or pretend you have eaten already.

❖ Because your body is deprived of a basic need, you may think about food a lot. You may be happy to cook for, and feed, others.

❖ As food restriction and weight loss intensify, your other interests disappear. Your energy levels and concentration diminish, and you may spend more time on your own.

❖ Ultimately, you often feel depressed, agitated and very anxious about any suggestion of change. Sometimes there can be huge feelings of guilt and shame, and also a real sense of hopelessness and despair.

You are often an 'all-or-nothing' perfectionist. You expect a lot of yourself and of others, but this often masks low self-confidence.

❖ You are often a person with an amazing capacity for attention to detail and may be very meticulous, hating to make mistakes. You are attracted to simplicity, clarity and rules. This paying attention to detail may be at the expense of seeing the bigger picture.

❖ You hold high expectations of yourself across most areas of your life. An underlying fear of failure or rejection, and a sense of not being good enough, drive these expectations.

❖ You often have a distorted body image, seeing yourself as bigger than you are.

As well as applying rigid rules to issues around food and eating, you may have other rigid routines or extreme standards. You may follow a punishing and inflexible exercise regime, which you stick to even if you are ill or injured. You may also clean or wash yourself to excess, or become rather obsessive about certain ideas or plans.

A person with AN may well be your friend. She is often shy, private, high achieving and eager to please.

❖ She often wants to please others and to be liked.

❖ She may not ask for help, or will push it away when it is offered.

❖ She often finds it difficult to express emotion. She may seem to undervalue emotions, and may be more comfortable with 'rational' discussion.

Health hazards

There are real health risks associated with starvation and weight-control methods. **AN has the highest death rate of all mental illnesses**. Some risks are evident in the short term (such as feeling faint and weak), some in the longer term (such as osteoporosis and organ damage) and some are dangerous because they are hidden (such as the risk of imbalance in blood salts like potassium, which affects heart and brain functioning).

Some of the main risks show up only after medical investigations, such as blood tests. If you or someone you know has AN, it is important to have a check-up with a medical doctor.

Starvation in AN leads to:

❖ Sensitivity to the cold. A person with AN wears lots of clothes, even on a sunny day, and her skin appears blue and mottled.

❖ Excess hair growth on the body, particularly on the back and sides of the face.

❖ Sleep disruption. Waking up repeatedly throughout the night.

❖ Poor circulation, slow pulse, low blood pressure, fainting spells.

❖ Thin bones (osteoporosis).
❖ Periods stop, or become irregular.
❖ Slow gut function, leading to feeling bloated and constipation.
❖ Susceptibility to anaemia and infections.
❖ Nerve and muscle damage. It may feel like a strain to climb stairs.

If you use additional methods of weight control, the risks are increased.
❖ Self-induced vomiting, and abuse of laxatives, diuretics or diet pills increase the health risks if you are very underweight. They can cause life-threatening changes in the salt and water balance in the body, which may lead to epileptic fits, irregular heartbeat or sudden death. There can also be damage to teeth, heart, kidneys and gut.
❖ If you have AN and exercise excessively, you risk fainting and collapse, and bone fractures.
❖ Starvation destroys muscle and causes the body to eat up its own flesh reserves.

Bulimia nervosa

What to look out for
The trademark symptoms of BN are bingeing and then compensating for it.
❖ You consume large quantities of food over a short space of time. This is a binge.
❖ Usually you try to compensate for the binge by getting rid of the food. This might include making yourself sick, taking diet pills, laxatives or diuretics.
❖ You may be in the normal weight range, underweight or overweight. You have been plump before, or alternatively you may have had problems with AN.

Beneath the surface, you often have difficulty in managing your feelings and beliefs.
❖ You usually have a low opinion of yourself. You may have had difficult experiences earlier in life, or find the pressures of life too much. You may feel inferior to others and plagued with self-doubt, or fearful of being rejected or abandoned.

❖ You often have a particularly painful relationship with your body and dislike the way you look – for example, avoiding looking in the mirror. You may constantly compare your appearance with other people's, using this as the main way to gauge your self-worth.

The person with BN might well be your friend. She can be a perfectionist, but may also be a bit disorganized and may tend to act on impulse.

❖ About a quarter of people with BN have other extreme behaviours. These include overspending, getting caught up in unwanted sexual encounters, misusing alcohol or drugs, shoplifting or even acts of self-harm, for example cutting or burning. These behaviours may seem to offer immediate relief, but in the long run they lead to feelings of helplessness and hopelessness.

❖ The person with BN often has a tricky relationship with emotions, either fearing their feelings will be too overpowering, or feeling eaten up by difficult feelings such as restlessness, boredom or emptiness.

Health hazards

The weight-control practices in BN cause a number of physical health problems (for details see above under AN). If you or someone you know has BN, it is important to have a check-up with a medical doctor.

What can be done to help?

Self-help

Self-help books can guide anyone with an eating disorder through the first stages of learning to understand herself and manage the problem. There are also books for carers and families, which provide advice on how best to talk to the person in a way that promotes change and defuses conflict.

Talking treatments

There are many treatments available for eating disorders and, with good support, many people get well. Many therapies are effective for AN, but the treatment of choice for BN is cognitive behavioural therapy (see p. 427).

The first step – increasing motivation for change

Eating disorders can help people manage difficult feelings and beliefs about themselves – so it may be terrifying and bewildering to think of parting with these ways of coping. In the early part of treatment, it is essential to focus on motivation. This is to encourage the person to consider the costs of their disorder and the benefits of change, and to broaden their perspective to include other ways of living.

Cognitive behavioural therapy (CBT)

CBT can help you to change how you think ('cognitive') and what you do ('behaviour'). These changes can help you understand and manage your thoughts and behaviour, and so feel better. Unlike some of the other talking treatments, CBT focuses on the 'here and now' problems and difficulties.

This is the treatment of choice for BN, and is also often used for AN. Therapist and patient work together. Treatment is time-limited (usually between 15–20 weekly sessions) and goals are set at the outset (such as increasing the variety or amounts of food eaten, or reducing the frequency of bingeing and vomiting).

During the first phase, the person works with her therapist to understand how the eating disorder developed and how it is maintained. This allows them to sketch out a 'formulation' that tracks the development of the eating disorder and highlights important core beliefs and rules for living that may maintain it. Examples could be 'I am bad and unlovable', 'If I don't perform perfectly, then I've failed', or 'If I lose partial control, then I lose total control'.

In the change phase, the person and their therapist challenge unhelpful or inaccurate beliefs and break unhelpful cycles (such as the binge–vomit cycle). The therapist introduces the person to useful change tools, such as diaries to monitor and work with painful thoughts; letter-writing to confront painful issues from the past; and distraction techniques.

Towards the end of therapy, the person plans for maintaining progress in the future. (See also p. 427.)

Cognitive analytic therapy (CAT)

CAT is also a collaborative time–limited therapy (20–30 sessions for eating disorders). The person and therapist work together to understand unhelpful patterns and ways of relating to oneself and to others.

After the first few sessions, the therapist presents the sufferer with a 're-formulation' letter, which summarizes how the difficulties developed, and are maintained, and the therapy goals. At the end of therapy, the two exchange 'goodbye letters', which acknowledge the gains made, the sense of loss at the ending of the therapeutic relationship and what the sufferer still needs to be mindful of in the future.

Compared with CBT, CAT places a greater emphasis on helping people become aware of unhelpful interpersonal relationships and ways of relating to themselves. It also puts more emphasis on exploring and understanding early-life experiences and how these have contributed to the development of the eating disorder. (See also p. 441.)

Interpersonal psychotherapy (IPT)

This is a time–limited, goal-based therapy, which concentrates mainly on rela-tionships with others and allows people to consider their roles and goals in life. (See also p. 442.)

Psychodynamic psychotherapy

This is a focused, time–limited form of psychoanalytical psychotherapy. The aim is to learn to understand the contribution of early relationships and life experiences to present-day difficulties and conflicts. This type of therapy takes time, because it requires people to uncover the conscious and unconscious processes that drive their ways of relating to others.

The main vehicle of change is through the relationship between the person and the therapist, and what the person can learn through this interaction and bond. (See also p. 441.)

Family–based treatments

This form of therapy works with the person and her family. There are different types of family-based treatments, with either the whole family attending together, separate parental counselling, or small groups of families meeting together.

The aim of all these approaches is to use the family's strengths, skills and knowledge of the sufferer to help her conquer the eating disorder. Family-based treatments are strongly recommended for adolescents with AN, and for those who are still very much involved with their family. (See also p. 444.)

Carers' groups

It is hugely stressful, and practically and emotionally challenging, to live with someone who has an eating disorder, and carers' workshops have been set up in different localities, run either by specialist eating disorder units or by the voluntary sector. These workshops allow carers to share their experiences, as well as offering tips for managing mealtimes, and difficult emotions and inter-actions. Staff may also be on hand to provide information, advice and support.

Medication

In BN, even if someone is not depressed, SSRI antidepressants can reduce bingeing and vomiting. They may 'kickstart' the recovery, so that the person can benefit from talking therapy. But without looking at the underlying issues, any positive benefits of drug treatments wear off after a while.

Which treatment is right for me?

All of the above therapies have much in common. It may be worth exploring them in more detail by using the library or internet. Here are a few guidelines.

- ❖ If you suffer from BN, CBT is the treatment of choice.
- ❖ If you are young, still living with your family or very much involved with them, and if you suffer from AN in particular, family-based treatment may be most helpful.
- ❖ If you want to focus on the 'here and now' (the eating disorder) and develop practical strategies for breaking unhelpful patterns and ways of being, CBT may suit you.
- ❖ If you like the sound of a more analytical therapy, with the focus on learning about yourself and your eating disorder through exploring developmental origins, and through understanding what emerges in your relationship with your therapist, CAT (which is time-limited and sets goals) or psychoanalytical psychotherapy may be best.

❖ If you have a hunch that your eating disorder is bound up with the types of interpersonal relationships that you find yourself in, IPT or CAT may be helpful.

Tips for families and friends

The self-help books detailed on page 106 are excellent resources for people with eating disorders, friends and family members.

❖ Do stick by the person and show calm, consistent support, even if she seems to push it away. Remember the prospect of change can be terrifying for people with eating disorders. Gentle guidance, rather than getting cross or being controlling, is most helpful.

❖ Underlying the eating disorder is a great deal of sadness and pain. If you can listen to the person's feelings, worries and thoughts, and show you care, you are doing them a huge service.

❖ Practically, you can try to support the person in eating regularly and enough. If she finds this too challenging, again it is best not to become angry or controlling, just try to be there for her, and let her know you care.

❖ If she is bingeing and vomiting many times a day, or is severely underweight, encourage her to get a medical assessment (see 'Health hazards', pp. 98–9).

❖ Remember, there is help out there, and many people recover or get significantly better through therapy. Encourage the sufferer to seek help via her GP, and perhaps offer to go with her to the first appointment.

Professor Ulrike Schmidt and
Dr Helen Startup

Dr Persaud's conclusion

Eating disorders are a favourite media preoccupation, perhaps because the media themselves are image obsessed. It may also be because several extreme-ly famous women have confessed to severe eating disorders. There are con-cerns that the media's preoccupation with perfect female bodies, such as those of the super-models, is driving what appears to be a new epidemic of eating disorders.

The fundamental cause for these problems is still controversial. Bulimia nervosa was first described as recently as 1979, suggesting the start of a genuinely new disease which has gone on to become extremely common.

Magazines devoted to male bodies and fitness are on the rise, and it is intriguing to note there now appears to be an increase in male body–image and eating problems. Some men appear so keen to 'bulk up' that they may abuse steroids with resulting severe physical and mental health side-effects – e.g. so-called 'roid rage'.

Some argue that important physical changes in the bodies of sufferers might pre-date the loss of weight, so that biological or organic causes for these disorders are being neglected in favour of more psychological accounts.

Whatever the final answer to why eating disorders happen, it is probably the case that widespread cultural factors, like what is considered a desirable body shape, will continue to play a bigger role in the cause and treatment of these problems than is the case for most other psychiatric difficulties.

i SUPPORT

SUPPORT ORGANIZATION

Eating Disorders Association, Sackville Place, 44–48 Magdalen Street, Norwich, Norfolk NR3 1JE; adult helpline (over 18 years of age): 0845 634 1414; helpline email service: helpmail@eda.org.uk; youthline (up to and including 18 years of age): 0845 634 7650; youthline email service: talkback@eda.org.uk; youthline TEXT service: 07977 493 345; www.edauk.com

WEBSITES OUTSIDE THE UK

Australia:
www.thebutterflyfoundation.org.au

New Zealand:
www.eatingdisorders.org.nz

Canada:
www.nedic.ca

South Africa:
www.recoveryspace.org

India:
www.indianpsychiatry.com

FURTHER READING

Self-help books for people with anorexia nervosa:

Overcoming Anorexia Nervosa. A Self-help Guide Using Cognitive Behavioural Techniques, Christopher Freeman and Peter Cooper (ed.), Constable and Robinson, 2001

Breaking Free from Anorexia Nervosa: A Survival Guide for Families, Friends and Sufferers, Janet Treasure, Psychology Press, 1997

Self-help books for people with bulimia nervosa:

Bulimia Nervosa and Binge-Eating: A Guide to Recovery, Peter Cooper and Christopher Fairburn, Constable and Robinson, 1993

Getting Better Bit(e) by Bit(e), Ulrike Schmidt, Janet Treasure and Tom Treasure, Psychology Press, 1997

11

Gender Identity

A man who was really a woman

BORIS HAD BEEN secretly cross–dressing since he was five, and at puberty his cross–dressing became sexually exciting. As time passed, the sexual excitement diminished. His cross–dressing became a way for him to 'express his feminine side'.

When Boris married, he told his wife of his cross–dressing and for some years there were no problems. In time, though, his wife became disturbed by the time and emotional investment Boris put into cross–dressing, and their sexual life diminished.

After a time Boris's marriage failed, and he went to a Gender Identity Clinic, wanting to spend the rest of his life in a wholly female role. He was asked to stop smoking and to turn his desire into reality by starting to live openly as a woman all the time.

Boris changed his name to Michelle. Her employer proved tolerant, and soon afterwards she was started on treatment with female hormones. She prospered in a female role and wondered why she had not changed very much earlier in her life. Two years later she underwent gender reassignment surgery. Soon after that she got a gender recognition certificate and changed her birth certificate to female.

A woman who was really a man

BERNADETTE HAD ALWAYS been masculine and had fought to get the school rules changed to allow her to wear trousers to school. At puberty she found herself attracted to other girls and was regarded as a masculine lesbian. Bernadette was herself not so sure of this; she felt as if she were a man. She did have a number of relationships with lesbians, but they all ended with the other woman saying that Bernadette was not simply a masculine woman but, rather, was like a man. She had come increasingly to feel like a man, and went to a gender identity clinic.

Bernadette was asked to start living her life as a man, and did this with more ease than she had expected, changing her name to James. He was given male hormones, and over the course of six months became so masculinized that he was always regarded as a man slightly younger than his actual age.

After living as a man for a year, James started a

relationship with a straight woman, and it seemed to be going better than had his earlier relationships with lesbians. He underwent a bilateral mastectomy (removal of both breasts) because, although always small, his breasts looked wrong.

A year later James was advised that he would be eligible for surgery to create an artificial penis. He and his partner were not sure whether this would be best, as a lot of surgery was involved, so they decided to think further about it whilst James acquired a gender recognition certificate and changed his birth certificate to male.

What is a gender identity disorder?

'Gender dysphoria' is when a person's sense of feeling male or female is either at odds with their physical form, or disturbed in some other distressing way.

Such feelings can occur for a variety of reasons. They can be a feature of depression (see p. 76) or bipolar disorder (see p. 42); they may be brought on because of substance misuse; or they can be a feature of a psychotic illness. In rare cases, they can be a feature of a partial androgen insensitivity syndrome (an inherited condition in which babies biologically 'intended' to be boys fail to show full normal male development), or another endocrine or chromosomal disorder.

If other causes for these feelings have been excluded, and if they have been present for at least two years, the person may be considered to be transsexual. People who are transsexual arrive at this situation from a variety of different backgrounds.

Most men born like this would, earlier in their development, have been described as dual-role transvestites, and before that as fetishistic transvestites (see p. 219). A smaller number would earlier have been described as very feminine gay men.

Most females would, in their earlier development, have been described by others, or themselves, as very masculine gay women. Only a small proportion of transsexuals, whether born male or female, would earlier have received a diagnosis of a gender identity disorder in childhood.

Children with such difficulties can be seen in the gender development clinic at the Tavistock and Portman NHS Trust in London. Adults have a wider variety of sources of help, with National Health Service clinics in London, Sheffield, Nottingham and Leicester. In addition, there are private providers. Most competent services are members of the Harry Benjamin International Gender Dysphoria Association and should be staffed by psychiatrists (sometimes along with chartered psychologists) and a specialized endocrinologist.

Treatment

The risks of unsupervised and illicit treatment

People who believe they are transsexual sometimes seek hormone treatment before they have changed their gender role or sought any professional advice. They may obtain hormones on the black market or from other sources. This is unwise, because hormone treatment without an established diagnosis may do great harm, and will prevent any later investigation for conditions such as a partial androgen insensitivity syndrome.

Illegal hormone treatment is almost always expensive. It can also be dangerous because of the uncontrolled nature of what is consumed and the lack of any proper assessment of the person's health, or possible reactions with other medications that the person may be taking. At the safest, the purchaser consumes a product that is without risk because it contains no active hormones.

Unsupervised treatment with high doses of oestrogens causes rapid breast growth, but after a short time the breasts stop developing. Small, hard, conical-shaped breasts result. No further hormonal treatment can later increase the size of such breasts.

Professional help

There is nothing to prevent anyone changing their social gender role at any time. No official permission is required, and no laws are broken. Patients who have already changed their gender role when they go to a gender identity clinic are likely to have the time they have already spent in their new gender role taken into account.

Before any treatment starts, a proper diagnosis should be made. This is the role of an experienced clinician, however certain the patient may be. Initial assessment should include a full study of the patient's history, with particular emphasis on gender development and sexual issues.

There should also be a full physical examination and blood testing to confirm good health, and to determine whether a partial androgen insensitivity syndrome or other endocrine disorder is present. These tests require that the patient be hormone-free. They are important because partial androgen insensitivity syndromes may affect patients' sisters' male children.

It is generally accepted that treatment should feature reversible changes first. Only if these interventions are successful should less reversible, or irreversible, steps be taken.

Nearly always, the patient should already have changed social gender role before hormone treatment starts. This would involve a change of name by Statutory Declaration to a name clearly of the opposite sex, and a change of all other official documents which can be altered without medical support. (To change one's driving licence and passport requires the support of a recognized gender identity clinic.)

The patient is required to be proactive about presenting their new gender role to the world. This means making it clear to everyone that they have changed gender role and are being accepted in that role. Others are not required sincerely to believe that the patient is of the new sex, but the patient must be able to 'come across' in such a way that others treat them as such.

If this step is successful, hormone treatment may be considered if it is clinically safe. The patient must be in good physical health and a non-smoker, since a smoker's risk of developing blood clots is unacceptably high.

Hormones are usually prescribed by the patient's GP for convenience, and because such treatment is likely to be lifelong. Properly supervised treatment carries no increased risk of overall mortality, but treatment with oestrogens does carry an increased risk of blood clots. The only reports of hormone-related cancers have been with unsupervised or illicit treatment.

Surgery

Patients are not considered suitable for any sort of gender-related surgery until they have lived and prospered in their new gender role for at the very least a year. After this time, a bilateral mastectomy might be considered for female-born patients.

Patients are usually expected to show an improvement, or at least no decline, in their social, occupational or psychological functioning. If of working age and ability, they are usually expected to spend at least a year in some sort of full-time occupation. This might be paid or voluntary work, education or a training scheme.

Those who are unable to work are expected to show adequate social function (consistent with their limitations) in their new role. Throughout, patients should be seen regularly to monitor progress and to deal with whatever problems may arise. Although counselling can be beneficial, it is often not available from local services, which may feel out of their depth in this area.

Genital surgery often comes after the patient has had two years of successful life in the new role. After gender assignment surgery, patients continue to require hormone treatment in order to preserve their feminization or masculinization, and to prevent osteoporosis. The dose is usually between half and a third of the pre-operative dose.

Born males continue to have a slightly elevated risk of thromboembolic disease but, because their hormone treatment does not contain progesterone, are not more at risk of breast cancer.

The longer-term outlook is quite good, provided that patients are carefully selected for gender reassignment surgery. Outlook seems to be better in patients who first presented at a younger age, and in those always sexually attracted to their own birth sex.

Conclusion

Gender identity disorders are more frequent in males, and are uncommon, very distressing, problems, the most severe of which is transsexualism.

Transsexual people may earlier have been viewed by themselves or others as feminine gay men, masculine lesbians or transvestites. The best help comes from specialist clinics because such clinics have psychological, endocrine and speech-therapy expertise.

The most important first step is to make a proper diagnosis, since many other conditions can mimic disorders of gender identity. Further, it is necessary to perform the physical investigations needed to make sure any treatment will be acceptably safe. This may take more than one assessment.

The guiding principle is to succeed in reversible steps before irreversible decisions are made.

Before any kind of hormone treatment, patients should first change their life so that they are accepted as living in the other gender role. If this succeeds, and if it is safe to do so, hormone treatment is started. Hormone treatment makes females look very masculine indeed. It is often less effective in males.

Gender reassignment surgery only happens if patients have successfully lived and thrived in the other gender role. Genital surgery is more effective in males than in females.

With careful assessment and a suitably measured pace, the outcome of these treatments can be very good. After treatment, patients need to continue with hormone treatment. If they were born in the United Kingdom, they can change their sex on their birth certificate.

Dr James Barrett

SUPPORT ORGANIZATIONS

Mermaids: a charity for gender dysphoric children and adolescents and their families. BM Mermaids, London WC1N 3XX; helpline (Monday–Saturday, 3.00pm–7.00pm only): 07020 935066; *www.mermaids.freeuk.com*

The Gender Trust, PO Box 3192, Brighton BN1 3XG; email: info@gendertrust.org.uk; *www.gendertrust.org.uk*

www.hbigda.org has links to other organizations around the world

WEBSITES OUTSIDE THE UK

Australia:
www.ftmaustralia.org

FURTHER READING

The following publications can be downloaded from *www.gendertrust.org.uk:*

Transitioning in the Workplace: A Guide for Employers

Transitioning in the Workplace: A Guide for Employees

A Guide to Transsexualism

Standards of Care for Transsexuals

A Guide to Sex Reassignment Surgery

12

Hysteria

A woman who was paralysed by stress

PEARL COLLAPSED IN the factory where she worked when she suddenly lost the use of her right leg. She was taken to hospital by ambulance with a suspected stroke. Although she had no movement in her leg, scans of her brain and spine showed no signs of a stroke. When the neurologists examined her, they could not find a physical cause for this weakness.

She had felt low for some time, finding it hard to eat and aware of aches and pains that kept her awake at night. She was puzzled when the neurologist said that he could find nothing 'physical' wrong with her. She did not feel her condition was related to stress, although she had been working very long hours to pay off debts her ex–partner had left her with. Her sister had recently emigrated to Australia.

Pearl started physiotherapy, saw a counsellor and was started on an antidepressant for her depression. It was during these counselling sessions that she described how her boss at work had been bullying her; she said that she couldn't stand up to him. She felt totally helpless and had been struggling to go to work every day despite feeling tired and miserable.

It seemed that Pearl's life had, in quite a short time, become extremely difficult. She had conflict at work, money problems at home, a recent relationship breakdown and had lost regular contact with her sister. She had become rather isolated and had become depressed. As is usual in these situations, Pearl had not seen her symptoms as stress-related, so her paralysis felt totally out of her control.

Over the next few days she gradually started to recover movement in her leg and, over the next few weeks, her mood, sleep and appetite improved. Pearl's counselling sessions and physiotherapy continued when she left hospital. Eventually she regained full movement in her leg. In counselling, she was able to talk about her problems with being assertive and coping with her anxiety. She soon felt well enough to apply for a new job, and saw a debt counsellor who helped her agree a monthly plan to pay off her debts.

What is hysteria?

Historically, the word 'hysteria' has been used to describe the sudden loss of function of a part of the body. It was first described over 3,000 years ago, when it referred to a range of unexplained physical complaints. Doctors don't use the term so often now, as its everyday meaning – a dramatic loss of emotional control – can be seen as quite insulting. Instead, they use the term 'conversion disorder' or 'dissociative disorder' to describe this situation: symptoms that look like neurological disease, but are in fact caused by emotional distress. Other phrases that can be used to mean essentially the same thing include:

❖ 'psychogenic' or 'stress-related' – emphasizing the role of the emotions
❖ 'functional', 'non-organic' or 'medically unexplained' – emphasizing the lack of physical disease
❖ 'somatizing', 'somatization' and 'somatoform' from the Greek word for body, *soma*

When making such a diagnosis, there is a risk that a doctor might be missing a physical disease. The diagnosis of hysteria became controversial in the 1960s, when it was proposed that many people were being diagnosed incorrectly with it when they actually had a neurological disease. However, research since then has shown that the doctors usually get it right. This is important because, without the right treatment, these conditions can be just as disabling as a physical disease.

People with these symptoms will usually see a neurologist or a physician before being referred to a psychiatrist. This can lead to unnecessary physical investigations – or even unnecessary treatments – if the psychological cause is not recognized early on.

What does it feel like?

Normally, we are aware of our ability to move or to feel emotion. Sometimes, usually under stress (see p. 241), one of these functions can become disconnected from our conscious awareness. This may seem strange, but there are everyday examples of this, such as when you have driven along a familiar route and you suddenly realize you have no clear memories of the journey; or of not hearing your name being called when you are absorbed in a particular task.

Hysterical symptoms usually start suddenly, sometimes after a stressful event. In some cases, physical disease can be ruled out by a simple examination, but often investigations are needed. Any function of the nervous system can be affected – the most common symptoms are listed below.

Movement

The muscles in an arm or leg will be paralysed. The paralysis may be complete or partial, and often varies in intensity. It may look like a stroke, but a brain scan will be normal.

Numbness

This often appears as patches of numbness affecting one half of the body. The pattern of numbness is different from that produced by damage to nerves or diseases of the nervous system. Scans of brain and spine will be normal.

Speech

The patient may have difficulty in speaking, stammer, or be completely unable to speak. 'Globus' is a word used to describe a distressing sensation of a lump in the throat.

Memory

This often follows a particularly traumatic event or intolerable life stress, and can be associated with a period of wandering or a 'fugue state'. It can be complete – so the affected person forgets everything, including who they are – or partial, relating only to the trauma.

Functional epilepsy

These are attacks that look like epileptic fits, but do not have the distinctive brain activity of epilepsy, which can be measured with an electroencephalogram (EEG). Other conditions – like fainting, panic attacks, post-traumatic stress disorder and sleep disorders – can also look like a fit (see pp. 24, 187 and 222).

Depersonalization

This is the feeling of not being real, or not connected to your body, and of having difficulty in experiencing emotions. Derealization is similar, but refers to the outside world not feeling real. These experiences can occur occasionally in normal people if they are extremely tired or panicky. If you have the disorder, these feelings keep on happening unpleasantly for no obvious reason.

Multiple personality

This condition involves the existence of at least two different personalities in the same person, each of whom to some degree lacks awareness of the other. It is much more commonly diagnosed in the USA. The diagnosis is controversial, with some psychiatrists arguing that it is actually created by some types of psychotherapy.

Pain

How we feel changes how much pain we notice. If we are very excited, we may feel little or no pain for a while, as sometimes happens in battle situations.

Unfortunately, the opposite can happen as well. We may feel aches and pains when there is no injury to the place where we feel the pain is coming from. The brain is 'fooled' by the nerves in the spine into thinking there are pain signals travelling up it. This pain feels as real as pain from any other cause, and can be thoroughly disabling.

Somatization

Symptoms arise in several parts of the body, for which no physical cause can be found. Neurological symptoms are often accompanied by pain, nausea and bloating, or sexual problems, such as impotence or irregular periods. The condition can continue for many years, with many medical specialists seeing the patient but being unable to find any definite physical diagnosis.

A hysterical or functional symptom feels as real as any other symptom. A patient with a conversion disorder really cannot move his or her limb. The symptoms are not consciously produced and the patient may be completely unaware of the influence of stress.

People with somatization disorder get very frustrated that doctors cannot find a particular physical disease to explain their symptoms, because it really feels to them as if something is wrong with their body.

What causes hysteria?

We do not know for sure.

❖ It can run in families, so genes may play a part.
❖ If you already have a neurological disease, then you are at higher risk.
❖ There is often a stressful event associated with the start of the symptoms.
❖ Childhood trauma, such as sexual or emotional abuse, is more common for sufferers.
❖ It may be more common in people who find it difficult to think or talk about their feelings or difficulties.

Recently, brain-imaging studies have been carried out on people with functional paralysis. They show that areas at the front of the brain, involved in emotions, become unusually excited when the person tries to move the affected body part. The theory is that their brain is trying to suppress or disconnect the bits that are needed to produce movement.

These findings give us a useful way to think about these puzzling problems, which don't seem to fit with our commonsense view of the world. It does look as though stressful experiences can disconnect the parts of the brain that are needed to perform a particular task – like moving or feeling. The damage is not permanent, however. The relevant parts of the brain can be reconnected and the function regained.

These brain-imaging studies have also scanned people who are deliberately faking their symptoms. They show quite different patterns of brain activation. This supports the idea that people with functional disorders do not deliberately produce their symptoms.

There may be other mental health problems: depression (see p. 76) is very common, but anxiety, post-traumatic stress disorder and personality disorder (see p. 157) may also need treatment.

Will it get better?

It usually does. Often it gets better quickly, by itself and without treatment, when the stressful experience passes. Extra support from the family or an employer might reduce the feeling of being stressed and help function to return. If it doesn't get better quickly, treatment helps.

If the condition goes on for a long time and stresses are not addressed, then the symptoms may not go away completely. Somatization disorder is a long-term problem that is likely to return at times of stress.

What can be done to help?

There has been very little research into the best treatments for functional symptoms, and different people may find different treatments work for them. Several different approaches can be used.

Physical therapies. These are designed to help someone get back to normal function – for example, a course of exercises from a physiotherapist for a paralysed arm, or breathing exercises for a stutter. Aerobic exercise, such as brisk walking for 30 minutes three times a week, can reduce stress levels.

Cognitive behavioural therapy (CBT). This type of talking treatment can be used to break unhelpful thinking patterns and to increase the level of activity gradually and safely. (See also p. 427.)

Relaxation exercises can reduce stresses and stop some of the bodily sensations that can be misinterpreted as signs of disease.

Psychodynamic psychotherapy can help if there are problems from childhood and continuing difficulties with other people (see p. 441). If someone finds it hard to talk about their feelings, a more practical approach, such as CBT or physical therapy, may be more useful.

Antidepressants have been shown to help in the treatment of some functional symptoms, even when there is no clear evidence of depression. People with somatization can be sensitive to the side-effects of the drugs, but these go away. It may be necessary to use lower than normal doses. Low doses of the older tricyclic antidepressants are useful in chronic pain.

Sedative drugs are sometimes used to produce a state of deep relaxation. This can allow discussion of difficult issues and, sometimes, the return of the lost function.

Hypnotherapy has been known to help, and probably works in a similar way.

Acupuncture is widely used in China. Although it is not used as much in the Western world, some patients find it helpful. Again, it may work by reducing feelings of stress.

Self–help
✔ Do
❖ see the symptoms as temporary
❖ stick with one doctor
❖ ask for practical help if you need it

❖ try talking to someone you trust about how you feel
❖ take regular exercise
❖ try relaxation exercises for stress
❖ keep active

✖ DON'T

❖ make plans that assume you are permanently disabled
❖ use alcohol or other drugs to try to feel better
❖ keep away from people

Tips for families and friends

Remember – these psychosomatic symptoms are not 'put on'. Your friend or relative really cannot do what they say they cannot do. This type of symptom is usually a reaction to stress of one sort or another – so there are probably ways you can help.

✔ DO

❖ be patient
❖ be supportive
❖ focus on getting things back to normal

✖ DON'T

❖ accuse them of putting symptoms on
❖ focus too much on the symptoms

Professor Michael Kopelman and
Dr Gavin McKay

Dr Persaud's conclusion

Hysteria hits the headlines when a person comes to media attention who cannot recall any of their past and has ended up in hospital, so appeals are made by the hospital for any information about the person. Sometimes this is an example of hysterical amnesia, where a profound loss of memory has occurred as a result, perhaps, of some emotional turmoil in that person's life. Whatever the complexities of the truth, they are rarely reflected in the lurid and simplistic media accounts of that person's life. Perhaps as a result of these press stories, hysteria has attracted a strong negative taint in public perception, as it is linked to deception or manipulation. The reality, however, is that sufferers experience undoubted and often very deep difficulties which need careful specialist psychological help.

i SUPPORT

USEFUL WEBSITES

www.dpselfhelp.com – source of information and online forum for sufferers of depersonalization disorder.

www.theacpa.org – American Chronic Pain Organization: US-based organization providing information and self-help to chronic pain sufferers.

www.mind.org.uk – UK-based mental health charity with a wide variety of information leaflets and contacts.

General information: *www.wikipedia.org/wiki/Hysteria*

WEBSITES OUTSIDE THE UK

Australia:
www.ranzcp.org

New Zealand:
www.ranzcp.org

Canada:
www.anxietycanada.ca

South Africa:
www.anxiety.org.za

FURTHER READING

www.trauma-pages.com – David Baldwin's Trauma Information Pages giving links to a large amount of information on traumatic stress and dissociation.

www.painandhealth.org – website giving links to various pain-related resources and organizations.

www.epilepsyfoundation.org – a factsheet about non-epileptic seizures can be found by looking under: answerplace, medical, seizures, types, nonepileptic, weinonepilepsy.

13

Jealousy

A man who constantly checked his wife's underwear

SHANE IS FORTY–TWO. He is divorced from his first wife, with whom he had two children. Their marriage broke up after six years, as Shane drank too much and gradually became over–possessive, jealous and occasionally hit his wife.

Now remarried, he has continued drinking regularly, has become sullen and morose, and for the last six months has suspected his wife of having an affair. She denies this, but he does not believe her. He has now started questioning her movements and checking her underwear for any semen stains. He is sleeping badly, not eating properly and seems to be quite depressed. He is angry with his wife but has not hit her.

Shane was referred to a psychiatrist who diagnosed him with morbid jealousy, depression and serious alcohol problems.

What wasn't clear, however, was whether the morbid jealousy had caused the depression, or whether the depression was caused by the jealousy.

The psychiatrist sought a second opinion from a colleague, another psychiatrist, and it was agreed that Shane should be admitted to hospital, hopefully as a voluntary patient. However, if he refused to be admitted, he would have to be compulsorily detained.

Although Shane had not expressed any suicidal thoughts, or shown any signs of self-harm, nor had he been violent to his wife, the psychiatrist was very concerned about his delusions about his wife, as such delusions are known to raise the risk of violence. He was acting on his delusions by questioning his wife and checking her underclothing. The psychiatrist discovered that this pattern of behaviour was recurrent, in that the same thing had happened to his first wife and he had been violent to her. He was also drinking too much, and this increases the risk of violence.

Detention in hospital is not a matter to be taken lightly, but the psychiatrist felt it was important to balance his human rights against the safety of others. Shane agreed to go to hospital as a voluntary patient, and, after a few weeks, there was a great improvement in his depression. It was necessary to treat his alcohol abuse, and to involve his wife in the process. The psychiatrist hoped that the morbid jealousy would also clear up.

What is jealousy?

Jealousy is a normal human emotion. You feel it when you think that someone else threatens your relationship with your partner. A relationship between two people is the norm in Western societies, but this has not always been so – in some cultures it is still normal for a man to have several wives.

Jealousy may occur in a heterosexual or homosexual relationship. It is often based on feelings of insecurity and low self-esteem, but because jealousy can be a normal emotion, it may have a role in preserving relationships. Indeed, if you have no feelings of jealousy at all, then some might say you lack commitment to the relationship.

Jealousy can be harmful if it becomes excessive, or if your thinking becomes distorted so that you believe that your partner is having an affair when they are not. When this happens, jealousy stops being protective and becomes destructive.

Trying to work out exactly when jealousy becomes abnormal is very difficult, and even experts will argue over this. Psychiatrists call abnormal jealousy 'morbid jealousy'. This form of jealousy can in some cases end in violence and death.

What is normal jealousy?

If your partner goes off with someone else you would expect to feel sad, hurt or angry. Your self-esteem will be dented. You may have normal feelings of jealousy towards their new partner.

These feelings can sometimes be extremely painful. You have lost the security and pleasure provided by the relationship, and now see someone else enjoying what you had. Usually, however, you will eventually be able to adjust to your loss and pain and will be able to get on with your life.

What is morbid (abnormal) jealousy?

There are two types of abnormal jealousy: obsessional jealousy, and delusional or psychotic jealousy.

Obsessional jealousy

If you are obsessed, you can't get a thought out of your head. The thought usually upsets you even though you recognize it as your own thought. You will often try to stop thinking about it, but it's hard, if not impossible, to get it out of your mind.

If you have obsessional jealousy, you will keep having a strong thought that your partner is being unfaithful. Deep down, you won't believe the thought, but it will be impossible to stop thinking it. You will be fairly certain that the thought is not true, but you cannot be totally convinced.

Psychotic jealousy

In this type of jealousy, you are convinced that your partner is cheating on you and you become convinced that there is evidence to prove that this is so, even when that evidence doesn't really exist. You will find yourself checking the bedding or your partner's underwear for signs of sexual activity.

You might follow your partner, or arrange for them to be followed. You will tend to misinterpret normal events as a sign of their cheating. For example, you pick up the phone and hear the line go dead, and you are convinced that this was your partner's lover trying to call him or her. You might accuse your partner of having an affair, or even become violent towards them. This can be a dangerous condition.

Sometimes psychotic jealousy is caused by another condition such as:

Schizophrenia. Here the delusional beliefs may be very strong. You may believe that someone is trying to kill you to get you out of the way. You may also hear voices when no one is there. These voices may tell you unpleasant things about what your partner is doing behind your back. (See also p. 196.)

Depression. If you are very low, you may come to believe that no one likes you, and that your partner is fed up with you and has found someone else. (See also p. 76.)

Brain damage. Jealousy can sometimes be triggered by a brain tumour, Parkinson's disease, or by dementia (see p. 13).

Substance abuse. Alcohol abuse can lead to abnormal jealousy. It can also be triggered by amphetamines or cocaine. (See p. 329.)

Sexual problems. Difficulties such as impotence can also lead to abnormal jealousy and are more likely to lead to violence. (See p. 212.)

What can be done to help?

If you are suffering from abnormal jealousy, you are likely to feel agitated and troubled. There is also a risk of you harming either your partner or the person you think is involved with them. You will have great difficulty believing that you are mistaken in your view and that your partner is, in fact, faithful.

The quality of your life and relationship can be improved with treatment. You don't need to go into hospital, but if there is a risk that you might harm someone else or yourself, then you would be better off in hospital.

Talking treatments

Cognitive behavioural therapy (CBT) seems to be the treatment that works best. CBT can help you to change how you think ('cognitive') and what you do ('behaviour'). These changes can help you understand and manage your thoughts and behaviour, and so feel better. Unlike some of the other talking treatments, CBT focuses on the 'here and now' problems and difficulties. (See also p. 427.)

Another form of talking therapy called psychodynamic therapy can also be used (see p. 441).

Medication

Tablets are often necessary, and can be given alongside a talking treatment. If your jealousy is of the obsessional type, then antidepressants are helpful. These tablets are also helpful if your jealousy is caused by depression.

If your jealousy is delusional, or due to schizophrenia, then you will need to take antipsychotic medication. This is usually given as a tablet, but can also be in the form of a depot injection, which means that you may only need to have one injection every 3–4 weeks.

It will also be important to look for, and treat, any other problems that may be making the jealousy worse, such as alcohol, drug use or impotence.

Could I be treated against my will?

Jealousy can be a dangerous problem. If the risk of your hurting someone is very high and your doctors think you are mentally ill and need help, but you are unwilling to accept help, then you may need to be admitted to hospital (sectioned) against your will under the Mental Health Act – see Appendix One, p. 463. Sometimes the temporary separation between you and your partner may help you begin to get better.

Any aggressive behaviour, even if caused by mental disorder, is unacceptable and illegal, and the police may bring criminal charges where appropriate. In addition to your mental health, the safety of others is very important, and this includes any children who may be drawn into the problem.

Which treatment is right for me?

The first thing is to accept that you need help, and to discuss the problem with your friends or family. You will need to speak to your doctor to get an idea of the sorts of treatment that can be offered to you. The treatment will really depend on the type of jealousy that you are experiencing.

Tips for families and friends

If you are concerned that a partner or someone you know is suffering from morbid jealousy, it is important to be aware that it is a psychiatric condition that could be helped with treatment. It is also important to realize that there is a risk of harm to others, especially the person at whom the jealousy is directed.

The jealous person should be encouraged to get help, but it is possible that they won't accept it, or that they will even become angry that you have mentioned it.

If there has been violent behaviour or threats, you should think about contacting the police, and find a way to separate the couple.

If the couple have been separated, there is still a risk of stalking (see p. 231). When this happens the police or doctors should be contacted.

Dr Harvey Gordon

Dr Persaud's conclusion

Jealousy represents a particularly difficult dilemma for clinicians. When a couple turn up at the clinic, one partner accusing the other of having an affair, it is often difficult to disentangle whether this is morbid jealousy or actually justified distress because of a secret affair.

Sometimes couples break up because the pathological jealousy finally drives an otherwise loyal partner away, but the break-up merely serves as confirmation in the sufferer's eyes that the jealousy was justified all along.

The treatment of jealousy will often involve both members of a couple and will require very skilled psychotherapeutic intervention. Clinicians often battle to get both members of a couple to a clinic, particularly when one claims that 'there is nothing wrong with me – get on and treat the patient'.

Certainly it's true that at the heart of much jealousy is personal insecurity and low self-esteem. Yet it's also vital for the sufferer's recovery that both members of the couple are fully involved in the treatment.

SUPPORT ORGANIZATION

RELATE: advice, relationship counselling, sex therapy, workshops, mediation, consultations and support face-to-face, by phone and through its website. Check your local telephone directory for the address and telephone number of your nearest branch. Helpline: 0845 130 4010; www.relate.org.uk

WEBSITES OUTSIDE THE UK

Australia:
www.ranzcp.org

New Zealand:
www.ranzcp.org

FURTHER READING

Uncommon Psychiatric Syndromes, David Enoch and Hadrian Ball, Hodder Arnold Publications, 2001

P. E. Mullen and L. H. Maack, 'Jealousy, Pathological Jealousy and Aggression', chapter in *Aggression and Dangerousness*, D. P. Farrington and J. Gunn (eds), Wiley and Sons Ltd, 1985

i SUPPORT

Learning Disabilities and Mental Health

A man who was left alone in a warehouse

TERRY IS FORTY-FIVE years old and has mild learning disabilities. He worked in an office supplier's business until eight years ago. At that time his mentor, one of the managers, Paul, retired and Terry found it difficult to continue with his employment. Since he left work he has been sharing a flat with Paul, who has become Terry's guardian.

Terry has been described as streetwise. He likes going out, watching TV and going to football matches with a friend. He has regular contact with his mother, brothers and sister. Terry has been helping Paul with housework, although Paul does the cooking and budgeting. Terry travels independently.

Recently, Terry's GP referred him to the community learning disabilities service because he had become worried about Paul's health. Paul has a heart condition that causes him to become breathless and occasionally he has to be taken to hospital. Terry is able to dial 999 and summon an ambulance.

Terry and Paul initially met a psychologist who thought that Terry might be depressed and suggested that they meet the psychiatrist together. Terry was visibly anxious and spoke in a hesitant manner. Paul said that he could not understand what had come over Terry, who could not concentrate, was not eating in case he might choke, was not sleeping well, and followed Paul around all the time. He wouldn't travel without Paul, and when he went to a football match he asked to leave early.

While Paul was speaking, Terry was wringing his hands and looking nervously at both Paul and the psychiatrist. When Paul asked him to say what he felt, Terry could not express himself clearly. However, he did tell the psychiatrist that he had thought of killing himself by taking poison, and that he had checked a kitchen cupboard to see if they had any cleaning materials that he could drink.

Paul talked about his own illness and about how the two of them had been coping with it. This allowed Terry to say that he feared that if Paul died, he might need to move elsewhere.

Paul mentioned that about six months earlier, Terry had tried to find another job. It seemed OK, but later Paul found out that Terry spent most of his time in a warehouse and had very little contact with other workers. He had been late returning home one day, and Paul had discovered that he had been left alone in the warehouse for several hours. Terry left the job after that, but Paul felt that his confidence had been dented.

The psychiatrist spoke to Paul and Terry about the diagnosis of Terry's problems. Terry had an anxiety disorder, which is a common mental health problem that gets better with treatment. Paul and Terry got some written information about it. It was important for Paul to understand that Terry was not 'making things up', and for Terry to feel that he would get better.

The decision made was for Terry to start on a course of antidepressants, with follow-up by a community psychiatric nurse (CPN). As the symptoms improved, Terry would be encouraged gradually to return to activities that he had enjoyed before his illness. In addition, Terry would be supported in expressing his feelings about Paul's illness and about his future when Paul died.

Terry did well with treatment, developing a good relationship with his CPN, and Paul told the psychiatrist that Terry was 'his old self again'. Paul and Terry decided that they would like help in talking about the future, so that Terry could make his own choices about it.

What is a learning disability?

A learning disability (also called mental retardation) is a condition of reduced intellectual capacity (an IQ of below 70). It is usually present from birth and affects a person's ability to cope with everyday life (adaptive skills).

Research has shown that adults, as well as younger people, with learning disabilities are more likely to suffer with mental health problems. The commonest disorders are psychotic illnesses like schizophrenia (see p. 196), and conditions like anxiety (see p. 24) and depression (see p. 76). Adults and young people with learning disabilities may also have problem behaviours, including aggression, disruption, hoarding, interfering with others, destructiveness or rituals.

Older people in general may suffer with memory loss and dementia (see p. 13). This appears to happen at a younger age, and more often, in older people with learning disabilities.

One of the main difficulties in diagnosing a mental condition in a person with learning disabilities can be communication problems; it is easier to diagnose the mental illness if a person has a mild learning disability and good communication ability. However, symptoms such as hallucinations (hearing voices when no one else is around) or delusions (firm beliefs of persecution, for example) do not always show themselves in the same way as they do in the general population. In people with severe learning disabilities, problem behaviours such as self-injury (see p. 250) may indicate the presence of mental illness.

There are several reasons why people with learning disabilities are more vulnerable to developing mental illness. For example, there may be some family history of the two conditions. And having any sensory impairment, like blindness, or a physical problem, like epilepsy, may lead to their being socially excluded.

What can be done to help?

If there is no other cause for the presence of symptoms that may have gone on for a few weeks, it is important to consider mental health problems. Sometimes, physical ill-health may be at the root of a psychological problem; an example is an underactive thyroid gland – hypothyroidism – which can seem like depression.

Family doctors can help decide whether the problem is likely to be due to a physical problem, or whether it is psychological. If the latter, they can then refer the person to a specialist service for people who have both learning disabilities and mental illness.

There are several treatment options that can be used to manage mental illness.

Medication

The choice of drug depends on the disorder that is being treated. Broadly speaking, the following types of medication are used: antipsychotics, antidepressants, mood stabilizers or antimanic drugs, and occasionally, for short periods of time, anxiolytics.

Medication can have short- and long-term side-effects, so it is essential that carers, as well as the person with learning disabilities, know about them and know how to change the dose and what to do if the person is not tolerating the medication. It is also important to know what other medication the person is taking to avoid any unwanted effects which could be harmful.

It is expected that the immediate symptoms will reduce within 4–6 weeks, but the treatment may need to continue for several months. Most community learning disabilities services have leaflets that explain the common side-effects and give information about the medication.

In Terry's case, antidepressants were helpful in reducing his anxiety and improving his sleep problems.

Talking treatments

For disorders like depression, and also for psychotic conditions, psychological approaches can be very effective.

Cognitive behavioural therapy (CBT; see p. 427) or psychotherapy (see p. 440) and counselling have been used to treat people with learning disabilities. These interventions may need adapting so that they are appropriate to the level of communication and understanding of the individual. Other means of making feelings and thoughts easier to understand are books, pictures or drawings. However, for people with severe learning disabilities, it can be difficult to introduce such approaches, and changing the home or work environment in a behavioural/observational context will work better.

Psychiatrists and psychologists have provided talking treatments like psychodynamic psychotherapy (see p. 441) since the mid–1980s, but there is limited research on how effective it is. Some reports of long–term psychodynamic therapy suggest that individuals gain in emotional intelligence and can make better sense of their experiences.

Other talking treatments include family therapy or group therapy (see pp. 444 and 443). The latter has been used with offenders, as well as with people who find it difficult to manage their anger, with positive results. Overall, there is increasing interest in extending learning disability services to offer the sorts of treatment that are well established in the rest of the mental health field.

Social interventions

People with learning disabilities are less likely to have friends, either with or without learning disabilities, or other social networks, or to be in employment. This isolation may help to maintain their symptoms, or may lead to more problems. An important part of the treatment is to encourage them to join various social groups that are run in the community.

Similarly, carers and relatives need information about support groups. 'Befriender' and advocacy schemes can be useful in helping people with learning disabilities and their carers to find their way through the complex world of services, and to ensure that some choice is available in developing a care plan.

Self–help

There are several organizations that can help people with learning disabilities or their carers. These organizations may provide support and information about specific syndromes, such as Down's syndrome, Fragile X syndrome and so on. 'People First', which is run by and for people with learning disabilities, provides information, training and advice, as well as helping individuals to develop self-advocacy skills.

In addition, people with learning disabilities are encouraged to access mainstream services, for example the 'Hearing Voices Network', which runs self-help groups for people with psychosis and their carers.

Complementary therapies

There is not enough information about the specific impact of complementary therapies on those with learning disabilities and mental health problems. However, aromatherapy, yoga, various relaxation techniques, drama or music therapy and acupuncture have become treatments that promote well-being and relaxation. New research suggests that yoga may be helpful for those with depression or anxiety.

What treatment is right for me?

❖ There should be thorough discussion with the doctor about the illness and the treatments available.
❖ If medication is offered, adequate and understandable information about the length of treatment and side-effects should be given.
❖ Issues about supervision of medication, and the dose, need discussion. It is likely that a community psychiatric nurse will monitor the person in the community, or outpatient appointments will be arranged. Sometimes, alongside medication, counselling or CBT may also be suggested.
❖ Sometimes a talking treatment may be tried first, before medication.
❖ It is important to remember that most people get better.
❖ A person with learning disabilities may need help to keep their appointments.
❖ A review of other problems that might be perpetuating the mental illness must be carried out. For example, is housing adequate, and is there enough assistance with the activities of daily living?
❖ Carers also need help, especially families, so that members do not feel exhausted or neglected. Use of respite care can provide breaks for both the person with learning disabilities and family members.

Tips for families and friends

People with learning disabilities and mental health problems may face long-term consequences as a result of their illness. For example, they may lose skills that they find difficult to regain, although in Terry's case he recovered. Carers should be warned that putting on pressure to get on with activities, or calling someone lazy, is unlikely to solve the problem.

Steps to improve the person's general quality of life, breaking tasks into smaller achievable steps, and finding alternative ways to change inappropriate behaviours are more helpful.

Most of all, carers should be aware of the symptoms that signal either the start or the return of a mental illness, and should ensure that they seek help early.

They can help the person with a learning disability to learn more about their health problems by using accessible information materials. They can work together to develop an action plan for issues of physical health, or plan what they would like to happen when there is a new episode of mental illness. Thinking ahead like this can reduce the stress of admission to hospital.

Dr Angela Hassiotis

Dr Persaud's conclusion

If psychiatry is a less popular speciality within medicine, then it could be said that learning disabilities is the Cinderella speciality within psychiatry. Because of the lack of services for people with learning disabilities, a particular problem is the tendency for those on the borderline between low and normal intellectual functioning to fall through the cracks in the system and not to be allocated to the kind of mental health professional who can really help them.

Another key problem is the need to involve educational systems and the difficulty in getting schools to recognize and respond to those, again, on the border between below-average and definitively abnormal functioning.

People with learning difficulties are often not in a position to advocate for themselves and their needs. It is very important, therefore, that people with normal functioning do more to raise awareness for those less fortunate.

SUPPORT ORGANIZATIONS

British Institute of Learning Disabilities. Tel: 01562 723 010;
www.bild.org.uk

Foundation for People with Learning Disabilities,
9th Floor, Sea Containers House, 20 Upper Ground, London
SE1 9QB; tel: 020 7803 1100; email: fpld@fpld.org.uk;
www.learningdisabilities.org.uk

MENCAP National Centre, 123 Golden Lane, London EC1Y 0RT; tel:
England: 020 7454 0454; Northern Ireland: 02890 691351; Wales: 02920
747588; helpline: 0808 808 1111 *www.mencap.org.uk*;
Ask Mencap: *www.askmencap.info*

WEBSITES OUTSIDE THE UK

Australia:
www.assid.org.au

New Zealand:
www.odi.govt.nz

Canada:
www.equalopportunity.on.ca

South Africa:
www.hst.org.za/index.php

FURTHER READING

The Royal College of Psychiatrists provides factsheets on mental
disorders as well as information for carers and other campaigns on
mental health issues: *www.rcpsych.ac.uk*

Books Beyond Words series: a series of more than 25 picture books for
use by people with learning disabilities or communication difficulties.
They can be ordered through the Royal College of Psychiatrists:
www.rcpsych.ac.uk

i SUPPORT

15

Less Common Disorders

Rare but distressing conditions

The disorders described in this chapter have little in common, except that they cause immense suffering – to both patients and carers alike – and are quite rare. It is easy to empathize with the anguish felt by a woman whose husband develops Capgras' syndrome and refuses to acknowledge her because he believes that she has been replaced by an exact double.

Some of the conditions have consequences of a forensic nature (people with mental illness who break the law may get involved in the criminal justice system) and therefore have implications for the wider society. Examples include a middle-aged woman, suffering from de Clérambault's syndrome, who stalked a male acquaintance for years until she attacked him with a knife and was charged. Another is a woman with Munchausen by proxy who tried to suffocate her four-year-old child to death.

These clinical conditions can be divided into psychotic (characterized by delusions – strange and unrealistic ideas – and hallucinations – hearing, seeing, smelling or feeling something that isn't actually there) and non-psychotic syndromes.

The case studies used in this chapter are made up from the author's clinical experience. They do not relate to real patients, but are a combination of some real symptoms that people may suffer, and are used to illustrate how these uncommon syndromes present in real life.

Psychotic conditions

Capgras' syndrome

Capgras' syndrome is an uncommon condition in which the individual believes that a person, usually closely related to him/her, has been replaced by an exact double. It is the best known, and most common example of a group of conditions known as delusional misidentification syndromes.

It rarely occurs by itself, more usually forming part of another serious mental illness. There have been attempts to explain the disorder purely in terms of disturbed nerve pathways within the brain. However, about 70 per cent of reported cases occur in the absence of any clinically obvious brain dysfunction.

Case study. A forty-five-year-old man was admitted to a psychiatric hospital because of a psychotic illness: he had been hallucinating and believed there was a conspiracy against him. While in hospital, he began to protest that his wife of twenty years, who visited him, 'is not my wife but a double', adding 'something has happened to her: she has been replaced. I love my wife very much but not that woman double.'

De Clérambault's syndrome

In this disorder, the person, generally a woman, suddenly develops the delusional belief that a man, with whom she may have had little or virtually no contact, is in love with her. The condition can exist in isolation, when it is referred to as primary erotomania. However, it frequently occurs as a feature of another mental illness – often paranoid schizophrenia or bipolar affective disorder (see pp. 196 and 42) – when it can be called secondary erotomania.

The object of the delusional belief is often someone of high social status – for instance, a doctor or lawyer. It is not unusual, in today's age of mass communication, for the object to be a well-known public figure.

Some patients bring chaos to the lives of the object, bombarding them with letters and telephone calls over long periods of time. Some may stalk the object or even carry out an assault. The psychological stress and personal strain experienced by the people who are the object of obsession can be immense. (See also Chapter 13, p. 123 and Chapter 25, p. 231.)

Case study. A forty-one-year-old single woman who worked as a secretary in a law firm suddenly developed amorous feelings for a married, highly respected solicitor who worked in a neighbouring firm. She became convinced that whenever he passed the window of the office in which she worked he sent her private and secret signals indicating that he was in love with her.

She 'knew' that he was planning to leave his wife and children in order to set up home with her. Over time, she plagued him, sending sexually explicit letters to his office, and on one occasion turned up at his home and confronted him in front of his wife.

The Othello syndrome

The Othello syndrome, also known as morbid jealousy, is an illness in which the central symptom is a delusion that the sufferer's spouse or partner has been, or is being, unfaithful. The sufferer is more likely to be male, and often seeks out minimal clues to confirm the 'truth' of the delusion. For instance, great effort may be spent on testing the partner in order to 'catch her out'; indeed, checking is the hallmark of morbid jealousy – checking, re-checking, cross-checking and always checking. (See also Chapter 13, p. 123.)

The person with the syndrome frequently becomes increasingly despondent and despairing, and may become irritable. The condition is an exception to the rule that most psychiatric illnesses do not necessarily lead to violence. There is a substantial risk of violence (including fatal assault) directed towards the partner.

The condition can occur in isolation, but more usually exists as a symptom of another psychotic illness – commonly a paranoid state, a depressive illness, in psychopathic personalities or in people with alcohol-related problems.

Case study. A fifty-year-old man developed a belief that his wife was unfaithful after she had been out alone with friends on a day trip. He 'knew' that she had developed a relationship with a friendly neighbour. He detected evidence of the liaison in the form of subtle changes in her demeanour when she returned from shopping trips.

He went to great lengths to verify her accounts of her shopping trips, for instance by checking that the bar codes on the goods she bought corresponded with the retail outlets which she 'claimed' she had visited. He checked her underwear for evidence of sexual activity, and would spend hours questioning and badgering her in order to obtain a 'confession'.

Folie à deux

The term *folie à deux* includes several syndromes in which mental symptoms, particularly paranoid delusions, are transmitted from one person to another, or to several others. The main feature is shared delusions in two or more persons who live in close proximity and who are relatively isolated from the outside world and its influences. The delusions are usually of a persecutory or hypochondriacal nature.

Usually, only one of the people concerned has a true inherent psychotic illness, often schizophrenia (see p. 196) or a delusional disorder. On separation, providing it is sufficiently complete and prolonged, the shared delusions in the second partner may clear up.

The majority of people with this disorder are blood relatives, most frequently two sisters. In non-blood relationships, husband–wife combinations are the most common.

Case study. Two sisters, Sarah aged seventy-six and Susan aged seventy-two, were both admitted to hospital, sharing delusions that their neighbours were trying to poison them by pumping gas into their home via the chimney. Sarah had been diagnosed with paranoid schizophrenia many years previously. Susan had previously been mentally healthy.

Cotard's syndrome

This is an uncommon condition in which the central feature is a nihilistic delusion. In its complete form, it may lead to the person denying his or her own existence and that of the external world. In more partial forms of the disorder, the person may believe that parts of their body have stopped functioning or are rotting or decayed.

The syndrome is typically, although not exclusively, seen as a symptom of a psychotic depression. Often, however, the nihilistic ideas have a grandiose quality (e.g. the world will end or time will stop because of the sufferer).

Case study. A seventy-year-old widow developed features of a depressive illness, becoming low in mood with considerable feelings of guilt, lack of worth and hopelessness. Additionally, she was perturbed by the fact that she had strange feelings about her own body, and believed she was turning into an animal, such as a dog. She then started openly to say, 'I have no body, I am dead.'

Ekbom's syndrome (delusional parasitosis)

This is a condition in which patients suffer from delusions of infestation. They believe that insects – lice, maggots or other small vermin – are living or otherwise thriving in the skin, and sometimes the body. The condition may occur as a feature of other psychotic conditions, such as schizophrenia or severe depression (see pp. 196 and 76), or may occur in isolation.

Typically, the person is able to give a detailed account of the parasites' behaviour, and frequently produces 'evidence' in the form of skin fragments or other kinds of debris. It is most common in females over the age of forty.

Case study. A woman aged forty-three years was referred to mental health services after she had first presented to a dermatologist. She had complained of an itching sensation under her skin, which, she believed, was caused by small insects that had invaded her house two years previously. She had gone to great lengths to sterilize and fumigate her house, and she frequently bathed her skin in antiseptics purchased from a supermarket.

Non-psychotic conditions

Ganser's syndrome

Ganser's syndrome is a condition characterized by the giving of approximate answers to simple and familiar questions, seemingly in a state of clouded consciousness. It is described as classically occurring in prisoners awaiting trial, or in similar situations where the individual is facing an intolerable, confining situation – physical or emotional – from which there is no easy escape.

The basis of the condition is not well understood, but it probably arises as a result of psychological processes operating at an unconscious level – that is, of which the person is unaware. The condition is time-limited, with full recovery expected once the precipitating stresses have resolved.

Case study. A man aged fifty-three, who was in prison awaiting trial for the murder of his wife, became increasingly disturbed and confused, and took to wandering about his prison wing. When examined by a psychiatrist, he appeared perplexed and anxious.

On being asked what month it was (December) he answered 'Wednesday'. When asked to do simple arithmetic, he gave approximate answers: for instance, $4 + 2 = 7$ and $5 - 2 = 2$. He was treated with small doses of tranquillizing drugs and his mental state improved so that he was able to stand trial.

The Couvade syndrome

The Couvade syndrome is a disorder in which fathers-to-be experience a variety of physical symptoms, the most striking of which resemble those commonly experienced by pregnant women. The symptoms are experienced during their partner's pregnancies or at the time of childbirth.

The most common symptoms are gastrointestinal disturbances, including loss of appetite, nausea and vomiting, and diarrhoea. Sometimes pregnancy cravings may occur. In rare cases, abdominal swelling may even be seen.

The cause of the condition is unknown. Traditionally, psychiatrists have tried to understand it in the context of unconscious emotional forces, such as over-identification with the expectant mother. Most people with the condition do not require treatment and indeed, in the majority of cases, the condition passes unrecognized.

Case study. A twenty-four-year-old man presented during his wife's first pregnancy, she was six months pregnant. He gave a history of morning sickness and when examined he was noted to have a swollen abdomen. The abdomen flattened when he slept.

Munchausen's syndrome

This is typically characterized by people who are admitted to general hospitals with apparent acute physical illness, which on further investigation turns out to be fabricated. The individual provides a plausible, often dramatic, history, which at a later date is found to be false.

Munchausen's syndrome is an example of a 'factitious' disorder; that is, the features are deliberately and consciously created by the sufferer, albeit because of pathological motives. The condition is often associated with pathological lying and other disturbances in personality functioning.

Munchausen's syndrome by proxy is a variant in which an adult, usually a parent or carer, deliberately fabricates symptoms or signs of illness in a dependent child. The subject has attracted a great deal of controversy in recent years, mainly because of the great difficulties doctors have distinguishing the disorder from other poorly understood, but genuine, physical diseases in children.

Case study. A thirty-two-year-old man had more than twelve admissions to hospital over a three-year period, presenting with acute abdominal pain. He underwent four abdominal operations. He used a variety of aliases, and always discharged himself suddenly, usually when he sensed that the doctors were becoming suspicious about the medical basis of his symptoms.

Gilles de la Tourette's syndrome

Gilles de la Tourette's syndrome is a motor disorder that just happens to be classified as a psychiatric disorder. It is characterized by generalized tics and involuntary utterances, which may be obscene and which start in childhood or adolescence.

The abnormal movements usually begin in the muscles of the face, especially around the eyes or mouth. The tics persist and gradually extend to involve other muscles in the neck, trunk, arms and legs.

In recent years much of the research into this condition has focused on potential brain dysfunction rather than the psychological or emotional aspects of the disorder.

Case study. An eleven-year-old boy started to cause concern among his schoolteachers because of the gradual development of swearing, screaming, grimacing and explosive obscenities. He also started to scribble vulgar messages on walls. The features persisted throughout his teenage years, despite the provision of treatment from a specialist adolescent mental health service. The tics and grimacing gradually resolved in his twenties, but would periodically reappear when he experienced stressful life circumstances.

Possession states

A possession state can be defined as the presence of a belief, delusional or otherwise, held by an individual (and sometimes by others) that their symptoms, experiences and behaviour are under the influence or control of supernatural forces, or an external being, such as an evil spirit, demon, ghost or the devil.

Such a presentation can be found in many psychiatric disorders: organic psychoses, schizophrenia (see p. 196), depressive psychoses, personality disorders (see p. 157), etc. Some writers (mostly non-medical) make a distinction between 'true' or 'genuine' possession and a 'possession syndrome' which arises during the course of medical or mental illnesses.

Psychiatrists make no judgement concerning the reality, or otherwise, of the demoniacal possession. What is acknowledged is the importance of the spiritual dimension to the majority of service users.

It is not surprising, therefore, that the anguish and distress associated with severe mental illness is, on occasions, manifested in pathological thoughts, perceptions and other abnormal experiences that contain a supernatural content.

Case study. A twenty-three-year-old man developed an interest in Satanism and other occult activities over a period of many years. He also regularly used illegal substances, such as cocaine and LSD. He started to complain that he would be visited by an external personage, who would instruct him to carry out acts of violence directed towards others.

What can be done to help?

For the conditions categorized above as psychotic, the best approach is generally the treatment of the underlying condition. In cases of schizophrenia and related disorders, newer, atypical antipsychotic drugs are the treatment of choice.

Cases of Capgras' syndrome require careful investigation, with brain scanning techniques to exclude organic disease. Cotard's syndrome may require treatment with electroconvulsive therapy, as the service user is likely to be suffering with a depressive psychosis.

The treatment of the conditions classified as non-psychotic is more complex. Generally, talking therapies are the treatment of choice (see p. 440). It should be noted that many of the features of Gilles de la Tourette's syndrome respond well to medications.

Tips for families and friends

Generally, the advice for families is the same as that applying to psychiatric disorders in general, and will be found elsewhere in this book. Specific advice will vary depending upon the underlying condition. With the exception of Othello syndrome (where separation is often the safest option), support and understanding from loved ones and relatives is extremely beneficial. This requires a full and thorough explanation of the condition to be provided by the relevant mental health professional.

However, it should be noted that some of the syndromes described in this chapter can cause enormous stress in the families of patients and 'victims'. The consequences of the obscene utterances in Gilles de la Tourette's syndrome are a good example of the former, while the strain for close relatives of the 'victim' of a patient with erotomania illustrate the latter.

Dr Hadrian Ball and
Dr David Enoch

Dr Persaud's conclusion

As a result of the stigma surrounding psychiatric and psychological problems, many who develop symptoms will keep them secret and will not discuss or explore them with others. This contributes to a conviction that they and they alone have developed these problems. As a result, many sufferers can believe for a long time that their particular psychiatric syndrome is uncommon. In fact, uncommon psychiatric syndromes such as those described here are indeed extremely rare, while most common psychological problems are astoundingly widespread in the general population.

However, whether a psychological symptom is common or rare is actually not as relevant as many might think, as even the rarer syndromes are often readily treatable. The key is to seek specialist help as early as possible in the course of the disorder, and not to postpone going to a physician for fear that one's particular problems will turn out to be completely unique.

SUPPORT ORGANIZATIONS

Community Legal Services Direct, *www.cisdirect.org.uk*, for victims of stalking and de Clérambault's syndrome.

Mind, 15–19 Broadway, London E15 4BQ; email: contact@mind.org.uk; Mind*info*Line: 0845 766 0163 *www.mind.org.uk*

Rethink: a voluntary organization providing advice and support to people with mental illness, their families and carers. 30 Tabernacle Street, London, EC2A 4DD; national advice service tel: 020 8974 6814; email: info@rethink.org; *www.rethink.org*

Sane, 1st Floor, Cityside House, 40 Adler Street, London E1 1EE; tel: 020 7375 1002; fax: 020 7375 2162; helpline: 0845 767 8000; *www.sane.org.uk*

Stop Abuse for Everyone, *www.safe4all.org*, provides information for partners of Othello patients.

Tourette's Syndrome (UK) Association, Southbank House, Black Prince Road, London SW1 7SJ; email: help@tsa.org.uk; *www.tsa.org.uk*

www.tourettesyndrome.net

www.wikipedia.org, for information on many of the syndromes in this chapter.

Women's Aid, *www.womensaid.org.uk*

*i*SUPPORT

(websites and further reading overleaf)

i SUPPORT

WEBSITES OUTSIDE THE UK

Australia:
www.tourette.org.au

New Zealand:
www.anzapt.org

Canada:
www.tourette.ca

FURTHER READING

Tourette Syndrome: The Facts, Mary Robertson and Simon Baron-Cohen, Oxford University Press, 1998

Enduring Love, Ian McEwan, Jonathan Cape, London, 1997
(de Clérambault's syndrome)

From the Edge of the Couch, Dr Raj Persaud, Bantam Books, London, 2004

Uncommon Psychiatric Syndromes, (4th ed.), M. David Enoch and Hadrian N. Ball, Hodder Arnold, London, 2001

Obsessive Compulsive Disorder

A woman who wouldn't touch her own clothes

SONIA IS EIGHTEEN. She has had a six–month fear of contamination by dirt and 'germs'. It all started after she watched a television programme about hepatitis and became worried that she might catch the disease. She realized that her fear was 'over the top', but felt unable to stop herself from taking elaborate precautions to prevent 'contamination'.

These precautions included washing her hands at least forty times a day, bathing for three hours a night, not touching doorknobs or other objects which had been handled by other people, or only touching these items using plastic gloves or paper tissues. Any clothes that she wore were placed in a plastic bag immediately after she undressed and were not allowed to come into contact with 'clean' clothes.

Following assessment, and explaining to Sonia and her mother about the behavioural treatment, Sonia agreed to start an 'exposure programme' at home with her mother's assistance. Her targets for the first week were that, with the help of her mother, she was to touch her 'dirty' clothes, systematically 'contaminate' all her clean clothes by touching them, and then sleep in her bed even if she did not feel perfectly clean.

The following week, Sonia returned with her mother to report on her success. To start with she had been tearful and very anxious when attempting the tasks. Her mother had firmly but kindly reminded her of the purpose of the treatment. Eventually she calmed down and agreed to touch her outside clothes, and then the outside of the wardrobe where her clean clothes were kept.

While she did this she was very shaky and tearful, but she succeeded. Once she had finished this 'contamination' exercise, she agreed to try to touch all her clean clothes. She was surprised to find that her anxiety reduced as she continued, although she remained concerned that her fear might escalate later. Before completing the session, Sonia volunteered to 'contaminate' the bedclothes of her clean bed.

She continued to make progress and reported that once she had 'taken the plunge', her anxiety got better. Over the next six weeks she was able to set herself more difficult targets, and managed to return to 'normal washing'. Two months after starting treatment she was able to return to work.

What is obsessive compulsive disorder?

People often talk about a friend or family member having an 'obsession' with football, films or a particular celebrity. In these cases, the individual enjoys the subject and spends many pleasurable hours engaged in their chosen activity. This is very different from what is meant in psychiatry by an obsession or obsessive compulsive disorder (OCD). People with OCD are tortured by worrying and frightening thoughts, and they may become very distressed.

Most of us will experience obsessions and compulsions from time to time, like worrying about whether we have switched the gas cooker off, or going back to check that we have locked the car. If you have OCD, these habits become very strong, so you feel compelled to check things or repeat actions even if that takes over your life.

Howard Hughes may have suffered from this condition. He was a famous film producer, aircraft manufacturer and playboy. However, obsessions about his health and fear of death led him to live the life of a recluse, in a bare room with no clothes and eating very little.

The good news is that OCD responds well to treatment. The vast majority of individuals who receive treatment will get better.

What does it feel like?

OCD consists of two parts – anxiety-producing obsessions and anxiety-reducing compulsions.

Obsessions

Obsessions are thoughts or impulses that intrude into your mind and make you upset and anxious. Everyone has these kinds of thoughts from time to time, but in OCD they can be very persistent and strong. You might try hard to stop having the thought, but the more you try, the stronger the thought becomes.

Your thoughts may fall into one of the following categories:

❖ fear of contamination with dirt and germs, and a worry that they will harm you or others
❖ fear of harming someone by forgetting to do something – e.g. a fear that there may be a fire if gas appliances are not switched off properly
❖ fear of harming someone by doing something wrong – e.g. a fear that if you get too close to a knife, you will pick it up and stab someone
❖ fear of throwing things away

Just having these thoughts will usually make you anxious, and you will usually be horrified or annoyed that you should be having the thought. You may see your thoughts as irrational, especially during a time of calm reflection. It is likely that you will try to avoid situations that bring on the thoughts.

Compulsions

These are things that you do in order to try to cope with the obsessional thought. For example, if you are a religious person but have strong thoughts that you are going to swear at God, you may believe that if you pray in sets of three, then this won't happen.

Or perhaps you have an obsession that you will go blind if you catch worms from dogs' mess. So every time you enter your house, you have to take off your shoes and clothes and wash them all to remove any traces of dogs' muck that you might have picked up on your travels.

Sometimes the compulsions won't have an obvious link to the thought. For example, your compulsion might be to avoid stepping on cracks in the pavement because, if you don't, something bad will happen.

Compulsions are your way of coping with the obsessional thoughts in an effort to feel better. Compulsions often make you feel much better for a few minutes, but the trouble is that the more you act them out, the worse you get in the long run.

What can be done to help?

There are effective treatments that can help the vast majority of sufferers to overcome this problem.

Self-help

The trick in overcoming OCD is to face up to your fears and to let the obsessive thoughts occur. This will make you anxious initially, but if you can then resist carrying out your compulsion, your anxiety will decrease. It may take as long as an hour, but once the anxiety reduces, you will have a great sense of achievement.

Start by writing down a list of your anxiety-provoking situations. Put the most scary situation at the top of the list and the least scary at the bottom. Then choose the least scary situation and put yourself in this situation for up to one hour without performing your usual compulsions, or until the anxiety has reduced by at least one half.

Once you have succeeded in this, then put yourself in the situation at least three times a day. You should find the anxiety decreases faster and more completely each time. Once you feel you have mastered the least scary situation, then try tackling the next one on the list. As you do this, you will begin to feel that you are getting control over the problem, instead of it having control over you.

There are three 'golden rules' about anxiety:

- ❖ anxiety is unpleasant, but it does no long-term harm
- ❖ anxiety will reduce if you persist with exposure
- ❖ regular practice makes exposure easier

A number of self-help books are available about this type of therapy, as well as a computer-aided and telephone-aided exposure treatment programme. See Support Organizations and Further Reading at the end of this chapter – page 156.

Talking treatments

The best psychological treatment for OCD is exposure therapy. This involves working on the techniques just described in the self-help section. Some people are too fearful or too overwhelmed to perform the exercises on their own, and do better when their treatment programme is directed by a therapist.

Traditional counselling or psychoanalytical psychotherapy is not helpful, as you need to face up to your fear and do something about it rather than talk about it.

Cognitive therapy can also help to challenge and control your obsessional thoughts.

Medication

Antidepressants can help reduce obsessional thoughts. The selective serotonin re-uptake inhibitors (SSRIs) have a few side-effects, the most common ones being nausea, stomach upsets and insomnia, and they can interfere with your sex life.

Just occasionally you may not respond either to drug treatment or to exposure therapy. If so, there are specialists to whom your doctor can refer you. They will be able to offer more intensive psychological treatment or different drug treatments.

Complementary therapies

Complementary therapies may sound attractive, but for OCD there is no evidence that any of them work for any length of time. The fact is that exposure treatment is difficult, but it's the only way to overcome the fears in the long run.

Other treatments

Very, very rarely brain surgery (neurosurgery) is used (about two cases a year in the UK), but only in extremely severe cases where nothing else has helped. One technique is to freeze the small areas of brain tissue that appear to generate the obsessional thoughts. Another technique is to insert electrodes to give electrical deep brain stimulation (DBS) – this is a newer procedure that is reversible.

Which treatment is right for me?

The two main choices for therapy are exposure therapy and drug treatment.

Exposure therapy
Good

* ❖ it's effective (75 per cent of people are helped by it)
* ❖ you might be able to do it yourself without needing a therapist
* ❖ no side-effects
* ❖ no long-term detrimental health effects
* ❖ no effect on fertility or the unborn child

Bad

* ❖ you have to be motivated, as it's hard work facing up to anxiety

Drug therapy
Good

* ❖ it's effective (50 per cent of people will improve)
* ❖ it's easy – just take one pill a day
* ❖ does not require motivation apart from taking the tablets

Bad

* ❖ you may get side-effects
* ❖ you may need to stay on treatment for years
* ❖ there may be long-term effects we don't know about
* ❖ need to be very careful during pregnancy

It's often possible to combine drug and exposure treatment.

Tips for families and friends

Try to encourage the sufferer to read about the condition and to seek help. As in the case study at the beginning of the chapter, you may be able to help or provide support, motivation and encouragement during the treatment.

Dr Lynne Drummond

Dr Persaud's conclusion

Most highly successful people are probably a bit more obsessional or obsessive-compulsive than the rest of the population. Perfectionism is linked to this disorder and the tendency to check excessively that everything really is all right often characterizes those people who get the job done to a higher standard than the rest of us.

However, there comes a point when OCD starts to affect your life and how you function.

One paradox at the heart of OCD is that people with the disorder find it very hard to understand that by being a little more sloppy, by taking more risks, and by accepting that everything isn't as they would like it to be, they will in the longer term achieve greater happiness and better mental health.

i SUPPORT

SUPPORT ORGANIZATIONS

OCD Action, 22/24 Highbury Grove, Suite 107, London N5 2EA; help and information line: 0845 390 6232; fax: 020 7288 0828; info@ocdaction.org.uk; *www.ocdaction.org.uk*

OCD-UK, PO Box 8955, Nottingham NG10 9AU; email: admin@ocduk.org; *www.ocduk.org*

No Panic: helpline: 0808 808 0545; *www.nopanic.org.uk*

Young People's OCD Clinic: an information website aimed at children and young people with OCD. Michael Rutter Centre, Maudsley Hospital, Denmark Hill, London SE5 8AZ; email: ocdyoutheditor@iop.kcl.ac.uk; *www.ocdyouth.info*

WEBSITES OUTSIDE THE UK

Australia:
www.anxietyaustralia.com.au

New Zealand:
www.mentalhealth.org.nz

Canada:
www.anxietycanada.ca

South Africa:
www.anxiety.org.za

India: *www.health.indiamart.com/mental-health/obsessive-compulsive-disorder.html*

FURTHER READING

Living with Fear, Isaac Marks, McGraw-Hill, 2005

Overcoming Obsessive-Compulsive Disorder: A Self-help Guide Using Cognitive-Behavioural Techniques, David Veale and Rob Willson, Constable and Robinson, 2005

Understanding Obsessions & Compulsions: A Self-help Manual, Frank Tallis, Sheldon Press, 1992

Personality Disorder

A man who kept getting the sack

BRIAN, A MAN aged twenty–seven, came to his GP asking for help with what he described as 'my mood swings'. He explained these by describing times when he felt very confident and positive about his life and relationships, and others when he felt 'like I was drifting towards disaster'. These periods in his life had become much more frequent.

What became clear from further questioning was that these changes were not confined to his mood, but affected all parts of his daily life. He never seemed to have settled; he had had many changes of job, almost as many changes of partner, and no certainty in life.

His parents had separated when he was only four, and he had been brought up by his grandmother. When she became ill, his stepfather looked after him. He was often violent, particularly after drinking, and picked on Brian.

Brian was bullied at school, and as he got older he started bullying younger children. After leaving school with no qualifications, he got a job in a supermarket, but was sacked for poor time–keeping and 'a disrespectful attitude'. He then had a series of other jobs as a warehouse man, a courier and a forklift-truck driver, all of which he either left early or was sacked from after arguments with his bosses. He had enjoyed his last job, but was sacked for drinking at work and damaging his truck by colliding with a pillar.

Brian met Fran at this time, and at first the relationship went well. They had a baby boy, David, and managed to buy a flat together. However, Brian's unpredictable behaviour, occasional excessive drinking with episodes of violence, and unsettled job record put strains on the relationship and after two years they separated.

Since then Brian had been unable to get into any sort of routine and had been unemployed at times. He'd started several new relationships that went well at first, but then broke down. He was hoping that someone could help him find a more stable path in life.

What is personality disorder?

We all have personalities; they are our unique mental fingerprints. Those of us with what can be described as 'normal' personalities are more adaptable, and can fit into other contexts, depending on the circumstances. For example, someone who is quiet and retiring can take a more dominant role and lead when they have to. Similarly, a naturally forceful person can take a back seat, and be passive, when put in a situation they have not experienced before.

'Abnormal' personalities are not as adaptable, and show themselves at the wrong times, often with embarrassing or harmful results. A fussy person may become so preoccupied by order and exact detail that he never finishes a task;

a shy person may become so bothered by meeting others that she never goes out of the house; and an impulsive person may be so unable to control his temper that he even hits his best friend during an argument.

Brian would be seen by most specialists in mental health as having an 'abnormal' personality. This is because a large number of his problems seem to follow a pattern and are related to his personality – his trouble keeping a job, his excessive drinking, his difficulty in having a long-term relationship, and his tendency to pick fights and arguments. His unhelpful mental finger-print always seems to sabotage his life, even when things are going well.

People in this group are sometimes described as having 'personality disorders'. Personality is best viewed as a range, in which everyone has some parts of 'normality' and some of 'abnormality'.

One way of differentiating whether difficult behaviour or feelings are down to personality or mental illness is to consider how long the problems have persisted. Those suffering from personality disorder cannot usually recall a time when life was fine – they always were plagued with difficulties, back to early childhood. Mental illness, on the other hand, seems to come along and strike down someone whose life was trundling along fairly OK before the illness began.

Personality disorder is one of the more controversial areas in psychiatry, but is now becoming more accepted, particularly the group called 'borderline'. The term used to be regarded as a pejorative label, which was used as an excuse for doctors to do nothing and take no responsibility for getting a patient better.

You might think that some of the people in the chart (overleaf) are wrongly placed, because the position and places in which they showed their abnormal personalities may themselves have been abnormal.

Judy Garland, despite her success as a film actress, felt uncertain about herself, who she really was, and where she was going. If any of us became an overnight celebrity (as Judy Garland did after the first night of *The Wizard of Oz*) we might be uncertain about what it all meant.

For some personalities, the obvious abnormality can be a cause of success. Sherlock Holmes, based on a real doctor whom Arthur Conan Doyle knew as a medical student, was so successful because he doubted everything until he was quite sure it was the truth.

Joseph Stalin lived at a strange time in a country where everyone was paranoid; he was just the king of paranoia. He was one of the few Soviet

TYPICAL PERSONALITY EXTREMES

Type of personality	Main features	Example of this personality type
Paranoid	sees conspiracy everywhere	Joseph Stalin
Schizoid	very withdrawn, isolated, no significant social contacts	Gollum (from Tolkien's *Lord of the Rings*)
Anti-social (dissocial)	aggressive, callous, irresponsible, with little feeling for others	James Bond/Blofeld
Impulsive	unable to control emotions or behaviour but regrets upsets afterwards	Bridget Jones
Borderline	uncertain about identity; emotional instability with tendency to self-harm	Judy Garland
Histrionic	always seeking attention, emotionally shallow	David Brent (of *The Office*)
Dependent	lacks confidence, relies excessively on others	Baldrick (of *Blackadder*)
Anxious	excessively anxious, neurotic, always expecting disasters to happen	Adrian Mole
Anankastic (obsessional)	abnormally fussy, preoccupied by detail	Sherlock Holmes

leaders of the time to survive long enough to die naturally – although some think he may have been poisoned.

What causes personality to be abnormal?

In most cases, we are not sure what causes personality to create problems. Half of the features contributing to our personality are genetic or inborn, and the other half are provided by the environment. What makes a personality is the mixture of genes and the environment, so we cannot assume that anyone's personality is predestined to happen.

A person might be at risk of getting personality problems, but doesn't show it because he or she has not had any unpleasant experiences. Someone else, who has a lower risk, can develop an abnormal personality because of awful experiences at an important age – for instance, child abuse between the ages of four and six. In such cases, the damage is done because the abuse happened at a particularly sensitive time in emotional development. If it had happened at another time, the personality might not have been affected so badly.

In Brian's case, it is easy to see how his early experiences might have affected him. He did not have a normal family life, and most of his experiences were the negative ones of a bullying stepfather. If these are the only experiences you have when growing up, it is not surprising that you imitate them yourself. This is called modelling.

What happens to personality as we grow up?

Although personality may seem to be permanent, it does change a lot over time. Personality development begins early in life and is often not completed until early middle age. Anyone between the ages of five and twenty-five should not assume their final personalities have been developed.

Many children have problems with their personalities as they get used to a changing adult world. What may seem a serious problem at the age of twelve can completely disappear in the next year.

A great deal of personality development takes place after other mental and physical development has finished. We can all remember people we knew at school who were quite impossible in some aspects of their feelings, behaviour or personality, but who turned out to be perfect citizens when they got older.

A lot of your personality depends on your environment. If you are a dependent, passive person (sometimes called a 'wimp'), you may do brilliantly at school and college where you have others to advise you, and on whom you can rely. But in the real world you may find it very difficult to adjust. Your schoolfriend, however, who was always in trouble with teachers, may do very much better after leaving school because of the extra freedom this offers to practise their ideas.

Can personality be changed?

It used to be thought that once you were grown up, you were stuck with the personality you had, and it could not be changed. One of the reasons why the term 'personality disorder' creates such negative feelings is the notion that, once you have got it, it is permanent – a nasty mental fingerprint that spoils your whole existence.

However, there is now good news for anyone who wants their personalities changed – treatments are available (see below). Research suggests, however, that only a minority of people do want to change; most people are very happy with the personalities they finish up with.

A lot of abnormal personalities become less abnormal as they get older. By middle age some features, such as impulsiveness, anger and irresponsibility, are less obvious – it is often described as 'mellowing with age'.

On the negative side, some features, such as being anxious, suspicious or fussy, can continue into old age and may even get worse. This can depend on whether the person is in tune with his or her environment.

People with abnormal personalities can lead very quiet and comfortable lives when they are in the right setting, and some people whom we would describe as having normal personalities can be quite disturbed if they are in situations where they feel out of place.

Old age can in many ways be like a second childhood, and when we are very old we may return to how we were as teenagers. Most of us will not be fit enough to dash about on motorbikes creating havoc (Granny's Angels), but we can become very bad-tempered and childish if we don't get our own way.

What can be done to help?

In recent years, a range of treatments for personality disorder have been developed, but they do require hard work. Many of them are psychological treatments, which means that the person being treated has to do a lot of the work, both during and outside treatment sessions (homework).

Other treatments concentrate more on changing things around the person concerned, rather than the person themselves. For example, in the treatment called nidotherapy (nest therapy), the person and the therapist examine everything that is going on in the environment. They look at what might be changed to make a better fit between the person's personality and the environment (just like a nest changing its shape to make a better fit for the bird sitting in it).

Other treatments can include:

❖ being placed in special settings with others who have the same problems, where the treatment is mainly in the form of a group (these are called therapeutic communities)

❖ other group treatments involving weekly sessions, with homework in between (group cognitive therapy)

❖ both group and individual treatments, in which new ways of living with underlying beliefs and attitudes are introduced (mentalization treatment and schema focus therapy)

So personality is not fixed. It changes in lots of ways, so in time we may be able to get rid of the term 'abnormal personality' altogether.

Positive personality

When we say that someone's got 'a great personality', what do we mean? It's clear we are not referring to the type of behaviour described earlier as 'personality disorder'.

For every negative aspect of personality, there is a positive one. So, let us describe another Brian. He was a singer in a pop group who had a big personal fan club. His concerts were full of people who felt he had a special relationship with them and seemed to be, as far as they were concerned, 'just singing for me'. Unlike many pop singers, success did not seem to have gone to his head, and he always had time to stop and chat to fans. He recognized many of the loyal ones and waved to them during performances. He was always modest about his achievements and insisted he was just an ordinary bloke. 'I'm just someone with a loud voice who gets on well with a great group of lads,' he used to say to interviewers when they were trying to make out he was another Frank Sinatra.

What distinguishes this Brian from the other? One word – success. If your personality fits the situation, you do well, but are obviously helped by other talents. There is often a thin line between repeated failure and continued success, and a small change can turn the tide. The two Brians can be the same person, and, you might have guessed, they are.

Research has found that what can save someone from personality disorder and lead to a change in life pathway is a new relationship, often perhaps with a partner or spouse who, if they are the right person, can sometimes seem to bring about fundamental change in personality.

There is much controversy within psychiatry and psychology as to whether it is possible that many people with apparent mental illnesses probably also harbour personality disorder. It may be, then, that the distinction between the two is more apparent than real.

Professor Peter Tyrer

SUPPORT ORGANIZATIONS

Mind, 15–19 Broadway, London E15 4BQ; email: contact@mind.org.uk; information helpline: Mind*info*Line: 0845 766 0163; *www.mind.org.uk*

Mental Health Foundation, London Office, 9th Floor, Sea Containers House, 20 Upper Ground, London SE1 9QB; tel: 020 7803 1100; fax: 020 7803 1111; email: mhf@mhf.org.uk; *www.mentalhealth.org.uk*

BBC Health: *www.bbc.co.uk/health/conditions/mental_health/disorders_person.shtml*

National Personality Disorder: *www.personalitydisorder.org.uk*

WEBSITES OUTSIDE THE UK

Australia: *www.sane.org*

New Zealand: *www.mentalhealth.org.nz*

Canada: *www.mooddisorderscanada.ca*

FURTHER READING

Stop Walking on Eggshells: Coping When Someone You Care About Has Borderline Personality Disorder, Paul T. Mason and Randi Kreger, New Harbinger Publications, 1998

Psychotherapy for Borderline Personality Disorder: Mentalization Based Treatment, Anthony Bateman and Peter Fonagy, Oxford University Press, 2004

i SUPPORT

18

Phobias

A woman who didn't go out for three years

S HARON WAS TWENTY-ONE and had been referred to me by her GP. She explained, 'If I leave the house, I get so anxious that it feels as if I'm rooted to the spot. I feel dizzy, I start to breathe too fast, my legs feel tense and my whole body goes rigid with fear. I feel as if I am not really there, but also everything around me seems unreal.

'It began three years ago, when I had a panic attack going for a job interview which I didn't get. Since then I've avoided going into crowded places. At first I couldn't go into my church, the supermarket or get on a bus. Then it got so bad that I couldn't even get into a car unless I knew the driver well. For the last three years I haven't been anywhere!'

There was nothing unusual about Sharon's background. She'd been a happy child who was good at school. It was after leaving school and failing the job interview that the agoraphobia started. For the last three years she had had no social life, though some friends still visited her at home.

One year into her agoraphobia, Sharon started individual psychotherapy. 'The therapist said my problem was linked to my insecurity in childhood. I was expected to talk about it, and most of the time the therapist said nothing. I didn't know what to say, so I sat in silence. Then he wanted to see me with my family. I think they were made to feel as if it were all their fault. It was a waste of time, and we stopped going.'

Sharon had already read a self-help book on agoraphobia and said she liked the sound of the treatment called systematic desensitization. 'I like the idea of very gradually getting used to going outside again, but whatever else you do, no more psychotherapy – and I won't take any drugs.'

I explained to Sharon exactly what systematic desensitization is, and that it involves gradually desensitizing the person with the phobia to the object of fear. This treatment is now seen as rather old-fashioned. Instead, I recommended that she try exposure therapy. Before her next appointment in two weeks' time, I persuaded Sharon to agree to try a short walk to her friend's house and to do this twice.

At the next appointment she said smilingly, 'That was so easy it was frightening!' She had surprised herself by completing this task, but it had not been that straightforward. She had had to go out at night (bright light is often a problem for agoraphobics), she had gone with her mother each time (companions make phobic situations more bearable) and her father had had to pick her up in the car.

Her next bit of homework was to try the same walk in daylight, and without her mother. Sharon managed this – a small step for most people, but a big step for her.

At this point the treatment seemed simple enough. She was to go out for increasing distances from her home, alone whenever possible, and explore places like parks and supermarkets. All did not go according to plan.

At the sixth session she reported, 'I am back at square one. Last weekend my parents went away for the weekend and I stayed indoors. Then I started to think about what might happen to me if I did go out, and this worked me up into a right state. I can't go anywhere now.'

Sharon was describing 'anticipatory anxiety', which means that the more you think about something, the worse it gets. One way of getting rid of anticipatory anxiety is to use a procedure called the 'two-column' technique. The patient makes a list of what they fear may happen in one column, and rational responses in the other.

Anticipatory anxiety	Rational response
● If I go out I'll collapse.	● When I did go out, nothing happened.
● If I go out I get dizzy.	● I also get dizzy indoors, but if I wait it goes.
● If I go out I'll die.	● I am still alive after my last outing.

After six sessions along these lines, progress was still slow. Sharon got as far as attempting a train journey, but had a panic attack on the platform. 'I just froze . . . it lasted only a few seconds. Then things around me looked unreal. I had a strange dizzy feeling. I felt as if I couldn't walk straight. This reduced my confidence about going out at all.'

At this stage, I felt that Sharon needed help with her panic attacks and that this should be in the form of a medication more widely used in the treatment of depression: imipramine. She agreed, despite her earlier refusal to start any drugs.

After about three weeks, she was able once more to go for

walks alone. She then agreed to go to a shopping centre for 45 minutes, and achieved this without panic attacks. Sharon's progress continued, and she was soon able to go back to her church and travel on public transport.

What are phobias?

Most people are afraid of something. A phobia is defined as an irrational fear. People with phobias experience extreme anxiety in situations that most people do not find troublesome.

Common phobias are agoraphobia (fear of open spaces, crowded places and public transport); social phobias (fear of social situations); animal phobias; and various other phobias such as fear of thunderstorms and flying in aeroplanes.

Phobias can prevent you from enjoying a normal life because you avoid the situations that make you feel anxious. This can actually make the problem worse over time. You may feel silly or inadequate at not being able to control your fears, which you know are irrational.

It is not clear why these fears develop, but they are always related to a high level of anxiety (see p. 24). Instead of looking for the causes, most treatments focus on gradually learning to control the fear.

The natural course of phobias

It is possible for a phobia to clear up completely after a few days or weeks, but once it has become established and has been present for a year or more, it is unlikely to disappear completely without treatment.

How common are phobias?

About 1 in every 10 people will have troublesome anxiety or phobias at some point in their lives. Agoraphobia accounts for 60 per cent of phobias, and is more likely to affect young women.

Are phobias inherited?

'My mother [or my aunt] had terrible agoraphobia. Does this mean I will get it?' is a question often asked by the relatives of phobic patients. There is some evidence that agoraphobia runs in families, and especially among female relatives, but the cause is still unclear.

Misconceptions about phobias

❖ Depression is an illness that often means a person does not want to go out or face people (see p. 76). This must not be confused with a phobia, and is treated differently.

❖ Obsessive compulsive disorder (see p. 149), and so-called 'dirt phobia', can be very like phobias, but again are different and require another treatment.

❖ Medical conditions, such as some kinds of epilepsy, or an overactive thyroid gland and other rare medical conditions, can mimic phobias.

❖ Sometimes stress produces panic and phobia-like symptoms (see p. 241).

Remember: if in doubt, seek professional help.

What does a phobia feel like?

If you have a phobia, you will suffer intense symptoms of anxiety that occur only in the particular situation that frightens you. For instance, if you have a phobia of dogs, you will feel fine when there are none around. If you know you may have to see or meet a dog, the mere anticipation of the event can cause intense anxiety, leading you to avoid the situation. The symptoms of anxiety may include one or several of the following:

Psychological
❖ feeling worried all the time
❖ tiredness
❖ lack of concentration
❖ irritability
❖ sleeping badly

Physical
❖ palpitations
❖ sweating
❖ muscle tension and pains
❖ breathing heavily
❖ dizziness
❖ faintness
❖ indigestion
❖ diarrhoea

These symptoms can be mistaken for a physical illness. A sudden intense experience of anxiety is called panic (see p. 24). This can be very traumatic, and is often the reason for people consulting a doctor.

Do people with phobias have other problems?

The effect a phobia can have on your life must not be underestimated. You may be unable to leave the house, and someone with social phobia can have problems making any relationships. This can mean that you are socially isolated, which can lead to depression and lack of personal fulfilment.

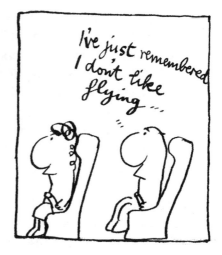

The depression may show itself as irritability, difficulty in getting off to sleep, lack of energy, and feeling gloomy and hopeless. Patients with agoraphobia are often depressed. However, if the depression only is treated, the phobic symptoms will remain.

If you have agoraphobia, you may have experiences that you feel are unreal and you may have the sense that you are out of your body. These are called derealization and depersonalization.

What can be done to help?

Treatment for phobias can be carried out on a self-help basis or by professionals.

Self-help

You can help yourself by managing the anxiety associated with phobias using the following three golden rules:
- ❖ anxiety is unpleasant, but it does no harm
- ❖ as you face anxiety, it gets less over time
- ❖ practice makes perfect

Think about how these rules can apply to you, and what practical steps you can take to begin to treat yourself.

Anxiety is unpleasant, but it does no harm

People often think they are going to die in an anxiety attack, as the symptoms are very unpleasant and uncomfortable: sweating, dry mouth, breathlessness and palpitations. (See Chapter 2, p. 24.)

One way of proving you will not die is to do some physical exercise, which brings on the same symptoms. Mild physical exercise, such as running up and down on the spot for 10 minutes, causes many people to have some of these symptoms. On the whole, physically fit people do not die from mild physical exercise.

Another way to try to prove to yourself that anxiety does no harm is to consider the normal anxiety you would expect to feel in a genuinely frightening situation.

As you face anxiety, it gets less over time

It is essential to remain in the phobic situation long enough to allow the anxiety to lessen. In the case of agoraphobia, you have to remain in the supermarket long enough for the anxiety to decrease, usually over 30 minutes, and often up to an hour. Brief exposure to supermarkets makes anxiety worse, so running out after 10 minutes, which is what you want to do, must be avoided.

Practice makes perfect

Learning to overcome anxiety is hard work. You are trying to break patterns of conditioning that have built up over the years.

Try to think of an example of where you have learned something difficult in everyday life. Did learning to drive, or type, come easily to you? How much practice did you have to put in?

The 'unlearning' of a phobia should be seen as a special kind of learning, because you have to break established patterns of behaviour that have been learned over many years. Can you remember having to unlearn something, such as how to use a different typewriter keyboard? Old habits die hard.

Practical steps

Using self-help therapy may be slower than getting professional help, but the principles are similar. Push yourself to experience the phobic situation, and remain in it long enough for your anxiety to lessen. This will have to be undertaken in a series of steps.

For example, a patient made the following list of steps in order to overcome her agoraphobia of thiry-five years:

1. Open front door and walk to garden gate (about 20 metres) with garden gate shut.
2. Walk to garden gate and open it.
3. Walk to post box at corner of street (about 50 metres from gate) with dog.
4. Walk to corner shops (about 100 metres) with dog.
5. Go into corner shop with dog.
6. Repeat 3 to 5 without dog.
7. Go to shopping centre and visit larger shops.

Cognitive approaches on yourself

You are often told by others to 'pull yourself together', and this is unhelpful. What can help is to think about what you say to yourself, and whether it is an unhelpful or unconstructive way of dealing with the problem. For example, you may feel a little faint when walking along the street, and you say to yourself: 'I feel faint – that means I am about to collapse. I shall lose control any minute and make a fool of myself. Perhaps I shall have a heart attack, or even die.'

This 'negative self-talk' is not at all helpful; it is what therapists call 'magnifying the symptoms'. The cure is to try to test out each of the negative ideas to yourself to prove that in fact the probability of their happening is rather low.

Medication

Many people don't want to take pills for their phobia. Others have the opposite view, and think that pills will solve the problem. The reality is somewhere in between. There are certain classes of medication that can help some aspects of phobic disorders.

Minor tranquillizers

Small doses of diazepam (valium) can help some people face the phobic situation in order to carry out exposure treatment. The danger of this class of medication is that you can become dependent on it.

Antidepressants

Antidepressants are often used in combination with cognitive behavioural therapy (CBT; see below), particularly when the person lacks the confidence to venture into the feared situation, and suffers from panic attacks.

There are three classes of antidepressants: tricyclic antidepressants, such as imipramine; SSRIs (specific serotonin re-uptake inhibitors), such as fluoxetine; and the mono-amine-oxidase inhibitors, such as phenelzine.

Beta-blockers, such as propranolol, have a useful effect in slowing down nervous activity. People who have tremors, palpitations or diarrhoea as their major symptoms can be helped by beta-blockers, together with CBT.

Talking treatments

Cognitive behavioural therapy (CBT)

CBT can help you to change how you think ('cognitive') and what you do ('behaviour'). These changes can help you understand and manage your thoughts and behaviour, and so feel better. Unlike some of the other talking treatments, CBT focuses on the 'here and now' problems and difficulties, instead of looking for the causes of your phobia in the past. It can help you change the way you think and how you act. (See also p. 427.)

CBT is a very successful treatment for phobias and is a way of talking about:

❖ how you think about yourself and your social situation
❖ how your actions affect your thoughts and feelings

CBT is available in GP practices, hospital outpatient departments or community mental health centres.

Tips for families and friends

The partner of a person with a phobia needs to understand that avoidance of a phobic activity makes it worse, so it does not help, for instance, to go to the supermarket for your partner. The best thing is to understand the therapy principles and to encourage the person to face up to phobic situations.

People often ask, 'What will I be left with if you take away my phobia? Will something worse take its place?' The answer is that all the evidence is against this. You will find that life becomes fuller and you are happier.

Planning for the future should be an important part of treatment. As agoraphobia lessens, you will find that you have time to do things that you could never have imagined before. An important part of recovery is to plan for this. Visit your long-suffering friends and family, who formerly had to visit you. Now is the time to join an adult education class, consider returning to work, or retraining for this if needed.

Dr Richard Stern

Dr Persaud's conclusion

Everyone experiences anxiety at some time, and indeed it is probably more common than depression, despite the fact that depression is more often discussed in the media and popular culture.

One key pointer to whether anxiety is becoming a medical condition is when it interferes with normal life, like work or relationships. For instance, a person with agoraphobia is so anxious that they will no longer go out.

The treatment of phobias is an action-orientated one focused on exposing yourself to whatever you are avoiding. This is often not popular with patients initially, but the scientific research on the subject is extremely clear that acting to confront avoidances is much more effective than merely talking about what makes you anxious.

i

SUPPORT

SUPPORT ORGANIZATION

National Phobics Society: formed by a sufferer of agoraphobia for those affected by anxiety disorders; a volunteer-led organization, run by sufferers and ex-sufferers of anxiety disorders. 339 Stretford Road, Hulme, Manchester M15 4ZY; tel: 0870 122 2325; email: info@phobics-society.org.uk; *www.phobics-society.org.uk*

WEBSITES OUTSIDE THE UK

Australia:
www.anxietyaustralia.com.au

New Zealand:
www.phobic.org.nz

Canada:
www.anxietycanada.ca

South Africa:
www.anxiety.org.za

India:
www.indianpsychiatry.com

FURTHER READING

The Feeling Good Handbook, David Burns, Penguin Books, 2000

Postnatal Depression

A woman who couldn't cope with her baby

FINDING OUT THAT she was pregnant came as a big shock to Joanne. Her son Jamie was barely one, and she had gone back to her job when he was six months. He was settled in nursery and, though she and Martin had talked about another child, they had planned to wait for a year or two.

Martin hadn't taken it well either. Although trying to be supportive, he was worried about money – they had just moved to a new house and really needed Joanne's salary to make ends meet. He had been angry when she told him, and they fell out for a couple of days.

As the pregnancy progressed, Joanne felt she was coming to terms with things, but she did keep thinking about how, after the birth of Jamie, she had stopped going out so much and had become cut off from her friends for several months. Her mother had been a good support and had helped get her back into the swing of things. But, since the house move, her mother was now much further away and Joanne knew nobody in this area. Work helped to keep her going, but she dreaded when she would have to stop. She worked to seven months, when sitting for long periods at her desk became more difficult. Once she was at home all the time the days seemed very long, but she tried to busy herself getting things ready for the baby.

The labour went well and, during the couple of days in hospital, Joanne felt fine. Back at home, her mother came to stay for a couple of weeks and Martin had some time off. They encouraged her to rest, but she found it difficult to unwind despite feeling tired all the time.

After her mother left, Joanne found herself worrying that she might not manage to cope. Jamie was more demanding, and baby Michael was still feeding three times a night. When Martin left for work in the mornings, taking Jamie to nursery, she lay in bed thinking of all the things she had to do through the day. Eventually she would have to get up for Michael, but she soon felt exhausted again. By evening, once Michael was down, she only wanted to go to bed. She was angry that Martin didn't seem to notice how much of a struggle it was for her.

Martin had noticed. Joanne seemed irritable and down. He didn't want to upset her, but when he asked how she was feeling, it only led to an argument. Things about the house became more of a chore for Joanne, and though Michael and Jamie were always well cared for, Martin felt she got little pleasure from the children. At times she seemed distracted and forgetful and, on a couple of occasions, he had come home to find her sitting crying, though she wouldn't say why.

Joanne's health visitor also thought something was wrong. Joanne always seemed on edge, frequently asking questions about Michael's weight and feeding. As a second–time mother, the health visitor had thought Joanne would be more confident, but Joanne seemed to have little faith in her own abilities.

On her fourth visit, the health visitor brought up the topic of postnatal depression. Joanne was initially angry, saying the health visitor must think she was useless. After some reassurance, however, she admitted for the first time that she had felt very depressed, had no energy throughout the day and saw no prospect of things getting better. The house seemed more and more of a mess every day. She thought this must be causing problems for Jamie and Michael, and described how guilty she felt that she couldn't even manage to be a good mother to her children.

After a long chat, the health visitor suggested some regular contact to give Joanne the opportunity to talk about her worries and help her to see how her thinking was being coloured by the depression. She also suggested a chat with Martin and Joanne together, so that Joanne would have the chance to explain to Martin how she felt and let Martin know how he could help.

A visit to Joanne's GP was arranged to see if there was anything else that she might suggest. Although Joanne knew she wouldn't feel better immediately, it was a great relief to have talked about the problems for the first time. It was also good to know that the health visitor seemed completely unfazed by her worries, saying that she had a number of women with similar difficulties who had been helped by the same strategies. It felt like a good start.

What is postnatal depression?

It's hard to pick up a newspaper or magazine without coming across accounts of film stars, actors or other famous people describing their experiences of low mood after childbirth. This can help women going through similar experiences to feel less isolated and encourage them to seek help.

At the same time, society places high expectations on pregnant women and new mothers. There is an expectation that this is a wonderful time, and that you should be radiantly happy. However, this is often far from the reality of adjusting to a new baby, and to the consequent changes in your lifestyle, particularly for first-time mothers.

Such high expectations make women, who may already feel low, also feel guilty and inadequate. This can prevent them from talking about the problem or from getting appropriate help. Western society, with its emphasis on the 'nuclear family', often leaves new mothers separated from the traditional support of the extended family.

More than half of all women will experience low mood in the first couple of weeks after birth ('baby blues'). This usually settles without the need for any specific treatment, other than the support of family and friends.

A much rarer condition, puerperal psychosis, is a severe mental illness that starts within days or weeks of childbirth. It usually requires urgent treatment, often in hospital. Women at risk can sometimes be identified during pregnancy and the illness prevented. Urgent treatment and early identification are essential as puerperal psychosis can sometimes, tragically, lead to infanticide.

PND describes a specific illness that occurs after childbirth. Research suggests that depression is not actually that much higher after childbirth than it is at similar life events (see p. 76). The symptoms of PND are not that different either. What makes depression at this time distinctive is the presence of a baby, the extra demands this places on you and your family, and the need for you and your baby to bond.

Focusing too much on PND can also mean that depression *during* pregnancy is overlooked. Contrary to popular belief, pregnancy is not 'protective' against mental health problems. However, the vast majority of women will not suffer any mental health problems either during or after their pregnancy.

What does it feel like?

Depressive illness affects around 1 in 10 women in the year after childbirth. The illness ranges from mild conditions, which get better over a few weeks with extra support, to severe illness, which may require admission to hospital. Symptoms can be thought of in terms of how they affect your *feelings, thinking* and *behaviour*, and can include:

❖ feeling 'low', particularly in the mornings
❖ feeling irritable and short-tempered
❖ having negative and pessimistic thoughts
❖ believing you cannot cope
❖ feeling guilty and blaming yourself

In severe illness, a woman may feel hopeless about the future, or even believe that her children or partner would be better off without her. In such circumstances, thoughts of self-harm or suicide may occur.

Depression can cause changes in your behaviour, such as:
❖ tearfulness
❖ sleep disturbance
❖ changes in appetite and weight
❖ reduced energy
❖ loss of interest in usually enjoyable activities
❖ problems with concentration and memory

These symptoms are usually present over at least two weeks. The difficulty is that some, such as sleep disturbance, which in other circumstances might indicate depression, can be due to caring for a new baby. A doctor or health visitor can usually distinguish between causes.

More frequent in PND are anxiety, excessive worries over the baby's health, and obsessional thoughts – recurrent, unwanted and upsetting thoughts or images, which frequently concern the baby. You may fear that the baby will fall ill or be harmed in some way – even that you may harm your own baby.

This can lead to your cleaning excessively, not allowing others to have contact with your baby, or even avoiding the baby yourself for fear that you might cause harm. Fortunately, it is extremely unusual for women to act on these thoughts. Despite feelings of guilt and inadequacy, most mothers with PND manage to care for their babies.

Puerperal psychosis usually starts soon after childbirth. It is a much rarer condition, in which depression – or the opposite, persistently elevated mood – is common. In addition, a woman can have false beliefs or odd experiences, and lack the ability to recognize that she is ill. The experience is often frightening and perplexing for the woman and for those around her. Fortunately, treatment is effective rapidly.

What causes PND?

There is rarely one single cause for depression; usually there are several factors, including a genetic predisposition, social pressures and problematic patterns of thinking, which make depression more likely.

Research suggests that social factors are particularly important. Women who feel unsupported, or have a number of other social or economic pressures, may be more at risk.

Previous mental health problems also increase risk. A personal or family history of severe mental illness (particularly bipolar affective disorder; see page 42) may place a person at much greater risk of puerperal psychosis.

Does it have any effect on the baby?

In some cases being depressed can affect a woman's relationship with her baby. Family members can make a difference by supporting the mother through her problems and caring for the baby until the woman is able to cope.

For her to get help to maintain and develop her relationship with her baby, even while she still feels depressed, is the best way of preventing any ongoing difficulties. A health visitor is often in the best position to provide advice and help.

Can women who go on to develop PND be identified in pregnancy?

Being depressed during pregnancy, or having previously experienced mental health problems, are perhaps the clearest risk factors. However, many other risk factors, such as lack of social support, are very common, and therefore make it impossible accurately to identify which women will become depressed.

What can be done to help?

All treatments for depression may also be helpful for PND. However, some medications should be avoided because they can cause side-effects, such as sleepiness, which could interfere with childcare and breastfeeding.

You may feel that if you admit you are not coping, your baby will be taken away from you. The reality is, usually, that everyone's main concern is to give you the support you need to cope while you get the treatment necessary to improve your mood.

Families can help by offering practical support, being sensitive to changes in the woman's mood, thinking and behaviour, and by allowing her to talk about her worries. GPs, midwives, health visitors and obstetricians all have experience in recognizing and helping with depression.

Self-help

There are a number of ways you can help to reduce the impact of PND:

❖ talk openly to family and friends
❖ let the health visitor or GP know about your problems
❖ read self-help books on PND
❖ accept that no one with depression can cope on their own, especially with a new baby
❖ if possible, take time out

Complementary therapies

Some women will want to use complementary or alternative therapies, although there is little evidence of their effectiveness with PND.

Complementary therapies may interact with other treatments, so it is essential to let your GP or health visitor know if you are using them. Complementary drug therapies can also transfer to breast milk, so are not recommended for women who are breastfeeding.

Talking treatments

Most women with PND will receive help from their health visitor. Health visitors have training in identifying depression, and may use a rating scale called the Edinburgh Postnatal Depression Scale (EPDS). In areas where it is used, an EPDS rating is usually given to *all* women, not just those who are suspected of having PND. Where depression is present, the health visitor will often offer extra contact and talking therapy – usually called *listening visits* – which have been shown to reduce the impact of PND.

Medication

A smaller number of women may require antidepressants. It is possible to take some antidepressants when breastfeeding. The decision should be made between the woman and her doctor, taking into account the woman's wishes and the age and health of her baby.

In a small number of cases, where the depression is severe or not responding to the original treatments, a referral to mental health services may be useful. Additional treatments may then be suggested, both drug and/or talking therapies. In some cases, admission to hospital can help. In many parts of the UK, facilities are available to admit mother and baby together. This allows the mother to receive treatment for her illness, while staff also help her maintain and develop her relationship with her baby.

Which treatment is right for me?

The choice of treatment will depend on the severity of the depression, the side-effects of medication, whether the woman is breastfeeding, and the wishes of the woman herself. These can be discussed with the GP.

Tips for families and friends

✔ Do

❖ listen to the woman's worries and concerns
❖ watch out for changes in mood, thinking and behaviour
❖ encourage her to seek extra help
❖ offer practical support, such as help with household tasks and baby care
❖ focus on, and encourage her in, the things she can manage to do, rather than concentrating on the difficulties
❖ seek help for yourself where needed
❖ remember that depression is common and that complete recovery is usual

✘ DON'T

❖ ignore or play down her worries
❖ 'take over' completely; she must not feel that others cope better than she can

Dr Roch Cantwell

Dr Persaud's conclusion

If we think about how women cared for babies in our evolutionary past, it was probably the case that women of childbearing age got together and helped each other at this demanding time. Looking after a baby was probably much more a group activity than it is today in the modern Western world. Instead, a mother now often finds herself bringing up a baby by herself much of the time, and it is this isolation which contributes largely to distress. A key issue appears to be support, from the wider family, neighbours and, perhaps most vital of all, from a woman's partner.

Postnatal psychological problems in mothers should always be taken very seriously because the health of not only a mother is involved, but also that of a baby. We now know from new research that these mental health problems have the potential to leave a long-term impact on a growing child.

The period shortly after giving birth carries a higher risk of mental illness for a woman than any other time of her life. This is a moment for which there needs to be much careful planning for assistance if good mental health is to be maintained.

If, however, things deteriorate to such an extent that admission to a specialist in-patient mother and baby unit might need to be considered, the mother and baby can be cared for together by a team specially trained to help with these problems. The lack of adequate provision across the UK and the rest of the world of these specialist in-patient services needs to be urgently addressed.

i

SUPPORT

SUPPORT ORGANIZATIONS

Association for Postnatal Depression: provides support to mothers suffering from postnatal illness. It exists to increase public awareness of the illness and to encourage research into its cause and nature. 145 Dawes Road, Fulham, London SW6 7EB; helpline: 020 7386 0868; *www.apni.org*

CRY-SIS, BM-CRY-SIS: provides self-help and support for families with excessively crying and sleepless babies. BM Cry-sis, London WC1N 3XX; helpline: 08451 228669; *www.cry-sis.org.uk*

Meet-A-Mum-Association (MAMA): self-help groups for mothers with small children and specific help and support to women suffering from postnatal depression. 54 Lillington Road, Radstock, BA3 3NR; tel: 01525 21704; helpline: 020 8768 0123; email: meet-a-mum.assoc@ btinternet.com; *www.mama.co.uk*

National Childbirth Trust: advice, support and counselling on all aspects of childbirth and early parenthood. Alexandra House, Oldham Terrace, Acton, London W3 6NH; enquiry line: 0870 444 8707; breastfeeding line: 0870 444 8708; *www.nct.org.uk*

Samaritans: confidential emotional support to any person who is suicidal or despairing. Tel: 08457 909090 (Ireland: 1850 609090); email: jo@samaritans.org; *www.samaritans.org*

WEBSITES OUTSIDE THE UK

Australia:
www.beyondblue.org.au

Canada:
www.sane.org

India:
www.seasonsindia.com

New Zealand:
www.mentalhealth.org.nz

South Africa:
www.pndsa.co.za

FURTHER READING

The Royal College of Psychiatrists' webpages on mental illness related to childbirth: *www.rcpsych.ac.uk*

Coping with Postnatal Depression, Sandra L. Wheatley, Sheldon Press, 2005

Post-traumatic Stress Disorder

A woman whose world fell apart

MARIE IS AN unusually small, friendly, middle-aged woman. She used to work as a cleaner with an early start every morning – but a year ago she was attacked on her way to work. She was crossing a narrow street towards the bus stop when she suddenly felt a pull on her handbag. A stranger, a woman with long, curly blond hair and wearing a black jacket, was dragging her along.

She was brutally beaten about her head, punched in the face and taken into a building. At that moment she thought she was going to be killed and repeatedly shouted for help. The woman managed to get Marie's handbag, leaving her on the floor feeling dizzy and bleeding from a cut on her forehead. The next thing she remembered was the police by her side and her attacker being escorted away by them. Her assailant went to prison.

Recently, the police told Marie that her attacker was soon due for release. Hearing that news, Marie's world fell apart. She became so convinced that the woman would be after her that she started to look for accommodation in another part of London. She felt continually depressed. Whenever she saw a person with long, curly blond hair, she panicked, which made it difficult for her to leave her flat. She had been sleeping badly, waking up with nightmares of her attacker. She argued more with her daughter and split up with her boyfriend – she felt they just didn't understand what she was going through. She often thought of the attack and was unable to relax when there were loud noises. She felt exhausted and frightened, and at times thought life was not worth living.

Finally Marie sought help from her GP, who first of all put her in touch with a therapist (psychoeducation) to talk about what happens when people suffer a traumatic event. They discussed how most people might improve spontaneously without help, but that others, like her, would develop post-traumatic stress disorder (PTSD) and would benefit from treatment.

Later on, when Marie felt a bit more relaxed, she started on talking therapy, focusing on her worst memories of the attack. She managed to remember details she thought she had totally forgotten, such as the face of her attacker and the two men who had come to her rescue.

Her nightmares and panic attacks decreased, and finally stopped. She can now go on public transport again and says, 'I now know what she looks like, and that not everyone with long blond curly hair is going to attack me.' She is happy to continue living in the same flat and is going to look for a new job. Moreover, she has got back together with her boyfriend and enjoys the company of her daughter again.

What is post–traumatic stress disorder?

During our lives, we all encounter painful and distressing moments. We usually get over these without professional help. However, extremely traumatic events cause unusual levels of stress. These are often events in which you believe that you (or other people, particularly if close to you) may be in danger of losing their life. These include serious accidents, violent assault, rape, terrorist attacks, earthquakes or other natural disasters, torture and warfare, or being diagnosed with a life-threatening illness.

Such traumatic events undermine the sense of security we usually enjoy and make us feel extremely vulnerable. After the initial reaction, most people adjust over the next few weeks. Others, however, get worse as time passes and develop the symptoms of PTSD. It is usually diagnosed only after the symptoms have been there for a number of months (six months in Europe, one month in the USA).

What does it feel like?

Many people feel grief-stricken, depressed, anxious, guilty and angry after a traumatic experience. As well as these understandable emotional reactions, there are three main types of symptoms produced by such an experience:

Flashbacks and nightmares. You find yourself re-living the event, again and again. This can happen both as a 'flashback' in the day and as nightmares when you are asleep. These can be so realistic that it feels as though you are living through the experience all over again. You see it in your mind, but may also feel the emotions and physical sensations of what happened – fear, sweating, smells, sounds, pain.

Ordinary things can trigger off flashbacks. For instance, if you had a car crash in the rain, a rainy day might start a flashback.

Avoidance and numbing. It can be just too upsetting to re-live your experience over and over again, so you distract yourself. You keep your mind busy by losing yourself in a hobby, working very hard, or spending your time absorbed in crossword or jigsaw puzzles. You avoid places and people that remind you of the trauma, and try not to talk about it.

You may deal with the pain of your feelings by trying to feel nothing at all – by becoming emotionally numb. You communicate less with other people, who find it hard to 'get through' to you. You may become absent-minded and accident prone.

Being 'on guard'. You find that you stay alert all the time, as if you are looking out for danger. You can't relax. This is called 'hypervigilance'. You feel anxious and find it hard to sleep. Other people will notice that you are jumpy and irritable.

Other symptoms can include:
* muscle aches and pains
* diarrhoea
* irregular heartbeat
* headaches
* feelings of panic and fear
* depression
* drinking too much alcohol
* panic attacks
* using drugs (including painkillers)

Rape victims often feel shame and so don't ask for help. An Iranian man left his country convinced that everyone knew what had happened to him and thought him gay. He had been raped by three military men, who threatened to tell his family. He was too ashamed to talk even to his teenage son.

Children

Children express their anxiety in a different way. They have sudden and extreme emotional reactions and may start behaving as if they are much younger. They may have upsetting dreams of the event and will often repeat behaviour that reminds them of it. For example, a child involved in a serious road traffic accident might play with toy cars, making them crash, again and again. They worry about dying young. Rather than talking about it, they may complain of stomach upsets or headaches and have problems at school.

How common is PTSD?

It can happen at any age in both men and women, although only some people exposed to a traumatic event will suffer PTSD. It is more likely if a traumatic event:

❖ is sudden and unexpected
❖ goes on for a long time
❖ traps you and you can't get away
❖ is man-made
❖ causes many deaths
❖ causes mutilation and loss of
   arms or legs

❖ attacks you intimately, e.g. rape
   or torture
❖ involves children

It is also more likely if you:
❖ believe you came close to death
❖ have little social support

What causes PTSD?

The symptoms of PTSD seem to be the normal reactions to trauma that are just too intense and go on for too long. When you feel these reactions in a situation of real danger, and for a short time, they can be very useful and even lifesaving. However, if they carry on when the danger is past, instead of helping you to survive, they make life more difficult. For example, being keyed-up and full of adrenaline is exactly what you need if you are in danger. But if it goes on and on you will just get tired, demoralized and exhausted. The numbness can protect us from the full impact of the trauma, but in the long run will stop us from getting involved in the real life around us. Flashbacks can, for a short while, be helpful by reminding you of what happened and making you think about better ways of dealing with it. But if they go on and on, they can distress you and make you feel out of control.

What can be done to help?

Talking treatments

Before talking therapy can start, you have to feel that you have some control and that you are safe. A woman who has been raped and beaten up by her husband, but is too frightened to leave him, will need shelter, protection and legal advice before considering trauma therapy.

The main proven talking therapies are:

Psychoeducation. Learning about the common reactions to trauma can help you to make sense of what is happening to you and to work out what you need. (See p. 444.)

Cognitive behavioural therapy (CBT) can help you to change how you think ('cognitive') and what you do ('behaviour'). These changes can help you understand and manage your thoughts and behaviour, and so feel better. Unlike some of the other talking treatments, CBT focuses on the 'here and now' problems and difficulties.

The therapist will help you to think about the ways in which you may overestimate threats, feel guilty at surviving, or blame yourself. They will also help you to cope with the stress and show you how to relax, so you can work on the trauma without feeling out of control. CBT is more effective if you have had a single trauma and were previously psychologically well. (See also p. 427.)

Eye movement desensitization and reprocessing (EMDR) is a technique that uses eye movements to help the brain to process flashbacks and to make sense of the traumatic memory.

We do not know exactly how EMDR works, but it seems to help you to reprocess traumatic memories into a more normal verbal memory. This fits with research showing that the language area of the brain functions less well in people who suffer from PTSD. This area seems to be reactivated after successful treatment. Another brain function that seems to improve with EMDR is Rapid Eye Movement sleep – and this is our normal way of processing what has happened to us, so we can deal better with our memories. (See also p. 443.)

Medication

Medication can be used to help with some of the symptoms. It is especially useful when the person is depressed, hearing voices or very troubled. It can be given on its own, or together with talking therapy.

The most common medications include antidepressants and, at times, a small amount of antipsychotic medication. Sleeping tablets can be helpful, but only for short periods of less than 2 weeks. If you are still in a dangerous situation, or feel too unsafe to start talking therapy, medication may be the only choice.

Complementary therapies

Many complementary therapies are available. However, none has been proved to resolve the symptoms of PTSD – although aromatherapy, osteopathy, homeopathy or massage may increase your sense of control and help you to relax.

Self–help

✔ Do

❖ keep life as normal as possible

❖ get back to your usual routine

❖ talk about what happened to someone you trust

❖ try relaxation exercises

❖ go back to work

❖ eat and exercise regularly

❖ go back to where the traumatic event happened

❖ take time to be with family and friends

❖ drive with care – your concentration may be poor

❖ be more careful generally – accidents are more likely at this time

❖ speak to a doctor

❖ expect to get better

✘ DON'T

❖ beat yourself up about it – PTSD symptoms are not a sign of weakness; they are a normal reaction, of normal people, to terrifying experiences

❖ bottle up your feelings: if you have developed PTSD symptoms, don't keep it to yourself because treatment is usually very successful

❖ avoid talking about it

❖ expect the memories to go away immediately; they may be with you for quite some time

❖ expect too much of yourself – cut yourself a bit of slack while you adjust to what has happened

❖ stay away from other people

❖ drink lots of alcohol or coffee or smoke more

❖ get overtired

❖ miss meals

❖ take holidays on your own

Tips for families and friends

 Do

❖ watch out for any changes in behaviour – poor performance at work, lateness, taking sick leave, minor accidents
❖ watch for anger, irritability, depression, lack of interest, lack of concentration
❖ take time to allow a trauma survivor to tell their story
❖ ask general questions
❖ let them talk; don't interrupt the flow or come back with your own experiences

✖ **Don't**

❖ tell a survivor you know how they feel – you don't
❖ tell a survivor they're lucky to be alive – they'll get angry
❖ minimize their experience – 'it's not that bad, surely . . .'
❖ suggest that they just need to 'pull themselves together'

Dr Nuri Gene-Cos

Dr Persaud's conclusion

Some sceptics believe that the diagnosis of PTSD has merely medicalized the inevitable tragedies of life, leading to unnecessary treatment and encouraging people to act like victims. Against this view, it is clear that, for some people, the psychological consequences of traumatic events are long-lasting, powerfully disabling and deserving of help.

USEFUL WEBSITES

www.survive.org.uk – UK and worldwide information about organizations dealing with domestic violence, male and female rape, sexual abuse. Mental health information pages have information on PTSD and Coping with Trauma

www.trauma-pages.com – David Baldwin's trauma pages: a very useful website, with a wide range of information

www.uktrauma.org.uk – website for the general public and for health professionals; information on PTSD

WEBSITES OUTSIDE THE UK

Australia:
www.acpmh.unimelb.edu.au

New Zealand:
www.everybody.co.nz

Canada:
www.ctsn-rcst.ca

South Africa:
www.csvr.org.za

FURTHER READING

Overcoming Traumatic Stress: A Self-help Guide Using Cognitive-behavioural Techniques, Claudia Herbert and Ann Wetmore, Constable and Robinson, 1999

Coping with Post-Traumatic Stress, Frank Parkinson, Sheldon Press, 2000

A Shattered World: The Mental Health Needs of Refugees and Newly Arrived Communities, John Reading and Meena Raj, CVS Consultants and Migrant and Refugee Communities Forum, 2002

Schizophrenia

A man who was followed by the Secret Service

STEPHEN WAS DOING fine until he was nineteen. He did well at school. He'd had no problems with exams. Looking back, he says that he felt shyer and more sensitive than his classmates, but not so anyone would notice. When he was younger, he had had some close friends, but when his family moved to the city, he became isolated.

Stephen went to university and immersed himself in his books. However, he soon began to have a 'weird' feeling that everything 'wasn't quite right'.

He kept this to himself, but wasn't able to read as much. He stopped going home at weekends. He hung around his flat, often not washing for days. At the beginning he was able to hide what was going on, but he became more and more irritable and impatient. He was preoccupied with the 'weird' feeling. Family and friends accused him of being distant. He confided in them even less and became more withdrawn.

One day, whilst on a bus, he passed a police checkpoint. He knew with 'crystal clarity' that the checkpoint was there to warn him that he was going to be killed by an Eastern European gang who had previously worked for the Secret Service. Everything now made sense.

Stephen became even more watchful. He took copious notes of news bulletins, the car numbers outside his flat, and who was scratching their nose in class. He was convinced his life was in danger and eventually went to the police. The desk sergeant listened carefully but told him that it was unlikely that a gang would target him. A few days later, he became convinced that the noises he had begun to hear were actually part of the electronic surveillance the gang had set up. These were voices discussing him, saying unpleasant and deeply personal things about him. They became so intense that he took the skirting board off the wall to work out where the bugging devices were.

Within a month everything came to a head. One day his local newsagent started scratching his nose. Stephen began screaming at him, 'You'll never get me', and that he 'would never break'. The police were called and Stephen was admitted to hospital.

He was so drained from the whole experience that he told the doctors and nurses everything. He was surprised by how relieved he was at telling his story. After a brief period in hospital, he felt well enough to go home and attended a day hospital. He stopped smoking hash, watched his diet and exercised again.

Stephen once stopped his medicine for a few weeks because he thought he was 'cured'. However, when his symptoms came back, he started his medication again. Now he views it in the same way as his younger brother, who has to take medication for his asthma: 'As long as I take it, I don't have to think about it too much.'

Stephen is now working full time and gets on well with his family and friends. He goes out a lot and runs regularly, but finds he has to work at staying well. 'You have to work hard at getting better, and it can take several years, and a lot of determination, to get your self-confidence back.'

What is schizophrenia?

Most people have very little knowledge of what schizophrenia is, what causes it and how it is treated. There is also widespread misunderstanding about what the illness is not.

Schizophrenia is *not* a 'split personality'. Schizophrenia is *not* caused by bad parenting, personal weakness or failure in an individual. It is one of the most misunderstood, and therefore most stigmatized, medical conditions.

Schizophrenia is five times more common than multiple sclerosis. It affects about 1 in every 100 people. This means that more than a quarter of a million people in the UK are affected.

What does it feel like?

Schizophrenia is a lonely illness. It distorts our senses and makes it difficult to tell what is real from what is not real; these experiences are termed 'psychotic' symptoms. They include believing people are talking in a nasty way about you. This leads to loss of concentration, loss of confidence and withdrawal from work, family and friends. Many people are so distressed that they turn to alcohol and drugs to get some relief from these symptoms.

If no action is taken, problems get worse, so seeking help early is important because treatment for schizophrenia does work.

Schizophrenia almost always involves a change in a person's work and social life, and a change in their personality. At first, the changes may be subtle and go unnoticed; eventually, they become obvious to family, friends, classmates or co-workers. The person who is ill may have trouble telling what is real from what is not real, and will often minimize or deny the symptoms completely.

People with schizophrenia often experience other symptoms, such as:

Thought disorder. Thoughts may be slow to form, come extra fast, or not at all. Thoughts may jump from topic to topic; an individual may seem confused, or have difficulty making even simple decisions. The person's thinking is often affected and coloured by 'delusions'.

Delusions. These are false beliefs totally out of keeping with a person's social and religious background. The belief is held with complete conviction. Some people may feel persecuted – convinced they are being spied on or plotted against. They may have 'grandiose' delusions and think that they are all-powerful and capable of anything. They may believe that they have a personal mission to right the wrongs of the world.

Ideas of reference. The person starts to see meanings in ordinary events. For example, they are convinced that radio or TV programmes are about them or that people are communicating with them in unusual ways, such as through the colours of cars passing in the street.

Personality change is common. There is a loss of emotion, interest and motivation. A normally outgoing person may become withdrawn, quiet or moody. Emotions may be inappropriate – the person may laugh in a sad situation or cry over a joke – or may be unable to show any emotion at all.

Perceptual changes turn the world of the ill person upside down. Sensory messages to the brain from the eyes, ears, nose, skin and taste buds become confused – and the person may actually hear, see, smell or feel sensations that are not real. These are called hallucinations.

It is important to remember that these false perceptions are real to the individual. The commonest problem is auditory hallucinations or 'hearing voices'. Sometimes the voices are threatening or condemning. They may also give direct orders and this can be very serious, as it may lead to the person doing things they would not do otherwise.

These misperceptions of reality trigger feelings of dread, panic, fear, depression (see p. 76) and anxiety (see p. 24) – natural reactions to such terrifying experiences. This is also a time of high risk of self-harm (see p. 250).

What can be done to help?

If you or someone close to you is experiencing any of the symptoms above, it is essential to get help early. Schizophrenia is treatable. Getting help early allows the person to get their life back on track quickly.

Medication is necessary to treat the most distressing symptoms of schizo-phrenia. You may not need to go into hospital; even if you do, it need not be for a long period. Usually, treatment can be continued at home.

With medication, most people notice an improvement within weeks, but sometimes it can take longer. You can begin to think more clearly, concentrate better, and find yourself less distracted and getting more done.

There are different types of medication, called antipsychotics. A common side-effect of these is weight gain, particularly if you have not been as physically active as previously. Most mental health teams recommend, after a medical screening, an exercise routine as well as a healthy diet.

Each of the drugs has particular advantages and disadvantages. If you have difficulty finding a medication that suits you, clozapine may be prescribed as this is thought to be the most effective drug.

In the case of schizophrenia, psychological therapies are not usually considered a complete substitute for antipsychotic medication, but are most helpful once drug treatment has got rid of your psychotic symptoms. They are usually used alongside medication and are most helpful once the drug treat-ment has got rid of the psychotic symptoms. Psychotherapy usually involves regular talks between you and a mental health professional. The sessions may focus on current or past problems, experiences, thoughts, feelings, or relation-ships, and could help explore why the illness started when it did in order to prevent a relapse in the future. (See p. 440.)

Another key to recovery is to learn more about the illness. Understanding the symptoms, what makes them better and what makes them worse will help you to control them. Education about the illness is also vital for the family. If there are any doubts, ask the members of your mental health team. They want to help.

Sometimes people need more help with their recovery, particularly if they have had more than one episode of schizophrenia. It may be necessary to undertake occupational therapy and/or coaching in how to begin socializing again. While many people do very well, some people will require continuing support in such activities.

Recovery from any serious medical or surgical illness can take months of rehabilitation. Recovery from schizophrenia can involve a lot of hard work, as well as a concerted effort by the individual and their family.

Tips for families and friends

❖ Learn to recognize the symptoms. Family members are usually the first to notice symptoms and suggest medical help.
❖ If you are worried that the person is becoming unwell, then ask your doctor for an assessment or referral. The assessment and treatment of schizophrenia should be done by people who are qualified. Choose a doctor who has an interest in the illness and has empathy with patients and their families.
❖ Work with the doctor/psychiatrist.

People with schizophrenia may not be able to volunteer much information during an assessment. Talk to the doctor yourself, or write a letter describing your concerns. Be specific. Be persistent. The information you supply can help the doctor towards more accurate assessment and treatment.

Make the most of treatment. There may be exchanges between doctor and patient that the patient feels are of a highly personal nature and wants to keep confidential. However, family members need information on care and treatment. You should be able to discuss the following with the doctor:
❖ signs and symptoms of the illness
❖ expected course of the illness
❖ treatment strategies
❖ signs of possible relapse
❖ other related information

Provide plenty of support and loving care. Help the person accept their illness. Try to show by your attitude and behaviour that there is hope, that the disease can be managed and that life can be satisfying and productive.

Help the person with schizophrenia maintain a record of information on:
- ❖ symptoms that have appeared
- ❖ all medications, including dosages
- ❖ effects of various types of treatment

Learn to recognize signs of relapse. Family and friends should be familiar with signs of 'relapse' – where the person starts to show the signs of schizophrenia again. These signs vary from person to person, but the most common signs are:
- ❖ withdrawal from activities
- ❖ deterioration of basic personal care

You should also know that:
- ❖ stress and tension can make symptoms worse
- ❖ symptoms lessen as the person gets older

Managing from day to day
- ❖ make sure the person takes their medication
- ❖ provide a structured and predictable environment
- ❖ be consistent
- ❖ maintain peace and calm at home
- ❖ be positive and supportive
- ❖ help the person set realistic goals
- ❖ gradually increase independence
- ❖ learn how to cope with stress together

It must be the mirror that's ill ...

Look after yourself and your family
- ❖ be good to yourself
- ❖ value your own privacy
- ❖ do not neglect other family members

And learn from others who have been through similar experiences.

Dr Mary Clarke and Professor Eabhardt O'Callaghan

Dr Persaud's conclusion

Schizophrenia has an unfortunate reputation as being an untreatable condition that is to be feared, when the reality is that, with a vigorous approach combined with early detection, your prospects can be excellent. Many high-functioning individuals, who have made enormous contributions to society, have suffered from schizophrenia.

One consequence of the inadequate provision of mental health services throughout the world is that correct treatment gets offered only to those who are very unwell. Yet psychiatrists can frequently recognize much more subtle signs that presage the advent of schizophrenia, sometimes years before the illness fully manifests itself. These signs are much more subtle than hearing voices or bizarre delusions and involve slight alterations in reasoning and thinking. It's a great pity that such early recognition, which offers the possibility of very early treatment and possibly even prevention, is not more supported by health services. Instead we seem to have to wait for sufferers to become severely unwell before services get involved.

i SUPPORT

SUPPORT ORGANIZATIONS

Rethink: a voluntary organization providing advice and support to people with mental illness, their families and carers.
30 Tabernacle Street, London EC2A 4DD; national advice service tel: 020 8974 6814; email: info@rethink.org; *www.rethink.org*

SANELINE: confidential helpline: 0845 767 8000; *www.sane.org.uk*

Schizophrenia Ireland: helpline: 1890 621 631; *www.sirl.ie*

The Royal College of Psychiatrists: information specifically relating to schizophrenia – *www.rcpsych.ac.uk/mentalhealthinformation.aspx*

WEBSITES OUTSIDE THE UK

Australia:
www.sane.org

New Zealand:
www.sfnat.org.nz

Canada:
www.schizophrenia.ca

South Africa:
www.schizophrenia.co.za

India:
www.scarfindia.org

FURTHER READING

Changing Minds: Our Lives and Mental Illness, Rosalind Ramsay, Anne Page, Tricia Goodman and Deborah Hart (eds), Gaskell Publications, 2002

Ian Chovil's homepage is a wonderful personal account of schizophrenia – *www.chovil.com*

Seasonal Affective Disorder

A woman who suffered from October blues

Hayley is thirty. She visited her doctor at the end of one October because she had been feeling tired and low in mood for about ten days. She had noticed seasonal changes in her mood for many years, and these became worse after moving to the north–east of Scotland.

In a typical year, she would start to feel tired and sleepy during the day from about the middle of October. Then, as the days grew shorter, she would need to sleep longer, so that by the middle of January she could sleep for up to fourteen hours a day. She would go to bed at 8.00pm, struggle to wake up in the morning, then often return to bed after she had taken her son to nursery. She would frequently have a nap in the afternoon, when she felt most tired.

In an average winter, she would gain around 12 lb (5.5 kg), as she would crave sweet foods, particularly chocolate. Her mood would become low, and her outlook on life gloomy and pessimistic. She felt at her worst in the mornings. She would withdraw socially during winter and dreaded Christmas.

In addition, her sex drive was non-existent during winter, and in her work as a freelance journalist she became much less productive, partly due to her bad concentration and short-term memory. January and February tended to be her worst months, and she usually started getting better by the end of March.

During the summer months, Hayley is bright, outgoing and energetic. At times she may become 'too cheerful', particularly when the weather is good, and friends have remarked that she can seem 'turbo-charged' at these times. She often wakes 'with the first light of dawn' in summer and cannot wait to get on with things, as she needs only around five hours of sleep.

Hayley spent the first ten years of life in the Middle East and recalls being very unhappy when her family moved to Surrey. She describes her mother as a 'lifelong worrier', and generally felt closer to her father. Her father's sister has been on antidepressants for most of her adult life.

Hayley had been prescribed the antidepressant, fluoxetine, for two winters, and had citalopram last winter. Both were helpful, but they made her feel slightly 'spaced out'. She also suspected that they further reduced her sex drive. She is contemplating another pregnancy and is keen to avoid antidepressants if she can.

Hayley was diagnosed with recurrent winter depression. Her doctor advised her to resume her exercise regime, especially if she was able to jog outside, as she would derive benefit both from the exercise itself and from daylight exposure.

Hayley began using a light box for half an hour at breakfast time initially, but she later increased this to one hour. She returned the following winter to report that the combination of the light therapy and making herself continue to exercise was helping, as she was less depressed than the previous year.

What is seasonal affective disorder?

For thousands of years, people have believed that the seasons affect our health. Hippocrates, in 400 BC, thought that it was 'chiefly the changes of seasons which produce diseases'. By AD 200 Aretaeus had already recognized the link between sunlight and depression, advocating that 'lethargics are to be laid in the light and exposed to the rays of the sun (for the disease is gloom)'.

Even our language suggests a link between mood and light. Examples include 'black moods', 'feeling brighter', 'ray of sunshine', or 'full of the joys of spring'. Many animals hibernate in winter and come alive in spring, as they begin to attract a mate and prepare for offspring.

The term Seasonal Affective Disorder (SAD) was first used in the 1980s, but there is still debate about whether it is an illness, or just a normal pattern of behaviour for many people.

What does it feel like?

Recurrent winter depressions start in the autumn and stop in the spring and summer. Most sufferers begin to experience symptoms in October or November. These reach a peak between December and February, and usually start to improve significantly in March and April.

Many symptoms of winter depression are similar to those seen in ordinary depression (see p. 76). They include low mood (often worst in the morning), loss of interest in things, experiencing less pleasure from enjoyable activities, lack of energy, low motivation, reduced sex drive, irritability and withdrawal from social relationships.

In ordinary depression, it is common to sleep less, to eat less and to lose weight. By contrast, in recurrent winter depression, you sleep more, often feeling very tired and sleepy during the day, and you tend to eat more and to gain weight. You might crave chocolate and other high-carbohydrate foods. You will usually become gradually less active during the course of the winter and consequently might find yourself in a vicious circle. As you become depressed and tired, you exercise less and go out less. This causes weight gain, and even less exposure to daylight, which in turn makes you feel more depressed.

By contrast, in the summer you are active, cheerful and outgoing. Some people become excessively energetic, cheerful and extrovert. To most people, this is an enjoyable asset, but to others it can be a problem and can even amount to clinical hypomania.

Who suffers most from winter depression?

Winter depression is uncommon in childhood, but when it does happen children can get irritable and sluggish, and schoolwork can suffer. Winter depression becomes more common after puberty. Women are three or four times more likely to suffer than men. After the age of sixty, men and women suffer equally.

In America, winter depression seems to be more common in the north. But this doesn't seem to be the case in Europe – so, for example, Iceland has low rates of winter depression. This may be because the people have developed a genetic protection against the disorder.

What causes winter depression?

We don't know the answer to this. Women are most at risk in their reproductive years, but this is true for all depressions.

It is perhaps obvious to point out that the cause of winter depression is almost certainly a lack of daylight. It is thought that the lack of sun affects serotonin and melatonin, two chemicals in the brain that control mood.

There are similarities to jet lag, in that people often feel tired in the day but more alert at night (phase shifted). This has implications for treatment, which are mentioned below.

What can be done to help?

Many of us will experience mood changes over the seasons. We call this an illness only when our life or health begins to suffer. The main treatments are light therapy, antidepressants or psychotherapy.

Self–help
There are four main things to remember:

❖ Exercise is good for all types of depression, so try to keep exercising throughout the winter months.

❖ Daylight exposure is good, so you should try to spend as much time out of doors (or at least sitting by a bright window) as you can manage.

❖ Try to keep optimistic. Tell yourself that the depression will go in the spring, and that from 21 December the days are starting to get longer. It is helpful if your friends and relatives know that you suffer, as they will help you to keep going and will tolerate you during the darker months of the year.

❖ Be on the look out so that you don't fall into a vicious circle. For example, if you don't exercise, your depression may get worse, and that will mean you won't get out, which will mean you get even less sunlight and so on. So the more areas in which you can intervene effectively (continuing to exercise, daylight exposure, continuing to socialize, etc.), the bigger the knock-on effects will be.

Light therapy

There are several ways to replace the 'missing' light during the winter months. Light boxes and dawn-simulating alarm clocks seem to work best.

Light boxes have been used for over twenty years. They are more effective when used early in the morning. Light boxes emit bright light that mimics sunlight, but with the harmful ultraviolet component removed so that they don't harm your skin or eyes. Most people use them for between half an hour and two hours each morning, depending on the brightness of the light.

Dawn-simulating alarm clocks are much less bright than light boxes. They produce a gradually increasing brightness of light in the hour or so before you would plan to wake in the morning. They are particularly helpful if your main symptoms include oversleeping and difficulty waking up. Some people will use a dawn-simulating alarm clock to help them wake up, and then a light box.

If light therapy is going to work, then you should notice its effects within a week. Manufacturers often give customers a three-week sale-or-return option, and this is long enough to know whether or not a light box or dawn-simulating alarm clock is going to work for you.

Light therapy is generally free of ill-effects. Occasionally it can cause headaches or blurred vision, and if you use it too much it can make you feel 'wired', as if you have drunk too much coffee. If light therapy is used too late in the day, it can cause insomnia.

Medication

There have only been a few research studies on the effectiveness of antidepressants, but they do seem to work. Selective serotonin re-uptake inhibitors (SSRIs) are usually used, such as fluoxetine, citalopram and sertraline. Venlafaxine and duloxetine may also be used. It's best to avoid drugs that cause sedation.

Talking treatments

The value of positive thinking and optimism has already been mentioned. Cognitive behavioural therapy (CBT) can help lift your mood and may help prevent future attacks. It can help you to change how you think ('cognitive') and what you do ('behaviour'). These changes can help you understand and manage your thoughts and behaviour, and so feel better. Unlike some of the other talking treatments, CBT focuses on the 'here and now' problems and difficulties. (See p. 427.)

Which treatment is right for me?

Most people like the idea of 'natural' light therapy. However, light boxes are not always convenient; you have to find half an hour in the mornings, and they are not cheap.

Some people think that taking an antidepressant once a day is a more convenient alternative. Cognitive behavioural therapy is also time-consuming, and may not be easily available near you.

Light therapy is best if you are oversleeping, have increased appetite and weight gain in winter, which go away completely in summer. If you are also prone to being 'down' at other times of the year, then antidepressants or CBT may be better.

Dr John Eagles

Dr Persaud's conclusion

Even on a cloudy winter's day, going for an hour's walk will top you up with much more light than staying indoors – no matter how bright the lights are where you live or work.

It's probably the case that many more people suffer from a range of seasonal mood problems than those who have the full-blown syndrome, and so maybe many more of us should top up on light during the winter rather than waiting for a diagnosis of SAD.

SUPPORT ORGANIZATIONS

The SAD Association: a good self-help organization. PO Box 989, Steyning, BN44 3HG; *www.sada.org.uk*

Manufacturers of light boxes and associated devices, while obviously being commercial enterprises, are usually knowledgeable and supportive.

WEBSITES OUTSIDE THE UK

Australia:
www.healthinsite.gov.au

Canada:
www.mooddisorderscanada.ca

FURTHER READING

Winter Blues: Everything You Need to Know to Beat Seasonal Affective Disorder, Norman E. Rosenthal, Guilford Press, New York, 2005

Seasonal Affective Disorder: Practice and Research, T. Partonen and A. Magnusson (eds), Oxford University Press, 2001

i SUPPORT

23

Sexual Problems

A man who can't enjoy sex

Francis is a forty-five-year-old man in a happy marriage. When he was made redundant about two years ago, however, he became very depressed and lost all confidence in himself. Francis went to see his GP and was treated for six months with an antidepressant. He made an excellent recovery and started a new job.

However, Francis returned to his GP a few months later as he and his wife were no longer enjoying sex and he now had difficulty maintaining an erection for intercourse. He felt somewhat embarrassed about this, and had not discussed it with his wife. He was worried what it would mean for the future of their relationship, as he now felt uncomfortable being intimate with his wife.

The GP referred Francis to the local psychosexual clinic, where a doctor interviewed him and arranged for some blood tests to exclude any physical causes. No exact cause was found, but Francis and the doctor agreed that, although he was no longer depressed, he had suffered a loss of confidence that was contributing to the erectile dysfunction. He was also a heavy smoker, mildly overweight and did little physical exercise.

Francis was given a prescription of sildenafil (Viagra) and was encouraged to talk openly with his wife about the problem. The treatment was successful, and Francis and his wife were able to enjoy intercourse again. Francis's self-confidence improved, he successfully gave up smoking and reduced his weight by joining a gym. After six months he no longer needed the sildenafil.

What is sexual dysfunction?

Sexual functioning is central to human life. It is the route to reproduction; it is a source of intense pleasure; and it plays a central role in the development of intimate human relationships.

Sexual functioning is very complex, involving both psychological and physical aspects. In sexual problems – sexual dysfunction – it is common for several factors to be involved, but psychological factors nearly always play a role and may sometimes be the main reason for the problems.

It is not easy to define sexual dysfunction. However, the following would be indications that specialist help is required:
❖ the problem occurs on most/all occasions
❖ has gone on for six months or more
❖ is causing distress or relationship difficulties
❖ leads to an inability to participate in a preferred sexual relationship

Common problems
Although often not discussed openly, sexual problems are extremely common.

In a large survey of men and women aged between eighteen and fifty-nine, it was found that:

In men

❖ 10 per cent suffer from erectile dysfunction, and this rises to 50 per cent over the lifetime
❖ 16 per cent have loss of sexual interest
❖ 30 per cent complain of premature ejaculation
❖ 8 per cent report delayed ejaculation

In women

❖ 33 per cent have a lack of interest in sex
❖ 24 per cent are unable to experience orgasm
❖ 21 per cent have a lack of pleasure in sex
❖ 18 per cent have poor lubrication
❖ 14 per cent complain of pain during sex

Most sexual dysfunctions are problems of desire, arousal or orgasm. Problems may be *primary* (occur throughout adulthood, but not necessarily on every occasion), *secondary* (occurred only recently), *situational* (only in specific settings or with specific partners) or *total* (occur on every occasion, in all contexts).

Disorders of desire

Desire refers to the general urge to be sexual ('sex drive' or libido). A disorder of desire should be distinguished from sexual aversion, lack of enjoyment during sex, depression (see p. 76) and physical causes, including alcohol and drugs.

Disorders of arousal

In men, arousal refers to the process of penile erection. In women arousal refers to lubrication and clitoral enlargement, which help intercourse. Erectile dysfunction is the most common sexual problem in men and is often referred to as 'impotence'. It leads to a failure to achieve sexual intercourse. Although physical causes are often not identified, and psychological/emotional factors play an important role, physical factors should always be looked for through a proper medical assessment.

In females arousal problems lead to vaginal dryness or lack of lubrication. This may be due to psychological factors (e.g. anxiety – see p. 24), physical problems (e.g. infection) or oestrogen deficiency (e.g. in post-menopausal women). It may also be secondary to a lack of sexual desire. As well as techniques to increase arousal during sex, and addressing common triggers (see table, p. 216), lubricating gels may be helpful.

Disorders of orgasm

Orgasm occurs in both sexes, and includes ejaculation in men. Problems with delayed or absent orgasm, despite normal sexual arousal, are the most common sexual complaints in women. Some people may consider this to be normal and not complain of a problem. Treatment may include a guided self-help programme such as 'sensate focus' (see box, p. 218), and the teaching of specific pelvic-floor exercises, though some cases will require referral to a specialist psychosexual therapist.

In men, problems with ejaculation are the most common complaint relating to orgasm. Premature ejaculation – where there is an inability to control ejaculation adequately for both partners to enjoy sexual interaction – is the most common, especially in young men. Ejaculation may occur immediately after penetration has begun, or even before erection. Delayed ejaculation is less common, though it is a common side-effect of some antidepressant medications.

What causes sexual dysfunction?

Usually there are a number of causes related to sexual dysfunction. Sometimes, however, a clear trigger or cause is apparent. The most common are listed in the table overleaf.

What can be done to help?

Many sexual problems are temporary and may resolve themselves without any treatment. This process may be helped by the person, or the couple, addressing some of the common psychological/emotional triggers (see table overleaf), and being aware of 'sexual myths' (overleaf), which commonly lead to inhibitions, communication problems or unreasonable expectations.

TRIGGERS AND CAUSES FOR SEXUAL DYSFUNCTION

Psychological/emotional problems

- relationship problems
- life stressors /feeling 'stressed'
- anxiety/depression
- low self-confidence
- performance anxiety

- guilt about sex
- fear of sexually transmitted disease
- previous negative sexual experience (e.g. rape, sexual abuse)

Medical/physical problems

- general ill-health
- diabetes mellitus
- cardiovascular disease
- endocrine/hormonal disorders

- liver disease
- kidney failure
- specific disorders of the genitalia or genital region (less common)

Medication/drugs

- decreased sex drive: alcohol, antidepressants, antipsychotics, some hormonal treatments, anti-epileptics
- impaired erection: smoking, alcohol, antidepressants, antipsychotics, beta-blockers, some diuretics, anti-epileptics
- impaired ejaculation: antidepressants, antipsychotics

Common sexual myths

❖ men should not express their emotions
❖ all physical contact must lead to sex

❖ good sex leads to a wild orgasm
❖ sex = intercourse
❖ the man should be the sexual leader
❖ women should not initiate sex
❖ men feel like sex all the time
❖ a woman should always have sex when her partner makes sexual approaches
❖ sex is something we instinctively know about
❖ 'respectable' people should not enjoy sex too much and should certainly never masturbate
❖ all couples have 'great sex', several times a week, have an orgasm every time, and always orgasm simultaneously
❖ if sex is not good, there is something wrong with the relationship

(Adapted from G. Andrews and R. Jenkins (eds), *Management of Mental Disorders* (UK edn, vol. 2), World Health Organization, Sydney, 1999.)

The more long-term problems, and those that cause a lot of distress, will need specialist medical help. Your GP will see you initially, but may refer you to a psychosexual clinic where necessary. It is usually advisable that the couple attend together. People may also access specialist help, information and advice directly by contacting RELATE.

Treatment will involve:
❖ excluding specific physical causes
❖ education about factors that affect sexual functioning
❖ improving communication between the couple
❖ identifying specific relationship factors which may be contributing

Relationship factors may include negative feelings between the couple (e.g. anger/resentment, lack of trust, hostility), excessive politeness, inexperience, or difficulty finding privacy in the home.

Medications are now commonly used when the main problem is male erectile dysfunction. The most common of these are: sildenafil (Viagra), tadalafil (Cialis) and verdenafil (Levitra) – all obtained by prescription. They work in a similar way, and they all require sexual activity or fantasy to initiate the sexual arousal process. The overall effectiveness is approximately 80 per cent in cases thought to be mainly psychological, and 50 per cent in cases with physical causes contributing to the problem.

Many couples will benefit from one of the various forms of 'couple therapy', which have proved very effective for a range of sexual dysfunctions; see p. 444.

'SENSATE FOCUS'

This entails a series of 'homework' exercises for couples to do together to reduce sexual anxiety. It also employs some specific techniques for specific problems. It begins with periods of prolonged non-genital foreplay, with a temporary ban on intercourse. Later stages progress to touching of breasts and genitals, but with the focus on awareness of sensations, and maintaining the ban on intercourse. Later, more genital contact is encouraged, reverting to non-genital contact if one partner becomes anxious or becomes focused on orgasm. In time couples will progress to full intercourse.

Masters and Johnson, 1970

Paraphilias

'Paraphilias' – previously known as 'sexual perversions' or 'sexual deviations' – refer to an attraction to something outside the normal range in relation to sex. It is only appropriate to make a clinical diagnosis of a paraphilia if the person's behaviour or desire is causing a degree of suffering or affecting their lives.

Many people engage in sexual activities or have sexual desires that are paraphilic (e.g. fetishes), but which do not lead to any problems for themselves or for others. What is regarded by a society as a paraphilia is partly dependent upon the current cultural context.

The most common paraphilias include the following:

Exhibitionism. A recurrent or persistent tendency to expose the genitalia to strangers (usually of the opposite sex) or to people in public places, without inviting or intending closer contact. There is usually, but not invariably, sexual excitement at the time of the exposure and the act is commonly followed by masturbation. Victims are usually strangers and commonly teenage girls.

Voyeurism. A recurrent or persistent tendency to look at people engaging in sexual or intimate behaviour such as undressing. This is carried out without the observed people being aware, and usually leads to sexual excitement and masturbation. Voyeurism appears to be carried out exclusively by men.

Paedophilia. A sexual preference for children, boys or girls or both, usually of pre-pubertal or early pubertal age. The majority of paedophiles are men, but some are women.

Sadomasochism. A preference for sexual activity which involves the infliction of pain or humiliation, or bondage. If the subject prefers to be the recipient of such stimulation this is called masochism; if the provider, sadism. Often an individual obtains sexual excitement from both sadistic and masochistic activities.

Fetishism. This involves intense, sexually arousing fantasies, sexual urges or behaviours, involving the use of inanimate objects – e.g. leather or rubber garments, women's underwear, stockings, bras, shoes and boots. A particular kind of fetishism is the erotic attraction to uniforms.

Fetishistic transvestism. The wearing of clothes of the opposite sex mainly to obtain sexual excitement and to create the appearance of a person of the opposite sex. Fetishistic transvestism is distinguished from transsexual transvestism by its clear association with sexual arousal and the strong desire to remove the clothing once orgasm occurs and sexual arousal declines. It can occur as an earlier phase in the development of transsexualism. (See also Chapter 11, p. 107.)

Other disorders of sexual preference include making obscene telephone calls, rubbing up against people for sexual stimulation in crowded public places, sexual activity with animals, and use of strangulation or suffocation for intensifying sexual excitement.

Causes of paraphilias

The origins or causes of paraphilias are not well understood. A number of theories have been put forward, including seeing the behaviour as an expression of real or fantasy experiences, desires or conflicts originating in the person's early psychosexual development. It is assumed that the person has got 'fixated' at a particular stage.

Another theory is the 'learning model' – a paraphilia is thought to arise from the association of a previously neutral object with a sexually arousing object, or a sexually arousing experience. Whilst the learning model probably provides a limited explanation, other factors, such as cultural and symbolic meanings of objects, also have a role to play.

Treatment of paraphilias

Paraphilias usually require treatment only if they are causing a lot of distress or harm to the individual or others, or are interfering with other important functions. It is essential not to 'over-medicalize' sexual behaviour which deviates from the norm but does not lead to significant problems. If treatment is required, this should be with a specialist in paraphilias.

The goals of treatment need to be agreed carefully, and it needs to be recognized that treatment may not be successful. There are specific psychological techniques available, such as covert sensitization or orgasmic reconditioning, but in general, controlling abnormal desires needs to be supplemented with gains in other more acceptable sexual behaviours for the beneficial effects to last.

Dr Andrew Parker

SUPPORT ORGANIZATIONS

RELATE: advice, relationship counselling, sex therapy, workshops, mediation, consultations and support face-to-face, by phone and through its website. Check your local telephone directory for the address and telephone number of your nearest branch. Helpline: 0845 130 4010; *www.relate.org.uk*

Institute of Psychosexual Medicine, 12 Chandos Street, Cavendish Square, London WIG 9DR; tel: 020 7580 0631; email: admin@ipm.org.uk; *www.ipm.org.uk*

Gender Identity Disorders in Children and Adolescents: *www.mermaids.freeuk.com*

The Gender Trust: *www.gendertrust.org.uk*

WEBSITES OUTSIDE THE UK

Australia:
www.adhd.com.au/sexual.html

Canada:
www.sexualityandu.ca

*i*SUPPORT

24

Sleep Problems

A woman with creepy-crawlies under her skin

S HEILA IS THIRTY–FOUR years old, married and has an eighteen–month–old son. She's had sleeping difficulties for as long as she can remember.

'As a child I remember having "creepy crawlies" under my skin, itching and driving me mad. I would cry to my parents to make it stop. They put cold cream on my legs or wrapped them in warm towels – eventually the best thing was to put on soft cotton trousers and run around the house to take my mind off it.'

As a teenager, she remembers being sleepy at school and being teased about falling asleep. After starting college, her falling asleep got worse. Teachers complained to her parents that she was sleeping through most of her classes and was having problems with her schoolwork.

'I dropped out of college with one A-level. Since then I have been found asleep under my desk on the floor at work; I have fallen asleep during a phone call and at the wheel of a car. I have never been able to stay awake much past ten at night and have been known to sleep in restaurants, parties and even nightclubs.'

Sheila felt that she was a total failure. 'Why can't I do things other people can and why do I fall asleep when I try to read?'

As she was growing up she saw different doctors who came up with different explanations for her problem. Eventually, she went to a specialist sleep clinic where she met a team of sleep specialists who carried out tests overnight in hospital. The tests showed that she had a disorder called restless legs syndrome (or RLS): during sleep, her legs move and jerk. As a result of this she is very sleepy during the day.

'I am now on treatment and have never felt better. I won the local dance championship recently and have started my degree course.'

What is insomnia?

We don't usually need to think very much about our sleep – it's a part of life we take for granted. But if we can't sleep it can be a real problem. In fact, most of us will find it hard to sleep at some point. We have a word for it – insomnia. It's often just for a short time, perhaps when we're worried or excited. After a few days, things settle down and we get back to sleeping normally. However, we need sleep to keep our minds and bodies healthy. If we carry on sleeping badly, we start to notice the effects.

There are a number of common patterns of insomnia:
- difficulty falling asleep
- difficulty staying asleep
- waking up too early in the morning
- unrefreshing sleep

223

Insomnia leads to:

❖ tiredness, fatigue and sleepiness
❖ lack of energy

❖ difficulty concentrating
❖ irritability

As many as a third of people seeing their GP have occasional difficulties in sleeping, and 10 per cent of those may have long-term sleep problems. About 30–40 per cent of adults have insomnia each year, and about 10–15 per cent indicate that the insomnia is long term or severe.

Types of insomnia

Acute insomnia. Periods of sleep difficulty lasting between one night and a few weeks. It is often caused by emotional upsets or physical discomfort. It can also be caused by having to sleep or be awake when your body clock doesn't want you to; this can happen when working shifts or when you get jet lag.

Chronic insomnia. Sleep difficulty at least three nights a week for a month or more. This can be caused by various health problems or it may occur on its own.

Insomnia caused by medical or psychological problems. Depression and anxiety commonly cause insomnia. Pain, immobility, difficulty breathing, dementia, pregnancy and the menopause are other common causes. Many medical problems can get worse at night and interfere with sleep, such as asthma, gastric reflux or back problems.

Insomnia caused by medicines or drugs. Stimulating antidepressants, steroids, nasal decongestants, beta-blockers, caffeine, alcohol, nicotine and street drugs (like Ecstasy) can all cause sleep problems.

Primary insomnia. When other causes of insomnia have been ruled out, the sleep problem is called primary insomnia. Chronic stress, hyper-arousal, poor sleep hygiene, or bad sleep habits contribute to this problem.

What can be done to help?

Medication

People have used sleeping tablets for many years, but:

❖ they don't work for long

❖ they make you tired and irritable the next day

❖ they lose their effect quickly, so you have to take more to get the same effect

❖ some people become addicted to them; the longer you take sleeping tablets, the more likely you are to become dependent on them

There are some newer sleeping tablets (zolpidem, zalpelon and zopiclone), but these seem to have many of the same drawbacks as the older drugs, such as nitrazepam, temazepam and diazepam.

Talking treatments

Cognitive behavioural therapy (CBT) has been shown to be helpful. CBT can help you to change how you think ('cognitive') and what you do ('behaviour'). These changes can help you understand and manage your thoughts and behaviour, and so feel better. Unlike some of the other talking treatments, CBT focuses on the 'here and now' problems and difficulties. (See also p. 427.) Research favours the use of a short course of medication combined with a course of sleep re-training CBT.

Self-help

Here are some tips that people have found helpful.

✔ Do

❖ Make sure your bed and bedroom are comfortable – not too hot, too cold or too noisy.

❖ Make sure your mattress supports you properly. It should not be so firm that your hips and shoulders are under pressure or so soft that your body sags. Generally, you should replace your mattress every 7–10 years to get the best support and comfort.

❖ Get some exercise. Don't overdo it, but try some regular swimming or walking. The best time to exercise is in the morning or late afternoon. Avoid exercise in the evenings after 6.00pm.

❖ Take some time to relax properly before going to bed. Some people find aromatherapy helpful.

❖ If something is troubling you, and there is nothing you can do about it right away, write it down before going to bed and tell yourself to deal with it tomorrow.

❖ If you can't sleep, get up and do something you find relaxing. Read, watch television or listen to quiet music. After a while you should feel tired enough to go to bed again.

✖ DON'T

❖ Don't go without sleep for a long time – go to bed when you are tired and stick to a routine of getting up at the same time every day, whether or not you still feel tired.

❖ Caffeine stays in the body for many hours after your last drink of tea or coffee. Stop drinking tea or coffee by mid-afternoon. If you want a hot drink in the evening, try something milky or herbal (but check there's no caffeine in it).

❖ Don't drink a lot of alcohol. It may help you fall asleep, but you will almost certainly wake up during the night.

❖ Don't eat or drink much late at night. Have your supper early in the evening rather than late.

❖ If you've had a bad night, don't sleep in the next day – it will make it harder to get to sleep the following night.

Other sleep problems

Restless legs syndrome (RLS)

This is a common yet under-diagnosed problem with unpleasant limb sensations occurring at rest and an irresistible urge to move. Periodic limb movements (PLM) may accompany these sensations and often interfere with sleep. RLS causes discomfort, sleep disturbance, tiredness and fatigue during the day. It often affects a person's quality of life.

If only my Doctor hadn't told me sleeplessness was a symptom of DEPRESSION – I'd never have known I had it

calma

Between 5 and 15 per cent of adults have RLS. It is easily diagnosed by sleep studies, such as polysomnography. RLS may be caused by a number of illnesses, such as diabetes, Parkinson's disease, rheumatoid arthritis, anaemia, pregnancy, neurological diseases and some drugs. It can be treated with medications such as clonazepam and some drugs used to treat Parkinson's disease.

Narcolepsy

This is a serious, but uncommon, problem in which people have sudden and uncontrollable attacks of sleep, which can last from 30 seconds to 30 minutes. Sometimes the attacks are accompanied by hallucinations or temporary paralysis. Narcolepsy can be quite debilitating, causing lack of muscle control and dream experiences throughout the day.

Sufferers often fall asleep in the middle of important activities, including driving and while playing sports. They also fall asleep during conversations and at work. People with narcolepsy often experience a temporary paralysis, which can lead to injury if they fall. So it is a dangerous and disruptive problem.

Narcolepsy can be diagnosed in a clinic familiar with sleep medicine, where a physical examination will be carried out.

Many people looking into the cause of this condition have become interested in a substance in the brain, called orexin or hypocretin, which seems to be lacking in narcolepsy sufferers.

Treatment consists of taking regular exercise and having a regular night-time routine. Depending on the symptoms, medication may be helpful – such as an antidepressant or a drug which increases wakefulness, such as modafinil.

Excessive daytime sleepiness (EDS)

This occurs in narcolepsy, but may have a variety of other causes, including obstructive sleep apnoea (see below) and restless legs syndrome. The main symptoms are feeling drowsy and tired; having an overpowering need to sleep during the day; being unable to stay awake in the day, even after a good night's sleep; and falling asleep at times when you need to be fully awake and alert.

The condition can affect work or cause dangerous driving. Sufferers are often frustrated and angry because they feel that they are misunderstood and seen as not interested in personal growth or learning. They often have low self-esteem or poor personal relationships as a result.

Obstructive sleep apnoea (OSA)

This is a condition where people temporarily stop breathing in their sleep. This sometimes causes them to wake with a start. Most people with sleep apnoea also snore, but not all snorers have sleep apnoea.

Disrupted sleep caused by frequent interruption of breathing leads to excessive daytime sleepiness, irritability, memory lapses, inattention, personality changes, poor work performance, increased driving and industrial accidents. Dangerously low levels of oxygen can cause heart problems and other health disorders, including depression (see p. 76), mood changes, memory loss, weight gain, impotence and headaches. There is an increased risk of irregular heart beat, high blood pressure, premature heart disease and stroke.

One effective treatment is a continuous positive airway pressure mask. This fits over your nose and supplies high-pressure air to keep your airway open.

REM sleep behaviour disorder

This causes vigorous episodes of behaviour such as shouting or violent movements during sleep, which may result in injury to oneself or others. The outbursts occur during rapid eye movement, or REM, sleep. Normally during this time we dream and our muscles are relaxed; however, in this condition people can move their bodies and act on their dreams.

This disorder is often misdiagnosed and has not frequently been reported in the UK. Up to 60 per cent of patients with this condition go on to develop Parkinson's Disease.

Sleep walking and sleep terrors

This is when the person typically leaves their bed during sleep and is active but confused and disorientated. They are likely to move slowly and clumsily, and they are at risk of injuring themselves. Sleep walking may be preceded by a scream or a sleep terror, with a marked increase in heart rate and breathing. If the person is in a state of terror, their movements may be more rapid; they may even run into walls or out into the street. They are not as responsive as someone who is awake, but they may shout or scream.

Trying to stop the person often leads to resistance. When they wake up, the sleepwalker will have no memory of what happened. There are safe and effective treatments, including tablets, psychotherapy (see p. 440) and hypnosis.

Dr Irshaad Ebrahim

Dr Persaud's conclusion

Difficulties with sleep are some of the commonest problems for which people go to their doctor. Sleep medications are some of the most prescribed of all drugs in the UK. The irony is that most drug treatments are now regarded as second best to non-drug approaches. Indeed, many drug treatments can become the cause of insomnia if prescribed for long enough.

Sleep disturbance can be an early sign of other psychological problems, such as excessive worry, anxiety (see p. 24) or depression, and these are often missed in the hurry to offer a prescription for a hypnotic.

A further irony is that the fear of insomnia which leads people to demand an instant fix from their doctors could itself be the root cause of sleep disturbance in the long run. Learning to be tolerant of not being able to sleep can be the best treatment of all – the body has a natural habit of delivering on the sleep front if deprived of it for long enough.

i SUPPORT

SUPPORT ORGANIZATIONS

The Sleep Council: promotes the benefits of sleeping well and provides information leaflets on sleep and beds. Tel: 01756 791089; www.sleepcouncil.com

Narcolepsy Association UK (UKAN): promotes the interests of people with narcolepsy and encourages better understanding of the illness. UKAN, 50 Culvert Street, Newent GL18 1DA; tel: 0845 450 0394; email: info@narcolepsy.org.uk; www.narcolepsy.org.uk

Ekbom Support Group: a patient support, information and advice group for people who have restless legs syndrome. 8 Rodbridge Drive, Thorpe Bay, Essex SS1 3DF; www.ekbom.org.uk; www.restlesslegs.org.uk

Sleep disorder clinics: there are a number of sleep disorder clinics, but referral to one of them should be made through your family doctor – patients cannot refer themselves. Try www.sleepmedicine.co.uk and www.sleeping.org.uk for links to other sleep clinics.

The London Sleep Centre – a comprehensive private centre for the diagnosis and treatment of all types of sleep disorders. NHS patients can be seen with prior approval from NHS Primary Care Trusts; www.londonsleepcentre.com. Also the **Edinburgh Sleep Centre**; www.edinburghsleepcentre.com

WEBSITES OUTSIDE THE UK

Australia:	**Canada:**	**South Africa:**
www.nodss.org.au	www.bettersleep.ca	www.sleepcentre.co.za

FURTHER READING

Get a Better Night's Sleep (Positive Health Guides), Ian Oswald and Kirstine Adam, Optima, 1990

Insomnia: Doctor I Can't Sleep, Adrian Williams, Amberwood Publishing, 1996

Beating Insomnia: How to Get a Good Night's Sleep, Chris Idzikowski, New Leaf Publications, 2003

AUDIO TAPES

Coping with Sleep Problems: a two-cassette audio pack with advice and self-help tips on how to deal with sleep problems. Available from the Royal College of Psychiatrists, tel: 020 7235 2351, ext. 146; www.rcpsych.ac.uk

25

Stalking

A woman who didn't want flowers

Ms A., a GRADUATE student, began to receive odd emails, both at university and at home, expressing affection and asking for a date. These were signed 'John' or 'You'll remember me', but she didn't recall meeting anyone called John or 'me'. She ignored them.

After several weeks she was approached by a fellow student whom she vaguely remembered from several years ago. They chatted casually and he asked why she hadn't responded to his invitations as they had been such good friends in the past. Ms A. made it clear that she hadn't answered because she didn't wish to start a relationship and politely added that it was nothing personal, but she needed to concentrate on her studies.

After that the flow of emails increased and flowers arrived at her flat. John began to hang around her at the university and approached her in the streets, trying to persuade her to go out with him because 'he still loved her'. The emails became more explicitly sexual and insistent. Ms A. sought out John, who was studying computer sciences, and told him to stop sending her gifts and emails. She became quite heated and made it clear they had never been friends and that she found his attentions distressing and wanted them to stop.

Several weeks passed. One evening, on opening up the files on her university computer (on which much of her research was stored), she found a series of obscene images. Over the next few weeks her computers at home and at the university were hacked into repeatedly, and material deleted, changed, or obscene pictures added.

She began to receive silent phone calls at all hours of the night, her car was vandalized and she suspected someone had entered her flat on a number of occasions.

She once again sought out John and confronted him. He denied everything and again attempted to persuade her to go out with him. Ms A. told John that if he kept harassing her she would report him to the university. She hadn't shared what was going on with her friends because she felt ashamed of what was happening.

A few weeks later, Ms A. received a notice from the university stating that, following the investigation of an official complaint, her access to university computer facilities had been suspended and she was not to enter certain specified areas of the university campus.

John had complained to the university that Ms A. had been stalking him and sending him harassing emails. He had the emails to prove it. When she checked the outbox on her computer email, she found dozens of emails addressed to John.

Not surprisingly the university treated her story with disbelief. They refused to investigate the matter further, insisting she was lucky not to be charged with stalking. She must have 'counselling' and apologize to the victim, John, if she wanted to stay on at university.

Fortunately, through the intervention of the head of the university's security section, a more thorough examination of the computer was undertaken. This revealed how Ms A. had been victimized.

After entering treatment 'voluntarily', John continued to express a bizarre mixture of erotomanic (delusional love) and persecutory beliefs about Ms A. Eventually he became obviously psychotic. Ms A. required help to overcome her ongoing anxiety and her loss of trust in the world as a safe and just place.

What is stalking?

Stalking involves repeated attempts to impose unwanted communications, or approaches, on another person in a manner which is likely to cause distress.

Stalking in its more extreme forms is immediately recognizable as a problem. For example, few would hesitate to use the term 'stalker' to describe a stranger who follows someone home from work every night, who stands outside their home, makes repeated silent phone calls and attempts to thrust letters expressing enduring love into the victim's unwilling hands. But what if it wasn't a stranger, but an estranged husband claiming all he wants is a chance at reconciliation?

Stalking is a problem behaviour which is made up of a series of actions each of which in itself is unremarkable. When do rude and insensitive intrusions become stalking? The simple answer is when they create fear or distress in the object of the unwanted attentions.

Even without necessarily producing fear, constantly repeated intrusions should perhaps be considered stalking when they persist despite responses which any reasonable person would realize indicated the intrusions were unwelcome and upsetting.

How common is stalking?

About 20 per cent of the population will be stalked at some time in their lives. Women are more than twice as likely as men to be stalked. Victims can be of any age, though the peak rates are for people in their teens and twenties. There is evidence suggesting that stalking is becoming increasingly frequent in Western nations.

About half of all stalking episodes involve short periods of harassment lasting for a few days at most. Though brief, these episodes can be very frightening, particularly as the perpetrator is often a stranger and the intrusions usually involve repeated approaches or being followed.

People who are stalked for more than a couple of weeks are likely to go on to suffer many months of pursuit. The more persistent stalkers are usually ex-intimates, acquaintances or work colleagues.

How does stalking affect victims?

Studies have shown that the victims of stalking, particularly if it goes on for a long time, often develop major psychological and social difficulties.

The psychological problems include anxiety, sleep problems and depression (see pp. 24, 222 and 76). Some victims become so frightened and depressed that they seriously consider suicide to escape from the situation.

The impact of being stalked on a person's life cannot be underestimated. Almost all victims of long periods of stalking restrict their social activities:
* many reduce or stop working
* some move home or even change the town or country in which they live
* some will tend to drink and smoke more

Fear for their safety is realistic, as between 20 and 30 per cent of stalking victims are threatened, and over 10 per cent will be physically and/or sexually assaulted.

Who is stalked?

Anyone can be stalked. You don't need to be a celebrity and you certainly don't need to act in a way that attracts stalking. The risks are highest for young women, but even old men can occasionally fall victim.

Stalking victims often blame themselves and all too often they are heard saying such things as, 'If I hadn't ever married him'; 'If I'd explained'; 'If I hadn't spoken to him and tried to explain'; 'If I'd made it clearer to her'; etc.

The answer is that people are nearly always stalked because they have been unlucky enough to have run across the wrong person at the wrong time. The explanation for the behaviour lies with the stalker not the victim.

Stalkers

Stalkers are usually young males, but no age or gender is exempt. They are generally one of the following types:

The rejected stalk following the breakdown of a close relationship, either seeking reconciliation or to express their rage at rejection. Attempts to restore the relationship often alternate with angry recriminations and vengeful outbursts. It's not difficult to understand why someone would have difficulty in accepting the unwished termination of a relationship. What is less obvious is why they persist in stalking often for months and sometimes years. One possibility is that the stalking becomes a substitute for the relationship – the continued contact generated by the stalking becomes an echo of a lost intimacy. For some dependent and vulnerable people, it may well be that the concrete reality of a stalking relationship, however problematic, is better than the uncertainty of ever finding a new companion.

The intimacy–seekers pursue people on whom they have fixed their affections in the hope of establishing, or asserting, a loving relationship. They will focus on a total stranger, or a casual acquaintance, who, without any basis in fact, they believe either already loves them, or will come to love them. It is the intimacy–seekers who make up the majority of those who stalk celebrities. Unlike other groups of stalkers, they are usually female and are often mentally disordered. All are lonely people, desperate to fill the emptiness in their lives with a relationship, even if that relationship is based on fantasy or delusion. Why do they persist? Better the illusion of love than no love at all.

The incompetent suitors are not looking for love but for a date, or a brief sexual liaison. They are nearly always socially incompetent males and make clumsy and insensitive approaches. They respond to rejection by ignoring the refusal or by angry insistence. This group often pester their victims repeatedly, but this rarely goes on for more than a day or so.

The resentful stalkers intend to frighten and distress their victim. The stalking begins in response to an actual or imagined injury or humiliation and is about revenge. This type of stalking often happens in work situations, or when people feel mistreated by professionals. The behaviour can become persistent because the stalking gives them a wonderful experience of power and control.

The predatory stalkers follow and observe their victims before a sexual attack. The stalking begins as an information-gathering exercise prior to a planned assault. The stalking often continues for longer than is necessary to learn about the movements of the victim because the predator starts to get pleasure from this secret hunt.

Predatory stalkers often indulge in fantasies and rehearse the attack as they observe their unsuspecting victims. They hide for most of the time, taking pleasure in making their victims suspicious of their presence. They do this, for example, by entering the victim's home and moving things around, but leaving no other trace of their passing. They make silent phone calls or knock on windows at night. They get a sadistic delight by producing fear and imagining the humiliation of the victim when their fears are ignored or laughed at.

Luckily, predatory stalkers are the least common type, but most sadistic and predatory sex offenders are predatory stalkers.

How do you stop stalkers?

Nearly 50 per cent of stalkers stop after a few days. They may go on to trouble new victims, but rarely return to the same person twice.

Stalkers who persist for more than two weeks are a serious problem. The rejected stalkers will sometimes stop when they are confronted with the police and know they will be prosecuted if they continue.

The resentful stalkers often respond well to the heavy hand of the law. However, the official police warning is not used enough with stalkers. In

California, there are special units where police and mental health professionals work together to manage the threat of stalking.

The intimacy-seeker, however, is usually unreceptive to such warnings, or even to any judicial sanctions. For instance, a stalker may be imprisoned a number of times, but on each release goes straight round to the victim's home, via the florist, to assert their love.

Once before the courts, stalkers should all undergo a mental health evaluation. Some, because of brain damage, strong religious beliefs, or a particularly unfortunate personality, cannot be managed. For them prison may be the only option. However, most stalkers can be treated. Occasionally the patient will be hospitalized because of the nature of their mental disorder or the level of risk they present of seriously harming their victim.

Managing stalkers involves:
- Ensuring the stalker faces up to the nature and effects of their behaviour.
- Increasing their understanding of what it is like to be the victim.
- Analysing their stalking process to identify key triggers. For instance, it may start after a weepy evening looking at the old wedding photos – no photos, decreased stalking.
- Coming to an understanding of what continues the behaviour – loneliness, difficulty falling out of love, continuing anger, etc. – all of which can be addressed by focused cognitive behavioural therapy (CBT, see p. 427).
- Increasing their social and interpersonal skills in the hope of their acquiring less damaging relationships.
- Setting up supports to try to prevent relapse.

Surviving stalking

Brief episodes of harassment from incompetent suitors are all too common experiences, particularly for young women. They are often frightening and confusing, but usually they cease within a day or so.

A person is most likely to be stalked long term by an ex-intimate (rejected stalker) or someone who has developed a grievance against you (resentful stalker). The misdirected love of the intimacy-seeker is also a possibility, particularly for those who come into contact in their work with the lonely and disordered.

The chances of surviving stalking without too much psychological, social and physical damage are increased if you:

Recognize early that you are being stalked. This is not as simple as it sounds, particularly when stalking starts in the context of the end of an intimate relationship or in a work situation. You have to face up to the fact that you are being stalked when uncertainty is overtaken by fear and distress.

Make clear that the communications and/or approaches are causing you distress and fear. This is not always possible, particularly if you are not sure who is sending the unwanted communications. Most stalkers deserve one clear warning that their attentions are unwanted and causing distress, but only one.

Avoid any direct contact or communication with the stalker. Once it becomes clear they are pursuing you, don't discuss, argue, try to persuade, or worst of all threaten your stalker. Make one clear statement of wanting the behaviour to cease, and from then on refuse any direct contact. In the case of ex-partners, particularly when there are shared children or property in common, refusing contact can be difficult, but it remains the best way.

Inform others. Being a victim can cause a sense of guilt and shame which means that you often don't tell anyone. It is essential, however, at an early stage to tell family, friends and work colleagues (where relevant) that you are being stalked. If left in ignorance, they may accidentally help the stalker. Those around you may be caught up in the stalking and need to know what is happening.

Keep records. The unwanted letters, unsolicited gifts, and text and phone messages should be kept. Contacts should be recorded in a diary, preferably noting the names of potential witnesses. This is the first stage of regaining control over your life and preparing to strike back. The evidence-gathering puts you in a position to obtain the assistance of the law when and if that becomes necessary.

Make use of the legal protections. In most countries, there are remedies available through both civil and criminal law. Reporting the stalking to the police and obtaining an appropriate response is helped if you come with your dossier/diary documenting the stalking.

Get professional help. Being stalked is at best distressing and at worst utterly terrifying. If you have a good GP they can help. If the stalking becomes a long-term problem, seeing a psychiatrist or psychologist with experience in helping victims is advisable.

Use stalking support groups. Being stalked is an isolating experience, but meeting others who have been in a similar situation can be comforting, informative and liberating. Support groups are emerging and they are an important resource for stalking victims.

Professor Paul Mullen

Dr Persaud's conclusion

What some term 'stalking', others might categorize as merely unrequited love. So stalking, like many other psychological problems, suffers from the issues of clear recognition and definition. For example, in the film *The Graduate*, Dustin Hoffman's character could be said to stalk the object of his affections towards the end of the movie, and yet the plot suggests he did the right thing because his 'victim' agrees to run off with him. This film could be interpreted as even encouraging stalking.

Because uncertainty over exactly what is going on can characterize the early stages of stalking, it's vital to seek specialist help or an opinion and even involve the police before the situation deteriorates into violence or extreme distress.

The problem is that many victims are afraid to seek outside advice or help for fear of appearing to overreact. It's better, however, to err on the side of caution and go for guidance than to suffer in silence.

SUPPORT ORGANIZATIONS

The Network for Surviving Stalking, PO Box 7836, Crowthorne, Berkshire RG45 7YA (please enclose a stamped addressed A4 envelope); fax: 01344 773446; email: help@nss.org.uk; *www.nss.org.uk*

www.antistalking.com/resource.htm has links to resources around the world.

WEBSITES OUTSIDE THE UK

Australia: *www.iinet.net.au*

FURTHER READING

Surviving Stalking, Michele Pathé, Cambridge University Press, 2002

Stalkers and Their Victims, Paul E. Mullen, Michele Pathé and Rosemary Purcell, Cambridge University Press, 2000

26

Stress

A woman who felt like a monkey in a cage

CATHERINE WAS FIFTY-FIVE and worked as a hospital secretary. She was very hard-working and proud of her high standards. Recently, though, she had found work a strain. There had been changes to the service, more forms to fill, and a number of managers whose only role in life seemed to be to monitor her work.

She decided to go to see her GP. She explained that she felt stressed, particularly when at work. 'I feel as if I'm a monkey being tested in a cage. Every time I sort out one task, they give me a more complicated one to do, and then two at the same time.'

Catherine was no longer happy with the standard of her work, had lost confidence in herself, and was worried about what she had and hadn't done when she went home in the evening. This was completely new to her – she had never worried before like this. She wasn't sleeping, suffered headaches and felt tense most of the time. When she was with friends or on holiday, however, she felt much better. She could relax and her tensions faded away – until the day before she had to return to work, when she felt all her worries come back.

Her big concern was that her work, in which she had always taken great pride and satisfaction, was now the main cause of her anxiety and stress. Even after she had gone on a course to learn a new computer package to make her job easier, she still felt the same.

Her doctor examined her and reassured her that all was well physically; he made an appointment to see Catherine in two weeks' time. He agreed with her diagnosis and thought that she was suffering from stress because of problems at work, but rather than treating her immediately, he thought it best to wait. A lot of people with stress–related problems get better without any treatment.

It was clear when Catherine returned after two weeks that she was no better. She was just as tense, still couldn't sleep and was having panic attacks at the thought of going back to work. The doctor decided to refer her to a practice nurse who had special expertise in anxiety and stress counselling. The treatment involved helping Catherine 'let go' of her worries through relaxation, positive thinking and carrying out some exercises.

After two months of treatment, Catherine was still unwell and couldn't return to work. She was referred to an occupational health physician. He contacted a psychiatrist and together they decided on a course of cognitive behavioural therapy (CBT). Although she got a little better with this treatment, she continued to feel very distressed and anxious at work and wasn't able to use the new technology that had been introduced.

Catherine's employers offered her early retirement on the

grounds of medical disability. Within days of her making the decision to accept, she felt dramatically better. 'I feel as though a concrete block has been taken off my head,' she said to her doctor, 'and I just know it's not going to return.'

She developed her interest in gardening and widened her social activities. A year later, she remained well and active in retirement.

What is stress?

Stress is not an easy thing to define. As in Catherine's case, work was her pride and joy, and yet it was work that was the main cause of her problem.

Stress is one of the most commonly used words in the language of medicine – and one of the most difficult to define. Wherever you go and read about illness, you will find that many conditions are said to be 'due to stress'. These include:

❖ heart disease
❖ stomach ulcers
❖ irritable bowel syndrome
❖ phobias
❖ depression

❖ some forms of arthritis and muscle pain
❖ dizziness
❖ migraine
❖ illness after childbirth
❖ even some forms of cancer

Stress must be a very powerful influence to cause all these problems.

Stress is a reaction of the mind and body to overload (or overwork). Overload puts the system out of balance: the parts of your mind and body that normally tick over without any trouble go badly wrong when you are stressed.

When the 'stressed' Catherine was asked to do a new piece of work at the office, she panicked and couldn't cope. Stress had led to changes that made her mind and body less flexible, so they couldn't cope with the new demands. Before the stress she would have dealt with these easily.

Catherine only noticed the anxiety and worry she was feeling. Her mind and body were saying to her, 'Cool off a bit – we're already doing as much as we can and we're not going to let you do any more.' Her mind reminded her just how serious things were by stimulating the production of hormones – chemicals that go round in the blood and affect all parts of the body – so that her body knew all about the stress as well.

Many of the hormones are produced by a little gland just by the kidneys, or renal organs. Because of its position, this gland is called the adrenal gland, and it makes the important hormones cortisol, adrenaline and noradrenaline. When too much of these hormones is produced, the following happen:

❖ your heart beats stronger and faster
❖ your blood moves from the skin to the muscles so you look pale, and feel tense and shaky
❖ you suffer from headaches and muscle tension
❖ your thinking is affected: you can't concentrate and are easily distracted
❖ you don't sleep well
❖ you feel mentally tense and anxious

So now we can see why Catherine couldn't cope with her new workload. Her body was out of order; she was inefficient through lack of sleep and poor concentration, and unable to process new demands on her mind or body. So a vicious circle developed. Catherine was given more work, which required increased concentration because it was new. She couldn't cope with this extra pressure, got even more anxious, coped even less well and became inefficient. Eventually she had to give up work. Sometimes a little time off, or a good holiday, is all that is needed to break this cycle, but in Catherine's case it had gone too far.

Distinguishing between stress and other problems

As feelings of stress are so common, they are found in many medical disorders. In deciding whether stress is really a major cause, we need to ask people three important questions:

❖ Did you feel under strain and have feelings of stress right from the beginning of your problem?
❖ Did something big happen in your life just before you had the stress symptoms?
❖ Can you identify what starts off your stressful symptoms and what makes them better?

Catherine could answer these questions without too much difficulty. The stress had come on gradually with the increase in her workload. Before this, she coped well. There was no obvious event that had brought on her stress, although a change in boss or a move to new premises could have contributed. She was also able to identify that the work was the main source of the stress because when she was on holiday, or away from work for any length of time, she felt better.

Although there was nothing dramatic that had changed in Catherine's life, other people can often pinpoint their stress starting after a serious incident, such as being mugged, losing a job, or the death of a relative.

Most people can identify stress, but some cannot and need someone else to point it out to them. The workaholic who drives himself into the ground, then puts in even more hours to try to make up, is a good example.

What are the effects of stress on health?

Everyone now knows that stress can do a great deal of damage. In Catherine's case, it turned one of the most positive things in her life (her work) into one of the most negative.

The relationship between work and rest becomes very unbalanced by stress. We all need somewhere between 5 and 10 hours' sleep a day to keep us healthy. Normally we have a good natural balance between sleeping and waking; stress interrupts this balance, making us short of sleep and therefore less efficient.

With the changes in blood flow in the body, our bodily organs become less efficient. Many common physical problems are caused by stress:

❖ fibromyalgia (a kind of arthritis) ❖ tension headaches
❖ irritable bowel syndrome ❖ giddiness and balance problems
❖ irregular heartbeats ❖ excessive tiredness
❖ constipation and diarrhoea

The long-term effects of stress can be even more damaging. You are more at risk of death from heart and circulation diseases, accidental death, suicide, strokes and some nervous diseases. Stress is a trigger that starts off the process, but then other things take over and create much more damage

Stress can lead people to drink alcohol more than usual. This is because alcohol, at least at first, is quite a good tranquillizer and calms you down. But when it is taken too often, and for too long, it leads to a host of problems, much illness and early death.

Stress can lead to a change in diet. 'The best tranquillizer in the world', it is often said, 'is a good square meal.' This may be so if you are under strain after a hard day of physical activity and have had nothing to eat. It is quite a different matter if you eat large meals after you have been sitting at a desk all day and have a quick nibble of fatty and high-carbohydrate foods when you think no one is looking.

The changes in diet created by stress can lead to weight gain, high blood cholesterol and high blood pressure. So in one sense stress can cause high blood pressure, but it is not a direct cause.

Is stress always harmful?

No. We all need some variety and change in our lives, and this involves some degree of stress. Variety and change can be stressful, but whether the stress becomes harmful depends on two factors: the amount of control we have over the stress, and our basic personality and temperament.

We all have two forms of control in our lives: external control, where we feel forced to do something because someone or some organization has told us to; and internal control, when we ourselves exercise choice and decide what we want to do.

Which type of control is better for stress? When our lives are externally controlled, we have much more stress than when we are exercising internal control.

Before the recent troubles, Catherine was very proud of her work. Even though at one level this was externally controlled – she had an employer who provided the job description and decided the nature of her work – this suited her, and she was able to exercise individual internal control. It was only when the extra work went beyond her capabilities and put pressure on her time that she became dominated by external control, and the vicious cycle of stress started.

It is who we are, as much as our fate in life, that decides if we are running under external or internal control. Who we are is decided by our personalities and how much stress we want in our lives.

Some people are naturally anxious and want as little change as possible in their lives. They will do everything possible to keep a regular routine. Others have more adventurous personalities, love change, and will take every opportunity to meet new challenges, both at work – where they may choose high risk, but potentially high-reward occupations – and at home. These people need excitement in their spare time, so they take up activities such as stock-car racing and go for wild parties. When asked by others if they suffer from stress, they will respond truthfully, 'Of course I don't suffer from stress; I enjoy every minute of it.'

It would be wrong to say that any particular activity or set of circumstances is or is not stressful. You cannot measure stress in isolation. It is the nature of the person's personality that decides whether something is stressful or not.

How to deal with stress

There are three ways of dealing with stress:
❖ overcoming the problem that is causing the stress
❖ avoiding it by using some other strategy
❖ living with it

Catherine tried all three of these at different times. She tried to cope with the changes at work that were making her anxious, and then went through a course of treatment to reduce her stress. She also tried the third strategy of trying to get back to work and learn new skills, but that did not work either.

So in the end she found the answer: she avoided the situation that caused the stress – her work – by taking early retirement. By doing this she was able to leave work with dignity and take up her interests, such as gardening, which she wasn't able to do before because of pressures of work.

People can choose any combination of these methods to deal with stress. Some tackle a problem face on, time and time again, until it is overcome. Others will do anything to go round it. It depends on our natures.

'You just have to live with it,' is often the message people get when under continual stress, but it should not be seen as a message of despair. Living with stress is becoming increasingly necessary in a world in which we cannot escape pressure. It is important to sort out the things in your life that make you feel better – what activities you get up to at the weekend, where you live, who your friends are and how often you see them. Exercising control will make you stronger for the future.

So it's best not to think of stress as a monster that invades your life without warning and terrifies you. It is more like a pet that won't behave – the cat that is always scratching the furniture, or the dog that won't stop barking. You can train yourself, and your stress, to fall into line with your wishes and, when this is done, what was previously a menace becomes a source of positive strength and, eventually, genuine pleasure.

Professor Peter Tyrer

Dr Persaud's conclusion

Contrary to popular belief, it is not scientifically clear if modern life is more stressful than in the past. Perhaps all that is changing over time is that we face different stresses. Our ancestors faced stress like bubonic plague and the Romans; we face stress like email spam and global warming.

Maybe why we feel more stressed than ever before is not because our environment is more arduous to survive, but we have lost the coping buffers our ancestors had, like religion, neighbours and a mercifully short life.

Life will probably never be without stress, but we can learn to improve our coping responses in the face of problematic stress – though this does require us to develop an interest in coping. Learning to cope with stress involves taking responsibility for our mental health – and who precisely should take responsibility for this, as well as our physical health, remains a thorny issue in the modern world.

SUPPORT ORGANIZATIONS

International Stress Management Association: an easy-to-use site offering information pages about various types of stress, as well as stress-relief tips and a referral service for stress counsellors. Lists of conferences and events, as well as a very extensive links section. ISMA UK, PO Box 26, South Petherton TA13 5WY; tel: 07000 780430; *www.isma.org.uk*

Health and Safety Executive: *www.hse.gov.uk/stress/standards*

WEBSITES OUTSIDE THE UK

Australia:
www.healthinsite.gov.au

Canada:
www.anxietycanada.ca

New Zealand:
www.headspace.org.nz

South Africa:
www.safmh.org.za

FURTHER READING

Self Help for Your Nerves: Learn to Relax and Enjoy Life Again by Overcoming Stress and Fear, Claire Weekes, HarperCollins, 2000

27

Suicide and Self-harm

A man who thought he had failed

Dear Joyce,

I am very sorry for all the misery I have caused you. I have failed in everything I have done, and have been a constant burden to you and the children. My whole life has been a succession of disappointments and there is no hope that I can ever come to any good. Every day is a struggle. When you read this I will finally be at peace.

Love from Andy

ANDY IS FORTY-SIX years old and is married with two children. Eighteen months ago, he used the money from a redundancy package to set up his own printing business. This was a risk because of a downturn in the economy and Andy worked long hours to keep his income steady, travelling around the country; he had little time to spend with his family.

He started to become very anxious and to feel depressed about his business.

He no longer enjoyed meeting his customers. He lost a lot of sleep worrying about work, and felt drained of energy. Soon he was unable to work and the business promptly collapsed.

Joyce, his wife, and the family were taken by surprise, but they responded by sorting out the finances and resolving problems with the business. Andy spent the next four weeks in the house doing very little – not dressing or caring about his appearance.

The family tried to help him. They tried to persuade him to go fishing – something he'd always enjoyed. But he wasn't interested; he had even lost the confidence to drive his car. Joyce suggested that he could do some part-time work for his friend, but he felt that this would end in failure. He felt hopeless, and explained to his wife repeatedly that his life was not worth living. Joyce tried to persuade Andy to go to see the GP, but he thought that the doctor wouldn't be able to help him.

One morning, when Andy knew that his wife would be out until late, he left the house and bought some painkillers and a bottle of spirits. He went to the bank, transferred all the money from his business accounts to his wife's account, then went home, wrote the short note above and left it on the kitchen table. He went to his bedroom and swallowed all the painkillers, together with the alcohol, and lay on the bed waiting for the pills to take effect. He was convinced his family would be better off without him once they had got over the shock of his death.

Joyce returned early from work, as she was feeling ill, and went upstairs to rest, only to find Andy unconscious. She called an ambulance and he was taken to hospital. He was kept in hospital for two days, where the doctors observed him and took blood tests to measure the level of the painkillers in his body and to check that there was no liver damage.

After he had recovered physically, he was seen by a

psychiatrist, who spent an hour talking to him and explained that he was suffering from severe depression. Andy continued to feel hopeless and regretted that he was still alive. He was very embarrassed and ashamed about failing to take his life. He didn't really believe that he had an illness, but felt that he was weak and a failure. He had always thought that depression was just an excuse people used to avoid difficult things in their life.

Andy was persuaded by his doctors to try a treatment for depression. He was transferred to a psychiatric hospital, where he was treated for six weeks with a combination of antidepressants and talking treatments.

After leaving hospital, he started to undertake simple activities again, such as fishing and walking. Gradually he returned to work, with the help of an occupational therapist. He continued to take antidepressants, and was seen regularly by a community psychiatric nurse for the first few months.

Six months later, Andy is enjoying his life and feels optimistic about his future. He understands about depression and is aware of the signs of it returning and the importance of asking for help at an early stage rather than waiting until he feels suicidal.

Joyce recalls how Andy told her that he thought that his life wasn't worth living. She never realized he might actually try to kill himself, as he had so much to live for.

How common is suicide?

❖ Worldwide every 40 seconds someone will die by suicide.
❖ Worldwide every 3 seconds someone will harm themselves intentionally.
❖ In the time taken to read this chapter, 25 people will have died by suicide.
❖ In the time taken to read this chapter, 400 people will have harmed themselves.
❖ Suicide rates have increased by 60 per cent worldwide in the last 45 years.

Although heart disease is one of the leading causes of death worldwide, this largely affects older people. Suicide affects both the old and the young. There has been a sharp increase in suicides by young men over the last decade in many countries; in fact, suicide is now the third most common cause of death among men aged between fifteen and forty-four. Suicide is a major public health concern.

Understanding and preventing suicide is a high priority for many politicians and health services. As well as suicide having an important impact at a population level, the death of an individual by suicide has far-reaching effects on family, friends, colleagues and the local community.

Attitudes towards self-harm and suicide differ between individuals, and especially between different cultures. In some countries it is still against the law to attempt suicide, and some religious communities view suicide as a sin. It is not surprising that people who experience suicidal ideas are reluctant to talk about them.

In some countries so-called 'assisted suicide' is legal for people with terminal illness facing severe disability. This raises important ethical questions about whether, and when, people have the right to choose to take their own life.

There are some important misconceptions about self-harm and suicide. Television, radio, newspapers and other media can have major effects on public perceptions of suicide. For example, there was an increase in the number of suicides by charcoal-burning in Hong Kong after a well-publicized case in the media, and of railway suicides in Germany after an episode of a popular television soap opera in which someone died by jumping in front of a train.

What are suicide and self-harm?

Suicide and self-harm are related, but distinct entities. Although suicide is relatively simple to define, as the intentional self-inflicted death of an individual, studies of those who have survived by chance following very dangerous suicide attempts suggest that the wish to die is not always simple. Some people wish to escape, or even to let fate decide.

Self-harm is a broad term that includes many different behaviours, which are sometimes referred to as parasuicide, attempted suicide, self-mutilation or deliberate self-harm.

At one extreme will be those who might cut their arms, with no intention of dying, but of inflicting physical pain to control unbearable emotions. At the other extreme are people who prepare for their death and survive only by chance.

Generally, there are two types of self-harm: those that are attempts to die, and those that are not. However, acts of self-harm are inappropriately dismissed as a 'cry for help'. Individuals who cut themselves to control strong emotions are more likely to make serious suicide attempts, and will sometimes die from these. Studies have found that after people have harmed themselves:

❖ 1 per cent die by suicide in the next year
❖ 5 per cent die by suicide within 10 years

Mental health workers have established a variety of useful approaches to dealing with suicide and self-harm, and some governments have implemented strategies aimed at reducing suicide rates.

Dispelling some of the myths – the truth about suicide and self–harm

Myth: People who talk about suicide do not kill themselves.
 Fact: Those who talk about suicide sometimes *do* go on to kill themselves.

Myth: People who are suicidal will kill themselves whatever you do.
 Fact: Those who are suicidal are usually not fully committed to the idea and *can* be helped.

Myth: Asking people about suicidal thoughts makes them more likely to kill themselves.
 Fact: People can often gain relief from talking about these ideas, and this may be the beginning of recovery.

Myth: People who self-harm are not at risk, just attention–seeking.
 Fact: Some of those who self-harm will go on to take their own lives.

Why does suicide happen?

Interviews with relatives and friends in the first few months after someone's death by suicide suggest that at the time of their death around 90 per cent were suffering from a mental illness which might have been treated.

Suicide is also linked with complex social, psychological and biological factors (see below). Mental illness is often only one of a number of factors contributing to any particular suicide.

The vast majority of people with a mental illness do not harm themselves. Researchers are beginning to discover how a variety of factors within a particular individual interact over time to result in suicide.

What methods do people use for suicide?

Some of the more common methods include:

❖ firearms
❖ hanging
❖ overdose of medicines
❖ poisons, such as weedkiller

❖ jumping
❖ car exhaust fumes
❖ drowning

More women are likely to self-harm, but suicide rates are higher for men. One reason might be that men use more violent and dangerous methods, which are more likely to be successful.

Factors associated with suicide

Biological

Brain chemical messengers: research suggests that abnormalities in the production and handling of the neurotransmitter serotonin within the brain are associated with increased risk of suicide.

Genetic factors: there can be a small genetic predisposition to suicide, but this on its own does not result in suicide. Specific genes may be inherited that increase the risk of suicide.

Physical illness: particularly cancers, HIV, chronic pain, and brain disorders such as multiple sclerosis and epilepsy.

Psychological

Mental illness accounts for around 90 per cent of suicides. All types of mental illness are associated with increased suicide rates – most commonly depression (in particular inadequately treated cases), drug or alcohol abuse, schizophrenia and personality disorders (see pp. 76, 329, 269, 196 and 157).

Many feelings that can lead to suicide can be brought on by mental illness:
- ❖ feelings of hopelessness
- ❖ feeling trapped (entrapment)
- ❖ thinking patterns: 'black and white' thinking, rigid thinking
- ❖ impulsiveness
- ❖ ideas about death: nothingness, heaven, reincarnation
- ❖ problem-solving difficulties

Social

Social factors that might lead to a risk of suicide include:
- ❖ social deprivation – low income, poor housing, overcrowding, living in a fragmented community
- ❖ unemployment
- ❖ occupation – more suicide in doctors, dentists, pharmacists and farmers
- ❖ available lethal method – e.g. possession of a firearm
- ❖ family history of suicide
- ❖ elderly and young people
- ❖ males more than females
- ❖ cultural acceptability, media portrayal
- ❖ social isolation

None of the reasons above is sufficient on its own to cause suicide. There needs to be a combination of factors over time. This means that to understand why someone takes their own life, we need to look not only at what was happening near the time of the event, but also at their whole life.

What are the signs that someone is planning suicide?

Sometimes suicide can come 'out of the blue', and friends and family are mystified. Suicidal feelings usually develop gradually and people find it hard to talk about them. Changes in behaviour are a clue that someone might be feeling suicidal:

❖ abusing alcohol or drugs
❖ getting their affairs in order
❖ becoming withdrawn

The person may talk about their suicidal ideas, using phrases like 'I can't go on any longer.' If this happens, then it is important to take them very seriously.

What can be done to help?

Advice to individuals with suicidal thoughts

If you are thinking about suicide, it is likely that there is another part of you, however small, that wants to stay alive. People who go on living after a period of very strong suicidal thoughts are nearly always glad they survived. They often say they didn't want to die so much as to escape from the pain.

When near to making a decision to end your life, it is difficult to see any future. So it is a matter of getting through a period in which life seems unbearable, when you become convinced that death is preferable. There is a well-worn saying: 'Suicide is often a permanent solution to a temporary problem.' There is a lot of truth in this, and those who work with people who have come close to ending their lives know that things can be very different, given time.

If you feel you would like to end your life:

✔ Do

❖ tell someone about your thoughts, such as a friend or family member
❖ call a helpline – it's sometimes easier to talk openly to someone who is independent
❖ speak to your GP – it's their role to treat mental illness, such as depression, as well as physical illness
❖ consider that you are very likely to be suffering from a mental illness that needs treatment
❖ get help sooner rather than later

✘ Don't

❖ try to cope on your own
❖ keep your thoughts to yourself, because you feel that others will feel burdened

❖ think others will be better off without you
❖ think you don't deserve help
❖ use alcohol or drugs, as these can make you more impulsive

Helping someone with suicidal thoughts

✔ Do

❖ listen, and believe them
❖ gently try to find out if they have made any plans to harm themselves
❖ consider keeping all medicines hidden
❖ consider seeking immediate help from your GP or emergency services
❖ help them to understand that there are alternatives
❖ help problem-solving

✘ DON'T

❖ immediately try to change their mind by pointing out all the good things in their life
❖ interrogate them, or try to rush them
❖ judge them, or take personal offence
❖ trivialize, or avoid talking about, their feelings
❖ leave them alone if there is an immediate risk

Ways of preventing suicide

❖ Better overall treatment of mental illness.
❖ Social policies to improve the welfare of deprived communities.
❖ Reducing access to means for killing yourself. This has been shown to be effective: for example, both the change in domestic gas supply to a less toxic substance in the UK, and the introduction of catalytic converters for cars reduced suicide rates. Other potential targets are reducing access to drugs used for overdose, or focusing on high-risk groups. Reducing access to lethal pesticides in areas such as Sri Lanka and China is also a target.
❖ Improving emergency treatment of poisoning.

Help for those bereaved due to suicide

Losing someone by suicide is similar to other bereavements, but can be particularly difficult to come to terms with because of:

❖ difficulty in accepting that
the cause was suicide
❖ guilt/self-blame
❖ realization of the emotional
distress of the deceased prior
to death
❖ feelings of betrayal/abandonment
❖ feelings of relief about the end of
suffering, and the stress of caring
❖ shame or stigma surrounding mental illness

It is not unusual to have suicidal ideas, so don't be afraid to talk to someone about these thoughts. (See also Chapter 29, p. 279.)

The nature and meaning of self-harm

The nature and meaning of self-harm varies significantly between individuals. There are different degrees of suicidal intent, but self-harm usually means that an individual is suffering from intense emotional distress.

Methods

The most common methods of self-harm are:

❖ cutting or burning
the skin
❖ taking overdoses of
tablets or medicines

Others include:

❖ ingesting poisons
❖ inserting objects into the body
❖ hanging
❖ jumping from a height

Why do people self-harm?

Risk factors for self-harm:

❖ females more than males
❖ teenagers to early adulthood
❖ single or separated
❖ inner-city living
❖ socially deprived
❖ psychological distress

❖ many are suffering from mental illness (depression, alcohol abuse, personality disorders, eating disorders)
❖ stressful or upsetting events, such as bereavement, loss of a job or breakdown of a relationship

Suicidal intent

❖ Self-harm may be an attempt to end their life. This may be an impulsive decision, or one that has been carefully planned for days or weeks.

Emotional control

For some people self-harm
❖ might give temporary relief from unpleasant emotions (e.g. emptiness, sadness, rage, self-hatred and guilt)
❖ converts 'mental pain' into physical pain, which may be easier for the individual to deal with or get help for
❖ allows them to feel emotions or to feel alive (as opposed to feeling numb or dead inside)
❖ is sometimes a form of self-punishment because of feelings of guilt and self-hatred
❖ harms a body which they have come to dislike (perhaps due to sexual abuse)
❖ offers a sense of control in a life that is otherwise out of control
❖ is a way of coping and carrying on living

Communication

Self-harm may be an attempt:
❖ to try to get help when there seems to be no other way
❖ to communicate feelings that are difficult to talk about

What can be done to help?

Drug overdose

After a drug overdose, a person will usually need to attend a hospital emergency department as quickly as possible. Monitoring and investigations will be required following all overdoses, but there are specific treatments for particular drugs:

Many drugs: activated charcoal is given as a drink to reduce the amount of drug absorbed into the bloodstream. The heart is often monitored, using an electrocardiogram, for drugs that can cause heart–rhythm problems.

Paracetamol: the amount of drug in the blood will be tested, and an antidote called acetylcysteine may be given, which prevents paracetamol from damaging the liver.

Benzodiazepines: if a person has become unconscious, or has breathing difficulties after an overdose of drugs like diazepam, then an injection of flumazenil can help to reverse the effects.

Opiates: after an overdose of a drug such as heroin, if there is loss of consciousness or breathing difficulties, then an injection of naloxone may reverse these.

After the immediate treatment

A person who has harmed themselves should be assessed by a healthcare worker trained in mental health (often a doctor or nurse). This is sometimes called a 'psychosocial assessment' and involves exploring the experience of the self-harm, as well as finding out about the person's life circumstances and mental well-being.

Following the assessment, the mental health worker may identify some particular need and recommend help or treatment. An important part of this assessment is to look for symptoms of mental illness and to direct the individual towards appropriate treatments if necessary.

Specific treatments for self–harming behaviour

These will be dependent upon the needs identified in the psychosocial assessment. Apart from the general treatment of any mental illness, alcohol abuse or drug abuse, the following may be specifically of use for self-harm.

Talking therapy: a number of different types of talking therapy (see p. 440) are used, including cognitive behavioural therapy (CBT; see p. 427) and problem-solving approaches. There is a more involved therapy for people who repeatedly self-harm called dialectical behaviour therapy (DBT; see p. 442).

Medication: self-harm is not a diagnosis, and there is no specific drug treatment that prevents self-harm. Some drug treatments, however, may help to reduce self-harm and suicide. For example, lithium is a mood-stabilizing drug that can reduce frequency of self-harm and suicide in people who have a diagnosis of, for instance, bipolar affective disorder (see p. 42). Clozapine, an antipsychotic drug, has similar effects in people with schizophrenia (see p. 196).

General support: people who have self-harmed may need intensive support, and may also require help with social problems regarding employment, finances, relationships and family. Support groups can be particularly helpful.

Advice for individuals

If you are self-harming, the chances are that you have reached a point in your life where it feels unbearable, and you seem to be running out of options. There are likely to be events in your life that feel out of control and are causing emotional distress.

Self-harming may seem to be your only way of coping. You may be suffering from low self-esteem. You may have had experiences such as abuse, bullying or neglect. You may be using drugs or alcohol to numb your emotions.

Getting help

You can:

❖ talk about and express your feelings, which can help you to start to make sense of things

❖ have access to someone whom you can trust, who can maintain confidentiality

❖ talk about any difficult experiences you may have had

❖ have far more options, and new ways of thinking about your life and your problems

❖ get treatment for depression, or another mental illness

❖ get in touch with others who may be experiencing similar problems

❖ make progress in sorting out the problems in your personal life

Advice to families and friends

When you find out someone close to you has self-harmed, you may feel shocked, angry, guilty or helpless. It is important to recognize and deal with these feelings, so that you can look after their needs.

❖ Self-harm is often kept secret from family and friends, but when it becomes apparent, it is important to respond in a helpful way.

❖ People who self-harm may have had experiences that are difficult to talk about, or they may have lost trust in others.

❖ They may be worried about what might happen if they talk.

❖ They may feel confused and unable to communicate their feelings. They may feel there is no way out, and feel completely lost or hopeless.

❖ The first step might be talking to a friend or family member, so that professional help can then be sought.

✔ Do

❖ listen, and try to understand how bad things are for them first, then gently challenge some of their hopelessness

❖ help them to find other ways of coping

❖ help them to start a plan to get help

❖ find out if they are considering suicide

✘ Don't

❖ get angry with them

❖ prematurely reassure them – they will feel you have not understood

❖ avoid discussing it, or change the subject

❖ think that discussing it will make things worse

❖ be embarrassed or afraid

❖ trivialize it, or tell them off

Dr Jonathan Evans
and Dr Lawrence Martean

Dr Persaud's conclusion

Suicide and self-harm are subjects surrounded by strong emotion. Some call suicide the ultimate selfish act. Freud suggested it was, at its core, a deeply aggressive act – a homicide turned inwards. Others argue that it can be a purely rational act pursued totally soberly, unrelated to psychiatric disorder.

Another perspective on suicide and self-harm is that they lie along a spectrum of self-destructive behaviours on which most of us will find ourselves at some time, from drinking too much, smoking or another self-injurious activity.

The taboo around suicide lingers and it is vital that opportunities are created for privacy and space for those seriously considering it to be able to confide without fear of judgement.

While specific suicide and self-harm services exist, given how impulsive a suicide can be – and as prevention is better than cure – it is vital that the mental health conditions that lead to suicide are treated early and vigorously. No-one should ever be afraid to raise the issue of whether suicide is or has been considered by someone they are worried about. This simple act has saved and will save innumerable lives – the suicidal greet such an enquiry with genuine relief at the opportunity to vent their feelings.

SUPPORT ORGANIZATIONS

Befrienders International: provides easily accessible information to crisis hotlines in over forty countries, and information on self-harm and suicide, www.befrienders.org (this organization works in partnership with Samaritans UK: www.samaritans.org.uk).

Survivors of Bereavement by Suicide: provides a helpline and information on local support groups for those who have lost someone due to suicide. Tel: 0870 241 3337; www.sobs.admin.care4free.net

Samaritans: offers free emotional support 24 hours a day. Tel: 08457 909090 (Ireland: 1850 609090); email: jo@samaritans.org or text 07725 909090; www.samaritans.org

WEBSITES OUTSIDE THE UK

Australia:
www.ranzcp.org

New Zealand:
www.ranzcp.org

Canada:
www.heretohelp.bc.ca

South Africa:
www.befrienders.org – this site will provide worldwide emotional support

FURTHER READING

The International Handbook of Suicide and Attempted Suicide, Keith Hawton and Kees van Heeringen, Wiley Press, 2000. (This is a comprehensive overview from an international perspective.)

Part Two

Managing the Mind

Preface

You may not be a dedicated follower of fashion but, unbeknownst to you, you do definitely have a certain style – and I'm not referring to whether you favour Prada over Chanel! The style I'm referring to is your lifestyle – and it acts as a kind of crystal ball to help doctors predict your future health and well-being.

The fact is, research is constantly evolving, helping us to understand psychological as well as other medical problems, and by examining your lifestyle your doctor is better able to predict with some accuracy the kind of medical or psychiatric disorder you will get in the future. This is why, for example, your family doctor has developed such an interest in your blood pressure and cholesterol. Few people realize that having raised blood pressure and cholesterol levels are not in themselves actually signs of illness. What they are instead are ominous indicators that unless certain changes are made to your lifestyle – and perhaps other preventative strategies taken (such as medication) – then you could find yourself being stretchered off to hospital suffering from a heart attack in the not too distant future. This is the heart attack you might have been able to prevent if you'd heeded medical advice and made those all-important changes to your diet and exercise regime. Since we all want to avoid the stretcher scenario, we're keen to crowd round the crystal ball to see what the doctor thinks our future holds – and we want to help him or her change it for the better, don't we?

Years ago, health was defined to our parents and grandparents whenever they turned up at a clinic by the 'present absence of disease'. So, if patients were not displaying any actual symptoms, doctors simply were not very interested in them.

But there has been a profound shift in modern medicine and it has had a radical impact on how we think about what it means to be healthy or ill. Today, health philosophers like Dr Ine Van Hoyweghen at the University of Maastricht point out that health is rather more complexly defined as the 'absence of an increased chance of future disease'. This approach has led to the proliferation of a whole series of new 'health states', and many of us are now identified as 'risk carriers'. So, for example, if your blood test and family history reveal you to be at high risk of, say, breast cancer, then you (as perhaps does the majority of the population) now inhabit an intermediate, almost twilight zone or disease state. You are neither completely healthy nor are you actually ill.

The dramatic power of predictive medicine, which is the medicine of today, is that it changes our understanding of what it is to be healthy or ill. Also, as genetics continues to advance, we are going to know much more accurately who carries genes that will predispose them to certain conditions. For example, who will be more likely to suffer psychosis if they smoke cannabis (this information is already available, albeit only in specialized research centres); who will be more prone to develop alcoholism if they begin to drink a little more than usual; and who will be more likely to take up smoking after just a few, seemingly innocent, puffs.

In the future, advances in genetics are actually going to turn the spotlight on our lifestyles and our choices even more intensely and, if we want to stay well, we're going to have to heed the advice on offer.

In this second part of our guide, we focus on how lifestyle choices impact on your health. In some cases, identifying potential problem areas in your life may lead you to alter or abandon certain damaging habits or behaviour patterns – and, like so many, you may find that you are able to alter some aspects of your life without any medical intervention at all. Indeed, research shows that positive self-change is often more effective than professionally inspired transformation. For example, several factors appear to be associated with the self-change process among substance abusers, but a key one appears to be a re-evaluation of the balance of positives and negatives of using these substances. For others, issues raised here will identify the need to seek professional advice, and the information provided in this section will offer you the help you need.

Knowledge is power – and the unbiased advice and information you will find here is the key to making the right decisions about the way you live your life now and in the future.

Dr Raj Persaud

References

Ine Van Hoyweghen, Klasien Horstman, Rita Schepers, 'Making the Normal Deviant: The Introduction of Predictive Medicine in Life Insurance', *Social Science & Medicine*, 63 (5), September 2006, 1,225–35.

Timothy P. Ellingstad, Linda Carter Sobell, Mark B. Sobell, Lori Eickleberry, Charles J. Golden, 'Self-change: A Pathway to Cannabis Abuse Resolution', *Addictive Behaviors*, 31 (3), March 2006, 519–30.

28
Alcohol

A man who kept a diary of his drinking

MIKE IS FIFTY–FIVE and his family doctor has referred him to the alcohol problems service. The doctor wrote, 'I have been seeing Mike frequently in recent months. He says he has been feeling depressed, and at times suicidal.

'Some years ago he had a car crash and was charged with drink–driving. He is often off work, usually with gastritis. Recently he damaged his ankle in a fall. The hospital report mentioned that he had smelt of alcohol.

'Mike is obese and has a slightly raised blood pressure. His wife, who is also a patient of mine, has mentioned that she thinks he is drinking too much. With some difficulty, I have persuaded Mike to seek advice from the alcohol problems service.'

At his first appointment Mike said, 'I have been feeling quite down recently. My work is very demanding and isn't going well, and I get so anxious about it that I can hardly drag myself out in the morning. I've been feeling run down, I can't sleep, my wife is fed up with me, and so are the children. She's even threatened to leave. She says I don't seem to care about them any more. All I do at home is drink to help me relax, and fall asleep in front of the television.'

The doctor in the clinic asked Mike more about his depression. He said that he found it hard to get up in the morning. Work was difficult, and he had no enthusiasm for it; he needed an early lunchbreak and a drink, and then felt more settled and able to cope. He insisted that he wasn't in any way 'an alcoholic' – lots of other people drank at lunchtime in his office.

The doctor asked Mike how much he drank. In addition to two pints of beer at lunchtime, he would often have two or three more in the evening on his way home, and a bottle of wine on Friday and Saturday with his wife.

He tried not to drink at all on Sunday in preparation for the following week. Occasionally, he and his wife would have something to drink at lunchtime. Of course, on special occasions he would drink a lot more than this.

His wife afterwards said he had had problems with alcohol for many years. She knew that he was a heavy drinker when they married, but he settled down at first. Over the last ten years he had been drinking more, and now he hardly ever spent time at home in the evenings with the family. He was either out at the pub or sleeping it off, but did not see that he had a problem.

The doctor discussed with Mike the part alcohol played in his life, and the advantages – and barriers – to changing his drinking habits. He explained how drinking might well be causing his depression. Mike agreed to keep a diary and set a target to cut down on his drinking. The doctor took some blood tests to assess his liver function.

Back at the clinic two weeks later Mike reported feeling less depressed. The doctor showed him the liver function tests and pointed out that they were very abnormal. In view of this, although Mike had cut down to about two pints of beer a day, the doctor recommended that he should stop drinking altogether.

At the next appointment Mike and his wife were both pleased that he had managed to stop drinking completely without too much difficulty, although he had been restless and a little shaky for the first day or two. In all respects their life together had improved. She even mentioned that their sex life, which had been non-existent for a long time, had become more satisfying.

Mike continued to attend the clinic. There were relapses, some severe, and his job was once more threatened. But he got through the relapses and has remained abstinent. He joined an outpatient group for people with similar alcohol problems, and they gain support and understanding from each other. Recently he was promoted at work to a more senior management position.

What is alcohol abuse?

Alcohol is our favourite drug. It is also the most easily available. Yet its social and economic costs far outweigh those attributable to 'illicit' drugs. Alcohol is a depressant drug which works on the central nervous system rather like an anaesthetic.

What does it feel like?

At first, alcohol reduces inhibitions and gives the false impression that it is stimulating you, but continued drinking leads to a loss of control, a slowing down of thinking, and eventually to sleep, unconsciousness, and death. Every year a number of people die from an unintentional overdose of alcohol.

In small amounts, alcohol has some social and psychological benefits. But, as we know only too well, inappropriate alcohol use causes problems ranging from fatal illnesses to general ill-health, accidents, crime and harmful effects on work and family life.

Some people think that it is only the amount of alcohol you have each week that causes problems. Not so. Many problems are created by having too much alcohol on a specific occasion, so-called binge-drinking. Being drunk messes up our judgement and may lead to antisocial behaviour, ill-judged sexual adventures, road traffic offences and violence. An alcohol binge can also cause acute stomach pains and other body problems.

Alcohol is loaded with calories, and obesity is a further complication of heavy drinking. (One pint of beer contains approximately 180 calories and one 175cc glass of wine 90.)

Alcohol is addictive. Tolerance (i.e. the amount you can drink before you get drunk) increases at first with regular use, so that the drinker seems to 'hold his or her drink better'. This shows that the brain is adapting to cope with larger amounts, but it is the first step on the way to becoming dependent on alcohol.

Then the drinker begins to have 'withdrawal symptoms', feeling anxious and uneasy when deprived of alcohol, and then craving develops, the need to have a drink above all else. At a more advanced stage, these withdrawal symptoms become severe, with visible tremor, agitation, sweating, nausea and vomiting, insomnia and recurrent nightmares. These symptoms may erupt into the waking state as hallucinations, which are characteristic of the extreme disturbance known as delirium tremens.

Continued alcohol misuse can also cause brain damage, with a loss of short-term memory that may progress to a condition similar to dementia.

Alcohol reduces the absorption of certain vitamins. Chronic drinkers who are poorly nourished can become acutely ill with confusion, double vision, weakness and signs of damage deep within the brain. This complicated condition, known as Wernicke's encephalopathy, requires urgent specialist treatment.

Controversies

There is a lot of misunderstanding about the word alcoholic – a term that is often used in a derogatory way. We can think of it as meaning severe alcohol dependence, as described earlier.

We know that alcohol problems run in families, and a genetic element is likely. However, only by drinking regularly and having ready access to alcohol will people, whatever their genetic make-up, run the risk of becoming dependent.

Another issue is whether the goal of treatment should be abstinence, as promoted by Alcoholics Anonymous, or controlled drinking for some people. Those in the early stages of alcohol dependence who are not physically addicted to it may be able to return to controlled drinking, although it is sometimes easier to aim for abstinence rather than to worry constantly about losing control. For those who are more damaged physically or mentally, abstinence is the safest policy.

There is little evidence for the idea that some people have an addictive personality. However, many people use alcohol to help them cope, particularly if they are always anxious, and this then develops into addiction. Dangerous drinking is a habit that undoubtedly causes physical and mental health problems.

Many think that people cannot change their drinking habits. Yet they can, and there is plenty of evidence that treatments work.

What can be done to help?

Self-help

Most of us underestimate how much we drink. The help needed depends on the nature and stage of the alcohol problem. Self-help is always important, and may be sufficient. Many people recognize that they have an alcohol problem and take steps to change, often helped by family members, friends or colleagues at work.

Self-help includes keeping a regular diary of drinking habits. This can show whether we are drinking too much, and highlight any risky situations – such as regular times and places when we drink more. Use the table overleaf to record your daily alcohol consumption.

Day	How much?	When?	Where?	Who with?	Units	Total
Monday						
Tuesday						
Wednesday						
Thursday						
Friday						
Saturday						
Sunday						
Totals						

Some drinks are stronger than others. The easiest way to work out how much we are drinking is to count 'units' of alcohol. One unit contains approximately 10g of alcohol and is the amount in a standard pub single measure of spirits, a half-pint of normal strength beer or lager, or a very small glass of wine. (Note that many pub measures of wine often contain 2 or more units.)

Guidelines for sensible drinking are up to 3 units a day for a woman and up to 4 units for a man, with a weekly maximum of 14 units for women and 21 units for men. Harm is more likely to be done above these levels, particularly for women who drink more than 35 units a week and men drinking 50 units or more.

Alcohol use in pregnancy is best avoided, or kept to very low levels, as it can affect the development of the baby.

Accepting the need to change is the most crucial stage in the recovery process. There may be setbacks along the way, and it is rare to achieve one's goals immediately. However, if the commitment to change can be maintained, there can be long-term recovery.

Available treatments

A crucial factor in successful treatment is a commitment to change. Sources of help include front-line services like the primary healthcare team and social work, and more specialized services like NHS alcohol treatment clinics and voluntary-sector alcohol counselling services. However, some people find it difficult to change.

Barriers to change may be:
- ❖ Social – for example, friends and colleagues pressurizing you to drink, or work involving entertaining with alcohol.
- ❖ Environmental – for example, in a hostel for homeless people, where drinking is the main social activity.
- ❖ Psychological – conditions such as anxiety, depression and social phobias, or feeling unable to cope without alcohol. These problems often disappear on stopping drinking.
- ❖ Physical – for example, using alcohol to relieve pain or insomnia (but excessive drinking can cause sleeplessness).
- ❖ Withdrawal symptoms – when a dependent drinker stops or cuts down, they may experience anxiety, tremor, agitation, nausea or vomiting. Drug treatment can help overcome the withdrawal symptoms, but is rarely necessary for more than a few days. It can be carried out at home, although sometimes admission to hospital may be necessary.

Detoxification is a treatment for the physical withdrawal from alcohol, and the start of the longer process of overcoming psychological dependence and learning about how to stay alcohol-free.

Preventing relapse. There are a number of specialist techniques to help prevent relapse. These mainly involve talking treatments (see p. 440), but there is also a place for drug treatment. Drugs which can reduce craving are acamprosate and naltrexone. Disulfiram (or Antabuse) makes you feel very ill if you take alcohol because it stops its breakdown in the body, but has no effect if you do not drink.

Lasting benefits can come from talking treatments aimed at changing lifestyle, overcoming barriers to change, and identifying and dealing with situations that commonly precipitate relapse, using a cognitive behavioural therapy (CBT; see p. 427).

Most talking treatments focus on examining the triggers to drinking, trying to increase personal motivation for change by a technique known as motivational interviewing, and a close examination of the factors which lead to relapse.

Group therapy can be helpful during the long task of changing our lifestyle and dealing with crises – see p. 443. In particular, Alcoholics Anonymous is of proven benefit, particularly to people with a severe addiction to alcohol. Members make a commitment to an alcohol-free lifestyle. The group social network of the organization can help people who have become isolated due to drinking, or find that their only companions are other problem drinkers.

Most people with drinking problems get help by going for treatment sessions in a clinic or community centre. Occasionally, residential treatment may be necessary if someone has severe withdrawal symptoms that require supervised detoxification in hospital, or if a person has evident brain damage or other specific physical problems requiring acute treatment.

Although there is good evidence that brief focused advice given on one or two occasions can be very beneficial, people with more severe alcohol dependence will need more specialist care for a longer time. This means that if lapses occur, they can be quickly identified and dealt with.

Complementary treatments. A variety of complementary therapies have been used to treat alcohol problems, including acupuncture, herbal medicines – such as oil of evening primrose – and various relaxation techniques. There are reports that these sorts of approach may help, although none has been shown to be more effective than another.

People can choose to use complementary therapies alongside more well-established and proven psychological approaches, such as cognitive behavioural therapy or certain drug treatments.

Which treatment is right for me?

The temptation to respond to comments about one's drinking with hostile denial is understandable, but counterproductive. Often the help of family or friends, and a self-help plan plus using a diary, will lead to reduced drinking.

With more severe problems, going to Alcoholics Anonymous may be enough for some people. Others may want the help of their family doctor or a counselling agency.

The family doctor should be able to refer people with more severe problems to a specialist addiction treatment agency with a range of treatments available. In many areas there are nurses who specialize in treating alcohol problems, and they will help with overcoming withdrawal symptoms and direct people to a continuing source of advice and support.

Even those who are severely damaged by alcohol, and have developed brain damage, may find help by abstaining totally and learning to adapt to the damage that their brain has suffered, perhaps through a period of residential care.

Prevention: tips for drinkers, their families and friends

- ❖ Keep a check on the amount of alcohol you drink, using the diary and guidelines above.
- ❖ Pace yourself to drink more slowly, and space alcoholic drinks with non-alcoholic ones.
- ❖ Avoid drinking on an empty stomach.
- ❖ Make weekly alcohol-free days.
- ❖ Remember it takes about one hour to eliminate one unit of alcohol.
- ❖ As a host, always have some non-alcoholic drinks available; you are responsible for the safety of your guests.
- ❖ Never force someone into taking an alcoholic drink.
- ❖ It is OK to say 'no'.

Dr Bruce Ritson

Dr Persaud's conclusion

Alcohol is not just widely available, it's a deep part of the fabric of Western society, making the non-drinker (perhaps a secretly recovering alcoholic) the one who will appear the odd one out at any social gathering. This means becoming alcohol dependent is one of the easiest of psychological problems to slip into without realizing it.

One test of how dependent any of us has become on anything is to challenge ourselves to do without it for an extended period. Maybe there is something rather profound to be said for the Lent tradition of giving up for forty days and nights any habit which might be bad for you. Yet another core problem with confronting alcohol dependency is just such a suggestion, as most abstinence ideas appear to be associated with a po-faced killjoy mentality. The reality is that when fun can be had only after a few drinks, the slippery slope is flying by beneath us.

SUPPORT ORGANIZATIONS

Drinkline – The National Alcohol Helpline: free, confidential information and advice on alcohol. Tel: 0800 917 8282 (England and Wales), Monday–Friday, 9.00am–11.00pm.

Alcoholics Anonymous, PO Box 1, Stonebow House, Stonebow, York YO1 2NJ; tel: 01904 644026; national helpline: 0845 769 7555; *www.alcoholics-anonymous.org.uk* – this website provides links to AA groups across the world.

Al-Anon Family Groups UK and Eire: self-help for friends and families of alcoholics. 61 Great Dover Street, London SE1 4YF; helpline: 020 7403 0888; *www.al-anonuk.org.uk*

WEBSITES OUTSIDE THE UK

India: *www.indianpsychiatry.com*

FURTHER READING

The Effective Way to Stop Drinking (Penguin Health Care and Fitness), Beechy Colclough, preface by Elton John, Penguin, 1998

The Thinking Person's Guide to Sobriety, Bert Pluymen, Griffin, 2006

29

Bereavement and Grief

A man who didn't want to forget his father's face

'MY PARENTS SEPARATED when I was a baby and I lived with my mother, but I spent every other weekend with Father. I loved staying with him, even though the flat was always messy and he spent most of the weekend down the pub. But I had my mates upstairs, two brothers who became my best friends.

'One weekend Dad complained of terrible pains in his chest and my friends' mother called the ambulance – Dad nearly died in hospital and I was with him. I wasn't allowed to tell my mother about it because Dad was worried that I wouldn't be able to see him again. When she picked me up from hospital, Dad told her that he had had an ulcer which had burst.

'Dad died not long after that – funnily enough on Father's Day. He died of alcoholism. I was eight. I find it difficult to talk about him, even to this day, because my mother and Dad were divorced and she was still angry with him. I also felt very guilty that I wasn't with him, as I am sure that I could have saved him. I get very down about that.

'When my schoolfriends found out that he had died, they didn't know what to say to me and somehow I always felt different to the others. Even if their parents were separated or divorced, they still had two parents and I only had one.

'I have two framed pictures of my dad in my bedroom, but I have forgotten his face and this makes me feel very guilty. Sometimes I dream of him, but he will always be the forty-six-year-old man that I loved and knew – he will never grow old.

'Recently Dad's brother died and I met up with all the grandparents, aunts, uncles, nieces and nephews from his side of the family. It was wonderful to speak about him openly and to remember him.'

What is grieving?

The loss of someone we love is one of the most painful experiences in life. Even so, most of us get through it with just the help of our family and friends. This chapter describes the normal process of grieving, some ways of coping, and why we may sometimes need extra help.

Normal grief

Grief is the price you pay for love, and most people accept it as worth paying.

When you grieve, you pine or long for the person you love – and have lost. You have waves or 'pangs', when you can't think of anything else and search desperately for some way to get the lost person back. Having cried, you feel a little better. For a while you can turn your mind to other things; then another pang comes and the cycle starts again.

Gradually, over time, the pain lessens. Between the pangs, you start to enjoy life again. Most people find that the first year is the worst. After that, you start to rebuild your life.

Grieving is not about forgetting the dead; it is about finding a new place for them in our hearts and minds.

Mollie, aged seventy-five, missed her husband terribly after he died: 'I could almost see him sitting in his favourite chair – it was quite disturbing. I couldn't talk to a friend or watch television without my eyes creeping back to the chair. It was as if I was searching for him.' This is quite common. Sometimes, for a brief moment, people may see or hear a lost person in a familiar place. It was not difficult to reassure Mollie that this was normal. She then said: 'Just lately I solved the problem – I go and sit in his chair. Now I feel as if I've got him inside me.'

Adjusting to other losses

There may be similar feelings of pain and sadness when adjusting to other losses – for example, the loss of a partner through divorce or separation, or loss of employment.

Traumatic loss

All bereavements are traumatic. They are particularly so if the death was unexpected, or took place in horrific or frightening circumstances.

'I can't believe it's true'

It can be hard to believe that a death has really happened, especially if it happened far away, and if we were unable to see or to hold or touch the lost person. We may find it hard to give up hope that they will be found alive, or that their body will be recovered. Information about the death may be limited or unclear. It can take a long time really to work out what has happened. You may never know exactly, and may have to live with this uncertainty.

What helps?
❖ Spend time talking it through – don't worry that you are being a burden, that's what friends are for.
❖ You may find it helpful to visit the place where the disaster took place, to talk with others involved, to place a wreath in a significant place, and to attend a memorial service or other rituals of remembrance.

'I can't get it out of my head'

You may be haunted by images of the way someone died. This is most likely if you witnessed the event, but television or other pictures can also 'bring home' the reality of what happened. Such images may:

❖ pop into your mind spontaneously

❖ be triggered by any reminder of the loss, e.g. loud noises, cries or shouts

❖ return as nightmares

You may try to avoid any reminders by shutting yourself up at home, avoiding any talk of the loss, or by being very busy. This kind of reaction is common and does improve with time, although sometimes it may become so painful and disabling that it becomes post-traumatic stress disorder (PTSD) – see p. 187.

What helps?

❖ Talking about the death again and again, until you can talk about it without getting so upset. If there is no one you can talk to, it can help to make contact with a bereavement volunteer (see p. 289).

❖ If this doesn't help, then you should consult your doctor. Effective treatments for PTSD have been developed in recent years. They do not necessarily involve medication.

Blaming

'I feel so guilty'

You may blame yourself for a death, or for not being there when needed, especially if it is a child who has died. You may ask 'Why should I survive?' or 'Why should I be happy now that he or she is dead?'

What helps?

❖ Even if you were not able to save someone, this does not make you guilty of their death. But if you still blame yourself, try to find a way to make up for it, to bring something good out of the situation. You could help others, or do something to commemorate the one who has died.

❖ Deep feelings of guilt can be a symptom of clinical depression (see p. 76). If you are deeply unhappy all the time, wake early in the morning, have lost your appetite and lost weight, you should see your family doctor. You may not believe that anything could help, but most depression can be relieved with proper treatment.

'I feel so angry'

It can be tempting to blame others for what happened. It may feel that by finding a culprit and punishing them, it will help your pain. It rarely does, and may even make things worse if you pick on the wrong person.

You may:
* feel jealous of other people – why should they be happy while you suffer?
* become irritable with children or other people who have done nothing wrong
* start to drive dangerously because you don't care any more

What helps?

* This anger is natural, but you need to control it. Try not to lash out, or, if you do, say 'Sorry'. Take extra care when driving – stop and take a break if your emotions are just too strong. If you are irritable with your children, or find it difficult to care for them, ask for help. Friends and relatives are usually happy to be of use, and you will not be letting the kids down if you admit that you are finding it hard to cope.
* Anger is a sign, not a sin – don't blame yourself. If you direct it where it can do good, you may help to prevent future suffering. Many disasters have been prevented because angry people took appropriate action.

Grieving

'I feel numb'

Numbness is the mind's way of protecting itself from mental pain that threatens to overwhelm you. This pain can be so strong that you can't think clearly, become confused and lose your bearings.

In an emergency, this emotional numbness helps us to keep going and cope with the crisis. But if it continues after the disaster is over, it can become a problem. This may happen if you worry that you might lose control if you allow yourself to be upset. Men, in particular, often feel this way and may use alcohol or other drugs to mask their grief – which does not help.

What helps?
❖ Express your grief – cry, rage or talk over and over about what has happened. Try to find someone you can trust who will be a good listener. Don't worry if, for a while, you let yourself lose control of your feelings. You will find it easier in the long run to live with, and to control, your emotions. Memories of the past are sometimes painful but they are your treasure – it is best not to bury them.

'I can't stop crying'
Grief goes on much longer than most people expect, so don't expect too much of yourself too soon. This said, grieving sometimes gets stuck – perhaps because you want to punish yourself, or because you have had feelings of depression or helplessness for a long time that the death has just made worse.

What helps?
❖ It can feel as though it is your duty to go on grieving, but the person you have lost would not have wanted you to suffer. It will usually help to talk to family and friends, but if you still feel constantly depressed or suicidal, you should see your family doctor.

Fear

'I feel so frightened'
We all know that disasters happen, but don't believe that they will happen to us. Most of the time we go through life confident that we are safe. Then disaster strikes. In a moment the world has become a dangerous place where you can take nothing for granted. You wonder what might happen next, and feel confused and lost.

Fear causes bodily changes – tense muscles, racing heart, sweating, breathlessness, sleeplessness. These can help us to stay alive in dangerous situations. But if they continue when you are safe, they can become a problem and may even be mistaken for symptoms of illness. This can make you feel more

anxious – which gives you worse symptoms, which makes you more anxious
– and so on. (See also Chapter 2, p. 24.)

What helps?

❖ Remember that these physical symptoms and feelings of panic are natural
reactions that will pass with time. They will not harm you. Relaxation
exercises, meditation techniques, prayer, or whatever makes sense to you,
can help you to control them.

❖ This said, you should not expect to go back to being the same person
you were before the disaster struck. You have learned the hard way that
life is never, and never was, completely safe. Disaster can, indeed, happen
to you. You may be sadder, but you are also more mature and you have
survived.

'Life has lost its meaning'

Your sense of purpose and direction in life arises from a hundred and one
habits of thought, assumptions about the world that you take for granted: 'I
know where I'm going.' Then, all of a sudden, you can take nothing for granted. Perhaps the person who died is the one you would have turned to in times
of trouble – and they are no longer there. It may feel that even God has let you
down. For a while you will feel crippled, as if a part of yourself is missing. It
takes time and hard work to adjust, like learning to cope with the loss of a limb.

Hidden grief

There are some circumstances when grief may be covered up, and you don't
get the support and love you need.

The gay or lesbian person may not be invited to his or her
partner's funeral; the macho man may cover up his emotions; or the over-
protective parent may not tell a child that a much-loved grandparent is dead.
Others may not understand the grief of those who have had a miscarriage or
who have lost a baby soon after birth.

The homosexual survivor may not realize that everybody knows his
'secret' and that many are not bothered by it; the macho man may not know
that by bottling up his feelings he may lengthen his grief; a child may imagine
that 'Grandpa went away because I was a naughty boy.'

What helps?

❖ People fear that disclosure will make things worse. It seldom does – grief can be therapeutic. Whether you choose to cry or not, it helps to talk. If you find yourself in tears, don't be alarmed. This just means that you care.

Children

Many children will not show how they feel, or will swing between great distress and apparent indifference. You can make it clear that you are there for them whenever they want to talk about the loss.

Children regularly deal with their problems by play – don't worry if they play at funerals or draw pictures of people who have died. If you join in the play, you can find out what is on their minds. A 'Memory Book' in which they can draw or stick pictures and mementoes of the lost person can be helpful. Try not to make the dead person sound so good that the child feels that they will never be good enough to compare with them.

Physical health

In the first year or so after a bereavement, it is usual to experience some changes in your health.

Normal changes

Anxiety and sadness may leave us feeling drained and lacking energy. The loss of appetite and weight that are common in the first month seldom last. By the end of the first year, many people have put on too much weight – our appetite for food may return before our pride in our appearance. Likewise, some people find their sexual feelings decline at first, but libido returns after a few weeks or months.

Health problems

Disorders that are affected by stress (see p. 241), like asthma and eczema, may get worse. So may psychological problems, such as insomnia, panic disorders or depression. Aches and pains, perhaps of osteoarthritis or rheumatism, are likely to bother us more if we are alone. Heart problems or high blood pressure may get worse.

You may stop looking after yourself properly, or even use alcohol or other drugs to numb your feelings. This will only work in the short term, and carries serious risk of addiction and damage to your health.

What helps?

❖ Eat a balanced diet.
❖ Take regular exercise.
❖ Smoke and drink moderately.
❖ Seek medical help if needed – don't ignore symptoms or postpone visits to the doctor.
❖ If you do start to smoke or drink too much, or use drugs, don't hesitate to ask for help.

Strange to say, the major changes – which are inevitable in all our lives when we lose someone we love – may help you to change habits that have been present for a long time. You may be able to achieve things that you would never have anticipated.

Who can help?

Friends: mainly by being there for you to talk to, but also to help with practical things.

The medical team: the family doctor and other members of the team can often help you to decide whether or not you need extra help. Many general practices have their own counsellors experienced in helping with bereavement problems.

If you have unanswered questions about a person's care or why they died, do ask. If there are grounds for complaint, you have a right to know how to proceed.

Voluntary agencies: see list, p. 289.

Dr Colin Murray Parkes

Dr Persaud's conclusion

Once a partner dies, the chances of a spouse following suit shortly afterwards goes up enormously and often heart disease is implicated, indicating that it really is possible to die of a broken heart.

The stress of bereavement is enormous, but one dilemma for mental health professionals is to plot the dividing line between normal grief and pathological bereavement in order to calculate who would benefit from services.

In many societies, talking about death is taboo; it may be that cultural attitudes and rituals contribute to bereavement difficulties, such as the way we deal with the dead and our approach to funerals.

There are always other reasons for carrying on living and finding a reason to be alive, and what the bereaved need is our support in helping them discover this.

SUPPORT ORGANIZATIONS

Cruse Bereavement Care: local branches in most parts of the UK except Scotland and offers support by telephone and the internet in all areas. Cruse House, 126 Sheen Road, Richmond, Surrey TW9 1UR; helpline: 0870 167 1677; email: helpline@crusebereavementcare.org.uk; email: info@crusebereavementcare.org.uk; *www.crusebereavementcare.org.uk*

Scotland: Cruse Bereavement Care, Lower Ground Flat, 8a Atholl Crescent, Perth PH1 5NG; tel: 01738 444 178; *www.crusescotland.org.uk*

Winston's Wish: for bereaved children and families. Clara Burgess Centre, Bayshill Road, Cheltenham GL50 3DW; tel: 0845 2030 405; *www.winstonswish.org.uk*

Cruse Young Person's Helpline: for bereaved adolescents and young persons. Tel: 0808 8087 1677; *www.RD4U.org.uk*

Terence Higgins Trust: lesbian and gay bereavement. Helpline: 0207 403 5969; *www.tht.org.uk*

WEBSITES OUTSIDE THE UK

Australia:
www.grief.org.au

New Zealand:
www.skylight.org.nz

Canada:
www.bereavedfamilies.net

South Africa:
www.lifeline.org.za

FURTHER READING

A Grief Observed, C. S. Lewis, Faber & Faber, 1976

Bereavement: Studies of Grief in Adult Life, Colin Murray, Penguin Books, 1998

Death and Bereavement Across Culture, Colin Murray Parkes, Pittu Laungani and Bill Young (eds), Routledge, 1996

i SUPPORT

30 Caring and Carers

A woman who had slipped into a world of her own

FATIMA AND I had been married for thirty years when, at the age of fifty-one, she was diagnosed with Alzheimer's disease. We had been happy and shared much in common – interests, pride in our only child, who recently qualified as a doctor, the loss of close family members and dear friends. We shared the worry when I was made redundant and was out of work for six months.

When our son left home, we began to talk about 'us' – how we wanted to spend the rest of our lives and whether we should remain in England. But then something indistinguishable came between us. Fatima became strangely less responsive, less interested in the home, and me, and 'us'. We were not together in the same comfortable way.

It took three or four years to show itself, and even then the unusual behaviour and uncharacteristic things Fatima said formed no discernible pattern. The undiagnosed, developing

Alzheimer's disease made it increasingly difficult for her to organize her thoughts logically, let alone articulate them. She hid a lot from me, but her difficulties became increasingly apparent.

I felt, instinctively, that it was something more than the 'mild neurosis' her doctor had identified. But it took two more years of increasing problems and bizarre behaviour before tests confirmed that she had Alzheimer's disease. As time went by, caring for Fatima became physically exhausting and emotionally draining; she relied more and more on me as the familiar became confusing, when she became agitated and when her memory let her down.

The seven years since diagnosis have been a terrible time, but also a time of great togetherness and fulfilment. Fatima no longer remembers or cares which day it is, cannot speak and can only stagger a few paces with support. But she is at peace with herself, is looked after and loved. For most of our friends, Fatima is no more. But to me she is still there, she is still composed of all that she was, all the life we shared. I know it will take her life, perhaps soon. When it does, it will be the disease that has been destroyed, not us.

[Fatima died at fifty-nine.]

What is a 'carer'?

'A carer is a partner, husband/wife, parent, son/daughter, other relative, or friend of a person suffering from mental health difficulties who provides care and supervision, on a regular and substantial basis, without which the patient concerned could not continue to live "independently" within the community or in their own home.'

Out of a total of nearly 6 million carers in the UK, the Princess Royal Trust for Carers has found that 1.4 million (23 per cent) care for someone with a mental health problem. About 230,000 of them care for more than 50 hours a week. If this were a paid job it would contradict the European Work Time Directive, which says that people should not work more than 48 hours a week.

'Proper' carers

If you are looking after someone with a mental health problem, you may not be considered a 'proper' carer because your responsibilities often do not include physical care. Caring for someone with a mental health problem can be variable, ranging from very little care when the person is well, to caring for every aspect of the person's life when they are unwell.

Carers perform a wide variety of tasks – for example, cooking, shopping, ensuring appointments are kept, dealing with medical staff, organizing transport, administering medicine, managing finances, personal tasks, and washing clothes and bedclothes.

If you are caring for someone with dementia, you may not be young yourself. You may be woken frequently in the night, perhaps suffer verbal abuse, and have to think and plan for the person you care for.

If you are caring for someone with a learning disability, you may have to carry out a lot of personal care, and you may encounter physical aggression.

If the person you are caring for has mental illness, you may have to cope with bizarre behaviour, or verbal and physical abuse. You may have to take financial responsibility – for example, dealing with benefits or housing.

What does it feel like to be a carer?

Exclusion from society

People with mental illness are stigmatized; sufferers and their carers often feel excluded from society. You may find that family, friends and colleagues visit less frequently, and eventually lose touch with you. As a carer you may feel embarrassed, and discourage contact with friends and family.

It is possible that you are caring for someone who used to be your closest companion and your main source of social contact. Perhaps you used to go on holiday together, go out for a drink, or have friends round for dinner. As their illness progresses, you are at risk of becoming increasingly isolated and lonely.

You may not have time to work, and this could result in financial hardship, even if you are in receipt of benefits. The combination of being unemployed and living on benefits makes social exclusion worse.

Exclusion from the health team

Dr Mike Shooter, past President of the Royal College of Psychiatrists, says: 'Carers are an integral part of the patient's support system ... They are the ones with the day-to-day experience of the patient's condition, and they carry the most intimate responsibility for the patient's welfare ... The carer's voice in decision making about admission and discharge is ignored at everyone's peril, and yet so often is.'

Unfortunately carers often feel excluded from the system.

Imagine that your daughter has been sectioned (taken into psychiatric hospital against her wishes) and since then you have been trying to speak to the team looking after her to find out what is going on. You find that people won't talk to you and never phone you back.

This is a common experience, as the mental health team often think that talking to a carer or a close family member is a breach of confidentiality.

Many carers are often very angry at the system, and it takes a long time for them to come to terms not only with the inevitable pain, distress and guilt that accompanies their loved one becoming ill, but also with their exclusion from the system and the lack of consideration.

Carers and professionals often have differing views about this. Carers often feel isolated, intimidated and frightened by mental health professionals, and professionals are often busy and harassed, and may have negative feelings about carers, perhaps thinking that they are interfering, or that they take up too much time.

Ideally, carers should be seen as 'partners in care'.

Health

In a recent survey, 37 per cent of carers said their health was 'not very good' and 10 per cent 'not at all good'.

Caring can affect your health by:
* getting you up in the night, coping with inconsistent, bizarre behaviour, dealing with verbal or mental abuse and physical aggression
* your worrying over financial problems and housing, and dealing with medical staff

These can lead to stress (see p. 241), nervous tension, depression (see p. 76), anxiety (see p. 24), back injury or high blood pressure.

Emotions

Many carers feel:
❖ mentally or emotionally drained
❖ frustrated
❖ sad for the person they care for
❖ physically drained
❖ stressed
❖ angry
❖ lonely
❖ guilty

Many carers also have disturbed sleep or sleep deprivation.

As a carer, it is likely that you have a close relationship with the person you care for. Their illness may have fundamentally affected that relationship. Many carers say they go through a bereavement, as they experience a sense of loss, isolation and social exclusion (see Chapter 29, p. 279).

Perhaps being a carer should carry the warning: 'Being a carer can injure your health and well-being'.

However, it is also likely that you are a carer because of love, a sense of responsibility and duty, and because you want to be. Many carers say there is a very positive side to caring. It gives them a sense of satisfaction and achievement; it helps them to develop new skills and to become more confident and assertive. So whilst the doors of opportunity to pursue your own career, education and leisure are often closed, other doors can open.

Concerns of carers

Carers have many worries:
❖ 'What will happen if I die, or cannot carry on caring?'
❖ 'I wish I had more help and understanding to do this job'.
❖ 'How would I cope if he comes to harm or tries to kill himself?'
❖ 'I wish people understood how I felt'.
❖ 'I wish her doctor would listen to me, rather than making me feel that I am in the way'.

You may be surprised to hear that a quarter of carers have, at some time, thought about harming the person they care for.

What can be done to help carers?

Most carers would like:

❖ more help for the person they care for, and to be more involved with the health team
❖ more help for themselves. This could include a realistic income for the caring work they do, as well as assistance to help them access opportunities for work, lifelong learning and leisure

Many countries are trying to tackle these issues. The UK government launched its National Strategy for Carers in 1999, setting out what the health service, social services and others should do for carers. There have also been various Acts of Parliament to improve provision.

In 1999 the government introduced the Mental Health National Service Framework. This required professionals to assess the needs of carers at least once a year, and to provide them with a written outcome of the assessment and a plan of action.

Family doctors in Britain can also earn points, which contribute to their salary, by identifying the carers of their patients and pointing them to appropriate local services.

Peter Tihanyi

Dr Persaud's conclusion

Carers are often torn between looking after their own needs and those of the person they care for, and these can come into conflict. Profound guilt leads many carers to neglect their own needs because they put those they care for first. The reality is that carers need to look after themselves because in so doing they are indirectly also caring for those they care for.

Society vastly undervalues the role of carers, and carers end up feeling miserable. Psychiatrists and other mental healthcare professionals, today more than ever before, recognize the vital role of carers in the management and treatment of psychological problems. They can be much more welcoming of carers' contributions and more likely to seek partnerships.

Carers' relationships with mental health services can be as much about gaining support for their role in caring as it is about direct care for the patient.

SUPPORT ORGANIZATIONS

Helplines

The Princess Royal Trust for Carers: a network of 120 carers' centres throughout the country, where information can be accessed in writing, by telephone or personally. 142 Minories, London EC3N 1LB; tel: 020 7480 7788; *www.carers.org*

Carers UK, 20–25 Glasshouse Yard, London EC4A 4JT; carersline: 0808 808 7777; email: info@carersuk.org; *www.carersuk.org*

Information

The Royal College of Psychiatrists and The Princess Royal Trust for Carers mounted a campaign from January 2004 to June 2005 called Partners in Care, specifically designed to raise the awareness of mental health professionals and patients about carers' needs, and to raise carers' awareness about a range of conditions and issues around mental health: *www.partnersincare.co.uk*

Finances

In the UK, the main benefit for a full-time carer is Carers' Allowance, which is payable until retirement age. To qualify, carers need to be caring for at least 35 hours a week. If the carer or family household additionally receives a means-tested top-up benefit, then they are entitled to an extra sum, known as Carers' Premium, to reflect the increased costs of caring. The Carers' Allowance:
www.dwp.gov.uk/lifeevent/benefits/carers_allowance.asp

Disability Benefits, Helpline (UK): 08457 123 456

WEBSITES OUTSIDE THE UK

Australia:
www.carersaustralia.com.au

New Zealand:
www.carers.net.nz

Canada:
www.ccc-ccan.ca

FURTHER READING

The Carer's Handbook, Jane Matthews, How to Books, 2006

The Essential Carer's Guide, Mary Jordan, Hammersmith Press, 2006

Children Caring for Parents with Mental Illness. Perspectives of Young Carers, Parents and Professionals, J. Aldrige, S. Becker, The Policy Press, 2003

i SUPPORT

Chronic Fatigue Syndrome

31

A woman who was too tired to walk

MARY KNEW SHE was ill. A fever, swollen glands and a sore throat that made even swallowing liquids hurt. It took all her energy just to get to the toilet and then back into bed. Glandular fever was confirmed by a blood test and she went home early from university to spend the next three weeks in bed. Every time she tried to get up, she felt ill and feverish, and had to go back to bed.

After four weeks her fever had gone and her throat felt better. She had lost a stone in weight, felt weak, and was dizzy if she got up too quickly. She was even exhausted after a short walk in the garden.

Eventually, after several months, she went back to university. She started lectures, but found it hard to concentrate. She worried about being behind in her work and about her continued ill–health. Her tutors expected her to work hard and her boyfriend expected her to go out with him most evenings. It was hard to sleep, so she took afternoon naps – which made it even harder to sleep at night. Deadlines brought back her sore throat and climbing a flight of stairs made her breathless. Blood tests showed no other causes and her GP decided that Mary had chronic fatigue syndrome.

Her plan for getting better involved several simple things – eating more regularly and drinking plenty of water, gradually stopping her afternoon naps, and regular times for going to bed and waking up.

Most importantly, she made a list of enjoyable activities that she could cope with, even on a bad day, and which she stuck to come what may – speaking with her friends on the phone and going out for a short, easy walk. Once she could cope with this, she slowly added activities every week. If she then felt worse, she kept her level of activity the same until she felt OK again. If she felt the same, she would increase them, but by no more than 20 per cent.

Her health, strength and stamina all gradually improved through the summer, despite a temporary setback with summer flu. Mary took stock of her life, split up with her boyfriend and decided not to return to university. A year later, she moved to another university, closer to her friends and family.

What is Chronic Fatigue Syndrome?

Chronic fatigue syndrome (CFS) is what most doctors call this illness, but other names include:

❖ myalgic encephalomyelitis (ME)
❖ post-viral fatigue syndrome
❖ post-infectious fatigue syndrome

CFS and ME describe a longer illness, usually lasting more than six months in adults or three months in adolescents. It doesn't necessarily follow an infection or viral illness. The term 'ME' is in fact somewhat misleading: myalgia (muscle pain) does happen in about half of patients with CFS, but encephalomyelitis (infection or inflammation of the brain or spinal cord) does not.

The main symptom of CFS/ME is persistent, disabling tiredness or utter exhaustion – fatigue, generalized weakness, lack of energy or 'running on empty' – made worse by physical or mental effort.

Other symptoms include:
- ❖ trouble sleeping at night (or oversleeping)
- ❖ poor memory or concentration
- ❖ muscle and/or joint pains
- ❖ headaches
- ❖ sore throat
- ❖ tenderness in the neck

Not everyone has all these symptoms all the time, and they may come and go.
Around 1 in 200 people will have CFS/ME at any given time.

Children and adolescents

CFS/ME is uncommon before puberty. It seems to be as common in boys as in girls. Glandular fever is a common cause in adolescents.

How is the diagnosis made?

By making an assessment of physical, psychological, emotional and social factors in order to rule out physical disorders such as:
- ❖ thyroid disease
- ❖ immune conditions
- ❖ sleep disorders

or mental disorders, such as:
- ❖ depression (see p. 76)
- ❖ anxiety disorders (see p. 24)
- ❖ obsessive compulsive disorder (see p. 149)
- ❖ somatization (psychological stresses causing bodily symptoms such as rapid heartbeat, feeling sick, chest tightness and light-headedness, tummy

pain or headaches; there is often a long history of several health problems; sometimes somatization may be connected to a difficult or traumatic upbringing)

Having more than one diagnosis

People with CFS/ME often, understandably, suffer from anxiety and depression at the same time. The illness creates worries, it can be hard to diagnose and the right treatment is not always available. Other problems include chronic widespread pain (sometimes called fibromyalgia) and irritable bowel syndrome (diarrhoea and constipation with bloating and tummy pain).

What causes CFS/ME?

Although nearly 3,000 medical papers have been published about CFS/ME since 1966, we still don't really know what causes it. One of the problems is that we cannot be sure that it is a single illness. It may be caused by several separate health problems. There are some clues, however.

What makes you more likely to get it?

❖ women are about twice as likely to get CFS as men
❖ other medical conditions, such as irritable bowel syndrome and chronic widespread pain (fibromyalgia)
❖ previous depressive illness
❖ it is not thought that allergic conditions, such as asthma and hayfever, increase the risk of CFS/ME

What triggers it off?

Viral and non-viral infections:
❖ 1 in 10 people with glandular fever (infectious mononucleosis) get CFS/ME
❖ other viral infections, such as parvovirus, hepatitis viruses and viral meningitis
❖ non-viral infections, such as Q fever and Lyme disease
❖ common upper-respiratory-tract infections, such as tonsillitis, **do not** trigger CFS/ME

We don't yet know why certain infections can cause CFS/ME. It may be the debilitating ones that keep you in bed for long periods, or there may be problems with the immune system of people with CFS.

It's not clear whether stress can trigger CFS/ME. Some evidence suggests that life difficulties for which there is no clear solution may make you more vulnerable.

What keeps it going?

Sleeping problems. About 9 out of 10 people with CFS/ME have problems getting off to sleep, waking in the night or even staying awake most of the night. Occasionally the opposite can happen, with sleep being too long and too deep. Either way, the sleep is usually unrefreshing.

Stress. This may be due to trying to continue the responsibilities of normal life while ill, but it is more usually to do with problems with another person – at work, in the family or amongst friends.

Boom and bust. It is natural to try to catch up with life when you are feeling a bit better. However, it's easy to overdo it and then to feel worse again – a 'boom and bust' cycle.

Prolonged inactivity. The body responds to inactivity by losing fitness and stamina. A week of bed rest reduces muscle strength by 10 per cent. You can also get consequent problems with temperature control, dizziness on standing and trouble sleeping.

Mood problems. If you've had depression or anxiety before, suffering from CFS/ME may bring this on again.

Unhelpful illness beliefs. If you believe that CFS/ME is caused by a persistent viral infection, you will tend to rest up if you feel worse. Your fitness and stamina get worse, making you rest more and feel more tired . . . and so on.

Social isolation. You may see little of your friends and family, will have less control over what you can do for yourself and may lose your self-confidence. The consequent stress can exacerbate the illness.

What can be done to help?

There are as many treatments for CFS/ME as there are theories as to its cause. However, two treatments in particular have been shown to help:

❖ graded exercise therapy   ❖ cognitive behavioural therapy

These seem to work when given to people individually who can get to clinics. Group treatments aren't so good.

Graded exercise therapy (GET)

You choose the physical activity that you most enjoy or want to do. Most people choose walking, some prefer swimming or cycling. You then work out how much of this activity you can cope with, even on a bad day (you may have to do less to start with).

You then work out how much you can increase this every week – up to 20 per cent, depending on what you can cope with. For instance, if you started with 5 minutes' walking a day, the next week you would try walking for 6 minutes.

After a week you review how you are doing. If some symptoms are worse, you stay at this level of activity until you feel OK. If not, you go on to the next level. The secret of success is always to keep the increases small.

At first, you just increase the time you spend doing something. Once you are doing half an hour, five days a week, you can think about increasing the intensity of the exercise.

Some people are put off GET, thinking that 'exercise' means going to a gym or going jogging. But it can start with the simplest of things – going for a walk around the garden or climbing a couple of stairs.

Cognitive behavioural therapy (CBT)

CBT can help you to change how you think ('cognitive') and what you do ('behaviour'). These changes can help you understand and manage your thoughts and behaviour, and so feel better. Unlike some of the other talking treatments, CBT focuses on the 'here and now' problems and difficulties. (See also p. 427.)

Treatment starts off, like GET, with you working out what you can cope with, even on a bad day – but includes mental as well as physical activities. Again, in discussion with your therapist you make increases in both physical and mental activity (such as walking or reading a newspaper), but in small chunks so that the increased activity is hardly noticeable. This helps to retrain your body and brain into becoming active again.

The therapist will also help you to identify links between what you think, feel and do, and then help you to address any unhelpful habits of thinking that may be keeping you unwell. Finally, CBT can help with the problems of insomnia, coping with stress, and coping with mood problems.

Pacing

Patient surveys suggest that pacing is the most helpful approach to coping with the illness, but it has not yet been supported by a scientific study. Pacing involves balancing activity and rest and mental versus physical activities. The idea is to try to use your energy wisely through the day, avoiding 'boom and bust' periods, to encourage natural healing.

Specialist treatment

This is usually arranged by your GP when the diagnosis is uncertain, when you have other health problems, you are severely affected, you have not responded to primary-care treatments or self-help advice, or are not able to see a therapist locally.

You may see a physician, a paediatrician, a psychiatrist or a therapist. The specialist will usually recommend one particular therapy approach (see above) after hearing your story. If their suggestion does not make sense to you, you should discuss this with them.

What doesn't help?

* Antidepressants help insomnia or depression, but **not** CFS/ME.
* Neither anti-viral, anti-bacterial or immune treatments, nor mineral or vitamin supplements have been consistently shown to be helpful.

Getting better

* People who are tired for a few weeks after a viral infection tend to recover on their own. If you have had CFS for six months or more, you will probably need expert help.
* Only about 1 in 10 people with established CFS/ME make a spontaneous recovery without any treatment.
* About 6 out of 10 people feel much better with either CBT or GET. About

a quarter of treated patients rate themselves as completely recovered from their CFS/ME after CBT and the same proportion still consider themselves recovered five years after treatment finishes.

It's easy to feel that you will not be 'really' better until you are back to doing what you used to do. However, for some people, this will mean going back to what made them ill in the first place. In some cases, CFS can actually be helpful in the long run – people see how out of balance and stressful their previous life was. They can then change those parts of their life that have been unhelpful.

Self-help

❖ Work out what makes you most tired and then:
  – change it
  – avoid it
  – change how you deal with it
❖ Work out if there is anything that is keeping you ill and see if you can:
  – change it
  – avoid it
  – change how you deal with it
❖ Work out what the minimum levels of various activities are that you can cope with on a bad day – then make sure you do them every day.
❖ Do a little more of each of these activities every week or fortnight – but don't increase by more than 20 per cent at any one step
  – if you feel worse, return to your previous level and stay there for another week or two
  – if you feel no different, increase what you do by a small amount
❖ Once you are quite active, increase the intensity of what you are doing – again, bit by bit.
❖ Improve your sleep – avoid stimulants like caffeine, and stick to regular times for going to bed and getting up.
❖ Read self-help guides.

Professor Peter White

Dr Persaud's conclusion

The treatment and recovery from chronic fatigue syndrome, like many psychiatric and medical problems, can be held back by conflict between clinicians and patients. This often arises because of the great uncertainty as to what precisely causes CFS and what the correct approach should be.

The anxiety that people go through with such an incapacitating set of symptoms means that not knowing what will succeed just adds to the distress of this condition.

Uncertainty and ambiguity lie at the heart of many psychological and medical problems, and learning to face these difficulties while maintaining a therapeutic relationship is an important challenge, particularly in the area of CFS/ME.

SUPPORT ORGANIZATIONS

Chronic Fatigue Syndrome/ME Service at St Bartholomew's Hospital: *www.bartscfsme.org*

King's College London: Chronic Fatigue and Treatment Unit: *www.kcl.ac.uk/projects/cfs*

WEBSITES OUTSIDE THE UK

Australia: *www.abc.net.au/health*

Canada: *http://hsl.mcmaster.ca/tomflem/top.html*

FURTHER READING

Coping with Chronic Fatigue, Trudie Chalder, Sheldon Press, London, 1995

Overcoming Chronic Fatigue, Mary Burgess and Trudie Chalder, Constable and Robinson, 2005

Chronic Fatigue Syndrome: The Facts, Michael Sharpe and Frankie Campling, Oxford University Press, 2000

i SUPPORT

Complementary
Medicines

A woman who wants an alternative

Steph is thirty. She has been depressed and is taking an antidepressant. She is visiting her doctor to discuss progress.

Steph: *I feel better, but I need something to keep me going. I have heard that St John's Wort is good.*

Dr W.: *In some countries it is used more than antidepressants. It is good for mild and moderate forms of depression, but if someone is seriously unwell or suicidal, they should stick with conventional treatment.*

Steph: *How does it work and how good is it?*

Dr W.: *We do not know how it works, but we think it increases the availability of the chemical serotonin to the brain. How good it is depends on the quality of the extract.*

Steph: *Surely, since St John's Wort is a natural remedy, it does not have any side-effects?*

Dr W.: *That's not quite true, but its side-effects are usually mild. You may get a dry mouth, headaches, nausea and stomach problems, tiredness, dizziness and sexual problems. It can also make your skin more likely to burn. This is called photosensitivity. If in doubt, it might be wise to use sunscreen.*

Steph: *Is it safe if I want to have a baby in the future?*

Dr W.: *It is not recommended for women who are pregnant or breastfeeding.*

Steph: *What about taking St John's Wort together with another antidepressant?*

Dr W.: *Not a good idea. There is a risk that it could lead to a surge of serotonin. This can make you feel uncomfortably hot and agitated. It could even cause seizures. A severe form of this is called serotonin syndrome, which can be potentially life-threatening.*

Steph: *Is it OK with the contraceptive pill?*

Dr W.: *No, St John's Wort can make the pill less effective, and you may end up getting pregnant. So if you take it, you need to think of alternative contraception.*

Steph: *Sounds like St John's Wort is riskier than I thought.*

Dr W.: *Many people benefit from St John's Wort, but it does interact with a number of other drugs. If you do decide to take it, then try to use a 'standardized extract', as it's easier to get the dose right. Also, it may be better to choose a product from a reputable provider. Of course another option, with even fewer side-effects, would be a talking treatment called cognitive behavioural therapy.*

What are complementary medicines?

People all over the world use complementary or alternative medicines. Some use them to improve well-being and enhance quality of life, others to treat an illness, either on their own as alternative treatments or together with conventional medicines.

Complementary therapies are popular because they are seen as 'natural' and safer than conventional medicines. Also, they are considered to be more holistic, seen to be treating mind and body entirely, rather than focusing on isolated symptoms only.

Some complementary medicines have been used for thousands of years. However, it's only in recent years that complementary medicines have been researched. Even now, relatively little is known about their effectiveness and safety.

Complementary medicines take many forms. Drug options include herbal medicines, foods and nutritional supplements. Physical treatments include acupuncture, massage and osteopathy. Treatments that claim to achieve their effects through changes in a person's energy flow include reiki, reflexology, healing and therapeutic touch, as well as homeopathy and traditional Chinese acupuncture.

Which complementary medicines can be used for mental health problems?

Many complementary options are available for anxiety and depression, but options are limited for conditions such as psychosis or schizophrenia (see p. 196).

At the end of this chapter, we suggest some internet resources that can help you to find more information about the individual therapies. However, you should not rely just on this information, but discuss your situation with a health professional.

Herbal remedies

Herbal remedies are derived from plants. It is often not clear what the active ingredient is, or exactly which part of the plant is needed to achieve an effect. It may also be hard to work out a safe and effective dose – doses are often based on experience rather than on the results of research. Plant remedies are not necessarily gentler than conventional medicines. All of them can have side-effects and can interact with other medicines.

In mental health, the most widely known herbal remedy is St John's Wort (*hypericum perforatum*). It is mainly used as an antidepressant, but it is also used to help sleeping and anxiety (see. p. 24). It is effective in mild and moderate depression (see p. 76), but if you are severely depressed or suicidal, then anti-depressants are better.

St John's Wort has few side-effects. It should not be taken with other antidepressants and it can interact with many other medications, often making them less effective: examples include the contraceptive pill, digoxin, drugs for AIDS and HIV, warfarin and some asthma drugs.

Valerian, passion flower, chamomile, lavender and hops are all used to help poor sleep, to treat anxiety and sometimes for addictions. They have been used for hundreds of years, but there has been very little research into their effectiveness. They may be helpful, but there is little proof that they are, or of how safe they are.

Kava, an anti-anxiety remedy, is effective, but there have been concerns that it might cause liver problems. It is no longer available in shops in the UK, but you can still buy it on the internet. We do not recommend Kava until the safety concerns have been clarified.

Ginkgo and hydergine are called 'cognitive enhancers'. They are taken to improve brain function, and are commonly used in dementia (see p. 13). Ginkgo is a blood-thinner, so people who have bleeding disorders or who take drugs like aspirin or ibuprofen may experience problems with bleeding. In rare cases this may lead to a stroke.

Ginkgo is widely available and is used by many people without problems. Hydergine can interact with anti-dementia drugs and many anti-depressants. There is also a risk that it may cause psychotic symptoms, such as hallucinations.

Commonly used supplements

Supplements include vitamins, minerals, and animal and plant products, such as cod liver oil or sunflower oil. All supplements can have side-effects or can interact with other medications. Any dose above the recommended level should be cleared with a health professional.

Omega-3 fatty acids, as contained in fish oils like cod liver oil, can improve general well-being. They may be helpful in depression, mood swings and psychosis. However, they are not as effective as conventional treatments, and many of the studies have only looked at their effectiveness when combined with regular medication.

Vitamin E (alpha-tocopherol) is an antioxidant that has been used to enhance cognitive performance, and to treat sexual problems (see p. 212), and a movement disorder caused by conventional antipsychotic medication (tardive dyskinesia). It may help a little in other movement disorders. Vitamin E can be dangerous in high doses.

Folic acid, selenium, S-adenosylmethionine (SAMe) and 5-hydroxytryptophan are supplements used in depression. Folic acid and selenium are best used in combination with antidepressants. Folic acid is commonly used in antenatal care for the prevention of birth defects.

Folic acid can interact with many medications. For selenium, it is important not to exceed the recommended daily dose. SAMe is not often used in the UK, though there is evidence that it may be effective. It has been traditionally used as an injection, but oral formulations have become available.

Acupuncture

Acupuncture has been used for depression, anxiety, agitation, sleep disturbance and fatigue (see p. 298). There are two schools – traditional Chinese and Western Medical. Traditional Chinese acupuncture is based on placing the needles along assumed energy channels – meridians – in order to restore a disturbed energy balance leading to illness.

The Western Medical approach uses similar techniques without using the energy concept. In the West, acupuncture is mainly used as a treatment for pain.

In electro-acupuncture, the needles are connected to a device which releases small amounts of electric current, thereby increasing the stimulus. This may be more helpful in the treatment of depression.

Most people tolerate acupuncture well, although the benefits and risks should be individually discussed. Some needle points require more caution than others; for instance, some can stimulate the womb and should not be used in pregnant women. Some people who suffer from fibromyalgia (ME) may tolerate acupuncture poorly because they are very sensitive to pain.

Homeopathy

Homeopathy uses 'like to cure like'. This involves using extremely diluted substances. The homeopathic medicines may be so diluted that only a few, or no, molecules of the original substance are present in the preparation.

Homeopathic medicines are prepared from minerals, plant and animal substances. The more diluted the solution, the stronger its effect. This is one of the most controversial aspects of homeopathy, which results in most people not being able to understand how homeopathic medicines could work.

There is a lot of doubt about their effectiveness, so they should not be used instead of conventional treatments in severe mental health problems. However, some people find it helpful to combine homeopathic and conventional medicines. The main advantage is that homeopathic remedies are safe because they are highly diluted. Occasionally, deterioration of existing symptoms can occur; this is called 'aggravation'.

Aromatherapy

Aromatherapy is based on the healing properties of essential plant oils. These oils are diluted in a 'carrier oil'. They are commonly used in oil burners, in bathwater, or massaged into the skin, so that the aroma of the essential oil evaporates and stimulates the sense of smell.

An aromatherapy massage is based on massage techniques that aim to relieve tension in the body and improve circulation. This, practitioners believe, allows oil molecules to be absorbed into the bloodstream during massage and to pass into the nervous system. Benefits of the aroma may also be obtained when oils are inhaled both directly and during the massage treatment, bringing about a general feeling of well-being.

People use aromatherapy for relaxation, sleep improvement, pain relief and reduction of depressive symptoms; it has also been used to reduce agitation in dementia. Evidence suggests that the effects are weak, and it may be advisable to use aromatherapy in conjunction with, rather than as an alternative to, conventional medicines.

For most patients, aromatherapy is safe. However, some oils should not be used in pregnant women, people with epilepsy, or babies and young children. Some oils can lead to allergies, or increased sensitivity to light.

How to use complementary alternative medicines

Since there is such a huge variety of remedies and techniques, it may be difficult to choose suitable options.

✔ Do

* keep an open mind about both complementary and conventional treatment options
* seek advice from your doctor, nurse or pharmacist
* tell professionals involved in your care, including your complementary therapist, about all your treatments and medication
* tell professionals if you are pregnant, plan to become pregnant or breastfeed
* tell professionals about your physical health, including seizures and allergies

❖ discuss openly your concerns about conventional treatments

❖ ask about your complementary therapist's qualification and experience

❖ ask your complementary therapist about the side-effects of any treatment

❖ seek medical advice if you experience unusual symptoms

❖ make special time for your treatment session

✘ Don't

❖ just stop taking your conventional medicines

❖ believe all information about remedies and therapies, unless from a reliable source

❖ believe in 'wonder cures'

❖ take high doses of supplements, unless confirmed with an experienced health professional

❖ combine many different remedies

❖ take complementary medicines without knowing what they are used for

❖ take somebody else's complementary medicines

❖ take remedies from an unreliable source

❖ pay large sums of money upfront

❖ practise acupuncture or any other physical treatment on yourself unless you have been trained in the technique

❖ blame yourself if a complementary treatment does not work for you

❖ be discouraged by unjustified criticism, but ensure that you are always safe

Finding a practitioner

Finding a well-trained practitioner can be difficult. You can always ask your doctor or mental health professional about this.

Herbal medicines and supplements. It may be useful to consult your local drug information service, and to find a health professional with special expertise in this area, or use services recommended by your doctor or hospital. There are also professional herbalists who belong to the National Institute of Medical Herbalists. They have had training in this discipline, and often work in a private setting. However, the majority are not medically qualified.

Acupuncture. The British Medical Acupuncture Society trains doctors and healthcare professionals. The British Academy of Western Acupuncture trains healthcare professionals. Physiotherapists and osteopaths have their own acupuncture training. The British Acupuncture Council represents non-medically qualified practitioners trained by several training colleges. Such practitioners are trained in traditional Chinese acupuncture.

Homeopathy. In the UK, the Faculty of Homeopathy trains medical doctors and other health professionals. The Royal London Homeopathic Hospital has been part of the NHS from its beginning in 1949. The Society of Homeopaths, which represents non-medically trained practitioners, is the largest organization.

Aromatherapy. There are a large number of training organizations. The Aromatherapy Organizations Council has a national register of aromatherapists.

Dr Hagen Rampes
and Dr Ursula Werneke

Dr Persaud's conclusion

One puzzle that faces doctors trained in 'conventional medicine' is why just at this moment in history, when medicine is at its most powerful, so many people, particularly in the West, are turning to 'complementary' or 'alternative' approaches.

One theory is that doctors increasingly speak in a 'foreign language' to the public, using alien scientific concepts. Alternative practitioners, on the other hand, use a language of 'energies' and 'channels' which strikes a chord with many more patients.

Another theory is that doctors don't have the time or skills to explore patients' anxieties properly. They feel more comfortable issuing a prescription.

However, most of us when faced with a medical emergency – such as sudden crushing chest pain and vomiting – will not go to the aromatherapist, but will take ourselves to the casualty department. When faced with a life-threatening emergency, we want to throw high-tech medicine at the problem. Perhaps the rise in alternative approaches reflects an increase in the number of people suffering from less acute, more chronic conditions for which conventional medicine offers no answer.

It might be that at the root of alternative approaches is a tendency for the person to feel more empowered, that they are looking after themselves, whilst modern clinics and hospitals make people feel that they are passive recipients of care.

Whatever kind of clinician a patient consults, certain fundamentals remain: it is useful to know what qualifications have been gained, who regulates the profession, what experience there is in the treatment of your particular problem, what the success rate is like, whether there has been independent evaluation of the approach, how much it is going to cost, and what the plan is if the initial approach doesn't work.

USEFUL WEBSITES

www.complementarymedicines.com

MedlinePlus: *www.medlineplus.gov* – this is run by the US National Institute of Health.

World Health Organization: *www.who.int/en* – an easy-to-use site which will tell you how complementary alternative medicine is practised in different regions of the world.

Food Standards Agency: *www.food.gov.uk* – from the home page, click on the 'nutrition' button on the menu. On the same website, see the Expert Group on Vitamins and Minerals' paper, *Safe Upper Levels of Vitamins and Minerals* by looking under: multimedia, pdfs, vitmin 2003

The Prince of Wales Foundation for Integrated Health: *www.flhealth.org.uk* – a UK website providing information on the integration between complementary and conventional health care.

FURTHER READING

'Complementary Alternative Medicine in Psychiatry: A Review of Effectiveness and Safety', U. Werneke, T. Turner and S. Priebe, *British Journal of Psychiatry*, 188, 109–21, 2006

33
Domestic Violence

*A woman who was thrown out
of her home with no clothes on*

MANDY MET HER partner, Steve, when she was seventeen and he was twenty–eight years old. Mandy was working as a trainee hairdresser at the time, and had ambitions to run her own salon. She was flattered by his attention and the fact that he bought her presents and treated her 'like a queen'. She believed that she loved him and he loved her. She moved in with him after knowing him for three months, and six months later they were married. There was no violence before their marriage; however, Mandy noticed that Steve was quite possessive towards her, and often questioned her about previous boyfriends and relationships.

The first episode of violence happened two weeks after their marriage. They had been out drinking at a local pub, and when they got home Steve started accusing her of 'chatting up' one of the men at the bar. When she denied this, he punched her in the face, giving her a black eye.

Mandy was shocked and distressed by what had happened. She thought about going home to her mother, but she was too embarrassed and didn't want to upset her mum, who had recently had a major operation. She couldn't understand why Steve had hit her, or what she had done to upset him.

Steve also seemed shocked and distressed by what had happened. He apologized and the next day phoned her up at work and sent her a bunch of flowers. Mandy decided to put the incident behind her, as she believed that it was a 'one off' and would never happen again. At work she told her colleagues that she had caused the black eye by walking into the wardrobe door by mistake.

A month later Mandy realized she was pregnant with their first child, and from this point she began to experience regular violence from Steve, as well as psychological and emotional abuse. He became more possessive and controlling of her. He made her give up work. He was rude and offensive to her friends when they came to visit, telling them to 'stay away'. He insisted on her keeping the house spotless, having his food prepared for him on time, and not going out unless she told him where she was going and whom she was seeing. He allowed her limited money for household provisions and wanted her to account for every penny. He accompanied her to appointments during the pregnancy and sat in during consultations.

The violence became more regular and serious. He would frequently shout at her, leaving her feeling frightened and vulnerable, and as the pregnancy progressed he criticized her for being 'fat and lazy'. He often threw things around the room, or broke things when he got angry. The violence progressed from slaps to punching and kicking.

Mandy feared going to bed, as she knew he would make sexual demands of her which, as her pregnancy progressed, she felt unhappy about. He became more and more jealous, accusing her of having affairs, which she denied, and telephoning home on a regular basis to check where she was.

As time went on he didn't seem to care any more about hurting her, and no longer apologized or appeared sorry about the injuries and distress he was causing. He threatened that if she tried to leave him he would find her and get her back. At times he threatened to kill her, and Mandy described one particularly terrifying incident when he put his hands around her throat so tightly that she believed she was about to die.

Mandy said that she didn't feel she could tell anyone what was happening. She went to her GP complaining of feeling tearful, unable to sleep and being 'on edge'. The GP did not examine her or ask about her relationship with Steve, but prescribed some antidepressants. She started drinking in order to 'calm her nerves'.

Mandy became more depressed and returned to her GP, telling him that she had recently been thinking about killing herself. Her GP advised her to cut down on her drinking and suggested a change of antidepressants. Again, he did not ask about her marriage or the state of her relationship.

When her baby was three months old, Mandy left home after Steve had assaulted her, head-butting her and throwing her out of the back door into the garden with no clothes on after she could not find his football shirt. She went to a refuge, but found it lonely and difficult to cope without Steve and her family around; against the advice of the staff, she telephoned him.

Steve persuaded her to come home, promising that he would 'never hit her again'. She believed him. But the physical and psychological abuse soon started again. The second time Mandy left, Steve found out where she was staying and turned up on the doorstep. Mandy felt she had no option other than going home with him again.

She didn't tell the police because she thought it would make things worse. That night, Steve locked her in the house and raped her. The next day Mandy took an overdose and was taken to hospital for treatment. A psychiatrist in the Accident and Emergency Department saw her. However, as Steve was present, Mandy couldn't tell the doctor about the domestic violence.

After this incident, Mandy made no further attempts to leave. She believed Steve when he told her that if she left she would lose custody of the baby as an 'unfit mother'. She also believed him when he told her that if she tried to leave him, he would kill her.

After four years of living in the abusive relationship, Steve was convicted of an unrelated offence and Mandy was eventually able to tell people about the violence. She got help and support from Women's Aid, her GP and members of her family.

She regained the sense of self-respect, self-esteem and dignity that she had lost through the years of abuse, and moved with her child to another part of the country. Two years on, she is working and has cut down on her drinking. She has come off the antidepressants and started a relationship with a non-abusive partner.

What is domestic violence?

We can describe domestic violence in a number of ways, but one currently used definition is: 'Any incident of threatening behaviour, violence or abuse (psychological, physical, sexual, financial or emotional) between adults who are or have been intimate partners or family members, regardless of gender or sexuality' (Home Office 2005).

Domestic violence is rarely caused by mental disorder, and is not a condition that requires 'treatment' as such. However, many victims of domestic violence develop serious mental health problems, which may come to the notice of mental health professionals or require psychiatric treatment.

Domestic violence is a crime that involves an abuse of power and control.

It is more likely to be experienced by women and to be carried out by men. Many victims experience considerable feelings of shame and stigma. Repeated negative encounters with the criminal justice system and other agencies, including health professionals, may make their distress worse.

How common is domestic violence?

❖ Domestic violence is the largest cause of ill-health worldwide in women between the ages of nineteen and forty-four.

❖ The rates of domestic violence reported by women around the world range from 19 to 69 per cent.

❖ In the UK there are around 16 million incidents reported annually; 4 per cent of women and 2 per cent of men report domestic violence over the course of a year, and 21 per cent of women and 10 per cent of men over their lifetime.

❖ Women are more likely than men to experience repeated assaults, to be injured, and to experience fear or emotional distress as a result of the violence.

❖ Any woman can experience domestic violence, although some factors increase the chance of this happening: poverty, low education, unemployment, marital conflict and alcohol use.

❖ There is a high rate of further domestic violence after an initial assault.

❖ Men who were beaten as children, or who saw their mothers beaten, are more likely to abuse their own partners. Women who experienced childhood abuse are more likely to become victims of domestic violence as adults.

❖ In many societies there is still public acceptance of men's right to discipline their wives.

Psychological and emotional effects of domestic violence

❖ Victims of domestic abuse develop feelings of low self-esteem, shame and being worthless. They become fearful and depressed. They lose their sense of competence and confidence.

❖ They often see themselves as to blame, or in some way deserving of the violence.

❖ They may become more and more socially withdrawn and isolated, making them more dependent on their partner and less able to find outside sources of help.

❖ They see their partner as dictating their feelings, behaviour and even their thoughts. Victims may appear passive, helpless and incapable of asserting control over their own lives.

❖ Many women seem to justify, make excuses for and minimize their partner's behaviour. Many women provide unbelievable explanations for their injuries, rather than admit to the fact that their partner has been violent to them.

❖ A picture of helplessness in response to repeated violence and abuse, and the often strong attachment between the victim of abuse and her violent partner, are characteristic features of many abusive relationships.

❖ Health professionals often express frustration and bewilderment at the apparent inability of many victims of abuse to remove themselves from the violent domestic situation, in spite of the escape options being suggested. However, women may find it impossible to leave violent partners for a number of reasons:
  – fear of the unknown
  – fear of revenge
  – lack of financial independence
  – concern for the children
  – lack of support from family and friends
  – a continuing hope that the man will change
  – in many societies, the stigma associated with being unmarried

Health effects of domestic violence

❖ Domestic violence in the UK costs public services £3 billion on an annual basis, which includes £1.2 billion to the National Health Service.

❖ The cost of domestic violence for mental health services in the UK is around £176 million on an annual basis.

❖ Apart from the poor physical health and injuries that can result from domestic violence, in a large number of cases it also results in the death of the victim. Two women per week are killed by a current or previous male partner, and in the majority of these cases there is a background of previous battering.

❖ Women appear to be at highest risk during pregnancy and the immediate post-birth period.

❖ Domestic violence is linked with poor psychological health and mental health problems, including depression (see p. 76), thoughts of self-harm (see p. 250), post-traumatic stress disorder (see p. 187), anxiety (see p. 24), and alcohol and drug abuse or dependence.

❖ Mental health problems may persist even after the woman leaves her abusive partner, and some women report becoming more depressed after leaving their partner.

❖ Women are reluctant to reveal domestic abuse unless they feel confident about getting a sympathetic response and informed advice about their options. The Department of Health encourages health professionals routinely to ask women patients about domestic violence.

❖ Health professionals need training and continuing support to make sure that women see such questioning as helpful and supportive, and to ensure that questioning does not endanger the woman's safety.

Risk in domestic violence

❖ 40–70 per cent of the female victims of homicide are killed by a current or former husband or partner, and the majority of these killings happen where there is a background of domestic abuse.

❖ In the UK, two women a week are killed by a current or former partner.

❖ Although leaving an abusive partner generally stops the violence, about 1 in 5 women complain of continuing stalking behaviours (see p. 231) and harassment by their partner. A high number of domestic homicides happen around the point of separation.

❖ When assessing the risk of homicide, it is important to look at:
  – the frequency of assaults
  – the severity of injuries
  – the frequency of alcohol intoxication or other substance misuse by the violent partner
    – forced or threatened sexual assaults

     – threats to kill

     – access to weapons

❖ There is some evidence that threats or harm to children in the home, extreme jealousy (see p. 123), and suicidal threats or attempts by the victim are linked with a higher chance of a fatal outcome.

How to assess risk

Ongoing risk assessment is important in order for women to be able to make an informed judgement about whether it is safe and/or necessary to get out of the relationship.

❖ Is the violence becoming more severe or frequent and is sexual abuse involved?

❖ Is there a recent change in the pattern of abuse?

❖ Is the couple separated or about to separate?

❖ Is there evidence of ongoing harassment or stalking?

❖ Has the woman sought help before? What was the response to her seeking help? What sort of support network has she?

❖ Is there actual or threatened harm to the children?

❖ Is there a history of self-harm or threatened suicide (by victim or perpetrator)?

❖ Is there a history of current alcohol or substance misuse?

❖ Is there past use of, or access to, weapons?

❖ Is there evidence of excessive jealousy?

❖ Has the woman sustained serious injuries, requiring hospitalization?

What can be done to help?

❖ Multi-agency partnerships are most effective in protecting victims and providing them with the services they need.

❖ Health professionals and health services must work in partnership with other voluntary organizations, charities and agencies that work with abused women in the community.

❖ Women want, and expect to be, listened to, believed and treated with respect – not blamed, criticized or treated as helpless victims.

❖ Victims of domestic abuse want to have information, advocacy (someone to help you by representing your rights and wishes) and support (both emotional and practical), and the time to discuss their experiences and explore their options with an informed and informative listener. At the end of the day, many women need the physical safety and security of a refuge.

❖ Some women want to see their partner prosecuted and punished, but many women are mainly interested in stopping the violence and in their partner getting whatever help and support he needs for this to happen.

Establishing a safety plan

This is likely to include:

❖ giving important telephone numbers to the victim and her children
❖ establishing a code word or phrase to use in an emergency
❖ identifying a place/places where she can go in an emergency
❖ leaving copies of documents, clothes, car keys and money with a trusted 'other'
❖ making a list of other important items to take in case of a rapid exit
❖ rehearsing escape routes with a support person
❖ telling a neighbour about the violence and asking the neighbour to call the police if there are suspicious noises

Tips for families and friends

One of the strategies used by perpetrators of domestic violence is to isolate the woman from her friends, family and external sources of potential support and help. Many women are encouraged or forced to give up work and end up becoming increasingly dependent on their partner for financial, as well as emotional, support.

This isolation makes it harder for families to know when abuse is going on. In addition, women may find it difficult to admit what is happening, even to close family members, because of feelings of failure and shame.

✔ Do

❖ ask directly about domestic violence, if there is the slightest element of doubt

❖ act on your suspicions if there is a change in personality or behaviour, evidence of unexplained bruising, or social withdrawal and depression, particularly in a situation with known marital conflict

❖ remember that many batterers are respectable, law-abiding individuals outside the privacy of the family home, and that domestic violence can happen in the most apparently respectable and affluent households – stereotypes of the 'typical' batterer or victim of domestic violence may prevent appropriate identification and intervention by those in a position to help

❖ understand that many women feel helpless and hopeless about changing the situation, and find it difficult to take what may feel like sensible and practical advice

❖ be aware of the potential risks involved in leaving violent partners

✖ DON'T

❖ criticize or blame the woman for what is happening

❖ reject her if she returns to her violent partner after leaving, and appears unable to separate effectively from him; it often takes several attempts before she can achieve separation both emotionally and physically

Dr Gillian Mezey

Dr Persaud's conclusion

It is puzzling to many on the outside why so many women stay for so long with an abusive partner when it appears so obvious that in the long term things will end up badly – the only real solution is escape and refuge.

The reality is that this situation is one that has to be faced by an enormous number of women all over the world. Most women have a very strong protective instinct towards their children; concerned relatives, friends and clinicians can therefore help these mothers to see that, regardless of their attitude to their own safety and health, their children are suffering in an abusive home. This is often the key to motivating women finally to escape this dreadful dilemma.

SUPPORT ORGANIZATIONS

For victims:

National Domestic Violence Helpline: a freephone number, available 24 hours a day, run in partnership with Women's Aid and Refuge. Helpline: 0808 2000 247; *www.crimereduction.gov.uk/domesticviolence40.htm*

Women's Aid: provides information, help and local refuge details for women experiencing domestic violence. Helpline: 0808 2000 247; *www.womensaid.org.uk*

www.survive.org.uk – information about organizations dealing with domestic violence, male and female rape, sexual abuse. Both UK and worldwide information.

Victim Support: Helpline: 845 30 30 900; *www.victimsupport.org.uk*

For perpetrators:

Domestic Violence Intervention project: PO Box 2838, London W6 9ZE; email: info@dvip.org; fax: (44) (0) 20 8741 4383; *www.dvip.org*

Women's Support Services: tel: (44) (0) 20 8748 6512; email: wss@dvip.org

Violence Prevention Programme: tel: (44) (0) 20 8563 7983; email: vpp@dvip.org

RESPECT, The National Association for Domestic Violence, Perpetrator Programmes and Associated Support Services, PO Box 34434, London W6 0YS; tel: 020 8563 8523; email: info@respect.uk.net; *www.changeweb.org.uk/respect.htm*

WEBSITES OUTSIDE THE UK

Australia:
www.lifeline.org.au

New Zealand:
www.preventingviolence.org.nz

Canada: *www.phac-aspc.gc.ca/ncfv-cnivf/familyviolence*

South Africa: *www.lifeline.org.za*

India: *www.indianchild.com/domestic_violence_in_india.htm*

i SUPPORT

FURTHER READING

Children's Needs, Parenting Capacity: The Impact of Parental Mental Illness, Problem Alcohol and Drug Use and Domestic Violence on Children's Development, Department of Health, 1999; *www.dh.gov.uk/Home/fs/en*

Domestic Violence: A Resource Manual for Health Professionals, www.dh.gov.uk/Home/fs/en

Domestic Violence, Royal College of Psychiatrists, Council Report 102; *www.rcpsych.ac.uk*

i SUPPORT

34 Drug Problems

A daughter who stole from her mother

Dr A.: *Well, Rachel, things seem to be going well – could we meet in a few weeks' time? I understand that you'd like your mum to come with you. Is there anything you'd rather I didn't discuss in front of her?*

Rachel: *I need her to understand that I'm sorting out my drug problem. It'll be easier to explain if she can check things out with you. I don't want to hide anything any more, so it's OK to talk about anything, really.*

Rachel's next appointment

Dr A.: *Hello Rachel, nice to see you again. Take a seat.*

Rachel: *Thanks. This is my mum.*

Dr A.: *Thank you for coming, Mrs White. It seemed very important for Rachel that you understand what's happening. She wanted to be totally open with you about her drug problems.*

Mrs W.: *I wasn't sure about coming at first. I've been at the end of my tether, not knowing what to do. But it's a relief now that I am here – perhaps I can understand how she got into this terrible mess.*

It was a complete shock when Rachel told me she was having treatment. I realized about five years ago, when she was eighteen or nineteen, that she had been messing about with drugs. I didn't know what she was using. Even if she'd told me, I probably wouldn't have known what it was, or how serious it was. I didn't know what to do or how to help, and she didn't want to talk to me about it.

Rachel: *That's why I wanted you to come today, Mum. I want to make a clean start and*

I can't do that if I'm still keeping things from you. You're right – I didn't tell you the truth when you found out about the drugs. I was afraid you'd throw me out.

Dr A.: So how do you both want to handle this?

Mrs W.: I'd just like Rachel to tell me how she started drugs, what she has used and what I could have done to help her more.

Rachel: To be honest, Mum, I don't think that at first I was doing anything different from my friends. We were all trying out something. I tried cannabis and amphetamines when I was fourteen or so – everyone else was doing it, and I made friends that way. It felt like sneaking a bottle of booze out of the house to drink in the park. It was just what we did.

It got a bit out of hand when I started mixing with some people who were older than me, who were using more regularly. I tried quite a few things then – LSD, Ecstasy, and often mixtures of things.

I couldn't afford to use regularly, but then I started hanging round with some heroin users who got money by dealing or shoplifting. It was about then that you found out. I wasn't injecting or anything, I never have – you know I don't like injections. I tried to play it all down and make out it was just experimenting, but I was needing to use more and more by then and I just couldn't stop.

I was spending all my money on drugs, and used to take money from the house and sold all my things. I got really desperate when I ran out of money. I just needed to get enough for my next dose and I didn't care about much else. I lost most of my friends who weren't using drugs – it took up all of my time, like having a job. I'd get the money, get the heroin, use it and then start all over again looking for money for the next fix.

Mrs W.: I knew things weren't right. I thought at first it was just you growing up, getting moody and falling out with your friends. It was when the money started to go missing from my purse that I realized things were serious – even so, I took a long time to realize it was drugs. When I did find out, I was really upset. I thought it must have been something I'd done, that I had been a bad mother. I didn't dare tell your father, I just kept it to myself – I didn't know how to get help.

Rachel: I can understand now how hurt and angry you must have been. We didn't talk about it, so I didn't know what to do. I thought if I just kept quiet then it would all be OK. I just wish we had been able to talk about it – I felt ashamed, and that I had let you down.

Dr A.: What I am hearing about here is two people who cared very much about each other, but who didn't know what to do. Now that Rachel has stopped using, perhaps you can talk through all of that without the drugs getting in the way. Rachel, perhaps you could ask your drugs counsellor if you and your mum could have some joint sessions together?

How common is drug use in young people?

Drug use among young people has increased over the last twenty years. Rachel is one of the many young people in the UK who started to experiment with drugs in her early teenage years. The older you are, the more likely you are to take drugs. At age eleven, 4 per cent have taken drugs in the last month and 8 per cent in the last year, compared with 23 per cent and 38 per cent respectively at age fifteen.

The use of drugs by young people in the UK is among the highest in Europe. About a third of youngsters have tried cannabis and 1 in 5 have used it in the last month. Nearly half of young people have been offered drugs at some point.

The most commonly offered drug is cannabis (27 per cent), followed by volatile substances such as glue and solvents (19 per cent), poppers (12 per cent), magic mushrooms (10 per cent), crack (9 per cent), cocaine (9 per cent) and heroin (7 per cent).

At some point in their lives, around 2.8 million people in England and Wales aged between sixteen and twenty-four have used an illicit drug; 0.5 million have used a class A drug in the last year. Older people tend to use drugs less – fewer than 5 per cent of them use drugs such as cocaine or amphetamines.

In 2002–2003, around 140,900 people received treatment from drug treatment agencies or general practitioners in England. Around 13 per cent of drug users recorded on regional drug misuse databases are aged under twenty – so around 18,000 young people are receiving some form of treatment.

Reasons for using

Rachel used because her friends were doing it, and to socialize. People may take drugs for many reasons, including:
❖ to celebrate
❖ to drown sorrows
❖ for pleasure, enjoyment and excitement
❖ for escapism and avoidance of stressful situations
❖ to feel socially comfortable
❖ boredom
❖ peer pressure

❖ to cope with withdrawal symptoms and craving
❖ to cope with depression and low self-esteem
❖ to increase confidence
❖ to relieve other psychological, psychiatric and physical symptoms or pain
❖ to increase energy and concentration, or to enhance performance
❖ to lose weight
❖ to unwind
❖ to have fun

We can't yet predict who will or who will not use drugs, or who will experience serious problems with drugs. Some family factors seem to protect young people:

❖ secure early relationships
❖ a good relationship with one parent
❖ affection and discipline in the family

❖ lack of family strife
❖ support for education
❖ disapproval of drugs by parents

As do these:

❖ female gender
❖ higher intelligence
❖ positive attitude
❖ good communication skills
❖ problem-solving approach
❖ supportive network of friends and/or relations

❖ higher standard of living
❖ schools that provide a range of opportunities
❖ sporting activity
❖ interests/leisure activities

Rachel was female and able to reflect on her situation, but she did not confide in her mother, who did not supervise her consistently. Her mother lacked support because she could not talk with Rachel's father.

What does it feel like?

Is there a difference between drug use, drug misuse and drug dependence (addiction)?

Rachel described the gradual change from casual, experimental use to being dependent on drugs. After a while, you:

❖ need to use more and more to get the same effect (tolerance)

❖ can't stop
❖ can't think about anything else apart from drugs
❖ spend all your money on drugs
❖ steal money and sell your stuff to buy drugs
❖ lose all your friends who don't use drugs

Quite apart from being illegal, drugs can harm your health and well-being. Problems can occasionally develop after just one dose of a drug, and may even prove fatal. If you use drugs 'recreationally' or 'experimentally', you may find that they make you feel unwell soon after you have taken them.

Heroin

Effects

❖ sleepiness
❖ feeling relaxed
❖ feeling content
❖ nausea and vomiting
❖ constipation
❖ reduced appetite
❖ reduced libido

It usually takes about six months of injecting it to become physically addicted.

Withdrawal symptoms

❖ shakiness
❖ hot and cold sweats
❖ stomach cramps
❖ watering eyes
❖ runny nose
❖ craving for the drug; this may be so bad that you sell all your stuff, borrow money and even start to steal it, often from your family or friends

Cocaine

Effects

❖ euphoria
❖ lots of energy
❖ agitation
❖ heart racing or beating irregularly
❖ nausea and vomiting
❖ some people become paranoid, grandiose, aggressive, argumentative and abusive
❖ some people get hallucinations
❖ sweats and chills
❖ epileptic fits

Withdrawal symptoms

- profound depression
- lack of energy
- feeling suicidal
- increased appetite
- craving for the drug

Cannabis

Effects

- relaxation
- altered sense of time
- happiness
- sleepiness
- increased appetite – 'munchies'
- reddened eyes
- dry mouth
- anxiety and agitation
- disinhibition
- hallucinations
- rapid heartbeat

Withdrawal symptoms

- anxiety
- tremor
- sweating
- muscle aches

General problems

Apart from the physical complications, there are legal consequences – if you are found in possession of drugs and supplying them, you can be arrested, prosecuted and even sent to prison.

In other ways, drug misuse is not really any different from misuse of alcohol, tobacco or volatile substances, e.g. glue sniffing. People can misuse, or be dependent on, more than one substance – sometimes many. People often smoke tobacco, drink alcohol and use cannabis, and so can be dependent on one, two or all of these substances. And alcohol and tobacco have their own withdrawal symptoms.

Withdrawal from different drugs can produce different symptoms:
- depressant drugs (e.g. benzodiazepines or alcohol) – confusion and disorientation
- stimulants (e.g. cocaine or amphetamines) – apathy and suicidal feelings

Drug use interferes with emotional, intellectual and social growth and development. Using several substances makes things even riskier.

Mental health problems and substance misuse can interact in a number of ways:

❖ drug withdrawal can cause mental health disorders
❖ drugs can cause mental health disorders; for example, one dose of LSD may precipitate a psychotic state
❖ if you have a mental health problem, you may use drugs to cope with your symptoms
❖ the combination of substance misuse with a mental disorder can lead to more risk-taking behaviour; this can lead to homelessness, prostitution, sexual exploitation, exclusion from school, truancy, crime and poverty

What can be done to help?

There are physical and psychological approaches. Each of these has its own advantages, and it is usually best to combine both. Medication and psychological treatment should be part of a comprehensive treatment package that takes into account the user's medical and social needs, such as accommodation, education or training.

While there are substitution treatments – for example, methadone and buprenorphine for heroin – it is important to emphasize that there are no medications for most other illicit drugs. Psychological treatments, which include counselling, motivational enhancement therapy, cognitive therapies and family therapy, are the *only* treatments available and should be offered even when medications exist. This is the case for cannabis, stimulants (amphetamines, cocaine) and Ecstasy. (See Chapter 44, p. 459, for information on medications used to help drug addicts overcome their problems.)

Where can you get treatment?

You can get drug treatment from a variety of organizations – your GP can often help you to get in touch with the right agency, or you can check out the websites listed on pp. 335–6. Treatment services can be community-based, residential or available in GP surgeries. Many voluntary agencies such as Turning Point provide 'drop-in' centres where you can go for help and advice.

Tips for families and friends

How would I know if someone was using drugs?

There are so many different drugs that there is no complete list of what to watch out for, particularly if someone is only using occasionally. Where someone is using more heavily or more regularly, you may notice signs (but there may be other explanations):

At home:
❖ unexplained mood changes
❖ unusual levels of evasiveness and secretiveness
❖ unexplained loss of possessions or money

Among friends:
❖ loss of contact with friends
❖ secretiveness about new friends

Personal issues:
❖ unusual smells
❖ deterioration in personal appearance
❖ increased 'ill-health'
❖ changes in routine, excessive drowsiness or overactivity

What should I do if I think someone is using drugs?

❖ get information from one of the websites
❖ try to talk to them about your concerns, but wait until they are sober or not under the influence of drugs
❖ get some support – talk to someone in confidence about the problem
❖ don't 'just leave it and hope it will be OK' – show that you care by talking about it

Dr Roger Bloor
and Professor Ilana Crome

Dr Persaud's conclusion

One approach to drugs problems is to assume that the person is not going to be able to resist temptation if it is put their way for quite some time following recovery from addiction. It is therefore important to ensure that it is extremely difficult for them to have access to their drug or illicit substance of choice. There are no drug addicts on a desert island with no drugs. This 'desert island' approach is not popular and it's tough, but if motivation is there to implement it, it can be extremely powerful.

Another factor worth considering is whether there are other issues in a person's life – such as low self-esteem, depression or boredom – that might lead them to turn to an addictive substance for alleviation. Perhaps it's only when these deeper underlying issues are addressed that drug problems can finally be cured.

SUPPORT ORGANIZATIONS

If you want to talk to someone, the following organizations all have helplines where you can get confidential advice, information and support:

Narcotics Anonymous (NA): helpline for people needing support and advice about the nature of drug addiction. Anyone from the using addict, their friends and family members, through to drug workers and the press are welcome to call. The NA helpline is now open 24 hours a day, seven days a week. Tel: 0845 3733366. *www.ukna.org*

FRANK (The National Drugs Helpline): freephone 0800 776600. This helpline can take calls in over 120 different languages via a three-way call with translators. The Parent Line number is 0808 800 2222. *www.talktofrank.com*

RE-SOLV: a national charity solely dedicated to the prevention of solvent abuse and volatile substance abuse. Freephone national helpline: 0808 800 2345. The line is manned 9am–5pm, Monday–Friday (excluding public holidays); outside these hours, an answerphone message provides details of an emergency contact. *www.re-solv.org*

Alcoholics Anonymous (AA): helpline 0845 769 7555, open 24 hours every day. Calls are redirected automatically to an AA member in your region. You may speak in complete confidence. *www.alcoholics-anonymous.org.uk*

i SUPPORT

i SUPPORT

USEFUL WEBSITES

www.turning-point.co.uk

www.drugscope.org.uk

www.na.org has links around the world

WEBSITES OUTSIDE THE UK

Australia:
www.healthinsite.gov.au

South Africa:
www.na.org.za

New Zealand:
www.nzs.com/health/addiction

FURTHER READING

Alcohol, Drugs and Addictions – leaflet for carers and professionals working with people with substance misuse problems. Available at *www.rcpsych.ac.uk*

Drugs, Dilemmas and Choices, Working Party of the Royal College of Psychiatrists and the Royal College of Physicians, Gaskell Publications, London, 2000; *www.rcpsych.ac.uk*

Street Drugs, Andrew Tyler, Coronet Books, 1995

Exercise and Mental Health

Exercise and mental well-being

The physical health benefits of exercise are well established. There is little doubt that exercise can play an important part in reducing your weight and improving your pulse rate, blood pressure and lung capacity. The mental health benefits of exercise are far less recognized, but there is a lot of good research which supports the positive and lasting relationship between regular exercise and mental health. Exercise has real psychological benefits, particularly for people suffering from depression or anxiety (see pp. 76 and 24).

The evidence for the psychological benefits of exercise is impressive for mentally healthy individuals, but even stronger for people with mental health problems. Several studies show that 30 minutes of exercise 3–5 times a week improves mood. This is usually in the form of aerobic exercise, such as swimming, walking or running, but non-aerobic exercise like yoga is thought to have similar benefits. The effects have also been seen in people with alcohol dependence, as well as those whose depression has arisen following a stroke.

One study suggests that exercise can actually prevent depression. In this research people were followed up for twenty-five years. Men who were doing 3 or more hours of sports a week in the beginning were nearly 30 per cent less likely to experience depression than men who did no sport. Some research suggests that moderate rather than strenuous exercise is better in helping someone with depression.

Patients have reported that exercise lifts the mood, reduces anxiety, increases self-esteem and boosts concentration. When a group of people with alcohol dependence were given a 4-week exercise programme, 60 per cent said that the exercise was of great value and 29 per cent said it was of considerable value.

When another group of patients were asked about what had helped them most during their stay in hospital, they reported that the physical fitness training was of more benefit than contact with nurses, psychotherapy or medication.

How does exercise work?

Distraction. Exercise may divert attention away from areas of stress, anxious concern and worry. It may be a useful way of helping people focus on events other than their particular life circumstances.

Self-esteem and mastery. Exercise can improve self-esteem and, for individuals who feel a loss of control over their lives, it can induce a sense of mastery that helps overcome depression.

Hyperthermia. Some people think that the elevation in body temperature from exercise helps to lift mood and reduce muscle tension. This is similar to the effect seen in people who use showers, saunas and steam rooms.

Chemicals in the brain. It is thought that exercise may work on chemicals in the brain, such as serotonin, that are thought to be involved in depression. Many antidepressants are also thought to work on these chemicals.

Endorphins. Beta-endorphins are also chemicals produced in the body that regulate pain and perhaps mood. They are thought to be responsible for the so-called 'runner's high', though the evidence for this is fairly weak.

Exercise prescription

There is little doubt that exercise is good for people who are depressed, and that the effect of exercise can be as good as talking treatments or psychotherapy (see p. 440). This suggests that medical prescriptions of exercise should be more frequently offered.

However, we all know that there are many things that prevent us from exercising – tiredness, embarrassment, motivation, lack of energy or time. This may be even harder for someone who is depressed, as they may also have feelings of hopelessness and low self-esteem.

An exercise programme should be realistic and should take account of the individual's circumstances. If you have not taken regular exercise for a long time, you should start gently – perhaps a few minutes of walking 2–3 times a week, gradually building this up over a fairly prolonged period.

The choice of exercise is up to you as an individual, but it is important that it should be something pleasurable. Group activity may be particularly useful for someone who is socially isolated. If the activity is carried out in the open, there is the added advantage of being outdoors, and if the setting is pleasant, this itself may enhance the beneficial effects of the exercise.

Walking or any other aerobic exercise for about 30 minutes, 2–3 times a week, is good. Benefits are more likely if you stick to the programme for four months or more. There is sometimes a temptation to over-exercise, but excessive exercising may itself become a problem, causing fatigue rather than raising your mood.

Professor Femi Oyebode

Dr Persaud's conclusion

Research is now showing that exercise can actually be one of the most powerful things a person can do regularly in terms of improving their health. If your doctor tells you to exercise regularly, you should not see it as a failure to grasp what you might be going through psychologically. There has even been some evidence to show that exercise might be helpful in preventing dementia (see p. 13) later in life.

One problem, however, is that most people seem unable to adopt an exercise regime which they can continue in the longer term. The key seems to be to take up an activity that you enjoy. Sport can be a good way of social-izing and, whereas simply going to the gym can be extremely boring, and often ends in nothing more than lapsed gym membership, taking up a more sociable activity can lead to longer-term benefit and enjoyment.

Another important consideration is to build exercise into your daily rou-tine, like getting off a stop or two early from your bus or train and walking the rest of the way to work.

Perhaps it is low self-confidence that prevents so many of us from taking up exercise – we feel we are going to be useless on the tennis court and so we avoid picking up a racket. However, going for lessons and recognizing that we are exercising for our own benefit, not to win a gold medal, are the keys to getting past these barriers.

It cannot be emphasized enough: **exercise is good for mental health**. The millions of people who regularly set out to run are aware of both the physical benefits of running and the psychological effects, including increased self-esteem, sense of accomplishment, and the incalculable benefits in confidence, alertness and concentration. This is probably one of the reasons why 40,000 people a year take part in the London and New York Marathons and this is just a fraction of those who apply to run in these events.

SUPPORT ORGANIZATIONS

Mental Health Foundation, London Office, 9th Floor, Sea Containers House, 20 Upper Ground, London SE1 9QB; tel: 020 7803 1100; fax: 020 7803 1111; email: mhf@mhf.org.uk; *www.mentalhealth.org.uk*

The Physician and Sportsmedicine Online: a source for primary-care sports medicine clinical and personal health articles. *www.physsportsmed.com*

WEBSITES OUTSIDE THE UK

Australia:
www.sane.org

New Zealand:
www.mindnet.org.nz

Canada:
www.mooddisorderscanada.ca

South Africa:
www.ssisa.com

FURTHER READING

Physical Activity and Mental Health, William P. Morgan (ed.), Taylor & Francis, 1997

36

Gambling

*A man who staked everything
on the spin of a wheel*

JIM'S GAMBLING STARTED with 'pitch and toss' and fruit machines
when he was very young. These became a part of his
everyday school life: he left school early most days to go to the
amusement arcades. By his teens, he was playing card games for
money with friends. When he was seventeen, his father, who
gambled quite heavily, asked him to place a bet for him at a
local bookmaker. While he was there, he also placed a bet for
himself. He vividly remembered winning £80.

In his early twenties, Jim began gambling regularly, visiting
bookmakers, dog tracks, race meetings and casinos. He
convinced himself that his gambling was not a problem and
that he could afford it. He even decided that he was a 'lucky'
gambler, and found the whole experience very exciting.

Shortly after his marriage, Jim's wife became pregnant and at this period he started to gamble more frequently. His local bookmaker installed a new roulette gaming machine that had a great impact on him. He went from a £1.50 spin to anything in excess of £50 when he was winning. He had several large wins, but often he would put his winnings straight back into the machine, with the result that he and his family rarely saw any of the money. He lied to his wife about what was going on in order to get out of the house to go to the bookmaker and play the machines. He started missing bill payments on important items, and used the money for his gambling instead.

However, Jim found that while abroad on holiday with his family, when there were no opportunities, the urge to gamble left him, only to return when he came home.

In view of his mounting debts, he thought he might make up his losses by internet gambling. He began by playing online fruit machines, and eventually blackjack, roulette and poker.

He had more rows with his wife. Sometimes he promised that he would never gamble again. At times, he would even recognize that his gambling was destroying him and his family. On one occasion, he felt so desperate that he took an overdose. However, the urge to gamble always returned. He began to steal money from his family and lied about it; while at work, he started using company money to cover his internet gambling in the hope of recouping his losses.

By the time his wife left him, Jim was many thousands of pounds in debt. After some months, the company for whom he worked became suspicious and called in the police. The investigation confirmed that all the money he had stolen had been spent on gambling.

What is gambling?

Gambling is a form of entertainment based on a contract between participating people. It involves a forecast of the outcome of an uncertain event. Various property, usually money, is staked on this forecast, so that when the result becomes available, some participants gain at the expense of others.

The participation of others is essential. However, sometimes, as in the case of gaming machines, this fact is hidden. The gambling appears to be with the machine, but is in fact with its operator, who sets the odds.

The popularity of gambling is due to the fact that it is a type of risk-taking, which provides thrill and excitement. In addition, as everyone taking part appears to do so on an equal footing, people with social anxiety and feelings of inadequacy may find gambling attractive.

Most gambling facilities are provided by commercial promoters, who arrange it so that the odds and the long-term outcome are in their favour. Alternatively, they charge a commission on winnings, with rising discounts for increasing participation. The industry has a vested interest in gamblers persisting in the activity, and doing so for prolonged periods, as this increases their profits. To do this, the industry heavily promotes the idea of winning.

Clearly, there is the *possibility* of winning money. However, the reality is that, while the occasional person wins, the majority will lose. Although there are some professional dog- and horse-race gamblers, their success is based on specialist knowledge. Similarly, in some card-game gambling, skill can be used to manipulate the situation. But for the vast majority of people who gamble, most of the honest devices promoted to improve the chances of winning are dubious.

Consequently, if gambling becomes a major preoccupation, especially if it is with a view to winning money, it is likely to result in serious problems. Excessive gambling can be as destructive as the misuse of drugs and alcohol.

What does it feel like?

Jim's case history illustrates many of the features of 'pathological gambling', which can also be referred to as compulsive or problem gambling. The most important characteristic is that the gambling is excessive in terms of money or time spent. Common features are:

❖ a history of heavy gambling in the family, or a family or cultural ban on gambling

❖ a large win early in the gambling career ('beginner's luck')

❖ preoccupation with gambling, to the exclusion of everything else, which decreases if the facilities for gambling are not available

❖ a growing tolerance of and craving for gambling, usually accompanied by concern that it is excessive in terms of the money spent or the time devoted to it

❖ in the end, a loss of control over gambling and 'chasing of losses', in spite of the person understanding the damage it is causing

The following problems usually develop so that the underlying gambling disorder may be missed:

❖ financial – such as debt and money shortages

❖ social – loss of employment and friends, running away from home, eviction, marital problems, divorce, behaviour disorders in the children of the family, criminality and imprisonment

❖ psychological – such as depression and self-harm

Why does excessive gambling happen?

There are many causes. However, there are a number of features inherent in gambling which affect people so that they can find it hard to stop.

Psychological effects

❖ Underlying all gambling activity is 'operant conditioning' – a process allowing a person to learn through rewards. Habits are most likely to be formed when the rate of overall reward is fixed but the timing of individual rewards is unpredictable.

As such, the long-term net gain or loss to those who gamble is almost irrelevant. This is dramatically illustrated in the use of gaming machines, which are also called 'one-armed bandits'.

❖ Casino gambling has a rapid turnover, which restricts the ability of those who gamble to apply any considered judgement. As a result, gambling becomes more impulsive, easily leading to excessive participation.

❖ The psychological probability of winning is different from the mathematical probability, even for a well-informed gambler. This results in success being overrated in gambles with a low mathematical probability of a win.

❖ The irrational belief that a string of losses makes a win more likely. This has been referred to as the Negative Recency Effect or the 'Monte Carlo Fallacy', since it forms the basis of many spurious gambling systems, especially in roulette. Strangely enough, it is also associated with the belief that a string of wins is likely to continue ('a lucky streak'), while a 'near win' may seem like a prelude to a win. These illogical ways of thinking encourage continuous gambling, and are exploited by gaming machines and scratch cards called 'heart stoppers'.

❖ Large prizes, even at very low probabilities, tempt the gambler because of the *possibility* of winning. The National Lottery is an illustration of this.

❖ Skill in gambling is usually overrated, and often implies an unrealistic ability to control the uncertain event. For example, in dog- and horse-race betting, punters tend to place their bets just before 'the off' in the fantasy that this will affect the result.

❖ Monetary credit reduces the likelihood that those gambling will set a limit on the amount of money staked.

❖ Heavy gambling is often associated with the loss of large amounts of money and, as the gambling industry promotes the idea that gambling is about winning, people who lose large amounts of money at it are seen as failures – indeed, recent public policy has referred to them as 'vulnerable'. The shame of being seen as a failure leads to denial and lying.

❖ Once large debts have accumulated, the only hope lies in the fantasy of a large win. Without this, calamity will strike whatever the person does. This results in the urge to lie and go on gambling.

These psychological effects have been increased as a result of recent developments in commercial gambling:

❖ Loyalty cards, which provide rewards to encourage the spending of more money.

❖ Unlike gambling in the social environment of licensed premises, gambling on the internet is usually done alone. Without the checks and constraints provided by the presence of others, the gambler is more at risk of acting on impulse. This also applies to gambling via interactive television and mobile phones.

❖ Electronic gambling machines, referred to as 'fixed odds betting terminals', have recently been introduced into betting offices. They are highly addictive.

Physical effects

❖ A gambling loss has been found to result in activity in the brain that is associated with subsequent *more risky* gambling choices. This accounts for the well-recognized Negative Recency Effect mentioned above.

❖ Disturbances in the reward pathways in the brain appear to be strongly associated with excessive gambling.

❖ Most people experience a great range and strength of emotions during gambling decisions. These are linked to responses in the brain to the expectation of winning money. In addition, people can lose track of time during a gambling session.

❖ Normal social levels of drinking alcohol alter self-control over decision-making. This may make it more difficult to decide at what point to stop when losing.

What can be done to help?

Excessive gambling involves a whole way of life. For management and treatment to be successful, the person needs to make major changes to their lifestyle.

Assessment

It is important to understand the extent of the gambling problem, as well as how it developed. The most accurate picture is usually obtained if the person gives a detailed written account. This is later useful as the basis of discussion with professionals attempting to help.

Many people who seek help for gambling do not recognize the need to restrict their gambling. Indeed, they may readily admit that they enjoy it, and only want help for the problems that it has caused. Such people are difficult to help. At least initially, the person must agree to stop gambling immediately for a period.

Management of finances

People who gamble excessively usually have a disturbed understanding of the value of money. Because of this, and the continued temptation to gamble, it is wise for the family finances to be controlled, at least for some time, by the partner or another trusted person.

Regular income from wages or salaries should be paid into a bank account over which the partner or trusted person has sole control. As the period of not gambling continues, the person who has been gambling excessively needs to become gradually involved in working jointly with whoever controls the finances.

It is important to obtain a detailed statement of all outstanding debts, as well as a record of the income and outgoings of the person seeking help and their family. The person with the gambling problem needs encouragement to draft a realistic plan of repayment.

Since debts are often considerable, the repayments may have to continue over many years, and the person needs to discuss the matter with their creditors. Repayments should be consistent with the person's regular income and circumstances. In the first flush of enthusiasm, they may commit to unrealistic repayments, which lead to a temptation to start gambling again.

Counselling

The person with the gambling problem needs to understand the nature of gambling. They should be made aware of traps, such as exaggerated ideas of the importance of skill (information from tipsters and various dubious numbers systems), as well as the subtle ways in which they can lose control. This will involve discussing the habit-forming process, and may be best done by a clinical psychologist.

The person and their partner should be encouraged to review their relationship. In particular, the couple need to consider how they spend their time, what friends they cultivate and what interests they pursue. It is often specific settings that have encouraged gambling in the past, and the couple need to make careful arrangements to avoid these situations or, at least, to be prepared for them. It may be helpful to draw up a joint contract that spells out the types of behaviour to be avoided, as well as those to be encouraged. This contract needs to be reviewed regularly.

Gamblers Anonymous

This is a form of self-help for excessive gambling, organized in regular local groups. As well as meetings for people with a gambling problem, there are also separate meetings for their spouses/partners (GamAnon).

Gamblers Anonymous can provide the opportunity to establish alternative social contacts to those that were preoccupied with gambling. Indeed, for some people, Gamblers Anonymous provides all the help they need.

Psychological treatments

Cognitive behavioural therapy (CBT) has been shown to be helpful. It can help to change a person's thinking ('cognitive') and also their actions ('behaviour'). These changes can help someone to understand and manage their thoughts and behaviour, and so feel better. Unlike some of the other talking treatments, CBT focuses on the 'here and now' problems and difficulties. (See p. 427.) Occasionally, treatment may enable a person later to gamble in a 'controlled' fashion.

Psychiatric treatments

Specialist treatment from a psychiatrist and/or a psychotherapist (see p. 440) for a neurotic disorder or severe depression (see p. 76) may be required, if these conditions underlie the excessive gambling.

Self–help
✔ Do

* only gamble for fun, and see any winnings as a bonus
* develop a wide range of interests and hobbies apart from gambling
* set a limit to the amount of money used for gambling
* stop gambling when ahead
* be cautious of a 'big win' – a winning streak is unlikely to continue
* remember that adverts for 'big wins' are to encourage more gambling
* bear in mind that prolonged bouts of gambling are bound to lead to losses
* keep a record of losses and winnings, liabilities and assets
* get a trusted person to control the money, if gambling is a worry
* understand that, if gambling becomes a habit, even when you win, you lose

✘ Don't

* gamble with money that, if lost, will cause problems
* borrow money to gamble

❖ attempt to deal with financial difficulties by gambling
❖ gamble every day
❖ chase losses
❖ put trust in an unbeatable 'system' for winning – in the long run, it won't work
❖ assume that 'luck will turn' when losing – losses are likely to continue
❖ allow gambling to interfere with work or studies
❖ let gambling become a major preoccupation
❖ allow your gambling to become a habit

If any of the don'ts apply to you, be concerned about your gambling.

Dr Emanuel Moran

Dr Persaud's conclusion

Gambling has become a deeply controversial part of public policy because governments, both national and local, have convinced themselves that opening casinos is a method of reviving an economy. National lotteries have also been found to be a relatively cheerful way of obtaining funding for causes which might otherwise have to be paid for through less popular taxation. Some would consider lotteries merely a tax on the poor or the gullible.

The gambling industry provides jobs and income and can appear as just a bit of fun or entertainment. While millions might be able to gamble fairly harmlessly and 'for fun', there are always also negative social consequences in the form of ruined lives.

The dilemma in a liberal society which values freedom is how to regulate the industry or educate the public in order to keep the fun element of gambling, whilst minimizing the considerable suffering it can also cause. Previously, this was achieved by allowing gambling to be easily available but not positively encouraged. In a situation where gambling is actively promoted, it is doubtful whether public education will be as effective.

Whatever the final answer, there is a danger that corporate forces at large in a free-enterprise society could be gradually transforming us into a nation of gamblers with profound negative consequences for our mental health.

SUPPORT ORGANIZATIONS

Gamblers Anonymous: self-help organization with links for people across the world who gamble to excess. Helpline: 020 7384 3040; *www.gamblersanonymous.org.uk*

GamAnon: support organization for families and friends of those who gamble to excess. Helpline: 08700 50 88 80; *www.gamanon.org.uk*

Gamcare: support organization, originally set up by the gambling industry. Helpline: 0845 6000 133; *www.gamcare.org.uk*

Gordon House Association: provides residential help for severe gambling disorder, outreach support and internet counselling. Helpline: 01384 241292; *www.gordonhouse.org.uk*

WEBSITES OUTSIDE THE UK

Gamblers Anonymous International Directory:
www.gamblersanonymous.org

Australia:
www.healthinsite.gov.au

New Zealand:
www.gamblingproblem.co.nz

FURTHER READING

Quit Compulsive Gambling: Action Plan for Gamblers and Their Families, Gordon Moody and Emanuel Moran, HarperCollins, 1991

i SUPPORT

Managing Your
Illness – and Your Life

A woman who felt controlled by outside forces

ANNE HAS HAD a long-term mental illness. She was diagnosed with schizophrenia twenty years ago, and has learned both to live with it and to manage it.

Anne started having mental health problems at university, but it wasn't until several years later that the problems returned. She started behaving in a strange way at work, and her employers insisted that she saw the occupational doctor, who referred her to a psychiatrist. Two weeks later, she took an overdose of antidepressants and was admitted to a psychiatric ward.

Anne was initially diagnosed as being depressed, then with manic depression. It was not until she admitted to hearing distressing voices and feeling influenced by an outside force that the diagnosis was changed to schizophrenia. Although the word 'schizophrenia' was scary, Anne was relieved to have a diagnosis, as it helped to explain her increasingly strange behaviour.

She was put on to antipsychotic medication, but was very sensitive to its side–effects. Over the next few years, she went through a cycle of coming out of hospital on a different drug, being unable to work or live comfortably, stopping the medication, getting ill again and returning to hospital.

Initially her partner was very supportive, but after she was admitted to hospital under a section of the Mental Health Act for the twelfth time, he told her she would have to manage her problems herself. He wanted to be her partner, not her carer.

Anne was then assigned a new care co–ordinator who was keen to do some counselling work with her. Anne decided that she would have to stay on medication for life. She took the lowest dose possible, so she 'didn't have to think through fog', of a drug with the fewest side–effects. This was one of the most important decisions in her life. With the support of her partner, she decided she should leave her stressful job and work freelance.

Anne took control of her illness as best she could. She and her partner learned to look out for early–warning signs, and identified other things that helped her stay well. She bought some exercise videos, and a Step, and worked out in front of the television at home. She started practising transcendental meditation. She became aware of the importance of a good diet and so began to eat healthily.

Anne now realizes that the way she lives today is much better than when she first became ill. She still has quite severe relapses, because her medication is at the lower end, and it is difficult to avoid stress. When she feels she is becoming ill, she asks to go into hospital for a short time, and this works well.

Anne does not like having a psychotic illness, but some aspects of it have been positive. It has given her insight, and compassion for others. She has got to know – 'and laugh with' – some interesting people she would not otherwise have met.

She remains open-minded about trying new medications – she is hoping that one day there will be one that will keep her well with no side-effects. She still works freelance, and sees the same care co-ordinator whose help is 'invaluable'.

Living with mental illness

Some mental health problems do not go away, and you need to work out how to live with them.

Your first experience of mental illness can be very difficult to understand. You may choose to seek professional help, or people close to you may urge you to do so. You will usually be offered some form of therapy – medication and/or talking treatments. A small number of people may need to be admitted to hospital.

You may only have one episode of illness, but for some this may be the beginning of a lifetime struggle with a mental health problem.

It can be difficult to accept that you will have to make adjustments to your lifestyle, or take medication for the rest of your life. It is very common for people to stop taking their medication – you feel better, and you don't want to be seen as an ill person.

There is often, however, a defining moment when you have to accept that some form of treatment is necessary. You may also find other ways of coping.

What does it feel like?

Mental health problems can be very frightening, both for you and for those around you. The most distressing aspect of the experience is the feeling of losing control of your mind.

For instance, with schizophrenia (see p. 196), it is about the sounds and experiences that others say are not present. In bipolar disorder and depression (see pp. 42 and 76), it is about out-of-control 'highs' or 'lows'. With this loss of control, you lose all your confidence. The experience of a psychiatric hospital can be very upsetting, because it may not be like anything you, or those close to you, have experienced before.

How you cope with a mental illness is a completely individual experience. This explains why two people with the same diagnosis often respond very differently to being ill. Similarly, your response to medication is extremely individual. It is not helpful to compare yourself with others. It can, however, be helpful to talk to other patients, as they may have good advice.

As a society, we are used to physical illnesses leading to treatment, which, on the whole, will make you better. If you develop a mental health problem, it can be very difficult to accept that it is not going to go away and that you will have to make changes in your life to cope with it.

Many people try to manage their illness without medication as soon as they feel better. However, if you do this two or three times and find that the illness returns, you should consider staying on a medication long term, or try to find another form of treatment.

Having a long-term mental health problem can mean that you lose your confidence and self-esteem. This can be especially true if you have resigned from your job because of the illness, or have become unemployed.

Some people become unwell before they are old enough to work or before they have finished their education. This can lead to the mental health system being their only contact with the outside world. Whilst it is valuable to get this mutual support from other patients and healthcare professionals, it is also good to make friends with people who are not connected to your illness.

There will be times when you will feel seriously frustrated with your illness.

Remember:
❖ It is not the doctors' fault, and shouting at them will not help.
❖ Even though you will feel that if you stop the medication you will be able to make your brain behave, the chances are that this will not work. All attempts to come off medication should be done with the support of professionals.
❖ Acceptable ways of dealing with the frustration are:
  – throwing (plastic) medication bottles against a wall
  – screaming at trees
  – trying to think positively (e.g. talking to a self-help group about how well you are coping)

It can be uncomfortable to be in the company of someone whose behaviour seems to be entirely self-centred, or that you don't understand. It is likely that your employers, family, friends or neighbours will see you do some strange, or even frightening, things. (It can be helpful to explain afterwards to those you trust how you were feeling and thinking at that time, even if it is embarrassing.) Carers and friends may become impatient with you, and feel that you could do more to help yourself.

Over the years, as you gain confidence and coping skills, you will be able to do more.

What can be done to help?

Explaining what's wrong with you
(mental health professionals, mental health charities, other service users, the internet)

Unless you have mental health problems in the family already, it is unlikely that you know what the disorder feels like, and what will improve things. It can be very helpful if you:

❖ Ask the mental health professionals to explain symptoms, behaviours, medication and other aspects to you.
❖ Get information from the many mental health charities and support groups who produce excellent information.
❖ Look for information and support on the internet.

Remember, you don't have to agree with any one explanation, and can always get a second opinion from another source.

Sorting the medication
(psychiatrists, family doctors, nurse prescribers, pharmacists)

Medication can have serious side-effects. Fortunately, there are a lot of different antidepressants, antipsychotics and mood stabilizers to choose from.

❖ It is important to think about what side-effects you can live with, and what will make you unhappy or uncomfortable. For example, if you have a job with an early starting time, there are medications which are less likely to make you feel really sleepy in the morning.

❖ Awareness of the side-effects of the medication you are taking can also help in other ways. Some drugs can make you put on weight, but if you know this, you can be careful about what you eat.

Talking treatments
(psychologists, counsellors, psychotherapists, arts-based therapists)

Some psychiatric disorders respond well to a talking treatment (see p. 440) or arts-based therapy. Even if you are on medication, it really helps to have someone to talk to. There are lots of different styles of talking treatments or arts-based therapies, and some work better than others for specific illnesses. It is quite common for people to reject a therapy at one stage of their illness, only to find it really useful some time later.

Help at work
(employers, Disability Rights Commission)

Employment and mental health problems can lead to a number of contradictions. If you are not working, and therefore not feeling very stressed, you will probably be keen to get a job. But when you do get work, and the stress starts to affect your mental health, you may consider stopping work. The law in this country says that employers have to make 'reasonable adjustments' if someone has a disability. It is important to speak to your employer about which aspects of your work may need to be changed.

When applying for a job, if you have the right qualifications you should not be discriminated against for having any disability, and this includes mental health problems.

Help with living in the community
(housing service, job centre, benefits office, community mental health services, faith institutions, GPs, Citizens Advice Bureau)

As there are for other people who may at some time struggle with living in our complex society, there are organizations that can help with aspects of it. Always try to be clear about exactly what help you want, and from whom. Having an advocate (someone who assists you to present your wishes and rights) to speak for you may also be helpful.

It is also good to remember that speaking for yourself, and getting it right, will increase your confidence.

Self–help

Alcohol: Go out with your friends, but remember that you should treat alcohol with great caution – it is addictive, and can make you depressed. Don't binge–drink, or exceed recommended drinking limits (14 units for a woman, 21 for a man per week). Have weekly alcohol–free days. The best advice is to drink in moderation.

Mind–altering (recreational) drugs: These are best avoided. There is evidence that they cause a relapse for some mental illnesses.

Early warnings: Learn to recognize the early stages of becoming ill. You can prevent a relapse just by taking action earlier. Common early warning signs include:

❖ negative thoughts
❖ louder voices
❖ sleeplessness
❖ difficulty with simple logic
❖ trouble dealing with social situations

Whatever it is for you, identify the signs. You will also need to identify what things keep you well.

Employment: The importance of employment cannot be underestimated. Apart from money, work gives you a sense of self-respect and self-worth. It can help you forget your illness and get you out of bed in the morning.

If it is not possible to get paid employment, try voluntary work, or ask if there is a sheltered work scheme in your area. Employment is one of the keys to good mental health.

Exercise: Exercise gives a huge boost to good mental health. Start with small amounts – swimming a few lengths of the pool, a brisk walk for half an hour, or a 5-minute run. If you don't like physical exercise, then try dancing – any kind of dancing.

It can be difficult to get started, but exercise lifts your mood in a way that nothing else can. You will feel you have achieved something, and be more positive about life. Try to build up your exercise routine so that you do at least one hour's exercise two to three times per week. (See also Chapter 35, p. 339.)

Food: Research has shown that eating good, wholesome food without harmful chemicals and additives can have a very positive effect on mental health. Try to eat fresh foods and drink ample water each day.

If you learn to cook, you will also save money because ingredients are often cheaper than pre-prepared meals and, being fresh, are more wholesome.

Feeling better about living: Try to distract yourself from worrying about life, and give yourself the occasional treat – whatever works for you.

Hobbies: It is important to find interesting and enjoyable things to do. Some people like to do things with other people, such as singing in a choir or supporting their local football team. You may rather do something on your own, such as birdwatching, running or gardening.

Relationships: Find someone you trust, to whom you can talk about your problems. This might be a professional, a carer, partner or friend.

Relapse: Even with the best coping strategies and support in the world, you may still relapse. Don't kick yourself, don't feel guilty, and don't feel a failure. It will pass, and you will get better.

Tips for families and friends

- ❖ **Do not despair:** With the right help, most people do improve or learn ways to cope.
- ❖ Together with other family and friends, recognize the early-warning symptoms and encourage action to avoid relapse.
- ❖ Do not treat your family member or friend as an invalid. There will be times when they will be well, so encourage them not to slip into the 'invalid role'.
- ❖ Explore the self-help techniques that work for you.
- ❖ Caring for someone with mental health problems can be emotionally draining. Make sure that you have your own protected time, and look after yourself.

Janey Antoniou and Vanessa Cameron

Dr Persaud's conclusion

Suffering from a longer-term mental illness can in turn lead to despair and disillusionment with doctors and treatments. Some illnesses, however, do take

a long time to improve, and many psychiatrists see patients who may have suffered for years yet who still make substantial recoveries given enough time.

It is important to set new key goals, such as focusing on avoiding relapse or increasing symptoms, and learn from the past about what has worked and what has gone wrong, leading to a worsening of the illness. If one treatment approach has lost your confidence or does not appear to be working, then you need to become more active in exploring alternatives and seeking second opinions.

There are psychiatrists and other mental healthcare professionals who specialize in illnesses which appear to have become more lasting (chronic) and an early referral to these services should be pursued vigorously.

It is really useful to have things you want to do with your life and to focus on achieving these goals, rather than letting the illness take over your life. Many people with very disabling and enduring illnesses have gone on to do astonishing things.

SUPPORT ORGANIZATIONS

Mind, 15–19 Broadway, London E15 4BQ; tel: 020 8519 2122; fax: 020 8522 1725; email: contact@mind.org.uk; Mind*info*Line: 0845 766 0163; *www.mind.org.uk*

Rethink, Head Office, 5th Floor, Royal London House, 22–25 Finsbury Square, London EC2A 1DX; national advice service: 020 8974 6814 (open 10am–3pm, Monday–Friday); email: advice@rethink.org; *www.rethink.org*

Mental Health Foundation, London Office, 9th Floor, Sea Containers House, 20 Upper Ground, London SE1 9QB; tel: 020 7803 1100; fax: 020 7803 1111; email: mhf@mhf.org.uk; *www.mentalhealth.org.uk/index.cfm*

WEBSITES OUTSIDE THE UK

Australia:
www.beyondblue.org.au

New Zealand:
www.mindnet.org.nz

Canada: *www.heretohelp.bc.ca/*
tellmeabout/managing.shtml

South Africa:
www.hst.org.za

India:
www.indianpsychiatry.com

FURTHER READING

Manage Your Mind: The Mental Fitness Guide, Gillian Butler and Tony Hope, Oxford University Press, 2007.

Mind and Body

The mind and body in medicine

The relationship between the mind and body has intrigued man for centuries. Over the years, Western medicine, with its origins in the sciences, viewed physical disease as a biological event with identifiable abnormalities. Emotions were seen as irrelevant to the practice of modern medicine.

Illness without measurable abnormalities still frustrates doctors. Yet 'medically unexplained symptoms' – where no concrete cause can be found – represent at least 30 per cent of all medical consultations. Examples of these distressing conditions are chronic fatigue, chronic pain and irritable bowel syndrome.

New research is giving us a better understanding of the relationship between mind and body, and shedding light on what makes us feel well and what makes us ill. It is helping us understand how the conscious mind (thinking, imagining, feeling and remembering) can change physical processes in the brain and affect our body (and vice versa). These findings have enormous implications for health care and are already contributing to new ways of maintaining health.

Brain chemistry

Neurotransmitters

The brain is made up of over 10 billion specialized cells called neurons. Neurons communicate with each other through the release of chemicals known as neurotransmitters.

Neurotransmitters, such as serotonin, adrenaline and dopamine, influence many physical and psychological functions – including mood, appetite, energy, sex drive, sleep and behaviour. The levels of these neurotransmitters are influenced by our genes and life experiences, as well as our thoughts, mood, behaviours, relationships, etc.

Hormones

Communication between the brain and body also takes place through hormones. The brain controls the release of various hormones into the blood, and these help to regulate bodily functions.

Some of these regulation systems are altered by stress and depression. This can have a wide-ranging effect on chemicals in our body, such as adrenaline and cortisol, our immune system, and on neurotransmitters such as serotonin.

The levels of other hormones, such as sex hormones, can change brain activity and even change the structure of the brain. Persistent hormonal disturbance can produce damaging effects on brain and body.

Cytokines

The discovery of small chemical immune messengers, known as cytokines, has revolutionized our understanding of mind/body communication. Cytokines can activate the nervous system, influence hormone levels and affect the immune system.

Over 100 cytokines have been identified, and it is known that stress, anxiety and depression can affect many of them.

Cytokines, hormones and neurotransmitters can have an impact on the brain, influence our thinking, mood and behaviour, and cause a wide range of physical symptoms. These naturally occurring chemicals have been called the *'molecules of emotion'*.

The central nervous system

One pathway of communication from brain to body is the central nervous system. The *autonomic nervous system* (ANS) is an important part of our central nervous system and one that is not under our voluntary control.

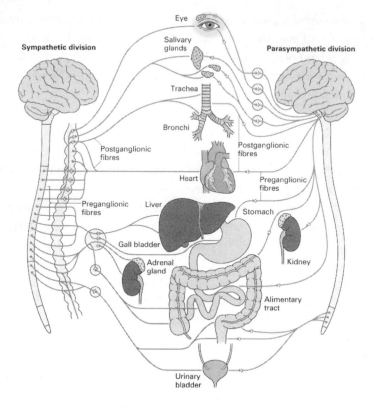

It is involved in controlling many functions, such as blood pressure, heart rate and body temperature. Stress affects this system, rapidly causing physical symptoms.

Memories

Adrenaline is a hormone which is released in the brain and body when we are frightened or stressed, and which improves memory. If you ask someone to recount major 'stand-out' moments in their lives, they often recall events that were associated with powerful emotions such as fear, anger, sadness, pride or happiness.

'Flashbulb memories' are often linked to higher levels of emotion, and so we can remember a lot of information about the experience. For instance, we are likely to remember where we were when we heard about 9/11, or Princess Diana's death.

Emotions

Emotions prime our body, and can then drive and dominate our thoughts and behaviour.

The response to thoughts, images or events can vary a lot between individuals, and at different times. For instance, many of us find our worries more difficult to deal with if we wake in the middle of the night. If several things go wrong at the same time, or if we become tired or exhausted, our ability to cope with even minor events can be compromised.

Our mood can also influence how we interpret events. When we are irritable, we can be easily triggered into anger; when sad, we tend to remember unhappy events and dwell on negative thoughts; when happy, we tend to focus on the positive. Our thinking style can maintain positive or negative emotional states.

For example, a woman is alone in her house at night, quietly reading in her bedroom, when she hears a noise downstairs. Believing the noise to be the cat creates little physical or behavioural response, and the woman carries on reading unworried. However, if the same sound prompted the thought that there is an intruder in the house, it triggers fear and the release of adrenaline, producing many of the symptoms listed in the box overleaf.

Fear

Fear can be useful, as it has a survival function. It is associated with widespread changes in the brain and the body, and the 'fight or flight' response – changes to help prime us to 'fight', 'freeze' or 'flee' (see box overleaf).

When the fear system triggers too easily or incorrectly, or remains 'switched-on' for long periods, it can become a problem. For example, a woman is mugged on a tube train. The mugger holds a knife to her throat and she experiences intense fear because she believes she might die. A lot of the contextual information may get 'logged' in memory – the mugger's aftershave, his accent and the music playing on his audio player. If, six months later, a man behind her in a queue smells of the same aftershave, she will experience fear and feel physically frightened, before she is even aware that she has smelt the aftershave.

PHYSICAL SYMPTOMS ASSOCIATED WITH STRESS, WORRY, FEAR AND ANXIETY – ADRENALINE

- rapid heart rate, palpitations, sweating, shakiness

- muscle tension, headache, neck stiffness, chest tightness

- breathlessness, dizziness, light-headedness, numbness, tingling in hands and feet

- faintness, tremor, feeling 'strange', 'detached' or 'spaced', blurred vision

- indigestion, nausea, heartburn, diarrhoea, irritable bowel syndrome, dry mouth, tightness in the throat

- fatigue, skin rashes, urinary frequency, feeling hot and cold

The unconscious mind

Some fears can be triggered by information we are not consciously aware of; this mechanism explains why we can feel anxious 'out of the blue', for no apparent reason. If someone with a spider phobia is shown a subliminal image (the image is flashed onto a screen for such a short time it cannot register in conscious awareness), it can still trigger a fear response.

The power of belief and the placebo effect

The power of belief can be witnessed in our daily lives. If you experience chest discomfort and believe that the cause was eating your lunch too quickly, it is unlikely to frighten you particularly.

However, if you believe that your chest discomfort is a heart problem, you are likely to become anxious and monitor your symptoms carefully. Once anxious, your brain chemistry changes, your attention becomes fixed on the threat and your body changes.

Placebos cause measurable changes in our biology.

❖ Knowing that other people, such as friends or family, are praying for you can produce some positive results.

❖ Over 50 per cent of us will gain pain relief from an inactive substance if we believe it to be a painkiller.

❖ Placebos can activate the same brain areas as proven treatments in Parkinson's disease, pain relief and depression.

❖ Placebo alcohol can increase aggressive behaviour, craving for alcohol and sexual arousal.

❖ Patients lost weight when they thought they were taking a weight-reducing drug, but not if they believed they were taking a placebo.

The reverse can occur if we believe something may harm us. This is known as the *nocebo effect*.

The power of the placebo is influenced by belief, the setting, the credibility of the intervention, the associated ritual, and the relationship with the therapist or doctor.

Worry

Repeated negative thinking about problems can lead to depression and anxiety. When anxious, we tend to consider unpleasant outcomes. These imagined scenarios often make us more anxious.

If anxious thoughts recur frequently, they are likely to become established inter-neuronal pathways. We can therefore 'hardwire' our patterns of thinking into the brain's circuitry, and then access them more readily.

Stress

Stress is normal and good for us. Deadlines motivate us to do things, such as revise for exams. What is stressful to one person may not be stressful to another. Some people seek out certain situations, such as skydiving or bungee-jumping, whereas others would strenuously avoid such situations. So defining stress depends not only on its context, but also on its meaning to the individual.

When pressure or stress is at a reasonable level it can improve a person's performance and is thought of as stimulation. But when this increases beyond that which a person finds beneficial, they will start to feel negative effects – they may become irritable and develop physical symptoms, such as poor sleep and fatigue. These effects can be illustrated by the graph below which shows that, in theory, for every person and for every task, there is an optimum level of stress that will result in the best performance.

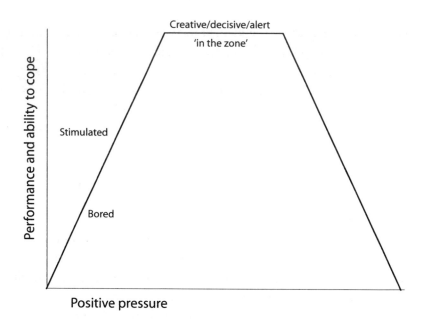

Stress and anxiety can be experienced as physical symptoms, because they result in natural biological responses and physical changes in our body. The bungee-jumper interprets this as excitement; the person with a fear of heights feels sheer terror.

Stress and anxiety can use up a lot of energy, leaving us feeling 'emotionally drained' or exhausted.

Major stressful events can cause depression. When stressed, we are more likely to avoid things and withdraw from normal activities. (See Chapter 26, p. 241.)

Case study

ALAN, A thirty-nine-year-old father of two, works as an accountant in a large firm. He has always enjoyed his work and thought his job was secure. But Alan's company has had a poor year and jobs are being axed. His workload has increased and he is now working longer hours. He is worried about losing his job.

Alan's wife has been diagnosed with postnatal depression and his ten-year-old son is being bullied at school. Alan wants to spend more time at home, but feels he must be seen to perform well at work. He spends over three hours commuting to and from work.

Alan starts to have difficulty sleeping; he feels tired in the day, and his concentration and memory are not as good as usual. He becomes worried that his impaired performance will be noticed at work and continues to worry that he might lose his job. He uses more coffee to try to stay alert.

anxiety symptoms ⟷ **frightening thoughts**

poor concentration, sleep disturbance   'I'll lose my job'
fatigue, poor memory

Over the next few weeks Alan experiences headaches, heart palpitations and chest tightness. These symptoms worry him because his father had heart problems and died of a heart attack in his mid-forties. Alan starts to monitor his heartbeat, taking his own pulse and scanning his body for symptoms. He becomes very aware of his heart thumping, and his anxiety seems to escalate immediately.

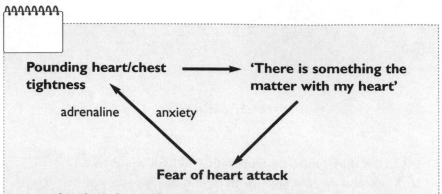

Alan finds himself constantly worrying about work and his health. He sees his GP. All his tests are normal but he remains concerned that there is something seriously the matter with his heart.

He also continues to worry that his memory is deteriorating. His worry and anxiety are making his symptoms get worse, his sleep deteriorates further, and he becomes more irritable at work and at home. He starts to drink more alcohol to try to calm himself down, and to improve his sleep.

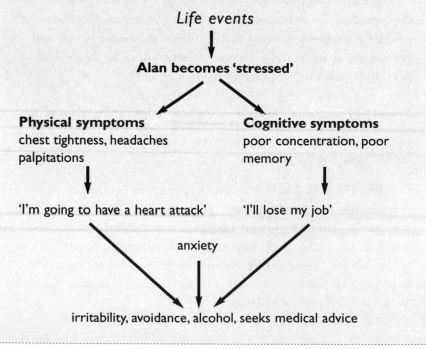

Emotions and the heart

Stress can affect the heart. It can lead to:

❖ raised pulse rate and blood pressure
❖ altered electrical rhythm of the heart

Anger can influence cardiac rhythm and change the size of blood vessels around the heart.

Over-breathing, a common sign of stress and anxiety, can cause dizziness, pins and needles, chest pain and breathlessness in some people. A recent study shows that stress at work can increase the risk of heart disease and diabetes.

The brain–gut axis – feeling 'gutted'

In the Western world 'unexplained symptoms' arising in the oesophagus, stomach or gut occur in up to a fifth of adults. Stress is strongly linked to abdominal pain and change in bowel habit.

The gut lining has receptors for the so-called 'molecules of emotion', so it is little wonder that emotions and stress can bring about changes in gastric activity and gut movement, and alter the blood supply to the gut. A lot of emotions create visceral or gut reactions, and the gut is commonly linked to feelings – 'feeling gutted' or 'gut instinct'.

Being worried or anxious is normal, and the human body is designed to cope with periods of feeling stressed. However, the physical symptoms of anxiety can feel unpleasant, and in themselves can be frightening. Their sudden arrival can become a source of anxiety and fear/concern, creating a vicious circle. Fortunately, there are effective treatments for stress and anxiety (see pp. 247 and 27).

Pain

Pain is defined as 'an unpleasant sensory and emotional experience' and is often frightening and distressing. Emotions change the level of pain we experience. Distress, anxiety and depression can alter the pain threshold and increase the level of perceived pain.

Bereavement

Bereaved close relatives have double the risk of dying within one year compared to close relatives who have not suffered a bereavement. This is particularly so with widowers.

Treatment

One of the most important findings of the past few years is the discovery that the brain can change in response to various stimuli and can repair itself. Just as exercise strengthens muscles, and prolonged rest causes wasting, so our neural connections can be strengthened and weakened.

We know that certain areas of the brain can be damaged by stress and depression. However, there is good evidence that alleviating stress and depression promotes brain repair.

Cognitive behavioural therapy

There is abundant evidence that beliefs, patterns of thinking and patterns of behaviour have a major impact on physical and mental health. Certain patterns of thinking and behaviour can set up different brain circuits, which then become reinforced and can be fired more and more readily.

Some patterns of thinking and behaviour can be damaging and destructive. Changing negative patterns of thinking and behaviour is the fundamental objective of cognitive behavioural therapy (CBT; see p. 427).

CBT is an effective treatment for many conditions, including anxiety, panic disorder, post-traumatic stress disorder (see p. 187) and depression (see p. 76) as well as chronic fatigue syndrome (CFS/ME; see p. 298) and rehabilitation from heart disease.

Medication

Antidepressants can activate areas of the brain concerned with mood.

The importance of love and support

Nurture and touch are basic human needs. Babies that are cuddled gain weight much faster than babies that are not touched. Traumatized children grow less well and there is evidence that unhappiness and distress in childhood is linked to poorer health in adulthood; some studies have shown links between child-hood abuse and several chronic conditions. As adults, we continue to benefit from human touch. Research shows that patients who are regularly touched by their carers tend to recover faster. Mood disorders in adulthood, such as depression, are associated with childhood adversity and are now recognized as risk factors for a range of physical illnesses. A growing number of chronic physical illnesses (irritable bowel syndrome, fibromyalgia, chronic pain and chronic fatigue) are more likely to occur in adults who have experienced emo-tional or physical abuse. We already know that a wide spectrum of chronic illnesses, such as ischaemic heart disease, are associated with mood disorder.

Being married, having children, spending time with people you care for, and feeling a sense of being connected are good predictors of happiness. We are communal animals and enjoy connecting with other human beings, experiencing nurture and social support.

Social support provides measurable health benefits, and protects the indi-vidual against the negative effects of stress. Lack of social support increases the risk of illness.

Even having a good relationship with your doctor can improve your health. Studies show that a good doctor–patient relationship is associated with improved adherence to healthcare advice, less prescribing, improved patient satisfaction, reduced Accident and Emergency department attendance, fewer complaints and less litigation.

Empathy is important in any therapeutic relationship. If you feel under-stood and listened to, then you are more likely to perceive an improvement in health. Being unhappy probably makes life seem longer, but in reality happiness appears to add years, as well as quality, to life.

The power of the positive

There is a growing interest in positive psychology, positive emotions and the science of happiness, because happier people are healthier, and tend to think faster and more creatively. Happiness can have a profound impact on our immune system, autonomic nervous system, hormone levels, health and illness.

What makes us happy? Well, it's not money; per capita income has quadru-pled in the UK since 1950, yet research suggests we are less happy.

It is the extent of an individual's social connections and social support – friends, family, community, workplace – and a sense of meaning in one's life that seem to be the best predictors of happiness and well-being.

Positive mental stimulation, positive mental challenges and physical exercise have been shown to stimulate new brain-cell growth and improve our health. Exercise can help lift depression.

Cognitive behavioural therapy can help the brain 'rewire' and develop more positive neural circuitry. There are strategies for promoting the brain's ability to self-repair, because the brain has been shown to respond positively to nurture, good company in the form of friends and family, a positive attitude, exercise, good diet and adequate sleep.

Sleep

Sleep is necessary for normal physical and mental health. The activity/sleep cycle is controlled by the mid-brain, which is affected by hormones. Stress and depression both have an impact on sleep.

Almost all medically unexplained symptoms are related to poor sleep. Sleep has an impact on the immune system and hormone levels. It is likely that the effects of stress on the immune system are mediated by sleep disturbance. Lack of sleep affects concentration, memory and speed of reaction. Twenty hours without sleep has about the same impact on a person's reaction time as being over the legal limit of blood alcohol for driving a car.

Just as with physical illness, recovery from any mental health problem will be greatly helped by regular and adequate sleep.

Dr Brian Marien

Dr Persaud's conclusion

A dilemma that lies at the heart of the relationship between our minds and our brains and bodies is whether we control our brains through conscious will, or whether we are the helpless victims of our brains and bodies. Do we need to take an antidepressant because biological changes in our brains need to be altered chemically, rather like pneumonia needs an antibiotic to help it clear up – or can we *will* ourselves better?

No one knows the answer yet. Research seems to show that difficulties such as depression benefit from both approaches. For example, taking an antidepressant, as well as using cognitive behavioural therapy – which asks us to take responsibility for the way we think, as this influences our emotions – seems to work better than just doing one or the other.

Until recently, the intimate relationship between mind and body, and emotion and disease, was poorly understood. Neuroscience, brain imaging and all the other scientific revelations provide only a glimpse of the complex, often unobservable, relationships between brain, mind and body.

Emotions impact on every area of our lives. They make us who we are, and they provide an excellent example of mind/body interaction. They influence how we think and they have a physical component – they can be pleasant or painful, creating pleasure or suffering.

Emotions are relevant to our survival, as they motivate or drive us to do things, or not do things, and they determine the quality of our lives.

We are now discovering just how important and relevant emotions are to our health and well-being. Knowledge of emotions and other mind/body interactions needs to be part of any science that is concerned with the physical and mental health of human beings. The way forward is to recognize the intimate and integrated relationship of mind and body in each individual.

'The nature of the body can only be understood as a whole,
for it is the great error of our day in the treatment of the human body
that physicians separate the soul from the body.'

Hippocrates

Parenting Problems

Families

Families are fascinating. However close we may have remained to our own parents, however distant we may have become, all of us started out in a family of some kind. And all of us have experienced the stresses and strains of family life along the way.

Families are the stuff of film, of TV soap operas and of newspaper headlines. Whether we laugh at them or cry, we are identifying with their story – remembering similar problems in our own family, or thanking our lucky stars that ours were not so bad.

Despite the horror stories that we hear so often, child abuse is rare in families. When it happens, it can be devastating. Even where the parents' intentions were misguided rather than wicked, it is the effect on the child that counts.

Research has helped to sort out reality from myths and anecdotes, but sometimes the parents' actual experience is more real than what the academics say. Much research, for example, has gone into disproving that there is any such thing as the 'middle child' syndrome, but parents with three children know that the middle one can have special difficulties of their own.

Every family is unique, and what works for one may not work for another. So here, instead, are some general thoughts distilled from the experience of families across similar situations. If that sounds like 'teaching your grandmother to suck eggs', at least it may be comforting to know that the eggs are the same for everyone, even if there is more than one way of sucking them!

Understanding children's behaviour

Parenting is a difficult job; it always has been. When things are going well, it is hard to think of a better vehicle than the family to carry children through all their phases of development to adulthood. But when things are going badly, everyone in the family can feel it.

Think of a child's behaviour as the central piece in a jigsaw of different factors:
- ❖ the child's individual characteristics
- ❖ the stage of development the child has reached
- ❖ the events the child and its family may be struggling with
- ❖ the peer group, culture and community in which the family lives
- ❖ the family structure, history and relationships that the parents bring to bear on the child's behaviour

It is impossible to appreciate the whole picture of the child's behaviour, the parents' problems and the interaction between them unless each piece of the jigsaw is put in place.

Individual characteristics

Children *do* differ, even within the same family. Whatever their sex, physical make-up or intelligence, they will differ in more subtle ways – personality, temperament and coping style. And the difference may be obvious very early on. Even the most sensible parents can be thrown by having a grizzly baby after several more placid ones.

Parents with one bubbly, extrovert child, who is popular with friends and the life and soul of every party, and a more introverted 'loner', who prefers reading or playing computer games in his bedroom, may worry that they have brought up one the right way and the other the wrong way, rather than be happy that their children are individuals.

We used to argue about whether these differences were due to nature (what we are born with – 'She's just like her mother!') or nurture (the influences of our environment – 'It's hardly surprising, living in that family!'). In reality, we are all a mixture of both, and it is this mixture that makes us unique.

Stages of development

Children develop through stages, one after another, as they grow up. Each stage presents a different set of skills to be learned. The young child learns about himself and the world within the safety of the family. The older child makes the first steps into friendships and more difficult relationships in the world outside. The adolescent comes to terms with sexual awareness, a wider sense of identity, how to compromise with the wishes of others, and becoming independent.

You watch your baby realize, for the first time, that just because they can't see the toy that fell off the table, it doesn't stop existing. You applaud your toddler's first hesitant steps. You wave goodbye at the school gate, or send your daughter off on her first 'date'. It's very exciting, but can be worrying too.

Primary school, for example, can be a bit like an extension of home – nearby, with lots of contact between parents and teachers. Everybody knows what is happening in each place and can back each other up in their 'parenting'. Then comes secondary school – 1,000 pupils, 20 miles and a tiring bus journey away, with its strange uniform, academic pressures, initiation rites, children of all ages (some almost adults in their own right) and all of them seeming more confident than your child. Both children and parents can be thrown off balance by this.

Events

On top of all that will be the life events that most families have to face up to. Some of these may seem traumatic – illness, death, house moves, financial disasters, even the break-up of the family itself. Parents wanting to protect their children from the trauma, and to hold their own feelings together in the process, will often shroud the event in secrecy: if we don't talk about it, it will be as if it had never happened.

In reality, if they are to deal with it healthily, children need to be able to share in the event on all levels – in any information, given in language appropriate to their age, and in packages they can take in; in the emotions that everyone will be experiencing; and in any of the rituals that go with it, funerals and the like.

If there is any 'golden rule', it is that children always know more than we think they know. So if a parent says they must 'be strong' for the children's sake, whatever their best intentions, they may trap the children in their lonely knowledge, unable to share their feelings, and perhaps even feeling wrong to have them. Crying *with* your children can sometimes be the strongest act of all.

And parents will need to beware of imposing their own hierarchy of disaster on their children. For the child, the loss of a pet or a girlfriend may be catastrophic. They should not be dismissed lightly with a glib 'There's plenty more fish in the sea.'

The surrounding community

Families do not live in a vacuum. Children move out from them into peer-group friendships, and hostilities, in the community. School is not just an academic hothouse, but a training ground for friendships too. Children who drop out of school miss out on the social opportunities, just as importantly as the work.

The 'good-enough' parent must tread the tightrope between too lax a hold on what is happening to their children outside the home and being so worried about the company they might keep that they smother them. The ability to make good relationships in adulthood begins in co-operative play and reciprocated sleepovers in childhood.

In a diverse world, there may be a contrast between the culture at home and the culture the child experiences outside. This can be enriching for parent and child alike.

Family dynamics

Families are held together by a spider's web of relationships, positive and negative, some closer than others, but all mutually dependent. There is no way of changing one relationship in a family without all the others having to shuffle over to accommodate it.

Upon these relationships are built the roles of family members (who does what) and the family rules (how we do it). There are huge differences, for example, in the way families settle arguments. Some sit down and talk it through together; some retire to opposite ends of the house until it all blows over; some 'elect' two of its members to carry all the feelings for them.

These patterns tend to be handed down through generations. They are part of the family history. This is fine if the method has proved a positive one, but some families are haunted by the ghosts of things going wrong in the past. For instance, it would be very unusual for a parent to allow their child to grieve openly for a loss if the parent had been prevented from doing so in their own childhood.

'Modern' complications

Many families now live in relative poverty. On windswept housing estates built round industries that have died, the tensions may lead to higher rates of family break-up, violence, crime, abuse, alcoholism, drug-taking and school drop-out.

Even in wealthier areas, professional families may struggle to keep up the mortgage, with both parents working flat-out, huge pressures on the children to succeed, and little time for true family feeling.

Traditional family structures may have crumbled. Children may no longer get the training for parenthood that they used to, by helping to look after younger brothers and sisters in large families. Parents are more mobile in their search for work and may have moved a long way from the rest of the family. Grandparents may not be the immediately accessible figures they once were.

Even in the most traditional communities, male and female roles have been shaken up, and adolescents have a commercial identity in their own right, with all its domestic demands and challenges. Good parenting, in some households, may be judged by the money spent on children, rather than the love and security given to them.

And there are now many types of family, none 'better' than others, but very different in structure, implication and needs. There are increasing numbers of single-parent families, by choice or separation, where one person shoulders the everyday burdens of parenting by themselves.

There are reconstructed families, in which step-parents struggle to build a relationship with the children of the partner's former marriage – often in the teeth of the children's resentment and with the 'natural' parent undermining things from the sidelines.

Foster parents give what security they can, over short periods of time, to children who have never known it and test it out at every step. Adoptive parents worry that their child's wish to seek out their family of origin will destroy the relationship they have so carefully built up.

Many adults now choose to have children later in life, facing up to dealing with demanding adolescents in relative old age, just when they might once have expected to be free of parental commitments. Teenage mothers are saddled with the responsibility of looking after a baby when they might still be enjoying the freedom of their own childhood.

Aspects of care

Acceptance: parents should try to accept each of their children for what they are, not what they want them to be. It is not fair for children to carry the frustrated ambitions of others. Finding their own identity and being respected for it is the basis of self–esteem.

Boundaries: this does not mean that you have to accept everything that your children do. 'I still love you, but I don't like what you've done,' is one of the most important messages a child may hear. If boundaries are clear, children will feel safe to experiment within them.

Consistency: parents need to decide on what rules are untouchable in their family, and back each other up – or any child worth their salt will divide and rule themselves. Punishments need to be appropriate, but rewards for good behaviour are always more effective.

Disputes: you wouldn't be human if disagreements did not occur! Many parents feel they should never argue in front of the children. But why not? It is good training for life to see that parents can argue in a civilized way and come to a compromise solution.

Example: contrary to what parents fear, most children grow up to be much like them. This means they take their examples, good and bad, from you. Parents cannot hope to stop children doing something they disapprove of if they are doing it themselves.

Fun: all this begins to sound desperately serious – and often it is. But despite all the work, academic, financial and social pressures, family life should be fun. Enjoy your children while you can – they won't be around for ever.

Generations: 'modern' parents stay younger in dress and outlook than parents were able to in the past. But the generation gap is important. Beware of stealing adolescents' thunder by joining in everything they do. How can they have an adolescent rebellion if there is nothing to rebel against?

Honesty: children do not need to be burdened with every detail of the parents' anxieties, but they do need to know what is going on. Remember, children will invariably find out. If they discover you have lied, how will they ever believe you again? If they remain in the dark, they may fill in the gaps from their imagination with something worse.

Invasions: having said that, privacy in families is important. Parents need time for themselves to foster and repair their relationship. And bodily privacy is crucial for adolescents. Try not to let family life be dominated by battles over the tidiness of their room, or time spent in the bathroom. And try not to read their diary, however tempting it may be!

Jealousies: are a normal part of family life. Young children may resent the arrival of a new baby, particularly if it has special needs that soak up a lot of the mother's time. Giving them a role in looking after the baby may help. Extra privileges earned with age and achievement are a role model for younger children to follow.

Keeping contact: relationships remain important, with parents after the children have left home and with children after a parent has left home through marital separation. And children are still children, however old they become. Sometimes they may need to retreat to you for comfort when adult life becomes unbearable.

Letting go: but parents must also honour their grown-up children's independence. No matter how much we cherish the memories of a time when they were little, we will need to let go – if we don't, our children may find less healthy ways of escape.

More serious scenarios

Despite all these difficulties, most parents get through without the need for help. But some situations are more complicated, and may need professional guidance.

Leanne (15)

Her parents report that Leanne spends hours locked in her room, dressed in black, listening to 'dirge-like' music. She was always a picky eater but now seems to eat very little. She says she is bullied in school, but doesn't want any-body to do anything in case it makes it worse.

She wears a brace on her teeth and has acne. They can't make head or tail of her mood swings – she can be nice one minute, and nasty the next – and they worry that she might be 'schizophrenic', like her great aunt ('who went strange, was admitted to hospital and never came out again'). Leanne has been taken to the GP (without much protest) after breaking up with her boyfriend. Her mother found her diary, in which she said she felt like killing herself.

Comment. Leanne's parents are right to seek help, and Leanne's lack of opposition may mean she's glad of it too. Much of her behaviour could be interpreted as normal adolescence and is unlikely to be a symptom of a psychotic disorder like schizophrenia (see p. 196).

But she might well be depressed (see p. 76), and she certainly needs assess-ing to see if she has an eating disorder (see p. 93). Writing in her diary may be a relief for feelings she might not act upon, but her break-up with the boyfriend could be the last straw. The GP will probably refer her on to a Child and Adolescent Mental Health Service (CAMHS; see Appendix Two, p. 471).

Adam (4)

His mother describes Adam as an 'evil' child, who was a grizzly baby and has had tantrums ever since. She had postnatal depression (see p. 177) after Adam's birth, and Adam's father walked out on them soon afterwards. When she is angry, Adam's mother says he is 'just like his father . . .'

She has remarried, and has a baby by her new partner, born several weeks premature. The baby spent time in the special care baby unit, and needs all his parents' attention at home. The health visitor alerted Social Services because Adam has been slapped for pinching the baby and hiding his toys.

Comment. This is a family under a great deal of pressure – from the anxieties about the baby and unresolved feelings about Adam's father. The relationship between Adam and his mother was undermined from the outset, and he has been the scapegoat ever since.

His behaviour has begun to live up to the role he has been given. He is missing out on any positive attention. Work needs doing with this family on all their relationships, and with Adam on his self-image. He may be as wor-ried about the baby as he is angry. But it will be difficult for these parents to switch from negative to positive feelings about Adam and a careful watch needs to be kept on his welfare.

Kirsty (8)

Kirsty is the eldest child of an Anglo-Indian family. Her father is a company director and her mother a solicitor. They have a big house and a big mortgage, and both are tired out, emotionally stretched and have little time for family life.

Kirsty is said to be a 'gifted' child, who tops all her exams. The parents worry that her potential won't be realized in the local school, are paying for extra tuition, and are considering an expensive boarding school. She is discouraged from playing with local children.

After a bout of flu, Kirsty has developed aches and pains in her legs that have kept her off school. The GP referred her for paediatric investigation, but nothing specific has been revealed. Kirsty's symptoms have worsened to the extent that she can only walk with difficulty, and is frightened to leave the hospital ward. The parents are demanding a second opinion.

Comment. There are many disputes about the nature of Kirsty's illness (which many would call chronic fatigue syndrome; see p. 298). The professionals need to avoid getting into a battle about it that would reflect and aggravate the tensions that already exist in this family.

Blame should be avoided. Everybody is trying to do their best for Kirsty, even if they are sometimes misguided. Tests have at least ruled out a serious physical illness. What Kirsty now needs is a programme of gradual rehabilitation, agreed by all, coupled with a sensitive exploration of some of the psychological issues.

What Kirsty's symptoms have effectively done is remove her from the academic treadmill. The parents may need a lot of support to see the implications of this and listen to what Kirsty wants for her own life.

Gavin (11)

Gavin is the middle of three children adopted together from Social Services care. All of them were abused in their family of origin. The older brother is good at sport and the younger sister is pretty. Gavin himself is physically unattractive; he has hearing difficulties, a slight stammer, is accident-prone, and wets the bed at night.

His teachers say he disrupts the class by playing the clown and he has just been found keeping lookout for older boys who were shoplifting. Only Gavin was caught. The parents wonder if he would be better off back in care.

Comment. It is not uncommon for one child to show the effects of earlier abuse more than others from the same family. Gavin's brother and sister both have positive identities to help them, but Gavin has nothing but problems. Bad behaviour, or plain silliness, may be the only way of getting attention from his peers.

He is a classic target for exploitation by older children. Help for Gavin might start with all his physical problems – none of them individually serious, but together ensuring that he struggles socially, and lowering his self-esteem.

His adoptive parents need to know what behaviour might be caused by the sort of abusive background he has come from, and the fact that only he is showing such behaviour is neither Gavin's fault nor theirs. Social Services need to offer as much support as they can to keep this family together. A further 'rejection' might be catastrophic for Gavin's future.

Dr Mike Shooter

Dr Persaud's conclusion

The children at the centre of these scenarios are all sad, but each of them shows that sadness in their own way – Leanne in her strange behaviour; Adam in his defiant aggression; Kirsty through her physical symptoms; and Gavin by his all-round difficulties. In each case, specialized help may be needed to break the cycle of childhood sadness and parental behaviour.

But this should not be a cause for pessimism. That help *is* there. And meanwhile, most parents and their children enjoy their family life, punctuated though it may be by internal squabbles and external events. We get little or no training for it, and yet most parents carry out their responsibilities with the aid of common sense. All that is needed, on top of that, is a good slice of luck!

Parenting is one of the most difficult things any of us will ever attempt and yet it often receives the least support from the surrounding community.

At the heart of great parenting is an ability to think clearly and dispassionately about a child, without the emotional baggage of a parent's own problems, personality and strong desires or fears for their child. An easier job said than done!

Given that family therapy (see p. 444) can often be of great assistance in a wide variety of parenting problems, it is a grave pity that there is neither more recognition of its value nor more funding for it by mental health services.

Don't worry, MUM— you're just going through a phase...

Physical Illness
and Chronic Pain

A woman who was cured, but didn't get better

M RS ALLEN WAS enjoying her retirement. Her children had left home, and she and her husband had more time to themselves. Then she began to feel increasingly tired. At first she put this down to getting older, but her husband became worried about how pale and ill she was looking, so she went to see her GP.

The GP took some routine blood tests, and then things happened very quickly. Mrs Allen was telephoned by her GP, who had arranged an urgent appointment for her at the local hospital to see a haematologist, a doctor who specialized in blood disorders. At the appointment, the doctor asked Mrs Allen to come into hospital straight away.

After a number of investigations, the doctors were able to give her a diagnosis. She had leukaemia – a blood cancer that had made her anaemic and tired, and had reduced her body's resistance to infection. Mrs Allen was determined to fight the leukaemia and agreed to a course of chemotherapy.

The side–effects of the chemotherapy made her feel sick, gave her diarrhoea and made her hair fall out. She began to feel sad and pessimistic about the future. She felt guilty about the effect that her illness was having on the family.

After a few weeks, the doctors gave Mrs Allen the good news that the chemotherapy was working and they made plans to send her home. However, she remained ill. She continued to feel tired, with no energy, and couldn't get out of bed.

The hospital staff felt that some of her problems could be due to her low mood and asked the hospital psychiatrist to see her. The psychiatrist asked her to tell him about her illness and how she had coped with it. She acknowledged that it had been difficult, and described how she usually dealt with problems in a practical way. If she couldn't tackle a problem directly, or get advice on what to do, she would distract herself by gardening or taking her dog for a walk. In hospital she couldn't do any of these things and felt trapped.

Mrs Allen had coped well at first, despite the painful investigations. The chemotherapy had made her feel sick and very low. Even though it was now finished, she still felt very flat. Things seemed hopeless; she wished she could go to sleep and never wake up again.

The psychiatrist asked if Mrs Allen's family were supportive. She replied that they tried to help, but were often very upset themselves. She had been the strong one in the family, to whom people turned for help. Now that she needed help, the family seemed to find it difficult to know what to do.

The psychiatrist explained that, like many people with a physical illness, she had become depressed. She had had to cope with the diagnosis of her illness, the uncertainty about the future, and all the investigations and treatment. In addition, chemotherapy can sometimes have a direct effect on the brain and contribute to depression. Being stuck in hospital, she had been denied her usual practical ways of coping.

Mrs Allen agreed to try antidepressant medication. The psychiatrist also arranged to meet regularly with her to discuss how she was feeling and he met with the family to discuss how they were coping. He also explained Mrs Allen's diagnosis of depression to the ward staff, who gave her and her family extra time to discuss practical issues about managing the leukaemia, as well as how they were feeling emotionally.

Within a couple of weeks Mrs Allen was feeling much brighter. Her energy started to return, she was able to get out of bed and walk around the ward. Her husband commented that his wife was returning to her old self.

Eventually she went home. The psychiatrist recommended that she continue with the antidepressant medication, particularly as she needed further courses of chemotherapy. The antidepressants were successful in preventing any more episodes of depression, despite the continuing treatment for the leukaemia.

Physical illness and psychological problems

We often talk about the mind and the body as though they were two separate things. It is easy to forget that physical illnesses have psychological consequences, or can trigger psychiatric illnesses – particularly anxiety and depression (see pp. 24 and 76).

Psychological problems are common in people with physical illnesses:
❖ they are twice as likely to be depressed as the general population
❖ one third of patients in a general hospital with physical illness have anxiety or depression
❖ more than half of patients with chronic pain have anxiety or depression

Long-term or chronic pain is a real risk factor for psychological problems. Chronic pain occurs in conditions when healing is slow or doesn't happen at all. You can still feel chronic pain after an illness or injury has healed.

Coping with physical illness

Coping with a physical illness raises many questions:
* what will the diagnosis mean to you?
* what treatments and investigations will you need to have?
* how will it affect your family life, relationships, work and social life?

Having to cope with a physical illness can go on for a long time, particularly in conditions that come and go or lead to a worsening in physical health.

How stressful is a physical illness?

Just how stressful an illness is depends upon a number of factors:
* the illness itself
* the treatments required
* your social situation
* your coping skills

Particularly stressful illnesses include those that involve the brain, such as a stroke or a brain tumour. These illnesses are long term, painful and disabling, and are more likely to lead to depression. Certain drug treatments can cause psychological problems, such as steroids, chemotherapy and some painkillers.

Having friends and family who can provide social support is important. It is helpful to have someone you can confide in, and who understands what you are going through. Without any social support, you are more at risk of psychological problems.

We all have our own ways of coping. Some people focus on practical things, such as seeking information about their illness. Others prefer to focus on their emotions, and can find it useful to join a support group and share their feelings with others.

Some attempts to cope may work against you, however.

❖ You may deny that you have an illness, which means that you don't get the care you need.
❖ You may put your energy into blaming someone else for your problem.
❖ If you have a history of mental health problems, you are more vulnerable to psychological problems, particularly with the stress of physical illness.

Difficulties in identifying and treating psychological problems

There are a number of reasons why psychological problems are not diagnosed in people with physical illness. These include:
❖ an assumption by health professionals or patients that feeling anxious and depressed is understandable, and you will not respond to treatment
❖ reluctance by health professionals to explore emotional issues, because of a lack of time, or a fear that they won't be able to manage them
❖ difficulty in telling the symptoms of depression from those of physical illness
❖ an assumption that your psychological symptoms are part of your physical illness
❖ your reluctance to discuss psychological issues with staff, as they are managing physical health problems
❖ you blame yourself for your health problems
❖ you consider psychological problems as a 'sign of weakness'
❖ patients with chronic pain do not believe that psychological factors play a role in their pain, or that psychological treatments can help

It is important for hospital staff to find out if you are anxious or depressed. Research has shown that simply asking the question 'Are you depressed?' is a simple and straightforward way of finding out if patients have psychological problems.

What does it feel like?

'Normal' distress or depression?

Although anxiety and depression are common in physical illness, it is not easy to distinguish when an emotional reaction to a stressful situation has become a psychiatric illness that requires treatment. This is especially true in the early stages of an illness, when an individual is coming to terms with bad news.

Generally, anxiety or depression go on for longer than 'normal' distress. These feelings will be more intense and will interfere with your life. Clues that someone with a physical illness might be depressed include:

❖ difficulty in coming to terms with their illness
❖ greater physical disability
❖ making a slower recovery than might be expected

Someone who talks about wanting to die, or has thoughts of suicide, is likely to be very depressed (see p. 250).

Symptoms of depression or a physical illness?

Symptoms of depression include:

❖ poor appetite
❖ loss of weight
❖ low energy

These can also be symptoms of the physical illness. When trying to identify depression in someone with physical illness, it is important to concentrate on symptoms such as:

❖ poor social communication
❖ being very 'down' and negative
❖ feelings of guilt or worthlessness

Consequences of anxiety and depression

Psychological problems not only affect your quality of life, but may also increase any disability you have.

Depression can affect your physical illness. You may smoke more and take less exercise. You are unlikely to take your prescribed medicines, or to take part in rehabilitation.

Depression and anxiety can have a direct effect on the physical workings of your body, which may be dangerous:

❖ Depression can make individuals with heart disease more prone to abnormal heart rhythms.

❖ Psychological factors can influence the long-term outcome for people with cancer.

Chronic pain

Chronic pain can make you more irritable than usual. You may feel guilty about being short-tempered. Pain can make sleeping difficult. When you are tired, it is harder to cope.

Pain isn't something we can see, and sometimes people feel that others don't believe how much pain they are in. You may be very frustrated with the health professionals for not being able to cure the pain.

For people in long-term pain, the misery of this can cause anxiety or depression. In turn, depression lowers an individual's pain threshold and makes the feeling of pain worse. A vicious circle of pain and depression can then arise.

What can be done to help?

When should you seek help?

If you have a physical illness, you must seek help if:

❖ your mood does not seem to get better over time
❖ the way you feel affects your everyday life, such as relationships with family or friends
❖ you feel that life is not worth living

It is important to talk about your feelings, or problems, with someone – such as your GP.

Self–help

❖ Just being able to share your problems with someone close to you can bring a sense of relief. It is helpful to talk freely with someone you trust and who doesn't pass judgement. They may be able to remind you that the way you feel is not a 'sign of weakness'.
❖ If there are things that are worrying you about your illness, or that you are uncertain about, ask the doctors or nurses who are treating you. You are likely to cope better if you know about your illness.

❖ Try to eat a healthy, balanced diet. Anxiety and depression can reduce your appetite and make you lose weight. This can make your physical health problems worse.

❖ Make sure that you build some enjoyable activities into your day. If possible, take regular exercise.

❖ Do not drink too much alcohol to lift your mood, or as a painkiller. Alcohol can make you feel worse and can interfere with any other medication.

Individuals with chronic pain may also find the following helpful:

❖ find things to do to distract you from the pain

❖ maintain a good bodily posture

❖ keep active, but don't overdo it

❖ gradually increase activity, and build up your confidence that you can cope with the pain

Medication for anxiety and depression

Sometimes health professionals or patients do not think that antidepressants will help, because the physical illness is an understandable cause of anxiety or depression. However, antidepressants have been shown to be helpful in treating anxiety and depression in a wide range of physical disorders. Just because depression is 'understandable' doesn't mean that it won't improve with treatment.

The choice of antidepressants prescribed depends upon your physical illness and other medications you are taking. Some antidepressants have a higher risk of side-effects related to the heart, and should be avoided in patients who have heart disease. People with physical illness are more sensitive to side-effects, and may need to start on a low dose of antidepressant: the general advice is 'start low, go slow'.

Antidepressants known as selective serotonin re-uptake inhibitors (SSRIs) and other newer antidepressants tend to be the safest and most widely used drugs in individuals with physical illnesses.

Medication for chronic pain

A variety of drugs are used to treat chronic pain.

❖ There are many sorts of painkillers (analgesics). Generally, they reduce or block the transmission of pain signals by the nervous system and the brain.

❖ Anti-inflammatory drugs work by reducing chemical pain messengers, which the body releases at the site of an injury.

❖ Some antidepressants can be an important treatment in chronic pain, even when someone is not ill with anxiety or depression. They can act as painkillers, reducing the transmission of pain signals in the nervous system.

❖ Anticonvulsant drugs, more usually used for the treatment of epilepsy, can help with certain types of pain.

❖ Muscle relaxants can help with pain caused by muscle spasm.

If you are prescribed medication for chronic pain, it is important to follow the advice of the doctors or nurses. Although the drugs can be very effective, they can also cause troublesome side-effects.

Talking treatments

Psychological and spiritual support is important in helping people come to terms with their illness, and may protect you against anxiety and depression. For those who do have psychological problems, talking treatments can be as effective as antidepressant drugs, and the two are often used together.

Talking treatments work by helping you to think clearly about what is happening, and to find ways of coping better with your feelings, thoughts and practical problems.

Which talking treatment should be used is based upon the nature of your problems and the treatments available. One of the most widely used talking treatments is cognitive behavioural therapy (CBT). CBT can help people with chronic pain. CBT can help you to change how you think ('cognitive') and what you do ('behaviour'). These changes can help you understand and manage your thoughts and behaviour, and so feel better. Unlike some of the other talking treatments, CBT focuses on the 'here and now' problems and difficulties.

The aim of the therapy is to help you manage and cope with the pain, and give you back some control over your life. CBT may include advice on stretching, exercise and relaxation, as well as planning everyday activities. This can be important in building up your self-confidence. The therapy can also address negative thinking patterns. (See also p. 427.)

Complementary therapies

Complementary and alternative therapies may help some people. They can make you feel that you are doing something positive, and that you have control in what can otherwise feel like an uncontrollable situation. If you are taking any other medicines, you must speak to your doctor.

Tips for families and friends

It is often those close to the person who notice the signs of anxiety and depression. If you are worried about someone, you should encourage them to seek help from the doctors and nurses who are treating them, or from their GP.

It can be helpful to remind the person that anxiety and depression are common, especially in people with physical illness, and that they can be treated. As a consequence, they will feel better able to cope with their physical illness.

Other things you can do to help someone cope:
❖ spend time with them and let them talk
❖ encourage them to do the things they normally do
❖ make sure they are eating a healthy balanced diet
❖ encourage them not to drink too much alcohol
❖ if they talk about not wanting to live any more, or have thoughts about harming themselves, make sure that their doctor knows this

Caring for someone with physical illness can be exhausting, especially if they also have anxiety or depression. If you are getting worn out, do ask for help yourself.

Dr Jim Bolton
and Dr Siobhain Quinn

Dr Persaud's conclusion

Many believe that disease is either physical (that is, real) or psychological ('all in the mind'), whereas most clinicians today now regard all illness as having psychological as well as physical components.

This view does place demands on specialist clinicians to have been trained in both psychological and physical medicine, so patients may want to consider how the biases of a particular training may slant their therapist in their view of a problem.

It is probably the case that the gold standard of care for all suffering should include physical as well as psychological components, and this remains a major deficiency throughout all of medicine.

SUPPORT ORGANIZATIONS

There are support organizations for people with many physical illnesses. Often these are national organizations that may have local branches. The doctors or nurses treating your physical illness may be able to give you details of these, or you can look for information on the internet. Examples include:

The British Epilepsy Association: *www.epilepsy.org.uk*

The British Heart Foundation: *www.bhf.org.uk*

The Multiple Sclerosis Society: *www.mssociety.org.uk*

Support is also available through organizations that focus on anxiety and depression – see pages 32 and 84.

USEFUL WEBSITES

The Royal College of Psychiatrists publishes a leaflet on *Physical Illness and Mental Health*, and a factsheet for parents and teachers on *Chronic Physical Illnesses: the Effects on Mental Health*. Both are available online at: *www.rcpsych.ac.uk*

The Royal College of Physicians publishes a booklet on Psychological Support for People in Hospital, which is available online at: *www.rcplondon.ac.uk*

i SUPPORT

WEBSITES OUTSIDE THE UK

Australia:
www.ranzcp.org

New Zealand:
www.ranzcp.org

Canada:
www.chp-pcs.gc.ca

South Africa:
www.mrc.ac.za

India:
www.indiatogether.org

FURTHER READING

Manage Your Pain: Practical and Positive Ways of Adapting to Chronic Pain, Michael Nicholas, Allan Molloy, Lois Tonkin and Lee Beston, Souvenir Press, 2000

41

Spirituality

A woman who thought the TV news was about her

A s a child, Nancy often went to church with her family but was always disappointed. 'I liked the surroundings and the services, but I couldn't connect. It was like something was missing. I was always aware of an enormous emptiness in my heart.' Later, she tried to fill this painful void with public acclaim: a naturally talented musician, she became an actress and television presenter. As a celebrity, she started drinking very heavily and using street drugs. She also had a number of unfulfilling relationships.

By her late twenties, Nancy had serious alcohol problems and was in another stagnant relationship. She was then introduced to the practice of meditation and chanting in a Hindu yoga tradition.

One day, after chanting, she began feeling kindness and

generosity towards others. She was uncharacteristically cheerful. 'I felt so merry that I began to feel very connected to the radio. Some points on the news seemed specially meant for my ears.' Further strange experiences, both frightening and wonderful, followed in the next few days. 'In the park, I felt connected to every tree, bird, dog, lake, person, in fact the whole of Nature. I waved at everybody without any fear and, to my amazement, everyone waved back. I really believed I'd cracked the secret of life.'

She began hearing voices and started seeing strange things. She was convinced that her mother had died and linked this with threats to Mother Earth. 'Mother Earth is weeping and we must act now,' she kept shouting loudly at work while preparing for a live television broadcast, to the surprise and alarm of colleagues. She was taken offstage and her parents contacted. That evening, after seeing her doctor, she was admitted to a psychiatric hospital, where she was medicated and detained for twenty–eight days.

Throughout this period a kind of 'Inner Voice' continued. Nancy found this reassuring and helpful. She was told, 'All there is, is love, Nancy. When you see this, you will understand.' She also had a vision of a radiant being in electric–blue robes. 'It communed with me with so much love, saying, "I am who you truly are. Be with me and you will truly understand that all there is, is love." My heart exploded. I have never felt so ecstatic.'

Nancy explained how the lessons continued through her 'Inner Voice' while in hospital. 'I was shown the stages of existence. They were likened to the floors of a house. I was shown that the responsibilities, from those of a cleaner all the way up to a king, were a direct result of soul karma. You couldn't skip a stage. We all had to experience everything.'

Nancy learned to behave properly and not mention her experiences to the nurses and doctors, although this was a life–changing episode for her. She gave up alcohol and drugs immediately; for the last seventeen years she has been a member of Alcoholics Anonymous and has never had a drink or taken drugs. Her career also changed direction. She is now running popular and highly successful singing and chanting workshops for people with mental health problems, particularly drink and drug addicts.

Nancy also recorded a CD of her own autobiographical songs. She has been in a new, loving and meaningful relationship for several years. When you meet her, you discover a generous, vibrant, creative, happy and contented person. She now says of her experience, 'I wish I could have avoided it, but it was really the best thing that happened to me.'

It is sometimes necessary to distinguish between severe mental illness and a period of rapid spiritual growth. Nancy's experiences of elated mood, high energy levels, loss of social inhibitions, grandiose thoughts, visual abnormalities, auditory hallucinations (hearing voices) and so on would normally make a psychiatrist think that she may be suffering from bipolar disorder (see p. 42). This, however, would be an incomplete and poor interpretation of the events in Nancy's case.

What is different about Nancy is her alert awareness and her detailed recall of her inner mental experiences and what was going on around her at the time.

This is just one example of *both* mental illness *and* spiritual emergence, leading to rapid spiritual growth. The psychological and spiritual dimensions are both involved. The consequences – for mental health professionals and patients alike – are that we are wise to be more aware of and sensitive to the spiritual dimension in our lives and work. For psychiatrists, taking a spiritual history or undertaking some form of 'spiritual screening' should be a requirement in each case under assessment.

What is spirituality?

Spirituality is a part of human experience in which psychiatrists are increasingly interested because of its potential benefits to mental health. It is not in itself the same thing as holding a particular religious belief, being religiously observant, or belonging to an established faith tradition.

The way 'spirituality' is described in this chapter is widely used in writing about health care. It can be defined as the experience of a deep-seated sense of meaning and purpose in life, together with a sense of belonging and of harmony in the universe. Spirituality involves a striving for answers about the infinite, and is particularly important in times of stress, illness, loss, bereavement and death. Such concerns involve feelings, and are equally important in young people and for those with learning disability.

While symptom-relief is important in health care, from the spiritual perspective the primary aim is 'holistic' – that is, towards healing of the whole person. This involves personal growth and developing maturity, sometimes through the experience of adversity, hardship and suffering, when we are forced to leave our regular comfort zone, as in encounters with mental ill-health.

How is spirituality distinguished from religion?

Genuine spirituality is inclusive and unifying. It creates a reciprocal sense that to harm another is to harm oneself, and equally that helping others is to help oneself. It applies to everyone, including those who do not believe in God or a higher being. While there are many religions, spirituality is universal, but also unique to each and every person.

What spiritual care can be offered to patients?

Healthcare professionals are increasingly discovering the benefits of paying attention to the spiritual life of people with mental health problems. They find that patients are searching for the following sorts of spiritual care:
- ❖ the opportunity to do something useful or pleasurable – creative art, structured work, enjoying nature
- ❖ to be treated with respect and dignity, producing a feeling of belonging, of being valued and trusted

❖ to be able to express feelings to staff members and to be listened to sympathetically

❖ encouragement to make sense of life's experiences, including illness

❖ permission and encouragement to develop a relationship with God or the Absolute (however the person conceives whatever is sacred); a time, a place and privacy for prayer and worship, reflection and meditation; the opportunity to explore spiritual (and sometimes religious) matters, encouragement in deepening faith, feeling universally connected and perhaps also forgiven

What are the benefits of paying attention to the spiritual dimension?

A group of patients identified the following:

❖ improved self-control, self-esteem and confidence

❖ speedier and easier recovery, helped by the healthy grieving of loss and the chance to attain one's full potential

❖ improved relationships – with self, others and with God/creation/ nature

❖ a new sense of meaning, which fosters hope and peace of mind, helping people to accept and live with continuing problems

Exploring the religious and spiritual aspects of life

A helpful way for psychiatrists or psychologists to begin to understand a person's spirituality is simply to ask, 'What helps and sustains you?' or 'What keeps you going in difficult times?' The answer to this enquiry will usually reveal someone's main spiritual concerns and pursuits, and the doctor will then have two important aspects to consider:

❖ what helpful inner personal resources does the person have that can be encouraged?

❖ what external supports from the community and/or faith tradition are available?

Spiritual concerns are usually deeply personal and few of us are used to talking openly about such things, so the doctor will normally take it slowly – it is probably more therapeutic. Here are some of the questions that doctors and patients are likely to explore together:

Setting the scene: What is your life all about? Is there anything that gives you a particular sense of meaning or purpose?

The past: Emotional stress usually involves some kind of loss, or the threat of loss. Have you experienced any major losses or bereavements? How has it affected you and how have you coped?

The present: Do you feel that you belong and that you are valued? Do you feel safe, respected and have a sense of dignity? Can you communicate freely with other people? Does there seem to be a spiritual aspect to the current problem? Would it help to involve a minister of your faith, or someone from your faith community? What particularly needs to be appreciated about your religious background?

The future: What does the immediate future seem to hold? What about the longer term? Are you worried about death and dying, or about the possibility of an afterlife? Would it be helpful to discuss this more? What are your main fears regarding the future? Do you feel the need for forgiveness about any-thing? What, if anything, gives you hope?

Remedies: What would you find helpful? How might you find such help? Have you considered self-help resources?

Spiritual practices

These span a wide range:

Mainly religious

❖ belonging to a faith tradition and participating in associated community-based activities
❖ ritual and symbolic practices and other forms of worship
❖ pilgrimage and retreats
❖ meditation and prayer
❖ reading scripture
❖ sacred music (listening to, singing and playing), including songs, hymns, psalms and devotional chants

Mainly secular

- ❖ acts of compassion (including work, especially teamwork)
- ❖ deep reflection (contemplation)
- ❖ yoga, t'ai chi and similar disciplined practices
- ❖ engaging with and enjoying nature
- ❖ contemplative reading (of literature, poetry, philosophy, etc.)
- ❖ appreciation of the arts and engaging in creative activities, including artistic pursuits, cookery, gardening, etc.
- ❖ maintaining stable family relationships and friendships (especially those involving high levels of trust and intimacy)
- ❖ co-operative group or team activities, sporting, recreational or other, involving a special quality of fellowship

Most people are spiritually active in some way, often without recognizing it fully. Asking them about this aspect of their lives can help bring it into useful focus when required. Whether part of the problem, as it can be when people experience personal religious or spiritual conflict, or part of the solution, as is also often potentially the case, spirituality is always relevant.

Spiritual values and skills

Spiritual practices help to create and sustain a certain state of mind. This fosters an awareness that serves to identify and promote values such as: creativity, patience, perseverance, honesty, kindness, compassion, wisdom, equanimity, hope and joy. All of these support good healthcare practice.

Spiritual skills include:

- ❖ being able to rest, relax and create a still, peaceful state of mind
- ❖ going deeper into that stillness and observing your emerging thoughts and feelings with emotional stability, in a way that carries over into everyday life
- ❖ using this capacity for deep reflection to connect with your spiritual essence and values, enabling additional skills:
  - being honestly and sincerely self-reflective, taking responsibility for every thought, word and action
  - remaining focused in the present, staying alert, unhurried and attentive
  - developing compassion and an extensive capacity for direct empathic communication with others

- emotional resilience: having the courage to witness and endure distress while sustaining an attitude of hope
- giving without feeling drained
- being able to grieve and let go

An important principle of the spiritual approach to mental health care is 'reciprocity', according to which the giver and receiver of care both benefit. Provided exhaustion and 'burn-out' are avoided, carers naturally develop spiritual skills and values over time, as a result of their devotion to those with whom they engage. Those who are cared for can often, in their turn, give help to others in distress.

Chaplaincy/pastoral care

NHS Trust chaplaincy and pastoral care departments now involve clergy and other people from many faiths and humanist organizations, as well as from Christian denominations. Chaplains, or spiritual advisers as they are sometimes called, are increasingly valued as contributors to the work of multi-disciplinary in-patient and community mental health services.

A modern mental health chaplaincy or pastoral care department should have access to sacred space. The chaplains will have made a point of establishing good relations with local clergy and faith communities and will provide a knowledge base about local religious groups and their traditions and practices. They will be alert to situations in which religious beliefs and activities may prove harmful, or when helpful spiritual practices are being ignored by the mental health service. They should be available for advice on controversial issues such as spirit possession and the ministry of deliverance. Close liaison with the mental health team supports a holistic approach in which the 'whole-person' needs of the individual can be best understood and met.

Psychiatrists, patients and carers should all be fully informed of local chaplaincy services.

Education and research

Research suggests that:

❖ belonging to a faith community
❖ holding religious or spiritual beliefs
❖ engaging in associated practices

are all helpful for mental health. Mental healthcare students and qualified clinicians are increasingly being taught about the value of patients' experiences of the spiritual dimensions of life.

Advice

Spirituality is a deeply personal matter. People are encouraged to discover 'what works best for you'. A routine daily practice involving three elements can be helpful:

❖ regular quiet time – for prayer, reflection or meditation
❖ study of appropriate religious and/or spiritual material
❖ time spent with others of a similar spiritual outlook

It is possible to find advice about spiritual practices and traditions through the resources of a wide range of religious organizations. Secular spiritual activities are increasingly available and popular too. For example, many complementary therapies have a spiritual or holistic element that is not defined by any particular religion (see Chapter 32, p. 308). The internet, especially internet bookshops, the local Yellow Pages, health food shops and bookstores are all good places to look.

Dr Larry Culliford

409

i SUPPORT

USEFUL WEBSITE

The Royal College of Psychiatrists Special Interest Group in Spirituality and Psychiatry:
www.rcpsych.ac.uk/college/specialinterestgroups/spirituality.aspx

WEBSITES OUTSIDE THE UK

Australia:
www.mentalhealth.asn.au

New Zealand:
www.mindnet.org.nz

Canada:
www.phac-aspc.gc.ca

South Africa:
www.sasop.co.za

FURTHER READING

Spirituality and Mental Health: Breakthrough, Philip J. Barker and Poppy Buchanan-Barker (eds), Wiley, 2003

Love, Healing and Happiness, Larry Culliford, O Books, 2007

Spirituality and Mental Health Care: Rediscovering a Forgotten Dimension, John Swinton, Jessica Kingsley Publisher, 2001

Happiness: The 30-Day Guide, Patrick Whiteside, Rider, 2001

Staying Well: Prevention and Mental Health

Preventing psychological problems

> 'Crises refine life. In them you discover what you are.'
>
> *Allan Knight Chalmers*

Most people's response when asked how to 'stay sane' is to suggest doing less, avoiding stress and relaxing more. If we could only withdraw from the problems life throws at us, then indeed we might feel better.

However, we're often caught up by so many demands that suggestions like 'taking more time off' are simply not possible. The key to 'positive mental health' and 'staying sane' is to deal actively with crisis, stress and difficulty.

Given these facts, you would think that 'prevention' would be given higher priority in mental health care. Modern physical medicine has, over the years, spent huge resources on preventative measures, such as vaccination programmes and public health campaigns – but mental health care is still in the Dark Ages in this area. One reason for this is that, whereas physical health is obvious to everyone, good mental health remains a little-known entity.

Perhaps the best way to measure mental health is not to look at how you react to good events, but how you respond to bad ones. The mentally healthy person is not as greatly affected by negative life events, such as bereavement or divorce, as someone who is mentally fragile.

For many years, psychiatry and psychology were focused on treating mental illness and psychological problems, rather than looking at why they start in the first place. This happened partly because of the belief that mental illness cannot be prevented, as its causes remain difficult to understand.

We now know enough about the links between poor coping strategies and future mental illness to be able to advise people on how to prevent most psychological problems.

There has been enormous progress in the prevention of physical illness, such as in the reduction of heart disease and the discouragement of smoking. The techniques used in preventing these illnesses have been very effective, even though their precise causes are still not fully understood.

It is important to identify those things in life that put us at higher risk of mental illness, as well as those which protect us against mental health problems. For instance, if you are having relationship problems and your thinking is irrational, you may become depressed. If you try to reduce or eliminate these risk factors, you will reduce your chances of psychological problems.

Helping yourself

In the past, there has been a lack of agreement about the best ways of coping. However, there are two basic strategies that everyone agrees can help.

Problem–solving

This involves doing something about the stressful circumstances that are upsetting you by removing or reducing them. So, a problem-solving approach to an abusive husband would be to get him to stop being abusive by counselling or, if all else fails, to leave him.

Emotionally focused coping

Put simply, this means that if you can't leave or change an abusive husband, you learn to put up with him.

All coping boils down to either changing the world, so it becomes a less stressful place to be in, or changing yourself, so you learn to put up with an unsolvable problem and become less upset by it.

When faced with a stressful event, you need to start by asking yourself:

❖ is this a solvable problem?
❖ has this problem been faced by others?
❖ how did they solve it?

Problem-solving often requires you to define the problem – that is, to think clearly about what aspect of it presents the most difficulty to you. Once you have a clear idea of what the problem really is, you are in a better position to solve it.

Sometimes the problem is not solvable, and there is nothing you can do about it. Then you need to switch to emotionally focused coping, and to change your 'internal emotional state' to being less upset.

Have you ever wondered how others cope? You hear in the news about those who are trapped under their overturned boat for days in the middle of the ocean, not even knowing if the rescue party has given up and gone home – yet these people seem to cope. How do they do it? You may think it takes a special kind of person to cope in these crises, but coping is really a skill, rather like riding a bicycle, that can be learned by anyone genuinely interested in coping.

At the early stages of upset, it is difficult to think clearly or calmly, and we tend to search wildly for a plan of action. There is a widely agreed really simple way forward in coping with stress, and this is called a 'coping "mantra"' or 'rational thought statement resonse to crisis'.

The coping mantra

Step 1. 'Because of this terrible event that has happened to me, I am certain to feel dreadful, indeed I should absolutely expect to feel bad. It would be all the more astonishing if I did not. However, let me just review exactly how bad I should feel about this. I should not try to deny or squash my feelings, but I should also not exaggerate them and get them out of proportion.'

Step 2. 'Even if this actually is the most horrendous possible thing that could happen to me, the best way of dealing with it is to see what practical, constructive thing I can do right now to improve it as much as possible.'

Step 3. 'If there really is no productive thing I can do right now, there is absolutely nothing to be gained by worsening my morale by dwelling or obsessing on a situation I can do nothing about now. After I have checked I really can do nothing more about this right now, I could absorb myself by doing something distracting, which will help my mood and my morale. If I am feeling a little better, I will be in a better position to help myself by being more positive and creative. In this crisis I need all the help I can get, so I shall try to help myself and not make things worse for myself.'

Explaining the coping mantra

This coping statement is divided into three parts.

Step 1. involves accepting upset as an inevitable part of crisis. Often people seek help to alleviate their distress, which is completely understandable, given their circumstances. Do not make your problem worse by adding in more work – trying to cope with your emotions, as well as coping with your problem. Allowing yourself to be panicky is something many people have difficulty doing, and some even seek therapy to get permission to be upset.

A good example of this is crying. Many people, perhaps especially men, try to avoid crying no matter how upset they may feel. However, the evidence is that crying usually leaves you feeling a little better. Exactly why crying achieves this is still unknown, although there is some evidence that tears shed from grief have a different chemical make-up than tears shed for other reasons. It is possible that crying relieves distress because it is a mechanism by which the body sheds some kind of toxin, which builds up as a result of distress.

Crying also signals to others our upset and need for help or comforting. Even crying in private seems helpful in relieving pain. So it may be the physical acknowledgement of our misery to ourselves that stops us fighting our own emotions and allows us to release and express our agony. This takes away some of our tension. Crying often signals the collapse of our ability to fight our distress, and can help us move on to the next stage of coping.

Step 2. involves checking to make sure your emotional reaction is based on a sound rational evaluation of your situation. What is the worst possible thing that could really happen to you now, or that you fear? What is the evidence for that appraisal? Is your dread a reflection of a realistic appraisal of how bad things are, or might be?

Do you need more information before you can properly judge how bad things are – in which case a good form of coping is to postpone your evaluation of just how bad things are until you obtain the relevant information, or advice from friends. A good way of coping is to seek the guidance of those who have been in the same situation themselves.

Step 3. It is only when you have checked just how bad things are, and tried to see what positive and constructive thing you can do to help yourself, that you should try to distract yourself or take your mind off things.

So learn the coping mantra and practise using it, and soon you will find your coping improves. Plan to cope, believe you can cope, learn to cope and you will find that you will cope.

The brain

There has been a lot of research looking at whether serious mental illness is caused by the brain not functioning properly. However, new research suggests the opposite – that severe distress linked to mental illness may actually produce physical brain damage.

Areas of the brains of soldiers who had seen military combat were measured using magnetic resonance imaging brain scanners. The part of their brain linked to memory, called the hippocampus, was found to be smaller than that of control subjects. The researchers concluded that the length of time soldiers were exposed to stressful conditions of combat is linked to a reduction in this part of the brain's volume. In other words, the more combat you saw, the smaller your hippocampus became.

Research has also shown that the exceptional release of stress hormones under conditions of extreme strain can cause brain damage. Similar reductions in hippocampal volumes were found in patients not exposed to stressful situations, but who had elevated stress steroid hormone release due to a medical hormone disorder.

You may feel that brain damage from experiencing extreme distress is unlikely to affect you if you steer clear of military combat. However, the more worrying finding is that this reduction in hippocampal volume has also been found in people who are depressed and have never been in a war. The length of time they were seriously depressed seems to predict how small their hippocampi became.

These new findings do raise the concern that poor mental health might in itself produce brain changes, and could make the person more vulnerable to psychological problems in the future.

Therefore the sooner you receive help for a psychological problem, the better your prospects for the future.

Dr Raj Persaud

WEBSITES OUTSIDE THE UK

Australia:
www.dhi.gov.au

South Africa:
www.hst.org.za

New Zealand:
www.mindnet.org.nz

FURTHER READING

Staying Sane: How to Make Your Mind Work for You, Dr Raj Persaud, Bantam Press, 2000

Physical Activity and Mental Health, William P. Morgan (ed.), Taylor & Francis, London, 1997

Understanding and Managing Stress: Readings, John D. Adams, Pfeiffer Wiley, 1980

Primary Prevention for Children and Families, M. Frank (ed.), Haworth Press Inc., Birmingham, New York, 1985

Preventing Mental Health Disturbances in Childhood, Stephen E. Goldston, American Psychiatric Publishing Inc., Arlington, Virginia, 1990

i SUPPORT

Stigma and Discrimination Against People with Mental Illness

The woman who wasn't allowed to drive

VERONICA QUALIFIED AS a librarian. After finishing her first degree she went on to complete her PhD. But after the start of her mental health problems she began to learn from her own experience about how her 'record' would limit where and how she could travel.

'My problem is actually about insurance and driving. I used to live in my car – I used to drive everywhere. And then I lost my driving licence, and to reapply I had to answer a long set of questions. One of the questions said, "Have you ever suffered from mental illness?" and like an idiot I said yes. Most of the people I know lie. So I lost my driving licence. One of the executives of the local mental health group was a barrister and she agreed to appeal it for me. We had to go to court for the appeal and they renewed my licence for a year.'

Veronica's experience of trying to regain her licence proved relentlessly frustrating. She reapplied, heard nothing, and just when she thought she was not going to get a renewal, 'One day this letter came saying that they had renewed my licence for three years. I was stunned, and I was very pleased. And then about two months later another letter came, saying that they had sought further medical advice and that they were only going to renew it for one year after all, which was very disappointing.' She was very, very angry. 'There are all these people driving around who've got endorsements. They drive when they're drunk. Younger men who are totally reckless, and I'm a very safe driver, and they won't give me a licence, but they do give them to these other people. It just feels very unfair. So I gave up trying to get my licence back.'

Veronica's freedom to travel has also been severely compromised by limits on her ability to buy travel insurance. In order to get a visa to go to Australia, she had to get travel insurance and health insurance, but was baffled by the blanket ban on people with mental health problems in the insurance policy. Now, reluctantly, when Veronica wants to travel to other countries, she lies. 'Nothing happens, and they don't find out. I don't know what would happen if I ticked the "Yes" box.'

Not being able to buy insurance has also stopped Veronica exercising other important civil rights, such as owning property. 'My partner and I did buy a flat, and we were told that if we wanted a joint mortgage we needed joint health insurance, and I thought "Well, I'm just not doing this, I'm just not going to put myself through it all again." But that did mean that I was not an owner of the flat – it was sole-owned by my partner. Because we weren't married, I don't know what would have happened if, say, he had died. What rights would I have had?'

Veronica has even found her credibility as a victim of crime questioned because of her mental illness. Once she went home for the weekend – her first visit home from hospital – and found that her maisonette had been broken into. 'My place was devastated. It was dreadful.' To make an insurance claim for a burglary she needed a police report number. When she told the detective sergeant that she had been in hospital, he obviously thought that people with mental records were not to be believed and added, 'You won't make a credible witness. No Crown Prosecution Service is going to put you on the stand with the record that you have got.' It wasn't until this detective sergeant agreed that she was 'to be believed', despite her record, that she could make an insurance claim.

What is stigma?

Put simply, stigma can be seen as three problems, all of which need to be tackled:
- ❖ problems of knowledge (ignorance)
- ❖ problems of attitude (prejudice)
- ❖ problems of behaviour (discrimination)

What does it feel like to be on the receiving end of stigma?

Money, employment and leisure

A major problem for many people with mental illness is finding and keeping a job. Rates of unemployment among people with mental illness are extraordinarily high, sometimes up to 90 per cent. Many people feel a terrible dilemma about whether or not to mention having a mental illness when applying for a job, and find themselves in a 'no-win' situation. Tell and you will probably not get the job. Don't tell and you cannot expect any special understanding or help later if you do get the job.

'My illness, depression and stress have been exacerbated by my debt problem. As a result I cannot get well enough to go back to work to earn money to pay the debts.'

A hard reality for people with mental illness who cannot find jobs is that their income on welfare benefits is very limited, so that many cannot afford new clothes or a holiday, for example.

> 'Due to medication I have put on a lot of weight and I have outgrown my clothes. Due to my income I cannot afford to buy new ones.'

Nor can they afford usual social activities, such as going out to a bar or café, which can have a demoralizing effect.

> 'All in all I find the experience of being on a low income degrading. I feel I am being punished for being ill and as if it is my fault, which in turn makes me more depressed. You see others buying such lovely things and I can have none of it. It really hurts.'

Travel and insurance

Another important limitation is the reluctance of doctors to allow people with mental illness to drive, as Veronica has found. A further important limit to travel is insurance. One survey in Britain found that a quarter of people with mental illness said that they had been refused insurance or other financial services. This may well be unlawful. In the UK, the Disability Discrimination Act 1995 makes it illegal to provide goods, facilities and services to a disabled person (including people with mental health problems) on terms which are unjustifiably different from those given to other people.

Not a full citizen

Some basic human rights can be put at risk for people with mental illness. Voting is one example. In the UK, in-patients are able to vote as long as they have a non-hospital address and they have 'capacity' to vote. In practice some compulsorily detained and long-term patients, who have only a hospital address, lose their right to vote. The loss of this vital democratic right is an important expression of social exclusion. As one person puts it, 'I vote, I count.'

Another right accorded to most citizens, but often withdrawn from people with mental illness, is jury service. In England, under the Juries Act of 1974, there is a blanket exclusion that means 'mentally disordered persons' are ineligible to serve on a jury. Since the lifetime prevalence of mental disorders is now understood to be about half of the adult population, such restrictions, consistently applied, might seriously deplete the pool of available jurors! By comparison, for people with physical disabilities jury service eligibility is considered on a case-by-case basis by the judge concerned.

Personal safety

People with mental illness are more often the victims of violence than the general population, and are sometimes even far from safe within mental health services.

> 'I've been abused in the street. I've had my house broken into twelve times and had a knife put through the door. All in an effort to try and drive me out. And I'm the one who's supposed to be nasty and violent.'

Unjust exclusion

Sometimes unexpected types of rejection and exclusion are found, for example not being able to book a hotel room for a meeting. In a letter to the Editor of the *Irish Times*, 24 November 2003, the Irish Advocacy Network (IAN), an Ireland-wide movement that fights for the rights of individuals who have experienced mental health problems, had this experience:

> ... 'IAN set about organising a three-day conference earlier this year. Employees telephoned several hotels asking if they were able to facilitate the conference. They were astounded at several responses and suspected that hotel staff were reluctant to facilitate a conference whose audience for the first two days would consist of people with mental illness.
>
> 'One hotel quoted an extraordinary price of €126,000. Another was concerned that medical or professional representatives would not be present during the conference to look after the "ill". We were finally accepted by Jackson's Hotel, Ballybofey, Co. Donegal. Jackson's turned out to be a warm, friendly place with excellent staff and a good quality of service.
>
> 'We are offended that people continue to believe that individuals with mental health problems are unable to be responsible and capable citizens. We believe that this experience confirms the extent of ignorance and prejudice of mental health that prevails in our society. This should be extremely worrying to us all as mental ill health is increasingly prevalent in our society.

'Our conference was a great success. We would like to thank the staff of Jackson's Hotel for their open-mindedness and for treating us as equal citizens in a respectful and courteous manner. Yours, etc.'

Paddy McGowan
Irish Advocacy Network Management Committee, Rooskey, Monaghan

What can be done to help?

At work there are many ways of helping someone with mental health problems (called 'reasonable adjustments' under the Disability Discrimination Act).

❖ For people with concentration problems, having a quieter workplace with fewer distractions rather than a noisy, open-plan office, with a rest area for breaks.

❖ More, or more frequent, supervision than usual to give feedback and guidance on job performance.

❖ Allow a person to use headphones to block out distracting noise.

❖ Flexibility in work hours so that the person can attend healthcare appointments, or work when not impaired by medication.

❖ A buddy/mentor scheme to provide on-site orientation and assistance.

❖ Clear person specifications, job descriptions and task assignments to assist people who find ambiguity or uncertainty hard to cope with.

❖ For people likely to become unwell for prolonged periods, it may be necessary to make contract modifications specifically to allow whatever sickness leave they need.

❖ A more gradual induction phase – for example with more time to complete tasks – for those who return to work after a prolonged absence, or who may have some cognitive impairment.

❖ Improved disability awareness in the workplace to reduce stigma and to underpin all other accommodations.

❖ Re-allocation of marginal job functions which are disturbing to an individual.

❖ Allow use of accrued paid and unpaid leave for periods of illness.

More generally, what types of change are needed?

Action	By
Introduce supported work schemes.	Mental health services with specialist independent sector providers.
Provide psychological treatments to improve cognition, self-esteem and confidence.	Mental health and general health services.
Give credit to applicants with a history of mental illness when hiring staff.	Health and social care agencies.
Provide reasonable adjustments/accommodations at work.	Mental health providers engaging with employers and business confederations.
Inform employers, service providers and educators of their legal obligations under disability laws – and wider equalities laws for people facing multiple discrimination, e.g. on grounds of race, gender, etc.	Employers' confederations.
Deliver and evaluate the widespread implementation of targeted interventions with targeted groups, including schoolchildren, police and healthcare staff.	Education, police and health commissioning and providing authorities.
Provide accurate data on mental illness recovery rates to mental health and primary care practitioners.	Professional training and accreditation organizations.
Implement measures to support care plans negotiated between staff and consumers.	Mental health provider organizations and consumer groups.

What can mental health staff do to reduce stigma and discrimination?

Action	By
● Develop new ways to offer diagnoses.	● Mental health staff.
● Have information packages for service users/consumers and family members that explain causes, nature, treatments and prognoses of different types of mental illness.	● Mental health staff, charities.
● Actively provide factual information against popular myths.	● Mental health staff.
● Develop and rehearse accounts of mental illness experiences which do not alienate other people.	● Mental health staff and consumer groups.

Conclusion

It is clear that consumer groups increasingly seek to change the terms of engagement between mental health professionals and consumers, and to move from paternalism to negotiation. It is time to stop thinking that stigma is inevitable and unchangeable, but instead to see exclusion from proper health care as one of the many ways in which people with mental illness are systematically discriminated against. One remedy is clear: to apply the Disability Discrimination Act equally for people with disabilities relating to both physical and mental illness. But this is much more than just a question of legal procedure. It means that winning full parity in how legal entitlements are put into practice for disabled people comes to be seen as part of a wider mental health civil rights movement.

Aliya Kassam, Dr Ann Law
and Professor Graham Thornicroft

SUPPORT ORGANIZATIONS

The goal of the **UK Disability Rights Commission** is 'a society where all disabled people can participate fully as equal citizens': *www.drc-gb.org*

The **MediaWise Trust** promotes, for the benefit of the public, compliance with ethical standards of conduct and with the law by journalists, broadcasters and all others engaged in or responsible for the media: *www.mediawise.org.uk*

A source of evidence-based information on a range of mental illnesses, provided by **Rethink** and the **Institute of Psychiatry**, King's College London: *www.mentalhealthcare.org.uk*

The Global Programme to Fight the Stigma and Discrimination because of Schizophrenia of the **World Psychiatric Association (WPA)** aims to: increase the awareness and knowledge of the nature of schizophrenia and treatment options; improve public attitudes about those who have or have had schizophrenia and their families; and generate action to eliminate discrimination and prejudice: *www.openthedoors.com*

The 'See Me' campaign challenges stigma and discrimination around mental ill-health in Scotland: *www.seemescotland.org*

SHiFT is an initiative of the **National Institute for Mental Health** in England (NIMHE) to tackle stigma and discrimination surrounding mental health issues. Its aim is to create a society where people who experience mental health problems enjoy the same rights as other people: *www.shift.org.uk*

*i*SUPPORT

i SUPPORT

WEBSITES OUTSIDE THE UK

Australia:
www.mmha.org.au

Canada:
www.canadian-health-network.ca

India:
www.indiatogether.org;
www.scarfindia.org

New Zealand:
www.likeminds.govt.nz

South Africa:
www.scienceinafrica.co.za
www.sahealthinfo.org

FURTHER READING

Shunned: Discrimination Against People with Mental Illness, G. Thornicroft, Oxford University Press, Oxford, 2006

Don't Call Me Nuts: Coping with the Stigma of Mental Illness, P. W. Corrigan and R. Lundin, Recovery Press, Chicago, 2001

Changing Minds, Our Lives and Mental Illness, R. Ramsay, A. Page, T. Goodman and D. Hart (eds), Gaskell, London, 2002

Therapies, Treatments and Medication

Cognitive Behavioural Therapy (CBT)

CBT is a way of talking about:
* how you think about yourself, the world and other people
* how what you do affects your thoughts and feelings

CBT can help you to change how you think ('cognitive') and what you do ('behaviour') and so feel better. Unlike some of the other talking treatments (see p. 438), it focuses on 'here and now' problems and difficulties. Instead of focusing on the causes of your distress or symptoms in the past, it looks for ways to improve your state of mind now.

It is as effective as medication for many problems, including:
* anxiety
* depression
* panic
* agoraphobia and other phobias
* social phobia
* bulimia
* obsessive compulsive disorder
* post-traumatic stress disorder (PTSD)
* schizophrenia

How does CBT work?

Most of us, when we are stressed, tend to dwell on our problems. We either get them out of proportion or underestimate our ability to deal with them.

CBT can help you to make sense of overwhelming problems by breaking them down into smaller parts. This makes it easier to see how they are connected, how they affect you – and how you might deal with them. These parts are:

❖ a situation (a problem, event or difficult situation)
❖ thoughts
❖ moods/emotions
❖ bodily/physical feelings
❖ actions – the things we do

Each of these areas can affect the others. How you think about a problem can affect how you feel physically and emotionally. It can also alter what you do about it.

So, identifying and understanding the connections between these areas is called a 'five-areas assessment'. Here is an example of how this might be done.

John's wallet

As John is about to go shopping, he suddenly realizes that he cannot find his wallet (**life situation/practical problem**). He jumps to the worst conclusion: that his wallet and credit cards were stolen the last time he was out. He fears that the thief will run up a large debt on his credit cards (**thinking**). This makes him feel anxious (**feelings/emotions**). He begins to notice a sick feeling in his stomach and a strong sense of tension throughout his body. He feels sweaty and clammy and a pressure in his head (**physical sensations**). He contacts his credit-card company and bank to cancel the cards (**behaviour**).

He phones his friend Anne to tell her what has happened. She is sympathetic and encourages him to try to remember where he last saw the wallet and to look around the house to see if he can find it. John is pleased that he has called her, because he now feels a little calmer. He promises to phone Anne back that evening to let her know what's happened.

Later that day he finds the wallet in his coat pocket, where he left it the day before. He doesn't phone Anne back to let her know he has found it because he is worried that she will think he is stupid. John feels angry at him-

self and beats himself up mentally about it ('You idiot – you're so stupid!') – and this makes him feel even worse.

How John interpreted the situation was both *extreme* and *unhelpful*. He ended up feeling both worried and down – he can't even buy anything now because he's cancelled his credit cards.

John's five–areas assessment

John's Wallet

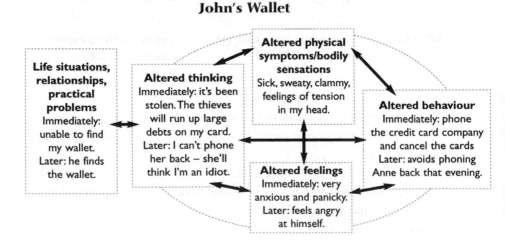

Each of the five areas affects the other four, for better or worse.

A friend who doesn't speak

There are helpful and unhelpful ways of reacting to most situations, depending on how you think about them:

		Unhelpful	Helpful
Situation:	You've had a bad day, feel fed up, so go out shopping. As you walk down the road, someone you know walks by and, apparently, ignores you.		
Thoughts:		He/she ignored me – they don't like me.	He/she looks a bit wrapped up in themselves – I wonder if there's something wrong?
Emotional feelings:		Down.	Concerned for the other person.
Physical:		Stomach cramps, low energy, feel sick.	None – feel comfortable.
Action:		Go home and avoid the person.	Get in touch to make sure they're OK.

The same situation has led to two very different results, depending on how you thought about the situation. How you *think* has affected how you *felt* and what you *did.*

In the example in the left-hand column, you've jumped to a conclusion without very much evidence for it – and this backfires, because it has led to:

❖ a number of uncomfortable feelings

❖ an unhelpful behaviour

If you go home feeling depressed, you may well then brood on what has happened and feel even worse. If you get in touch with the other person, there's a good chance you'll feel better about yourself. If you don't, you won't have the chance to correct any misunderstandings about what he or she thinks about you.

We can also give this situation a five-areas assessment:

This 'vicious circle' can create new situations that make you feel worse. When we are distressed, we are more likely to jump to conclusions and to interpret things in extreme and unhelpful ways.

CBT can help you break this vicious circle of altered thinking, feelings and behaviour. When you see the parts of the sequence clearly, you can change them – and so change the way you feel and respond. CBT aims to get you to a point where you can 'do it yourself' and work out your own ways of tackling these problems.

Walking Down the Street

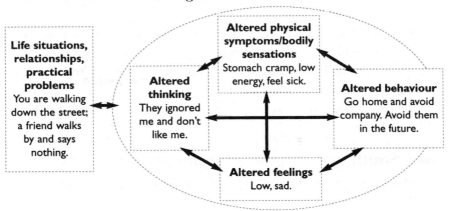

Life situations, relationships, practical problems
You are walking down the street; a friend walks by and says nothing.

Altered thinking
They ignored me and don't like me.

Altered physical symptoms/bodily sensations
Stomach cramp, low energy, feel sick.

Altered behaviour
Go home and avoid company. Avoid them in the future.

Altered feelings
Low, sad.

What does CBT involve?

CBT takes place in many different areas – GP practices, outpatient departments of hospitals, or community mental health centres. The therapist may be a doctor, nurse, social worker, occupational therapist, counsellor or psychologist.

CBT can be done individually or with a group of people. It can also be done from a self-help book, by attending a group or further education class, or via a computer program. If you have individual therapy:

❖ You will usually meet the therapist for between 5 and 20 weekly or fortnightly sessions. Each session will usually last between 30 and 60 minutes.

❖ In the first 2–4 sessions, the therapist will check that you can use this sort of treatment and that you feel comfortable with it.

❖ The therapist will also ask you questions about your past life and background, as well as how you are feeling now. This will lead to a 'formulation' summary (see below) to help you understand why you are feeling as you do.

Example formulation summary

Joan Smith is a forty-year-old married woman whose husband left her three weeks ago after she found out he had been having an affair. Since then, Joan has been distraught, feeling low, weepy and unable to enjoy anything.

Even though it was he who had the affair, she blames herself and thinks, 'I've been a terrible wife'. She thinks that 'I'll never get another man', and that her life is over. She is also 'mind-reading' her friends and the rest of the family – 'They will think I was responsible for ruining the marriage' – which isn't what they think at all.

She is sleeping fitfully and waking earlier than usual, still tired. This makes her feel worse and she is not answering the phone or door when people call. She is exhausted and is drinking more than usual to get off to sleep. This does not help her sleep and is making her mood worse.

She has thought of taking an overdose, and is storing up paracetamol tablets with this in mind.

Joan Smith's five–areas assessment

This analysis of the problem will help you to decide what you want to work on. You can then set short-, medium- and long-term targets that you can approach step-by-step in the next therapy sessions.

Your therapist may ask you to keep a thought diary. This will help you to identify your individual patterns of thoughts, emotions, bodily feelings and actions.

Together you will look at your thoughts, feelings and behaviours to work out:

❖ if they are unrealistic or unhelpful
❖ how they affect each other, and you

The therapist will then help you work out how to change unhelpful thoughts and behaviours. For any particular thought, you can use the 'Thought

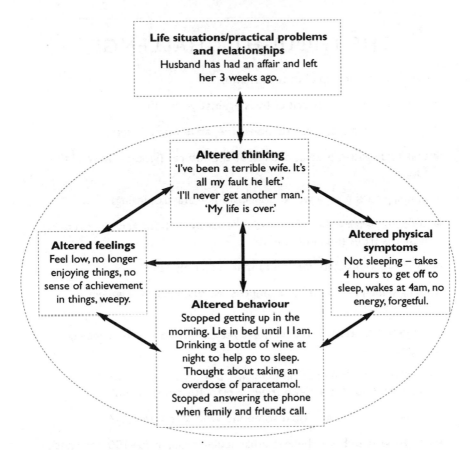

Life situations/practical problems and relationships
Husband has had an affair and left her 3 weeks ago.

Altered thinking
'I've been a terrible wife. It's all my fault he left.'
'I'll never get another man.'
'My life is over.'

Altered feelings
Feel low, no longer enjoying things, no sense of achievement in things, weepy.

Altered physical symptoms
Not sleeping – takes 4 hours to get off to sleep, wakes at 4am, no energy, forgetful.

Altered behaviour
Stopped getting up in the morning. Lie in bed until 11am. Drinking a bottle of wine at night to help go to sleep. Thought about taking an overdose of paracetamol. Stopped answering the phone when family and friends call.

Challenge' (see box overleaf). Finally, you may need to learn some new skills – problem-solving, managing your time or being assertive – and ways of tackling problems (like reduced activity, avoidance, unhelpful behaviours or drinking too much) that are making you feel worse.

Homework tasks: putting things into practice

It's easy to talk about doing something, but it can be much harder to actually do it. So, after you have identified what you can change, your therapist will recommend 'homework' – where you can plan ways of putting into practice these changes in your everyday life. Depending on the situation, you might be asked to:

❖ question a self-critical or upsetting thought, using the thought review approach

❖ experiment and try out new skills to test how well they work

THE THOUGHT CHALLENGE

Label it as an unhelpful thought. Am I:

- being my own worst critic? (bias against yourself)

- focusing on the bad in situations? (negative mental filter)

- making negative predictions about the future? (gloomy view of the future)

- jumping to the very worst conclusion? (catastrophizing)

- second-guessing that others see me badly without actually checking if that is true? (mind-reading)

- taking responsibility for things that aren't my fault?

- using unhelpful, extreme or impossible *must/should/ought/got to* statements?

Stop, think and reflect: don't get caught up in the upsetting thought.

Move on: don't be put off from what you were going to do. Keep active. Face your fears. Keep to your plan. Respond helpfully.

Ask yourself what would someone who loved you say?

Rate how much you believe a particular thought (0–100 per cent).

Ask the seven Thought Challenge questions:

- What would I tell a friend who said the same thing?

- Am I basing this on how I feel rather than the facts?

- What would other people say?

- Am I looking at the whole picture?

- Does it really matter so much?

- What would I say about this in six months' time?

- Do I apply harder standards to myself than I do to other people?

Experiment: test it out. Come to a balanced conclusion.

- Act against the original extreme. Act on your new balanced conclusion. See what happens.

- Finally, come to a summary based on everything you have learned.

Re–rate how much you believe the original upsetting thought (0–100 per cent), and the new balanced conclusion.

Remember this process takes time. By practice, you will build up your confidence in using the approach.

NB: A downloadable credit-card sized version of this process is available free of charge for download from *www.livinglifetothefull.com*

At each therapy session, you discuss how you've got on since the last session. Your therapist can help with suggestions if any of the tasks seems too hard or does not seem to be helping.

Your therapist will not ask you to change things too quickly – you decide the pace of the treatment and what you will and won't try. There won't be any surprises in treatment – everything is done at a pace that helps you move forwards, but not so quickly that things seem too difficult.

The strength of CBT is that you can continue to practise and develop your skills after finishing the sessions. This makes it less likely that your symptoms will return.

Problems getting cognitive behavioural therapy

There aren't enough qualified CBT therapists to go round – so, as a start, it might be worth trying a CBT self-help book, computer package or website (see p. 437) .

How effective is CBT?

❖ It is one of the most effective treatments for conditions where anxiety or depression is the main problem. (See pp. 24 and 76.)

❖ It is the most effective psychological treatment for moderate and severe depression, and is as effective as antidepressants for many forms of depression. For severe depression, CBT should be used with antidepressant medication. When you are very low, you may find it hard to change the way you think until antidepressants have started to make you feel better.

❖ There is some research to suggest CBT may be better than antidepressants at preventing depression coming back. If necessary, you can have a 'refresher' course.

❖ CBT may be slightly more effective than antidepressants in treating anxiety, and it is the treatment of choice for panic attacks (see p. 26).

However, CBT isn't for everyone, and another type of talking treatment may work better for you (see p. 438).

What problems might I have in using CBT?

If you are feeling very low and have difficulty concentrating, it can be hard, at first, to get the hang of CBT – or, indeed, any psychotherapy. This may make you feel disappointed or overwhelmed. A good therapist will pace your sessions so you can cope with them. It can also be difficult to talk about feelings of depression, anxiety, shame or anger.

How long will treatment last?

A course may last from six weeks to six months. It will depend on the type of problem, and how treatment is working for you. The availability of CBT varies and there may be a waiting list.

Dr Chris Williams

Dr Persaud's conclusion

While CBT is now widely regarded as the treatment of choice for many of the commonest psychological problems, it still needs a competent therapist. Check, not just that your therapist is delivering CBT, but that he or she has adequate experience and training in this area – membership of some of the key organizations might be a helpful guide.

USEFUL WEBSITES

British Association for Behavioural and Cognitive Psychotherapies: *www.BABCP.com*

Free online CBT life-skills course using the five-areas model supported by the Scottish NHS: *www.livinglifetothefull.com*

Mood Gym site to prevent depression: *www.moodgym.anu.edu.au*

WEBSITES OUTSIDE THE UK

Australia:
www.healthinsite.gov.au

New Zealand:
www.rational.org.nz

FURTHER READING

Overcoming Depression and Low Mood: A Five Areas Approach, Christopher J. Williams, Hodder Arnold, 2006

Acknowledgements: The five-areas model examples and the thought review questions are reproduced by permission of Dr C. Williams. The cartoon illustrations are by Keith Chan and are taken from *Overcoming Depression and Low Mood* (second edition) by C. Williams (2006), published by Hodder Arnold Publishers. Reproduced with permission.

i SUPPORT

Other talking treatments

A girl whose parents blamed themselves

MIRIAM IS NOW seventeen, and she was diagnosed with anorexia nervosa when she was ten years old. She suddenly stopped eating and lost weight quickly; eventually she had to be admitted to hospital. It was a terrible shock for the family.

In hospital, with the help of a dedicated team of paediatricians and nurses, Miriam gained weight quickly, but once she went home it started all over again. Within eight months she was re-admitted to hospital. This time she stayed for three months, and when her target weight had been achieved, her parents were pleased to have their girl back in a healthy state. But Miriam became more and more depressed. She was seen by a child psychiatrist, who prescribed antidepressants and saw her from time to time.

Eventually, at thirteen years old, she tried to kill herself. She was then admitted to an adolescent unit, where she stayed for over six months. Once Miriam was discharged, everything went back to square one – she started dieting again. Her parents threatened to take her back to hospital if she lost any more weight. Soon she had to be re-admitted.

Afterwards, Miriam stopped going to therapy. She tried to join the youth group at her synagogue, but everyone seemed so different and in control of their lives, so she stopped attending. In the end she couldn't see any way out and tried to take her own life again. It became a desperate fight for the parents to save their child. Family therapy was offered and, very reluctantly, Miriam agreed to take part.

Her parents blamed themselves for Miriam's problems. The therapist, however, encouraged them to work closely together to fight Miriam's eating disorder. They focused on deciding when and how much Miriam should eat, and what the consequences would be for her not doing so.

The parents were put firmly in charge, though this led to protests from Miriam, who accused them of not caring enough, of being insensitive and authoritarian. The therapist also thought it might be useful for the parents to learn more about the illness, and to meet parents of other children with eating disorders.

Miriam's mother remembers: 'We went to an introductory evening without Miriam, and met other families who had teenagers with anorexia nervosa. Everyone had been through similar problems. We learned about the mistakes we had made because of our ignorance about the disorder. Knowing about the illness is important.'

As well as the family sessions, they also went to 'multiple-family group therapy'. Miriam's mother said, 'Each family seemed to be in a different phase of the illness, but we were always able to discuss new problems and situations. This led to us re-thinking and learning about the illness, so that we could talk about any new difficulties.'

Over the next three months, Miriam recovered her weight at home, without any further admissions to hospital. She and her family continued to attend single-family sessions, as well as participating in multiple-family group therapy. Her eating disorder was no longer in evidence.

When Miriam was sixteen, she asked to have individual psychotherapy to deal with her poor self-esteem and episodes of depression. She received ten cognitive behavioural therapy (CBT) sessions and is now in good mental health.

What are talking therapies?

Psychotherapy is often referred to as the 'talking cure' – a treatment relying on the power of words rather than on medication. There are almost 500 different forms of talking therapy, but only the most common and established ones are described here. Sometimes the terms 'counselling' and 'supportive psychotherapy' are used.

Talking therapies vary a great deal, but what they all have in common is that they help us to understand how we 'work' as people, and how to make appropriate changes if necessary. They are also all treatments based on talking to another person, and sometimes doing things together.

The main psychotherapeutic approaches are all quite different, and can involve work with individual clients, couples, families and groups. The person carrying out the talking treatment is usually called a therapist, the person being seen is usually referred to as the client.

Psychoanalytic and psychodynamic psychotherapy

Psychoanalysis was invented by Sigmund Freud more than 120 years ago, and many of his ideas and those of his followers survive and are used in different ways in the twenty-first century.

Psychoanalytic psychotherapy

This is based on the idea that our minds have both conscious and unconscious parts: we are aware of and remember many experiences and events, but others get stored away – into 'the unconscious'.

Freud argued that from infancy and early childhood, we develop defence mechanisms to manage serious conflicts, and that difficult early experiences and feelings get repressed and are not accessible to our conscious minds.

Initially, Freud used hypnosis, which enabled his patients to speak freely about themselves, allowing their repressed 'unconscious' memories to emerge. Some of these came out in the form of dreams, fantasies and slips of the tongue. Freud asked his patients to lie on a couch and, sitting behind them, encouraged them to 'say anything that comes to mind'. Sometimes he interpreted what he thought was going on in the patient's unconscious mind, pointing out to them fears, secret wishes and repressed desires.

The relationship between patient and psychoanalyst was very important to Freud's work. He noticed that patients often 'projected' and 'transferred' their thoughts and feelings on to him, and he called this 'transference'. The aim of this approach was for the patient to be less ruled by the unconscious repetition of earlier relationship patterns, and to test out new ways of relating with the analyst.

Over the past hundred years this 'pure' psychoanalysis has given way to psychoanalytic psychotherapy, with the couch rarely used and the client and psychotherapist facing each other. This treatment is about the relationship between the therapist and the client. The psychotherapist is no longer the detached observer, but examines his own 'counter-transference' – the feelings that arise in the therapist during the therapeutic work.

Psychodynamic psychotherapy

This treatment has evolved from a 'one-person psychology' to a two-way process. It aims to help clients by putting their problems in the context of personal experiences and development, with the developing relationship between the therapist and client being essential.

Psychodynamic psychotherapy takes place at least once a week, usually at the same time and place. Sessions tend to last 50 minutes, and treatment can go on for many months, if not years. Changes are often slow and difficult to measure, but the process helps clients to take responsibility for their problems and actions. The approach can be effective with depression, anxiety, personality disorders and other disorders (see pp. 76, 24 and 157).

Other newer individual psychotherapies

Cognitive Analytic Therapy (CAT)

As the name suggests, cognitive analytic therapy combines psychodynamic and cognitive behavioural therapy techniques (see above and p. 427). During the first session, the therapist and client work together to develop an understanding of current problems and how they evolved, linking the present problematic situation with past thinking patterns and feelings. As part of this process, two or three problems are identified, and strategies to deal with them are discussed.

CAT also focuses on recognizing unhelpful relationship patterns. For example, if your parents have been over-controlling, this may lead you to be very controlling of others and of yourself. Some abused children abuse themselves or others. CAT aims to help you understand why you behave in these ways. CAT also aims to bring together different parts of your personality.

The duration of CAT is 16–24 sessions, depending on the underlying personality difficulties. The work has proved particularly helpful to people with eating disorders, anxiety and depression.

Motivational enhancement therapy (MET)

Also known as 'motivational interviewing', this is a client-centred, collaborative and non-confrontational way of counselling. MET aims to help clients explore and resolve their feelings about changing specific behaviours.

The client's motivation to change is helped with a gentle process of negotiation. It involves exploring the reasons a person continues to behave in specific ways, and helps the client to shift their decision-making processes in the direction of change. Motivational interviewing reduces negativity, and the approach is often used in conjunction with CBT techniques.

Dialectical behaviour therapy (DBT)

This is a treatment for people with borderline personality disorder (see p. 157). It is mostly based on CBT techniques to bring about change, but also on the Zen principle of 'radical acceptance'. It helps clients to understand that their responses to things are valid, but also problematic.

Change can happen only when the client accepts that there is a problem. This acceptance in itself is a step in the process of change. DBT can be done on an individual basis, but also in group sessions.

Interpersonal therapy (IPT)

Initially developed as a brief treatment for depression (see p. 76), IPT combines techniques from behavioural and psychodynamic approaches (see above), including role-play and improving interpersonal communication skills.

IPT is used when people have relationship problems, aiming to strengthen the client's social support network and reduce interpersonal difficulties with family and friends. The goals are to reduce depression and to increase social support. The therapist has an active role in coaching the client, and also in educating them about depression.

Eye movement desensitization and reprocessing (EMDR)

This is a technique to treat post-traumatic stress disorder (PTSD; see p. 187), which uses eye movements to help the brain to process flashbacks and to make sense of the traumatic experience.

The therapist asks the client to think about the traumatic event, and actively bring back disturbing memories and troubling images. The client is asked to move their eyes by following the therapist's eye movements. This is done over one to two minutes, with feedback obtained about any noticeable physical, emotional or cognitive changes.

Based on these, further eye movements are made until the patient experiences and reports reductions of distress related to the trauma. The average duration of EMDR treatment is 6–8 sessions, but further treatment may be needed in more complex traumas, such as childhood sexual abuse.

Group psychotherapy

The idea of putting individual clients together in groups can be traced back to the beginning of the last century, when doctors in the USA brought together patients with tuberculosis. This led to major improvements in their physical health and emotional well-being.

One hundred years later, group therapy is still a popular and cost-effective form of psychotherapy. The most common approach is based on the psychodynamic model (see above), with patients providing the 'material', which is interpreted by the therapist(s).

Between 6 and 8 clients, usually equal numbers of men and women, who do not know each other, meet regularly for 90 minutes, once a week, for between 18 months and 3 years. Clients sit in a circle, together with the therapist or a pair of co-therapists. Strict confidentiality is observed – clients must not disclose anything that comes up within the sessions to anyone outside the group. Group members should not meet each other outside the group-therapy session.

The aim of group therapy is for clients to 'open up' about their problems, and to find solutions through a fuller understanding of themselves and their relationships. Being with other clients, often with similar problems, can provide peer support but also challenges.

Specialized groups can be particularly helpful when clients share very similar experiences. Being familiar with similar issues allows group members to give each other 'expert' support and advice, as well as sharing experiences. In therapeutic groups for victims of abuse, for example, clients are more able to voice their experience in the presence of other abuse survivors.

There are also groups for clients of specific ages – for children, teenagers, young adults and older people. Clients of similar age groups can more easily identify with each other.

A more recent arrival is multi-family group work. Here 6–8 couples or 6–8 whole families spend hours or even days together. By exchanging ideas and experiences with members of other families, they can compare notes and learn from one another.

Family and couple therapy

Love them or hate them, families play a central role in most people's lives. Who and what we are is strongly influenced by our upbringing – and family life is full of drama, from birth to death.

People's problems will often not be theirs alone, but are affected by their relationship with other members of the family. Like any other organization, no family is the same. Each has its own rules and specific characteristics.

If the family cannot cope with a crisis or change, and finds it difficult to readjust, then one or more members may develop problems that affect others. For example, a child's behaviour affects the mother, whose response, in turn, affects the father and the other children, who cannot help but affect the child.

Family therapists see it as their job to help 'unblock' families who can be stuck in this pattern of behaviour, and to help families and their individual members to learn new ways of dealing with their difficulties.

In couple therapy, the therapist may be working with, for instance, a woman who is depressed, with low self-esteem. Her partner's response is to protect her too much, and this increases her feelings of being inadequate.

Psychoeducation is one specific form of family intervention. Carers and relatives are educated about the causes, and the course, of their family member's psychiatric illness. They are also taught about what is helpful, and less helpful, for the person with the problem. The general aim of psychoeducation is to reduce the strong emotions in the family, and to provide the client with more physical/personal space.

There are a number of different models in family and couple therapy. On average, family and couple sessions last for 60–90 minutes, with an average frequency of 6–10 sessions, spread out over 3–6 months. The therapy can take place in a clinic, at the family home or in another setting, such as a community centre.

Many clients seen for family therapy do not have a single clearly defined mental health problem. With children and adolescents, this type of therapy can provide effective help for:
- ❖ conduct disorders
- ❖ anorexia nervosa
- ❖ substance misuse

It can also be a secondary treatment for:
- ❖ depression
- ❖ chronic physical illness

Family therapy can help treat:
- ❖ childhood physical abuse and neglect
- ❖ attention-deficit hyperactivity disorder (ADHD)
- ❖ anxiety
- ❖ grief following bereavement
- ❖ psychosomatic problems

With adults, family therapy is effective for the treatment of:
- ❖ psychotic disorders (schizophrenia in particular)
- ❖ substance and alcohol misuse
- ❖ mood disorders, such as depression
- ❖ distress in couple relationships

Family and couple therapy can be used both on their own and with other treatments.

Dr Eia Asen

445

Dr Persaud's conclusion

Psychotherapists come from a whole range of different disciplines – psychology, psychiatry, nursing and social work. They will all have qualifications in psychotherapy or counselling. In the UK, public psychotherapy services are not well developed, and a lot of people receiving psychotherapy have to do so privately.

You can get information from your GP about psychotherapists in your area. Many health centres now do employ practice counsellors and psychotherapists. Adult psychiatric and psychology services often provide some form of psychotherapy, but it remains a major resource issue and availability varies widely. However, in the field of Child and Adolescent Mental Health Services (CAMHS), individual and family psychotherapy is now widely available.

One of the really confusing things about entering the world of psychotherapy for the first time is how to choose between the myriad of very different schools of therapy which exist. Given the richness of the field, some encourage patients to 'shop around' and be experimental about which treatment approach they try out before settling on one or another.

Another view is that the differences between the schools might be more imagined than real. Some research suggests it's not the particular school of thought a therapist has been trained in which really matters, but the personality and charisma of the clinician themselves. What has been termed 'empathy', 'genuineness' and 'warmth' have been found to be the key characteristics of a therapist; these can predict a good outcome for the therapy regardless of what treatment approach is taken.

Whichever therapist you opt for, it's wise to enquire what training they have had, which qualifications they possess, who regulates their profession and what their experience is of treating your specific kind of problem.

While the drugs used in psychiatry are often criticized for their side-effects and possible dependency, psychotherapists often escape similar questioning of their approach when in fact talking therapy does have side-effects and can create dependency.

It's wise to approach all treatments critically and have a clear sense of when it might be wise to think of switching strategies.

PROFESSIONAL ORGANIZATIONS

British Association of Psychotherapists, 37 Mapesbury Road, London NW2 4HJ; fax: 020 8452 0310; email: mail@bap-psychotherapy.org; *www.bap-psychotherapy.org*

British Psychoanalytic Society, West Hill House, 6 Swains Lane, London N6 6QS; tel: 020 7267 3626; email: mail@psychoanalytic-council.org; *www.psychoanalysis.org.uk*

British Association of Counselling and Psychotherapy, BACP House, 15 St John's Business Park, Lutterworth, Leicestershire LE17 4HB; email bacp@bacp.co.uk; *www.bacp.co.uk*

British Association of Behavioural and Cognitive Psychotherapies, The Globe Centre, PO Box 9, Accrington, BB5 0XB; tel: 01254 875277; email: babcp@babcp.com; *www.babcp.com*

UK Council for Psychotherapy (UKCP), 2nd Floor, Edward House, 2 Wakley Street, London EC1V 7LT; tel: 020 7436 3002; email: ukcp@psychotherapy.org.uk; *www.psychotherapy.org.uk*

USEFUL WEBSITE

Sigmund Freud and the Freud archives:
http://users.rcn.com/brill/freudarc.html

WEBSITES OUTSIDE THE UK

Australia: *www.healthinsite.gov.au; www.psychotherapy.com.au*

New Zealand: *www.nzap.org.uk*

Canada: *www.psychotherapycanada.com*

South Africa: *www.psychotherapy.co.za*

India: *www.indianpsychiatry.com*

i SUPPORT

Medication

Why medication works in mental illness

Many mental illnesses respond well to drug treatment. This is probably because mental illnesses are due, in part, to alterations in brain chemical messengers called neurotransmitters, and most drug treatments work to adjust the balance of particular neurotransmitters in the brain.

For example, in schizophrenia (see p. 196), it is thought that excess activity of the neurotransmitter dopamine system (perhaps caused by stress, or drugs such as cannabis) leads to the psychotic symptoms, such as hallucinations and delusions. Antipsychotic drugs (e.g. chlorpromazine, haloperidol, etc.) block one of the brain targets of dopamine – a binding site called the dopamine d2 receptor. This reduces the overactivity in the system and allows the symptoms to die down.

Other disorders, including depression and anxiety (see pp. 76 and 24), are thought to be due to a relative deficiency in the production of other neurotransmitters such as serotonin (5HT). Antidepressant drugs restore normal levels of 5HT by preventing its clearance from the nerve terminal regions where it is needed. Tranquillizers like diazepam (Valium) augment the brain's natural calming chemical GABA.

Side-effects

Drugs used to treat psychiatric illness often cause some unwanted side-effects. This is because these medications affect brain neurotransmitters, which often mediate many different functions in the brain and sometimes elsewhere in the body.

Adverse effects are usually harmless and most often shortlived. For example, antidepressants called selective serotonin re-uptake inhibitors (SSRIs) can cause nausea and abdominal distress, such as diarrhoea, at the start of treatment, but this usually wears off over a few days. Tranquillizers can cause sleepiness and unsteadiness.

It is very important that patients understand that the side-effects are normal and shortlived, so that they do not stop taking the medication. Most treatments take some time to work (e.g. up to four weeks for antidepressants) and if stopped, no benefit is likely. Some side-effects can be helped by other medication, so tell your doctor if they are bothering you.

In rare cases, psychiatric drugs can cause more serious adverse effects. These include blood disorders (e.g. with clozapine, a treatment for schizophrenia, which is why blood tests are regularly used with this antipsychotic), and problems with face and body movements (tardive dyskinesia). For the latter, there are antidotes that can be prescribed. However, some forms of these face and body movements, such as tardive dyskinesia, can occasionally be irreversible.

In all cases of adverse effects, it is vitally important that the patient, or their carers, tell the prescribing doctor in order to obtain appropriate advice. Starting at a lower dose can often minimize side-effects, and in some cases alternative medicines can be tried instead.

Stopping drugs

There are many evidence-based guidelines on how long to treat most psychiatric illnesses, and when to stop treatment. In the case of schizophrenia, medication is recommended for many years, if not for life.

In the case of depression, a period of treatment of six months or longer is best to allow complete recovery. This should be longer if there have been recent previous episodes. We now know that almost all people who have a depressive episode will have another in the next twenty-five years. Those unfortunate enough to have had three prior episodes have a 90 per cent chance of another episode in the next five years.

Antidepressants are even more effective in preventing further episodes of depression than in treating a current one, and so people with a high risk of relapse, due either to prior episodes or incomplete recovery, may need to stay on medication for many years.

When it is appropriate to stop treatment, it should usually be done slowly. This is to minimize the risk of distressing withdrawal reactions, which can mislead patients and doctors alike into thinking that the illness is coming back.

Antidepressants

Antidepressants are drugs that relieve the symptoms of depression. They were first developed in the 1950s and have been used regularly since then. There are almost thirty different kinds of antidepressants available today, and there are five main types:

❖ The original older drugs
  - tricyclics
  - MAOIs (monoamine oxidase inhibitors)
❖ The newer ones
  - SSRIs (selective serotonin re-uptake inhibitors)
  - SNRIs (serotonin and noradrenaline re-uptake inhibitors)
  - receptor-blocking drugs, e.g. mirtazapine

For a list of commonly used antidepressants, see the box on p. 453–4.

How do they work?

In depression, there appears to be an underactivity in some of the neuro-transmitter systems, particularly those of serotonin and noradrenaline. Antidepressants work by increasing the activity of these chemicals in our brains.

What are antidepressants used for?

❖ moderate to severe depressive illness
❖ severe anxiety, panic attacks, post-traumatic stress disorder (PTSD; see p. 187)
❖ obsessive compulsive disorder (OCD; see p. 149)
❖ chronic pain (see p. 389)
❖ eating disorders (see p. 93)

If you are not clear about why an antidepressant has been suggested for you, ask your doctor.

Are the newer ones better than the older ones?

In some ways they are. The older tablets (tricyclics) are just as effective as the newer ones (SSRIs), but the newer ones have fewer side-effects. A major advantage of the newer tablets is that they are very much less dangerous if someone takes an overdose.

Antidepressant side-effects

Tricyclics may cause a dry mouth, a slight tremor, fast heartbeat, constipation, sleepiness, and weight gain. Particularly in older people, they may cause confusion, slowness in starting and stopping when passing water, faintness through low blood pressure, and falls.

If you have heart trouble, it may be best not to take one of this group of antidepressants. Men may experience difficulty in getting or keeping an erection, or have delayed ejaculation. Tricyclic antidepressants are *very* dangerous in overdose (currently the most common drugs associated with successful suicide in the UK).

SSRI antidepressants, suicidal feelings and young people

As there is some evidence of increased suicidal thoughts (although not actual suicidal acts) and other side-effects in young people taking antidepressants, SSRI antidepressants are not licensed for use in people under eighteen. However, the National Institute for Clinical Excellence (NICE) has stated that fluoxetine, an SSRI antidepressant, can be used in the under-eighteens.

There is no clear evidence of an increased risk of self-harm and suicidal thoughts in adults. Overall, antidepressants do not increase the risk of suicide. In fact, they may decrease the risk of suicide, because this is very high in untreated depression.

Are antidepressants addictive?

Antidepressant drugs don't cause the addictions that you get with tranquillizers, alcohol or nicotine:

❖ you don't need to keep increasing the dose to get the same effect
❖ you won't find yourself craving them if you stop taking them

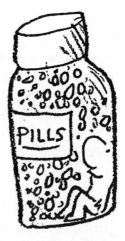

When antidepressants are stopped, however, people can experience withdrawal symptoms:

❖ stomach upsets
❖ flu-like symptoms
❖ anxiety

❖ dizziness

❖ vivid dreams at night

❖ sensations in the body that feel like electric shocks

In most people these withdrawal effects are mild, but for a small number of people they can be quite severe. It is generally best to taper off the dose of an antidepressant, rather than to stop it suddenly.

Pregnancy and breastfeeding

It is always best to take as little medication as possible during pregnancy, especially during the first three months. There is recent evidence of an increase in congenital malformations in babies of mothers who took antidepressants during this time. However, some expectant mothers do have to take anti-depressants and the risks need to be balanced.

There is some evidence that babies of mothers taking antidepressants may experience withdrawal symptoms soon after birth. Just as with adults, this seems to be more likely if paroxetine is the antidepressant concerned. Until we know more, doctors have been advised to consider alternative treatment in pregnancy, so advice from a doctor should be sought.

Some women become depressed after giving birth (see postnatal depression on p. 177) but usually get better with counselling and practical support. However, if you are unlucky enough to get it badly, it can exhaust you, stop you from breastfeeding, upset your relationship with your baby and even hold back your baby's development. In this case, antidepressants can be helpful.

The baby will get only a small amount of antidepressant from mother's milk. Babies older than a few weeks have very effective kidneys and livers. They are able to break down and get rid of medicines just as adults do, so the risk to the baby is very small.

Some antidepressants are better than others in this regard, and it is worth discussing this with your doctor or pharmacist. On balance, bearing in mind all the advantages of breastfeeding, it seems best to carry on with it while taking antidepressants.

COMMON ANTIDEPRESSANTS

Medication	Trade name	Group
amitriptyline	Tryptizol	Tricyclic
clomipramine	Anafranil	Tricyclic
citalopram	Cipramil	SSRI
dosulepin	Prothiaden	Tricyclic
doxepin	Sinequan	Tricyclic
fluoxetine	Prozac	SSRI
imipramine	Tofranil	Tricyclic
lofepramine	Gamanil	Tricyclic
mirtazapine	Zispin	NaSSA
moclobemide	Manerix	MAOI
nortriptyline	Allegron	Tricyclic
paroxetine	Seroxat	SSRI
phenelzine	Nardil	MAOI
reboxetine	Edronax	SNRI
sertraline	Lustral	SSRI
tranylcypromine	Parnate	MAOI
trazodone	Molipaxin	Receptor-blocker
venlafaxine	Efexor	SNRI
duloxetine	Cymbalta	SNRI

Anxiolytics

Although many antidepressants are the first-line treatment for anxiety disorders (see p. 24) as well as depression, they do take some time to work. During this period, doctors often prescribe a rapid-acting anxiolytic, sometimes called minor tranquillizers, for a few weeks to provide rapid relief of symptoms.

Most commonly, benzodiazepines are used for this purpose, although some antihistamines are also used. In the past, barbiturates were popular, but they are rarely used now on account of their poor safety record and increased risk of dependence.

Anxiolytics may be used on an intermittent, as-needed, basis to help people cope with short periods of increased anxiety. They also promote sleep, and so can be used for various forms of insomnia (see p. 222).

How do they work?

Anxiolytics act to dampen down brain activity. Benzodiazepines, the most common, increase the actions of the brain's own calming chemical, GABA. Antihistamines block the action of another neurotransmitter – histamine – that activates the brain, causing arousal and anxiety.

There are two other types of drugs that can be used to help reduce anxiety. One is buspirone, a drug that acts on 5HT systems to reduce tension and worry, which is used for the treatment of GAD (generalized anxiety disorder). Like antidepressants, it takes a few weeks to work.

The other type is beta-blockers, which are drugs used primarily to treat high blood pressure. As they block hormones that cause some symptoms of

THERAPIES, TREATMENTS AND MEDICATION

anxiety, especially tremor and racing heart, they can provide relief for people where these symptoms are prominent.

What are anxiolytics used for?

They are primarily used for the short-term treatment of anxiety:

❖ in acute situational anxiety – to help people cope with periods of extreme anxiety
❖ to counter a side-effect of antidepressants, which can be feelings of anxiety
❖ to improve sleep
❖ to reduce muscle tension and tension headaches
❖ in some cases, when other treatments have not worked, they may be used for long-term treatment

Benzodiazepines

Though once very popular, these have been replaced by the SSRIs (see above) as the mainstay of anxiety treatment. However, they are still used, especially to help with sleep and transient episodes of situational anxiety. They work quickly, and many patients carry a few tablets with them 'just in case' they are needed.

Benzodiazepines have a number of adverse effects, including sedation, unsteadiness and memory difficulties, which may prove problematic for driving and operating machinery. They also increase the action of alcohol and other sedating drugs, such as some painkillers.

The major problems are that some people find themselves needing increasingly large doses and also many people have difficulty stopping after long-term use. This can lead to unpleasant withdrawal symptoms. Between 10 and 25 per cent of people experience these so badly that they go back to taking the benzodiazepines and become long-term users.

Benzodiazepines are often abused by drug-users as a substitute for other drugs that are in short supply.

Antipsychotics

These are sometimes called major tranquillizers. They have been in use for over fifty years, initially in the form of drugs such as chlorpromazine and haloperidol, the 'typical' antipsychotics. More recently, a new class, the 'atypicals', has become popular. These include risperidone, olanzapine, cloza-pine and quetiapine.

The antipsychotic drugs have changed the treatment of psychotic disor-ders, especially schizophrenia (see p. 196), where they are often used for many years to prevent relapse.

How do they work?

All antipsychotic medications reduce the actions of the neurotransmitter dopamine. It is believed that many of the symptoms of schizophrenia, espe-cially the hallucinations and delusions, are caused by excessive dopamine activity.

However, dopamine has many functions in the brain, especially the facilitation of movement. These drugs frequently partially block this action, leading to the characteristic adverse effects called 'extra-pyramidal symptoms', a form of Parkinsonism (slow movements, a tremor), as well as restlessness of the legs (akathisia), and odd involuntary movements of the face and body (tardive dyskinesia).

The newer atypical antipsychotic drugs produce fewer adverse effects on movement, though some (especially olanzapine) have other problems, in particular excessive weight gain.

Clozapine works in a rather different way from the other drugs, and can succeed when others have failed, though we do not yet know why this is. It causes fewer movement problems, and may also lead to a greater improvement in thinking and motivation. However, it causes weight gain and, very occasionally, epilepsy. It can cause excessive saliva which can be easily overcome by further medication. In rare cases it can stop blood cells being produced, which is why regular monitoring of the blood count is necessary.

Many antipsychotics can occasionally elevate the hormone prolactin, which can cause breast growth in men and lactation in women. Clozapine, quetiapine and aripiprazole are least likely to do this.

What are antipsychotics used for?

As well as the treatment of schizophrenia – both acute episodes and preven-tion – antipsychotics can be used to:
* reduce mania
* help sleep, especially in psychotic states

❖ reduce aggression
❖ calm agitation in a range of psychiatric disorders
❖ treat depression in combination with other drugs

Long–lasting injections (depots)

Some antipsychotics are available as injections that can be given up to a month apart. These work in the same way as tablets but, because they are made in a form that releases the medication slowly, the treatment is longer lasting.

This approach has been shown to improve the outcome of schizophrenia. This is because treatment is more reliable and relapses less frequent – and often slower in onset, which allows them to be caught before they become too severe.

Different classes of antipsychotics

Older 'typical' antipsychotics:
❖ e.g. haloperidol, chlorpromazine, flupenthixol, fluphenazine

Newer 'atypical' antipsychotics:
❖ dopamine receptor antagonists (blockers): olanzapine, risperidone, clozapine, quetiapine, sertindole, ziprazidone, sulpiride and amisupride
❖ dopamine receptor partial agonists: aripiprazole – this blocks dopamine in brain regions where it is in excess, and may increase its function where it is relatively lacking

Mood stabilizers

These are medicines that help prevent mood swings – from mania and hypomania to depression. There are two main types of mood stabilizers. Lithium has been used for fifty years to reduce the number and severity of manic mood swings in bipolar disorder (manic depressive illness, see p. 42). More recently, a number of anticonvulsant drugs have been shown to have mood-stabilizing actions; these include sodium valproate, carbamazepine and lamotrigine.

How do they work?

At present we do not fully understand why some people have mood swings, or how these drugs work to reduce them. Current theories suggest they affect the production of certain regulatory chemicals in brain cells, making them less likely to undergo the changes in activity that lead to mood swings.

What are they used for?

Mood stabilizers prevent mood swings in bipolar disorder. Some of them, especially lithium and lamotrigine, can reduce recurrent depressive episodes.

Sometimes lithium is used to treat mania. In depression, it can also be added to antidepressants to assist their effects. Carbamazepine is sometimes used to reduce anger attacks.

Lithium

This is a metallic ion that needs to be held at a level between 0.4 and 1.0 mmol/litre in the blood to produce its benefits. If levels go below this, it is ineffective, and if they rise above 1.2 toxicity is experienced. Levels above 2 are very dangerous and require medical help.

Because of this, lithium levels in blood need to be measured on a regular basis until the correct dose is found. Side-effects may include tremor, dry mouth, extra urine production and weight gain. Occasionally, lithium can lead to an underactive thyroid, but this can be corrected. However, lithium is highly effective at reducing bipolar mood swings and, in general, the benefits outweigh the adverse effects.

Anticonvulsants

These share a range of adverse effects, especially sedation (which can often be reduced if they are given at night) and skin rashes (which are minimized by slowly increasing the dose).

In some places, sodium valproate levels in blood are measured to achieve the effective dose – though this is not essential. Often, if lithium is not working adequately, an anticonvulsant is added – so-called double, or on occasions when two are added, triple, therapy.

Sleeping pills – hypnotics

A number of drugs are used to help patients get off to sleep and stay asleep longer. Most are like the benzodiazepine anxiolytics, in that they increase the action of the brain's own calming neurotransmitter, GABA. Traditional benzo-diazepine hypnotics include nitrazepam and temazepam.

The newer hypnotics are called the z-drugs – zopiclone, zolpidem and zaleplon. They last for a shorter time in the body and so cause little hangover. Their different chemical structures also mean they produce less dependence and withdrawal than the older drugs.

However, all hypnotics can lead to some worsening of sleep when they are stopped, so in general, long-term use is to be avoided. Recently, a refined version of zopiclone – eszopiclone – has been licensed in the USA for the long-term treatment of insomnia, as it has been shown to be effective for six months or longer.

Medication for addiction

There are a number of drug treatments for addiction. Some work to block the effects of abused drugs, and are called antagonists. Others mimic the effects of abused drugs. They are prescribed as a substitute (substitute treatments) and are a method of taking away the need for addicts to commit crime to buy drugs on the street.

For opiate (heroin) addicts there are two substitute drugs – methadone and buprenorphine. Methadone is a longer-acting variant of morphine and is taken once a day, usually under supervision. Buprenorphine is a safer, less powerful, alternative drug that acts partly as a blocker. It can be given daily, or even three times a week, depending on the dose.

The only opiate-blocker in current use is naltrexone. When taken daily, it blocks the effects of any other opiate, and so stops street use. However, because it has no pleasurable effects, it is difficult to get addicts to take it, unless legal sanctions can be put into place.

Recently, drug treatments for alcoholism have become available. One is acamprosate, a drug that seems to dampen down excitability in the brain and possibly acts to stop craving. The other is the opiate antagonist naltrexone, which seems to reduce the pleasure that alcohol gives, thereby reducing the amount drunk.

Nicotine in tobacco is very addictive, with a well-defined withdrawal reaction. Substitution therapy, in the form of nicotine patches or gum, can help in stopping smoking.

Buproprion, an antidepressant available in the USA and some other countries, is available more widely as Zyban, for preventing relapse. It probably works because, in nicotine withdrawal, there is a relative deficiency of dopamine and buproprion acts to increase this neurotransmitter. Zyban can cause fits if the dose is increased too fast, so it is best to build up from 150mg to 450mg in weekly instalments. (See also Chapter 6, p. 59.)

Professor David Nutt

Dr Persaud's conclusion

Drugs used in the treatment of mental health problems are frequently extremely effective, but they need to be prescribed and then monitored by a trained practitioner. Sometimes drugs appear not to work, but this is usually because a wrong diagnosis has been made or the drugs have been prescribed for too long to be effective any more.

Ultimately it is highly unlikely that most psychological problems are going to be cured simply by the prescription of a pill – usually the problems that patients face in their lives that have led to the emotional disturbance will need to be addressed as well. There is often a mistaken faith in the ability of a mere tablet to solve many of life's ills.

The offering of a prescription by a doctor has profound psychological implications as well as pharmacological ones. It often carries the implicit message that the pill contains the solution and therefore if the patient isn't getting better there is something wrong with the tablet or the doctor's treatment plan. Often when it comes to psychological problems the patient enters a therapeutic alliance with a clinician and, although the doctor is providing guidance and advice, the patient will also have to do a fair amount of work themselves in order to get better.

Patients may not be aware that many doctors feel enormous pressure to end a consultation with a prescription as a symbol that the physician has

indeed tried to help and taken the problem seriously. Instead a prescription should be offered only when both doctor and patient understand the true extent of the role of medication in correcting these kinds of difficulties.

SUPPORT ORGANIZATION

UK Medicines Information: *www.ukmi.nhs.uk*

WEBSITES OUTSIDE THE UK

Australia:
www.ranzcp.org

Canada:
www.chp-pcs.gc.ca/CHP/index_e.jsp

India:
www.indianpsychiatry.com

New Zealand:
www.ranzcp.org

South Africa:
www.mentalhealthsa.co.za

i SUPPORT

Appendix One:
Mental Health Legislation

A girl who tried to hang herself

YASMIN WAS ONLY twenty when she was first admitted to a psychiatric hospital. She was in her second year at university, studying geography.

Her parents were thrilled when she got her six AS–levels and four A–levels and became the first person in the family to go to university. Yasmin had spent her last four years at school studying hard, and had spent most of her time locked away in her room working. Her parents didn't worry about her because she was ambitious and they knew she would excel.

The university was in the north of England and this was the first time that Yasmin had left home. She had a room in halls of residence, but although she made a couple of friends in the same block, they were not studying geography and so she felt very alone. She spent a lot of time in the library, where she met Ali. Yasmin was very flattered by his attention and thought that she was in love with him. Ali then met someone else and dumped her shortly after.

Yasmin stopped going to lectures and seminars. She felt very depressed and couldn't get out of bed. Nobody really noticed that there was a problem until she was found in a shower, having failed to hang herself. The shower wasn't very secure and came away from the wall. She refused to see the university doctor.

The police and members of the local mental health team were called and she was admitted to the local psychiatric hospital, under Section 2 of the Mental Health Act (28 days assessed). After several weeks' treatment, Yasmin was able to understand how ill she had become. Doctors advised that she stay in hospital a little longer and she agreed to stay as an informal patient. She finally left hospital after two months and returned home. Everyone agreed that it would be better for her to go to a university nearer to home so that her parents could look after her.

Mental health and the law

From your eighteenth birthday onwards you are said to be competent to make, and take responsibility for, all decisions which affect your life. Of course you may be unable, from time to time or all the time, to make decisions. Sometimes you might be able to make simple decisions, but not more complex ones.

In this chapter, we look at the current legal framework for those people who are unable to make decisions, either permanently or temporarily, due to some form of mental disability.

In the UK, there are six Mental Health Acts (each having different rules), two Mental Capacity Acts, the Common Law (i.e. law made by judges as a result of court cases), and several laws relating to people with mental disorders who are accused of criminal behaviour. Then there are additional laws in relation to children and young people.

The range of decisions which you make, or which may have to be made on your behalf, is considerable. Within the mental health service the main focus, not surprisingly, is on ensuring that people receive the health care and medical treatment which they need. This may include compulsory admission to hospital (being admitted to hospital under law, against your will).

However, far more common are decisions about whether or not the person:
❖ should go into a home when they get older
❖ can look after their own finances
❖ can make a will
❖ is able to make decisions about marriage
❖ is able to sign contracts

When accused of a crime, there are decisions to be made about whether or not the person:
❖ is fit to stand trial
❖ if convicted, should go to prison or hospital

Common Law

Common Law applies only if there is no statutory law – i.e. law passed by Parliament (an Act). It is a Common Law principle that you are entitled to make treatment decisions for yourself.

As a judge put it in a recent case, 'a competent patient has an absolute right to refuse to consent to medical treatment for any reason, rational or irrational, or for no reason at all, even when that decision may lead to his or her death.' It would be an offence for a doctor to force treatment on you, without your consent, other than in particular, well-defined, situations. The most obvious example is in an emergency, when your consent, as the patient, is not normally asked for, because you are unconscious or disorientated, or because your consent could not be obtained until it was too late.

In England and Wales, the Common Law has, for the most part, been changed by the Mental Capacity Act (April 2007) in relation to care and medical treatment. In Scotland, the Adults with Incapacity (Scotland) Act, 2000 is already in force. Northern Ireland will continue to rely on the Common Law for the time being.

Mental Capacity Acts

These laws describe how medical, social and financial decisions are to be taken, by professionals and others on your behalf, when you are unable to make the decisions for yourself. For example, any decisions made for you must be in your best interest, taking into account what you would have wished (if this is known).

The law also allows you, if you wish, when healthy and able to make decisions, to plan for your care and treatment should you become incapable of decision-making at some time in the future (for example because of Alzheimer's or a head injury).

In the same way as you may make a will, you can set out what care and treatment you would or wouldn't wish to receive. You might, for example, say that you want a particular antidepressant if you get very depressed, because it has worked in the past, or that you wouldn't want to be given particular medical treatments to keep you alive if you became terminally ill. If you request a treatment it is called an advanced statement; it must be taken into account by doctors, and others, but is not binding on the professional staff.

If you say that you don't want a particular treatment in the future, it is called an advanced refusal of treatment or an advanced directive and *is* binding. A doctor or nurse must not give you treatment specified in your advanced directive (unless there are specific and exceptional circumstances – e.g. you are detained under the Mental Health Act). In Scotland, however, advanced refusals are not binding.

Alternatively, you can authorize someone else to consent to, or refuse, treatment on your behalf.

There are special regulations in relation to sterilization, termination of pregnancy or the withholding or withdrawing of life-sustaining treatment.

Children and young people

The Children Act is important here. Children aged sixteen and seventeen can agree to medical treatment in exactly the same way as an adult; however, they are not thought to be competent to refuse treatment.

Children under sixteen may be able to consent if it is decided that they have enough understanding and intelligence to understand fully what is proposed.

Children under eighteen cannot refuse treatment. Parents can consent on behalf of children of any age up to sixteen. Where there is a major disagreement, it might be necessary to ask the Court for a decision.

In Scotland, you are an adult at the age of sixteen and the Court's power to overrule a refusal of treatment does not apply.

Mental Health Acts

Mental Health Acts set out the rules for the compulsory admission to hospital, for assessment or treatment, of people with a mental disorder. In some countries (e.g. England and Wales, where it is used over 50,000 times a year) this is irrespective of whether or not the patient retains the ability to make decisions for him- or herself.

In other countries (e.g. Scotland), the person with a mental disorder must usually have some form of incapacity, in the same way as someone with a physical illness, before treatment can be forced upon them.

The processes described in a Mental Health Act must require:
❖ that there are clear reasons (criteria) for your detention, admission to hospital and the giving of treatment
❖ that you cannot be treated safely without use of the Mental Health Act
❖ that decisions are made by more than one professional
❖ that there are time limits to your detention and proper reviews of it, and that you must be released if the criteria are no longer met
❖ that you can appeal to an independent body against your detention or treatment
❖ that there are particular safeguards in relation to specific treatments

So, you can only be detained in hospital under a Mental Health Act if:
❖ You suffer from a mental disorder. There is sometimes argument over what should 'count' as a mental disorder. Mental illnesses such as schizophrenia or severe depression are easy. Less clear are difficulties such as addiction to drugs or alcohol. There is also a lot of argument about people with so-called personality disorders. Those with a learning disability are defined as having a mental disorder, but this is not grounds for compulsory admission to hospital, or for treatment, unless the person is very aggressive or irresponsible. It is important that people aren't

labelled as mentally ill just because they are different in some way. The current Mental Health Act deliberately excludes people with a sexual deviancy or promiscuity or those who are dependent on alcohol or drugs.

❖ It is in the interests of your health or safety or for the protection of others, and you are severely ill enough to need admission to hospital.

❖ You cannot be treated safely or effectively at home.

Who is involved in the process?

Two doctors are required (other than in an emergency, when one is enough). One of them should, if possible, know you – e.g. your general practitioner – and the other must be approved as having special experience in the diagnosis or treatment of mental disorder (and is therefore usually, but not always, a psychiatrist). The two doctors should not normally work together. Once the two doctors have recommended that you require compulsory admission to hospital, an approved social worker (ASW) decides whether or not to ask the hospital to accept you, taking into account your views and the opinions of the doctors, your carers or family.

Time limits

An emergency order, requiring only one doctor (or, in special circumstances, a police officer) lasts up to 72 hours. More usually the initial admission for assessment is for up to 28 days. This cannot be extended. If the doctor in charge of your treatment, called the responsible medical officer (RMO), believes you need a further period of detention in hospital for treatment of your mental disorder, it again requires two medical recommendations and an ASW. This time the order lasts for up to six months. If you have had compulsory admissions before, then you might be put on a longer-term order straight away. In Scotland the Tribunal authorizes the extended periods of detention.

The RMO can discharge you at any time. The RMO can also give you permission for periods out of the hospital, if he or she thinks it's safe to do so. If you have what the law calls a 'nearest relative', he or she can also order your discharge, although this can be overruled by the RMO if you are thought to be dangerous. In Scotland, the 'nearest relative' is called a 'named person' and this person cannot order the patient's discharge.

Your 'nearest relative' is very precisely defined. You cannot choose. It is your husband or wife (or civil partner) if you are married; if not married, then your oldest child, if over eighteen, or your older living parent and so on.

There are different rules if you are in trouble with the law, and the decision is to be made by a judge in court. However, it still requires one or two doctors to recommend compulsory admission to hospital before the judge can make such a decision.

Right of appeal

When you are admitted to hospital, you will have your rights explained to you. For each period of detention (except the 72-hour emergency order), you have two separate routes for appeal.

You can appeal to a panel of three specially appointed people experienced in mental health issues. They are called hospital managers, although they have nothing to do with running or managing the hospital (this appeal is not available in Scotland).

You can also appeal to a totally independent judicial body called a Mental Health Review Tribunal (MHRT). This is also a three-person panel consisting of a lawyer or a judge, who chairs the hearing, a senior doctor and a third person who is neither a doctor nor a lawyer.

Both types of appeal will take written evidence from the doctor in charge, a nurse, a social worker and perhaps other people. You will be shown the reports written about you, unless there are very good grounds for the information to be withheld. There will then be a semi-formal 'court' hearing in the hospital. For the MHRT you are entitled to be represented by a solicitor paid for out of legal aid. The doctor has to explain why you are being detained, usually supported by the nurse and social worker. You can challenge what they say with the help of your solicitor.

Safeguards

Once in hospital, you will be required to stay on the ward, or within the grounds of the hospital. If necessary, you may be put on a ward which is locked. If you have been sent to hospital by the courts having been convicted of a serious offence, then you may be put in a more secure hospital.

You can be treated (preferably with, but occasionally without, your consent) with medication and psychological therapies. Basic nursing care must be provided. The state of the ward and the overall quality of care provided should be monitored by an independent body, based in Nottingham, called the Mental Health Act Commission.

If you are detained in hospital for more than three months, then you can only be made to take medication if you agree to it, or if an independent medical opinion is provided by the Mental Health Act Commission. The Commission will send a senior psychiatrist, chosen by them, who will interview you, along with a nurse and another professional (not a nurse or doctor) involved in your care, before deciding if you do have to take the medication.

Electroconvulsive therapy also can only be prescribed if you consent to the treatment or, if you lack the capacity to consent or refuse the treatment, with the authority of the Commission's second-opinion doctor.

Dr Donald Lyons and Dr Tony Zigmond

SUPPORT ORGANIZATIONS

The Mental Health Act Commission, Maid Marian House, 56 Hounds Gate, Nottingham NG1 6BG; tel: 0115 943 7100; fax: 0115 943 7101; *www.mhac.org.uk*

Mental Welfare Commission (Scotland), K Floor, Argyle House, 3 Lady Lawson Street, Edinburgh EH3 9SH; telephone enquiry line: +44 (0)131 222 6111 or freephone 0800 389 6809; tel: +44 (0)131 244 + ext.; fax: +44 (0) 131 222 6112; email enquiries: enquiries@mwcscot.org.uk; *www.mwcscot.org.uk*

Mind, 15–19 Broadway, London E15 4BQ; tel: 020 8519 2122; fax: 020 8522 1725; email: contact@mind.org.uk; information helpline: Mind*info*Line: 0845 766 0163; *www.mind.org.uk*

USEFUL WEBSITE

www.hyperguide.co.uk/mha – Nigel Turner's HyperGUIDE to the Mental Health Act the Institute of Mental Health Act Practitioners

WEBSITES OUTSIDE THE UK

Australia: *www.health.gov.au*

Canada: *www.qp.gov.bc.ca/ statreg/stat/M/96288_01.htm*

India: *www.psyplexus.com/ excl/lmhi.html*

New Zealand: *www.moh.govt.nz/ mentalhealth*

South Africa: *www.info.gov.za/ gazette/acts/2002/a17-02.pdf*

Appendix Two:
Mental Health Services

A man who couldn't be bothered to speak

S HARIQ WAS TWENTY-EIGHT and happily married with two young children. His wife, Amina, had started to notice that he was becoming more and more depressed and was drinking very heavily in the evenings after work. He had even been very aggressive with her and the children, which was not like him at all – he was a very gentle man. In a fit of temper, he had smashed up their best kitchen plates. Amina was very worried that both parents-in-law might notice that something was wrong and think that the marriage was breaking up, and that it was her fault.

Shariq eventually stopped going to work; he didn't even have the energy to wash himself any more or to speak. He sat all day, slumped in front of the TV. Amina was now at her wits' end. She was worried that he would lose his job at the local DIY shop and that they wouldn't be able to pay the mortgage.

Shariq then stopped eating and couldn't be persuaded to go to the GP, especially as he was a friend of the family. Amina finally persuaded the GP to visit them at home. Shariq refused to answer any of the GP's questions. The GP was very concerned to see how Shariq had changed so much in such a short time, although he couldn't find anything physically wrong with him.

The family doctor referred Shariq as an emergency to the local mental health service. He was assessed by a community nurse and a psychiatrist, who decided to treat him at home and arranged for treatment to be prescribed by the GP. Members of the crisis team visited him at home every day to monitor his progress and to provide support to Shariq and the family.

After a few weeks on antidepressants, Shariq was well enough to start visiting the day hospital. The crisis team stopped visiting, but the community nurse continued to meet with him regularly until he was fully recovered.

What are mental health services?

Mental health services refer to the organized system for the delivery of assessment, treatment and support to people with mental health problems and their families.

Who works in mental health services?

The mental health professionals who work in specialist mental health services in the UK include:

❖ in-patient nurses (RMNs)
❖ community psychiatric nurses (CPNs)
❖ occupational therapists (OTs)
❖ social workers – including approved social workers who are involved in Mental Health Act work (ASWs)

❖ psychotherapists
❖ pharmacists
❖ psychologists
❖ psychiatrists

In addition, there are many people without a professional qualification who have important supporting roles.

Policies surrounding mental health

Mental health services differ a lot between different countries. What's available, and how to access services, depend on many things:
❖ how health and social welfare services have developed
❖ the priority attached to mental health problems
❖ the enthusiasms of governments/policymakers
❖ the ability of the rest of society to provide the support and care that people with mental health problems need

In the UK, specialist mental health services are paid for by service commissioners, who receive funds from the Department of Health and the local Social Services Department.

It is important to remember that the staff are almost always trying to do their best. However, there is always a gap between what might be done in ideal circumstances and what the commissioners choose to pay for (on your behalf, and within the resources available for all aspects of health and social care).

Referral to mental health services

Most treatment for mental health problems is delivered by general practitioners (GPs) and therapists at the GP practice. However, if specialist care is needed, the GP will refer you to a psychiatrist or to a mental health team; this is the same as with any medical specialist working in the NHS.

Many people with mental health problems receive most of their care and support from family members, friends, carers and organizations that have no links with the health or social care system.

Why do we need mental health services?

Services are there to provide assessment, treatment, care and support for people with mental health problems, or to assess and (if appropriate) meet their needs.

The needs of people with more severe mental health problems are not only about helping their distressing symptoms (for example, hearing voices and ideas of being persecuted in schizophrenia). Often, severe mental health problems come back – there can be good times, but also bad ones which can lead to a crisis. People with more severe problems may be a danger to themselves (through neglect, vulnerability or a desire to harm themselves) and/or to other people.

Severe mental illness also interferes in our work, how we manage our finances, make relationships and, occasionally basic self-care. Social isolation and lack of supportive relationships are common problems. So some people may need help with getting their benefits and managing their money, finding housing and accessing leisure activities, education and getting work.

Mental health problems are often 'co-morbid' – they exist with other problems. The commonest is a form of mental illness with drug and/or alcohol abuse. It is important to get effective help to tackle both problems.

We are now more aware of the role of people with mental health problems as parents. Supporting this role may require close working between different services such as: Mental Health Services for People of Working Age; Children and Family Social Services; the health visitor; the school; and Child and Adolescent Mental Health Services (CAMHS).

Complaints and second opinions

If you are unhappy about the help that you or your relative is receiving, do raise your concerns and, if necessary, make a formal complaint. Complaints are taken very seriously and help services learn about how things could be done better.

Everyone has a right to a second opinion. If you feel you have (or the person you are caring for has) a particular problem, ask for an opinion from someone with relevant expertise.

Carers

Mental illness does not just affect the patient, but can have a profound impact on those around them, friends and family. Much is known about the stress of being a carer. Services in the UK are now obliged to assess the needs of carers and to identify the support they require to help them with the burdens of care. The commonest issues identified by carers are the need to be listened to, and getting help in crises. (See also Chapter 30, p. 290.)

Getting help and information

The care system in the UK is complex and often confusing. One main respon-sibility for staff working at the interface between primary care (GP) and sec-ondary care (range of specialist services) is to help patients and carers find their way through the system.

Specialist services are expected to provide written information about what they offer. In many areas there are guides detailing local provision, including how to contact mental health and social care organizations, and local self-help groups.

It is also important to ask for written information about your problem and the local services that are available to help.

Mental health services across your lifetime

Mental health problems occur throughout life. There are therefore specialist needs for children and adolescents and for older people.

The boundaries between Child and Adolescent Mental Health Services, Old Age Services, and Mental Health Services for Adults of Working Age are complicated and vary locally.

❖ Specialist mental health services in the UK are generally similar and work along the same lines.

❖ Multidisciplinary teams (MDT): professionals and other staff from a range of backgrounds.

❖ Staff must work according to the Care Programme Approach (CPA). The CPA states that services must assess the needs of people accepted by the service; develop a care plan that sets out who should do what; share this care plan with the patient; and regularly review the plan. There should be an allocated 'care co-ordinator', a member of the team who takes responsibility for this.

❖ The care plan should look at all relevant health and social care needs. It should not just focus on getting rid of the symptoms of the illness.

❖ Services include both health and social service staff, working together in joint teams.

❖ Services depend on many other agencies, including GP practices, social, educational, leisure, employment and welfare services, and private and voluntary providers.

Child and Adolescent Mental Health Services (CAMHS)

CAMHS services include:

❖ GPs and other members of the primary healthcare team

❖ specialists working in general hospitals and schools

❖ Children and Family Social Services Departments

❖ youth workers

❖ Youth Offending Teams

CAMHS deal with a wide range of severe mental health problems from severe depression, to attention deficit hyperactivity disorder (ADHD), to conduct disorder.

The move from CAMHS to adult mental health services can be a problem, because CAMHS offer treatment for problems such as ADHD, autistic spectrum disorders and conduct disorders that adult services traditionally don't.

Old Age Mental Health Services

Old Age Mental Health Services have expertise in assessing and treating people with dementia, and those suffering from mental illness complicated by the physical problems linked to ageing.

These services work closely with services which provide domiciliary care and housing for elderly people.

Mental Health Services for Adults of Working Age

Between youth and old age lies 'working age' – a term only recently adopted. There are currently four recognized psychiatric specialities in the UK devoted to the treatment of working-age adults:

❖ general adult psychiatry
❖ psychotherapy (which includes psychodynamic psychotherapy, cognitive behavioural therapy (CBT), marital therapy and family therapy – see Chapter 44, p. 427)
❖ learning disability (some specialists work with children and the elderly)
❖ forensic psychiatry (which involves the treatment of people who have committed offences)

Psychiatrists also have other areas of expertise with specialist services:

❖ addictions (treatment of abuse of drugs and/or alcohol)
❖ liaison psychiatry (work in the general hospital with people who have physical illnesses or complaints, and emotional or psychiatric problems)
❖ psychiatric rehabilitation (treatment of people with severe disabilities)
❖ perinatal psychiatry (which involves the welfare of mothers when pregnant, and in the year after they have had a baby)
❖ neuropsychiatry (assessment and treatment of people with psychiatric symptoms occurring in the context of neurological disorder)
❖ eating disorders

Adult Mental Health Services

Previously these services consisted of:

❖ a Community Mental Health Team (CMHT)
❖ an in-patient unit that provided hospital beds for people needing to be admitted to hospital
❖ some access to psychological treatments
❖ a presence in the local general hospital (at least to assess people who had harmed themselves)
❖ a day hospital
❖ in-patient and community rehabilitation services for people with the most severe illnesses

Things have got rather more complicated in recent years. The CMHT still exists, although it now generally relates to the GP you are registered with.

The CMHT is now supplemented by a number of other teams:

❖ the Assertive Outreach Team (AOT), for people with severe problems with whom it is difficult to connect

❖ the Early Intervention in Psychosis team (EIP), which provides intensive support to people in the first three years of their psychotic illness

❖ the Community Forensic Team (CFT), which provides treatment to people who have committed serious offences because of their mental illness

❖ the Crisis Resolution/Home Treatment Team (CRT/HTT), which provides an alternative to hospital admission

Dr Frank Holloway

Dr Persaud's conclusion

Widespread complaints about mental health services haven't managed to change things. Perhaps one reason for this might be that services cannot realistically provide what a patient expects or hopes for from a service. Can a service, for example, be expected to improve all emotional distress if and when it arises in all the thousands of its patients, or is it best devoted to and used as a way of dealing with a severe crisis where a hospital bed is required?

At a policy and administrative level, services might need to be clearer about what they aim to do. Similarly, patients might need to obtain this clarity for themselves about what their own corner of the service might be best used for. It is useful for those trying to use a service to think about and investigate what drives and governs how that service works internally. It might be, for example, a fear of untoward incident inquiries which drives the way staff work and therefore this dictates how the service works.

Increasingly, users of services are getting together to work with those who provide a service to plan how it will operative.

One new tension that is developing, particularly in the planning and operation of modern psychiatric services, is that what delivers the most patient satisfaction is often not what produces the most fulfilled mental healthcare workers.

SUPPORT ORGANIZATIONS

National Service Frameworks for Mental Health, Children and Old Age: *www.dh.gov.uk*

NICE Guidelines: disorder-specific guidelines, Including versions specifically designed for users and carers. *www.nice.org.uk*

Mental Health Foundation: helps people survive, recover from and prevent mental health problems. 9th Floor, Sea Containers House, 20 Upper Ground, London SE1 9QB; tel: 020 7803 1100; *www.mentalhealth.org.uk*

Mind: a leading mental health charity in England and Wales. 15–19 Broadway, London E15 4BQ; tel: 020 8519 2122; Mind*info*line: 0845 766 0163; *www.mind.org.uk*

WEBSITES OUTSIDE THE UK

Australia:
www.mhca.org.au

India:
www.nimhans.kar.nic.in

Canada:
www.healthservices.gov.bc.ca

New Zealand:
www.mhc.govt.nz

South Africa:
www.scienceinafrica.co.za/2002/march/mhic.htm

Editors and Contributors

Dr Raj Persaud (Consultant Editor) is a consultant psychiatrist at London's Maudsley Hospital. He has received a number of awards and prizes for his work and was appointed Gresham Professor for Public Understanding of Psychiatry in 2004. He has appeared on numerous television programmes, is a regular radio broadcaster and has written several books, including most recently *Simply Irresistible: The Psychology of Seduction* and *The Motivated Mind*. He lives in London.

Editors

Janey Antoniou has a background as a scientist in genetics and molecular biology. A user of mental health services, she currently works as a freelance writer and trainer on mental health issues and lives in London.

Dr Martin Briscoe is a consultant psychiatrist. He works as a consultant for the NHS and has a private practice in Exeter. He is the website editor for the Royal College of Psychiatrists and helps to produce their public information materials.

Vanessa Cameron is Chief Executive of the Royal College of Psychiatrists. (See page 482.)

Professor Hamid Ghodse is professor of psychiatry and of international drug policy at the University of London; Director, International Centre for Drug Policy, St George's University of London; President, European Collaborating Centres for Addiction Studies; Director of the Board of International Affairs, Royal College of Psychiatrists; Non-Executive Director,

National Patient Safety Agency (NPSA); member of the WHO Expert Advisory Panel on Drug Dependence and a (past-president) member of the United Nations International Narcotics Control Board.

Deborah Hart is Head of External Affairs at the Royal College of Psychiatrists where she has worked for the last twenty-five years in different guises. She is committed to producing accessible information for the general public and to campaigning to reduce the stigma of mental illness.

Jill Phillipson is a medical communications specialist, with a particular interest in mental health. She has worked in health care public relations for many years, and has also practised as a couple counsellor.

Dr Ros Ramsay is an adult psychiatrist working as a consultant at the South London and Maudsley NHS Foundation Trust. She is a member of the Royal College of Psychiatrists' Public Education Committee and works on the production of information for service users and carers.

Dr Philip Timms has worked for fifteen years as a consultant psychiatrist with homeless people in South London. He chairs the editing group for the Royal College of Psychiatrists' series of mental health leaflets for the general public.

Professor Peter Tyrer is the Editor of the *British Journal of Psychiatry* and professor of community psychiatry at Imperial College. He has been interested in personality and stress for many years since being gardener to Spike Milligan as a medical student.

Alexi Wedderburn, who has an interest in psychology and mental health, worked for the Royal College of Psychiatrists for six years. She lives in London and Italy.

Contributors

Janey Antoniou ('Managing Your Illness – and Your Life' and 'Diagnosis: What Have I Got?') (see above).

Dr Eia Asen ('Therapies, Treatments and Medication: Other Talking Treatments') is both a consultant psychiatrist in psychotherapy and the Clinical Director of the Marlborough Family Service (Central and North West London Mental Health Trust) in London.

Dr Hadrian Ball ('Less Common Disorders') is a consultant forensic psychiatrist by background. Since July 2000 he has occupied the post of medical director of a specialist mental health NHS trust. He lives in Norfolk.

Dr James Barrett ('Gender Identity') is Lead Clinician at the Charing Cross Gender Identity Clinic. He has worked with disorders of gender identity for nearly twenty years and seen several thousand patients. He prefers to travel by pedal cycle.

Dr Roger Bloor ('Drug Problems') is a former RAF psychiatrist. He returned to the NHS twenty years ago as a consultant with special respon-sibility for drugs and alcohol. He is Medical Director of an NHS trust and senior lecturer in addiction psychiatry at Keele University Medical School.

Dr Billy Boland ('Cravings') is a clinical lecturer in addictive behaviour at St George's, University of London and a specialist registrar in psychiatry. He lives in London.

Dr Jim Bolton ('Physical Illness and Chronic Pain') is a consultant liaison psychiatrist working in a general hospital in Surrey. He is also an honorary senior lecturer at St George's University, London. He lives in London.

Dr Peter Byrne ('Diagnosis: What Have I Got?') is a consultant NHS psychiatrist in East London with an academic base in University College, London. He has been researching and publishing about mental health stigma since 1996. He has worked on the Royal College of Psychiatrists' Public Education Committees in Ireland and, since 1999, the UK, and chaired the media section of the College's Changing Minds campaign for five years.

Vanessa Cameron ('Managing Your Illness – and Your Life') was diagnosed with bipolar disorder over thirty years ago. With the help of her husband and her doctors, she has learned how to live with and manage her illness.

Dr Roch Cantwell ('Postnatal Depression') is a psychiatrist specializing in the treatment of pregnant and postnatal women, and honorary senior lecturer at Glasgow University. He runs a Mother and Baby unit which serves half the delivered population of Scotland. He lives in Glasgow.

Professor Patricia Casey ('Bipolar Disorder') is professor of psychiatry at University College Dublin and the Mater Misericordiae Hospital. She is the author of three books including *A Guide to Psychiatry in Primary Care*. Her research interests include personality disorder and suicide; she is one of the principal investigators of the Outcome of Depression International Network Group and Editor of the *Quarterly Journal of Mental Health*. She is a regular contributor to the Irish media and currently has a weekly column in the *Irish Independent*.

Dr Mary Clarke ('Schizophrenia') is a consultant psychiatrist with a special interest in psychosis in St John of God Hospital, Stillorgan, Co. Dublin, Ireland. Her research interests are in schizophrenia, particularly in the area of early intervention.

Jessica Colon ('Body Image Disorders') is a final year psychology student at Siena College, New York. She is planning to pursue a PhD in clinical psychology.

Professor Ilana Crome ('Drug Problems') is Professor of Addiction Psychiatry and Academic Director of Psychiatry, Keele University Medical School (Harplands Campus) and Lead Clinician and Consultant in Addiction, North Staffordshire Combined Healthcare NHS Trust. She has been directly involved in national clinical research, training and policy developments in substance misuse since the 1980s.

Dr Larry Culliford ('Spirituality') is a consultant psychiatrist and successful author (see www.happinesssite.com), closely involved with the Royal College of Psychiatrists' Spirituality and Psychiatry Special Interest Group. A practising Christian with strong affinities for Buddhism and other faiths, he currently lives in Sussex.

Professor Chris Dowrick ('Depression') is a general practitioner and professor of primary medical care at the University of Liverpool. His book

Beyond Depression, which explores the limits of conventional medical understanding of depression, was published in 2004. He lives in Liverpool.

Professor Colin Drummond ('Cravings') is head of the Addictive Behaviour Research Group at St George's University of London and is a psychiatrist leading NHS alcohol treatment services in South West London. He has published many articles and books in the field of addiction, and advises on addiction policy in the UK and to the World Health Organization.

Dr Lynne Drummond ('Obsessive Compulsive Disorder') has been a consultant psychiatrist and senior lecturer in behavioural and cognitive psychotherapy at the University of London and SW London and St George's Mental Health Trust since 1985. She is Consultant in charge of the National Obsessive-Compulsive Disorder (OCD) Service providing inpatient and outpatient treatment for severe, chronic resistant OCD.

Dr John Eagles ('Seasonal Affective Disorder') is a consultant psychiatrist at Royal Cornhill Hospital in Aberdeen and an honorary reader at Aberdeen University. He has published research in several areas, including seasonal affective disorder, suicide, eating disorders and the epidemiology of schizophrenia.

Dr Irshaad Ebrahim ('Sleep Problems') is a specialist neuropsychiatrist in sleep disorders, and medical director of the London Sleep Centre. He has published original research in the role of novel neuropeptides in narcolepsy, has a special interest in insomnia and parasomnias and is a member of the British Sleep Society and Fellow of the Royal Society of Medicine.

Dr David Enoch, ('Less Common Disorders') formally senior consultant psychiatrist at the Royal Liverpool University Hospital, is an internationally acknowledged authority and pioneer of Uncommon Psychiatric Syndromes, the title of his best-selling book (fourth edition). A broadcaster and author, his other titles include *Healing the Hurt Mind* (eleventh edition) and the recently published *I Want a Christian Psychiatrist*.

Dr Jonathan Evans ('Suicide and Self-Harm') is a senior lecturer in psychiatry at the University of Bristol and practises as a consultant psychiatrist in South Bristol. He has conducted research on depression in mothers and fathers both during pregnancy and after childbirth, and has also conducted studies on suicide and self-harm. He has a clinical interest in bipolar disorder and runs a bipolar clinic in South Bristol. He strongly believes in the importance of improving public understanding of mental health and has acted as an adviser to the BBC.

Dr Mona Freeman ('Your Brain and How It Works') is a specialist registrar in child and adolescent psychiatry at the Tavistock Clinic in London. She is involved in various public education projects in conjunction with the Royal College of Psychiatrists.

Dr Nuri Gene–Cos ('Post-traumatic Stress Disorder') is consultant psychiatrist in the Traumatic Stress Service at the Maudsley. She has trained in EMDR and sensorimotor therapy and has a special interest in conversion disorder (hysteria) and PTSD. Her main research is in brain electrophysiology.

Dr Harvey Gordon ('Jealousy') is a consultant forensic psychiatrist at the Oxfordshire and Buckinghamshire Mental Health Partnership NHS Trust and honorary senior lecturer in forensic psychiatry at the University of Oxford. He has previously worked as a Consultant Forensic Psychiatrist at Broadmoor Hospital and the Maudsley and Bethlem Royal Hospitals. He is Secretary of the Forensic Section of the Association of European Psychiatrists.

Dr Nori Graham ('Alzheimer's and Other Dementias') is Emeritus Consultant in Old Age Psychiatry at the Royal Free Hospital, London. She is former Chairman of the Alzheimer's Society, England and of Alzheimer's Disease International (ADI), and remains Vice-President of both organizations.

Professor John Gunn ('Dangerousness and Mental Disorder') is the former head of the Department of Forensic Psychiatry at the Maudsley in London and former chairman of the Faculty of Forensic Psychiatry. He is the author of books and many papers on forensic psychiatry.

Dr Cosmo Hallstrom ('Anxiety and Panic') is a consultant psychiatrist with a special interest in anxiety disorders. He has published widely on the medical treatment of anxiety and depression and also addiction to tranquillizers.

Deborah Hart (Various case histories.) (See page 481.)

Dr Angela Hassiotis ('Learning Disabilities and Mental Health') is a senior lecturer and consultant psychiatrist at the Royal Free and University College Medical School and the Camden Learning Disabilities Service. She is a member of the Royal College of Psychiatrists' Faculty of Learning Disability Executive and her research interests include epidemiological studies, ethics, and mental health interventions. She lives in London.

Dr Frank Holloway ('Mental Health Services') is a consultant psychiatrist and clinical director working in the Croydon Integrated Adult Mental Health Services. He is also the current Chair of the Royal College of Psychiatrists' Faculty of Rehabilitation and Social Psychiatry.

Dr Aliya Kassam, ('Stigma and Discrimination Against People with Mental Illness') a psychiatric epidemiologist, moved to London from Calgary, Alberta, Canada, in 2005 to work for the Institute of Psychiatry at King's College London. She is currently pursuing a PhD at the Institute of Psychiatry in Health Services Research.

Dr Hind Khalifeh ('Your Brain and How It Works') is a specialist registrar in General Adult Psychiatry with a special interest in neuropsychiatry. She works in London.

Professor Michael Kopelman ('Hysteria') is professor of neuropsychiatry at King's College London, Institute of Psychiatry, based at St Thomas's Hospital. He is particularly interested in memory disorders of all varieties, and he runs a neuropsychiatry and memory disorders clinic.

Dr Ann Law ('Stigma and Discrimination Against People with Mental Illness') trained as a linguist and is Research Administrator at the Health Service and Population Research Department at the Institute of Psychiatry, King's College London.

Dr Donald Lyons ('Mental Health Legislation') is Director of the Mental Welfare Commission for Scotland. He is an Old Age Psychiatrist and previously worked in Glasgow and in the Trent region. He lives in Glasgow.

Dr Gavin McKay ('Hysteria') is a specialist registrar in psychiatry at Guy's Hospital and has a special interest in neuropsychiatry. He lives in London.

Dr Brian Marien ('Mind and Body') is a doctor of medicine, health psychologist and cognitive behavioural psychotherapist. His main clinical interest is in mind/body medicine where advances in the brain sciences are providing remarkable insights into how the 'mind' influences our physical and psychological health and well-being.

Dr Lawrence Martean ('Suicide and Self-Harm') is a junior doctor specializing in psychiatry. He lives and works in Bristol where he graduated from Bristol University, and was a Royal College of Psychiatrists' prize-winner.

Dr Gillian Mezey ('Domestic Violence') is a forensic psychiatrist who has published extensively on the psychiatric and psychological effects of physical and sexual violence. She has contributed to the Department of Health's and the Royal College of Psychiatrists' Policy Guidelines on Victims of Rape and Domestic Violence, and recently, for the Department of Health's and NIMHE's Victims of Violence and Abuse Prevention Programme. She lives in London.

Dr Emanuel Moran ('Gambling') is a widely published psychiatrist who first delineated the condition of pathological gambling. The World Health Organization has adopted his description. He is the Royal College of Psychiatrists' adviser on pathological gambling.

Professor Paul Mullen ('Stalking') is professor of forensic psychiatry at Monash University and Clinical Director of the Forensic Mental Health Services in Victoria, Australia. His research interests are the relationship between mental disorders and offending, the long-term effects of child abuse, and problem behaviours such as stalking, threatening and chronic complaining.

Professor David Nutt ('Therapies, Treatments and Medication: Medication') is professor of psychopharmacology at Bristol University and honorary consultant in the Avon and Wiltshire Partnership Trust. He runs a specialist anxiety, depression and sleep-disorders clinic and has conducted many research studies into these disorders.

Professor Greg O'Brien ('Autism and Asperger's Syndrome') is Associate Medical Director, Learning Disabilities and Professor of Developmental Psychiatry at Northumbria University, and also Associate Medical Director and Consultant Psychiatrist at Northumberland Tyne and Wear NHS Trust. He is Associate Dean of the Royal College of Psychiatrists and President of the Penrose Society. He has published more than eighty papers, books and chapters on various themes concerning the mental health of people with a learning disability.

Professor Eabhardt O'Callaghan ('Schizophrenia') works as a psychiatrist in Dublin and is professor of mental health research at University College Dublin. He collaborates with colleagues in the UK, Denmark and Sweden on the aetiology, course and outcome of mental illness, particularly schizophrenia.

Professor Femi Oyebode ('Exercise and Mental Health') is a psychiatrist and poet. He is head of the Department of Psychiatry at Birmingham. He contributed to the *Oxford Companion to 20th Century Poetry* and has appeared at both the Hay-on-Wye and Cheltenham festivals. He lives in Birmingham.

Dr Andrew Parker ('Sexual Problems') is a psychiatrist at the Maudsley Hospital. He specializes in adult severe mental illness and substance misuse. He also has interests in the philosophy of mind and the nature of religious belief. He lives in London.

Dr Colin Murray Parkes ('Bereavement and Grief') is a psychiatrist and author who, through his research and teaching, has pioneered the development of volunteer-based bereavement services. He is Life President of Cruse Bereavement Care and Editor of the international journal *Bereavement Care*.

Dr Siobhain Quinn ('Physical Illness and Chronic Pain') is a London psychiatrist. She specializes in older people's mental health and the interface between physical and psychological disorder. She prefers a broad and holistic approach and combines conventional psychiatric treatment with nutrition, exercise and relaxation techniques.

Dr Hagen Rampes ('Complementary Medicines') is a general adult psychiatrist who has a longstanding interest in complementary and alternative medicine and mental health. He is the Chair of a working group of the Royal College of Psychiatrists and the Prince's Foundation for Integrated Health. He has recently become Chair of a steering group which will produce national guidelines for the use of complementary and alternative medicine in mental health.

Dr Bruce Ritson ('Alcohol') is a consultant psychiatrist and Chairman of the Scottish Intercollegiate Group on Alcohol. He was formerly Chairman of the Addiction Faculty, Royal College of Psychiatrists and is an honorary Fellow of Edinburgh University. He is the author of books and papers concerning the treatment and prevention of alcohol-related problems.

Professor Ulrike Schmidt ('Eating Disorders') is a consultant psychiatrist at the South London and Maudsley NHS Foundation Trust and Head of the Section of Eating Disorders at the Institute of Psychiatry. She chairs the Eating Disorders Special Interest Group of the Royal College of Psychiatrists and is an Associate Editor of the *European Eating Disorders Review*.

Dr Mike Shooter ('Parenting Problems') has been part of mental health services in every sense. He was a consultant working with children and families, he is a past-president of the Royal College of Psychiatrists, and he has a recurrent depressive disorder of his own.

Dr Helen Startup ('Eating Disorders') is a clinical psychologist who trained at the Institute of Psychiatry and currently works at the Eating Disorders Unit, Maudsley Hospital and Bethlem Royal Hospital. Prior to this she worked at the CBT unit, Maudsley Hospital. She completed a PhD in 2001 that explored cognitive mechanisms of pathological worry.

Dr Richard Stern, ('Phobias') a former member of a Medical Research Council–funded team at the Institute of Psychiatry developing therapeutic studies into phobias and obsessive compulsive disorder, has been consultant psychiatrist at St George's and Springfield Hospitals, London. He currently works in private practice, based at St Anthony's Hospital, Surrey.

Professor Pamela Taylor ('Dangerousness and Mental Disorder') is professor of forensic psychiatry at Cardiff University and adviser on forensic psychiatry to the Chief Medical Officer for the Welsh Assembly Government. She co-edited a recent book on treatment of personality disorder and, with John Gunn, is preparing the second edition of their forensic psychiatry textbook.

Professor Graham Thornicroft ('Stigma and Discrimination Against People with Mental Illness') is Consultant Psychiatrist and Director of Research and Development at the South London and Maudsley NHS Foundation Trust, and Professor of Community Psychiatry and Head of the Health Service and Population Research Department at the Institute of Psychiatry, King's College London.

Peter Tihanyi ('Caring and Carers') is a qualified social worker and has a masters degree specializing in the voluntary sector. From May 1994 to October 2006, he worked for the Princess Royal Trust for Carers. He is now an independent consultant on health and social care. He co-chaired the campaign Partners in Care with the then President of the Royal College of Psychiatrists, Dr Mike Shooter.

Professor Peter Tyrer ('Personality Disorder' and 'Stress') (see page 481).

Dr David Veale ('Body Image Disorders') is a consultant psychiatrist in cognitive behavioural psychotherapy at the South London and Maudsley NHS Foundation Trust and the Priory Hospital North London. He is an honorary senior lecturer at the Institute of Psychiatry, King's College London. He is currently President of the British Association of Behavioural and Cognitive Psychotherapists. He was a member of the NICE guidelines for the recommended treatment of obsessive compulsive disorder and body dysmorphic disorder.

Dr James Warner ('Alzheimer's and Other Dementias') is a consultant in old age psychiatry at St Charles Hospital, London. He is co-author of the popular book for carers *Dementia at Your Fingertips* (translated into seven languages) and author of the dementia chapter of *Clinical Evidence*.

Dr Ursula Werneke ('Complementary Medicines') is a consultant psychiatrist and liaison psychiatrist. She actively practises complementary medicine, including herbal medicine and acupuncture. She has published widely in this field, psychopharmacology and public health, and her work has gained broad international attention.

Professor Peter White ('Chronic Fatigue Syndrome') is professor of psychological medicine at Barts and The London, Queen Mary's School of Medicine and Dentistry, University of London. He specializes in the treatment and research of chronic fatigue syndrome.

Dr Chris Williams ('Therapies, Treatments and Medication: Cognitive Behavioural Therapy') is senior lecturer at the University of Glasgow. His main clinical and research interest is in providing wider access to cognitive behavioural therapy (CBT) approaches and he was lead developer of the popular life-skills course www.livinglifetothefull.com. He has published several written and computer-based self-help treatments for anxiety, depression and bulimia and is a well-known CBT trainer and teacher.

Dr Tony Zigmond ('Mental Health Legislation') is a psychiatrist who practises and lives in Leeds. He is the lead on mental health law for the Royal College of Psychiatrists and trains doctors in mental health legislation.

Index

support organizations 230
treatments 225, 459
insurance 418–19, 420
interpersonal therapy (IPT) 80, 102, 442
Irish Advocacy Network 421–2
irritability 27, 61, 181, 208
irritable bowel syndrome 245, 301, 364, 375

jealousy 124–7, 128–9
case study 123–4
in children 384
getting help and support 126–8, 129
tips for families and friends 128
see also Othello syndrome
jury service 420–21

kava 311

labelling: and diagnosis 88–91
lamotrigine 45, 46, 457, 458
lavender 310–11
learning disabilities, people with 132–3, 136, 467
and carers 134, 135, 136
case study 130–32
getting help and support 134–5, 137
treatments 133–5
legislation 464–70
leukemia: case study 389–91
Levitra *see* verdenafil
Lewy body disease 16, 20
lifestyle 267, 268
light therapy 209–10
limbic system (of the brain) 7, 9
lithium 45, 46, 47, 457, 458
lofepramine (Gamanil) 453
lorazepam 30, 45, 64
love, importance of 374–5
Lustral *see* sertraline

magic mushrooms 331
Manerix *see* moclobemide
manic depression *see* bipolar disorder
MAOIs *see* monoamine oxidase inhibitors
masochism 219
massage 30, 63, 192, 310
ME (myalgic encephalomyelitis) 299–300
see chronic fatigue syndrome
medication 448, 460–61
addiction to 60, 61, 64, *see also under*
antidepressants
and overdoses 260–61, 451

and sexual dysfunction 215, 216
side-effects 19, 21, 224, 358–9, 448–9
see also anxiolytics; anticonvulsants;
antipsychotic drugs; complementary
medicines *and specific conditions*
memory 9, 366
memory loss 19
and Alzheimer's 13–14, 18, 20, 21
due to hysteria 117, 121–2
and learning disability 132
Mental Capacity Acts 464, 465, 466–7
Mental Health Act Commission 469, 470
Mental Health Acts 464, 467
detention under 73, 127, 467–70
right of appeal 469
Mental Health Review Tribunal 469
mental health services 471–3, 474, 475–8
complaints and second opinions 474, 478
referrals to 473
mental retardation *see* learning disabilities
methadone 64, 65, 335, 459
'mini-strokes' 22
mirror-checking 50, 51, 52
mirtazapine (Zispin) 450, 453
moclobemide (Manerix) 453
'molecules of emotion' 365, 373
Molipaxin *see* trazodone
monoamine oxidase inhibitors (MAOIs) 174, 450, 453
mood swings, bipolar disorder 43, 44, 45
and stabilizers 457–8
motivational enhancement therapy 442
muggings, victims of 187–8, 367
multiple personalities 117
Munchausen's syndrome/by proxy 138, 143–4
muscle relaxants 397
myalgic encephalomyelitis *see* chronic fatigue
syndrome

naltrexone 64, 275, 459–60
narcolepsy 227
Narcotics Anonymous 63, 65
Nardil *see* phenelzine
'nearest relative' 468
Negative Recency Effect 348, 349
neurotransmitters 7, 11, 12, 364–5, 448
see also adrenaline; dopamine; serotonin
nicotine addiction *see* smoking
nightmares 189
see also sleep terrors
nitrazepam 225, 459